Zionism Imperialism and Racism

Edited by A.W. KAYYALI

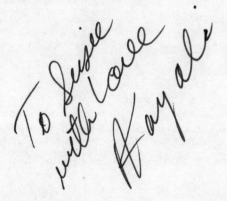

CROOM HELM LONDON

© 1979 A.W. Kayyali
Croom Helm Ltd, 2-10 St John's Road, London SW11

British Library Cataloguing in Publication Data

Zionism, imperialism and racism.
   1. Zionism — History
   I. Kayyali, Abdul-Wahhab
   956.94'001   DS149

   ISBN 0-85664-761-6

Printed in Great Britain by offset lithography by
Billing & Sons Ltd, Guildford, London and Worcester

CONTENTS

Introduction

INTRODUCTION

> Right and wrong are the same in Palestine as anywhere else. What is peculiar about the Palestine conflict is that the world has listened to the party that committed the offence and has turned a deaf ear to the victims.
>
> Professor Arnold Toynbee

In our era of unprecedented global interdependence and lethal military technology the world may ignore the issues of potential intercontinental conflict only at its peril. This is particularly so in the case of the dangerous situation in the Arab Middle East. The *'casus belli'* in that part of the world is the Arab-Zionist conflict, which owes its origin to the imperialist inspired alien Zionist invasion of Palestine and threat to the future of the entire Arab Nation.

Zionism, as the contributors to this volume point out, is a colonial movement based on racist, supremacist and distant religious notions perceived and launched as a political project within the imperialist framework of late nineteenth and early twentieth-century Europe. Both the antagonistic Western attitude towards the Arabs and the Zionist colonial ideology are now clearly anachronistic and actually threaten the interest and well-being of the West, the Jews and humanity. That these Western attitudes and Zionist ideas are presently at variance with the spirit of our times, is borne out by the liquidation of colonialism and racist entities in Africa and elsewhere and by the United Nations Resolution 3379 of 10 November 1975 which determined that Zionism is a form of racism and racial discrimination.

It was on the first anniversary of that momentous resolution that the University of Baghdad invited prominent thinkers and scholars from 46 countries to participate in a seminar on 'Zionism and Racism' to examine Zionism in theory and practice. The seminar was singularly successful, and it is my privilege to present a selection of the papers submitted to that seminar in the hope of contributing to a greater understanding of the underlying factors of the Arab-Zionist conflict. Unless the West is prepared to admit the justice of the Palestinian claim in the Middle East, there can be no hope of peace in the region. Such an understanding is vital to the future of the Western industrial societies and will help future efforts to build peace on the firm foundations of justice. It is time the West listened.

A.W. Kayyali

Part One

ZIONISM: ITS PHILOSOPHIC AND
HISTORICAL FOUNDATIONS

1 THE HISTORICAL ROOTS OF THE IMPERIALIST-ZIONIST ALLIANCE

Abdul Wahhab Al Kayyali

In as much as imperialism is an international politico-economic system based on the concept of moral and material inequality of nations, entailing subservience and exploitation of the ruled by the ruler through the oppressive use of force as well as by other means, it is necessarily a racist phenomenon. This is borne out by the historical record of imperialism throughout the world, and without such a basic view, no correct reading of racism and modern history is possible.

Historical evidence points to the fact that Zionism, as we know it, was born within the framework of imperialist thoughts and designs of the early decades of nineteenth century Europe and enthusiastically embraced by some Jewish intellectuals and activists who were influenced by the prevalent chauvinist and racist ideas of the latter part of that century. The common denominator was the interest to find solutions for European problems and needs at the expense of other people, in this case the Arabs. The use of the term 'alliance' refers to the partnership and the nature of the link between the two parties and not to any semblence of parity between the two as it is quite obvious that Zionism is merely one of the offshoots of the tree of imperialist ideology. The peculiarities of the Zionist ideology and entity tend to assert rather than negate its racist character.

Zionsim as a modern political creed and as an effective organised movement can only be correctly conceived as an artificial or temporary solution to three interacting challenges facing Europe in the nineteenth century, the heyday of Western imperialism.

1. The growth and expansion of European imperialism, which necessitated the search for new sources of raw materials and markets for the finished products, in addition to securing the lines of commercial and military communications. The importance of the Arab lands as the gateway to Africa and the bridge to Asia was made abundantly evident by Napoleon's campaign (1797-1799) and by the "dangers" of Mohammed Ali's attempt to form an independent state comprising Egypt and the Arab States. Thus the need for stifling any nascent independent state, doubly more threatening to imperialism in the wake of the spread of Arab-nationalist sentiment, became increasingly

persistent as the "Ottoman Empire", the "sick man of Europe," drifted further toward disintegration.

2. The failure of European liberalism and the ideas of equality and democracy to incorporate and assimilate the Jew coupled with the capitalist crisis in Eastern Europe. The adoption of industrialization led to a loss of vocation for a great number of Jews who could not easily adjust to the transformation of the feudal economic system. It is important to note that Jewish "apartness" was, in the past, a contributory factor to the phenomenon of anti-Jewishness.

3. The spread of aggressive and chauvinist expansionist nationalism in Europe which stressed the racial basis of the national state as well as racial superiority and the need for expansion (Lebensraum) was diverted to overseas colonies and possessions. Superiority, exploitation and domination were upheld as a civilizational mission under the notion of the "white man's burden."

The first two of these challenges were known as the "Eastern Question" or the "Syrian Question", and the "Jewish Question". The inter-European rivalries and the scramble for colonies precipitated world wars and revolutions and was transformed into the "colonial question." The first question prompted the major imperialist figures to propose the idea of creating a client Jewish settler-state in Palestine primarily designed to block the fulfillment of unity and independence in that important area of the world and to serve the interests of its sponsors. The events of the latter part of the century were conducive to the creation of a consensus of opinion among the imperialist and Western politicians, with the cooperation of Western Jewish millionaires and anti-Semites everywhere in favor of Zionism and Jewish emigration to, and the establishment of, a Jewish state in Palestine. The interaction of the challenges and the persistence of the problems and issues fed into the imperialist design and directed events toward finding solutions at the expense of peoples of the Third World.

The Growth of Western Influence

Toward the end of the eighteenth century the Western powers' interest in the Arab area intensified as the aging Ottoman Empire became increasingly dependent on the European powers which obtained privileges, footholds and spheres of influence within the Empire itself. These powers sought to establish direct links with the various populations and religious sects in the area. Thus France became the protector of the Catholic communities in Syria, Lebanon and Palestine while the Orthodox Christians came under Russian protection.

It was during his Palestinian campaign (1799) that Napoleon, motivated by his war needs and later by his ambition to attract the loyalty
of the Jews as agents throughout the world, issued his call for the rebuilding of the Temple in Jerusalem and the "return" of the Jews to
Palestine for political purposes. Napoleon's campaign itself had aroused
British interest in Palestine as it had posed a threat to the British overland route to India. When Mohammed Ali (Al-Kabir) of Egypt embarked on his ambitious plan to modernize Egypt and build a strong
independent state comprising Egypt, Greater Syria and the Arab Peninsula during the first decades of the nineteenth century, the British
government adopted a course of direct military intervention and was
instrumental in driving the armies of Ibrahim Pasha (son of Mohammed
Ali) back to Egypt.

Mohammed Ali's advance into Syria opened the Syrian Question (a
question which still remains as it is synonymous with Western schemes
and endeavours to prevent Arab unity). New British policies were formulated. One of the keys to the new approach was Palestine, the Jews
a prominent part of its spearhead. In 1838 the British decided to
station a British consular agent in Jerusalem and in the following year
opened the first European consulate in that city. During the 1840s and
the 1850s the British government, which had no protégées of its own,
established a connection with the Jews in Palestine (around 9700 in
all), the Druze in Lebanon and the new Protestant churches. "Behind
the protection of trade and religious minorities there lay the major
political and strategic interests of the powers." [1]

From its start the British presence was associated with the promotion of Jewish interests. "This question of British protection of Jews
became, however, and remained for many years the principal concern
of the British Consulate in Jerusalem."[2] The formulation and framework of British imperial policy in the area was best drawn out by its
architect, Prime Minister Viscount Palmerston. In a letter to the British
Ambassador at Constantinople explaining why the Ottoman Sultan
should encourage Jewish immigration to Palestine, Palmerston wrote
" . . . the Jewish people if returning under the sanction and protection
and at the invitation of the Sultan would be a check upon any future
evil designs of Mohammed Ali or his successor."[3]

It is remarkable indeed that Palmerston used the term "Jewish
people" in reference to racial-religious unity as there were no other
bonds between the Jews at a time when even prominent Jews were
speaking of Jewish "communities," and when the Jewish assimilationist
movement, the Haskalah, was making headway. Also noteworthy was

the use of the word "returning" in reference to mistaken racial ancestry — as if history stood still for two thousand years — and taking religious memories as a title deed with utter disregard, nay in studied direct opposition, to the will of the inhabitants of the land. All this preceded the conversion of the father of Zionism to Zionism and the official birth of the movement by more than half a century. Nor was Palmerston's concept a bolt in the sky of British imperial policy. This particular idea of erecting a colonial Jewish settler-state in Palestine to serve imperial interests and a variety of moral pretentions, was shared and upheld by a number of prominent British imperialist prime ministers, statesmen, military leaders and adventurers. These included Palmerston, Shaftesbury, Colonel Gawler, Disraeli, Rhodes, Colonel C.H. Churchill, Lawrence Oliphant, Joseph Chamberlain, General Smuts,[4] A.J. Balfour and W. Churchill, to name but a few.

Many of these patrons of Zionism were not philo-Semites as is sometimes commonly assumed. Balfour's pro-Zionist stance was initiated by Herzl's argument before a British Royal Commission on the immigration of Jews to Britain (1902) that diverting the Jews to Palestine was the solution to that British problem. Lawrence Oliphant provides a very clear-cut case of the contradiction between the moral and idealistic pretensions of gentile Zionists and their actual imperialist motivation. According to Lawrence's biographer, the man "shared much of the facile anti-Semitism of his time."[5] A more recent example is provided by President Richard Nixon who provided more arms and money to Israel than all the preceding American Presidents combined and who, according to press reports about the White House tapes, was not above derisory remarks about Jews in his private counsels.

The British imperialist Zionist seed did not sprout immediately and had to await the rains of wider imperialist interest in the area — the opening of the Suez Canal in the 1860s and the British occupation of Cyprus and Egypt in the seventies and eighties respectively. An additional impetus was the spread of anti-Semitism in Eastern and, later, Western Europe.

The growth of Western influence "caused the Western Jewish communities to play an increasingly important role in the Holy Land."[6] This role was conceived within the confines of these interests under the protection of the privileges (capitulations) granted by the Sultan to the Western powers. It was financed as well as guided by rich Western Jews closely associated with the ruling circles in the West.

The first organizations to promote the proposed colonialization program were British and inspired by the Palmerston-Shaftesbury line of thought — The British and Foreign Society for Promoting the Restoration of the Jewish Nation to Palestine, The Association for Promoting Jewish Settlements in Palestine, The Society for the Promotion of Jewish Agricultural Labour in the Holy Land. *The Jewish Chronicle* was established and became "an important vehicle for the popularization of Palestine colonization in Jewish circles."[7] In 1861 the London Hebrew Society for the colonization of the Holy Land and the French Alliance established the agricultural school of Mikveh Israel near Jaffa, obviously aiming at the settlement of Jews in Palestine on a considerable scale. Richard Stevens explained this surge of French interest: "Following the Crimean War there was generally a renewed interest in extending French influence in the Levant and various political writers championed not only the protection of an autonomous and Christian province of Lebanon but also an autonomous Jewish province of Palestine."[8]

At that stage several British writers wrote pamphlets promoting the idea of Jewish settlement in Palestine. Byron's *Hebrew Melodies,* George Eliot's *Daniel Deronda* and Disraeli's *Tanored* conveyed a romantic touch and stimulated public acceptance of the self-interested British-inspired idea of a Jewish "return" to Palestine.

These Western attitudes and efforts provided the necessary background for the emergence of Zionism. As previously noted, two European developments in the second half of the nineteenth century provided the necessary birth conditions of the imperialist-conceived Zionist idea and implanted it in Jewish minds as if it was a natural and inner-motivated Jewish development. The first was the direct and indirect result of the intellectual and political growth of European chauvinist nationalism. It was no accident that the first proponent of the Jewish national idea as a modern creed, Moses Hess, entitled his book *Rome and Jerusalem* (1862) in direct reference to the nationalist movement in Italy, and in which he embraced the racial concepts and the pseudo-scientific racist theories of the nineteenth century. Hess stressed that Jews should avoid assimilation and reassert their uniqueness by "reconstituting their national centre in Palestine." For all his attempted logic, Hess, like most Zionist thinkers, betrays the intrinsic superstitious and messianic traits in what is often otherwise non-religious Zionism, when he speaks of imminent victory of the Jewish idea thus heralding the "Sabbath of History." It is not the immediate impact of *Rome and Jerusalem* that is of primary historical importance but rather the intellectual and political climate that produced it. To the intellectual and political founders of Zionism the realpolitik of European statesmen was of tremendous influence, that of Bismarck a virtual inspiration.

The second European development which pushed the Zionist idea to the fore was the Russian pogroms in 1881. These pogroms led to a mass exodus of Jews to Eastern and Western Europe and brought about the collapse of the Haskalah assimilationist movement. Its place was taken by a new movement, Hibbath Zion (the Love of Zion), inspired by Leo Pinsker's pamphlet *Auto-Emancipation* (1882). Societies were formed in Jewish centres to discuss the question of settling in Palestine as an immediate and practical prospect and the revival of Hebrew as a living language. The first Jewish colonists belonged to an organization of Russo-Jewish students, known as Bilu, which was formed at Kharkov for the specific purpose of colonizing Palestine.

Herzl and the Growth of Zionism

Despite the sprouting of colonial-oriented Jewish organizations no central leadership emerged. The continuing flow of Jewish immigrants into Western Europe brought anti-Semitism and intensified the interest of prominent Western Jews in the fate of the Jews of Eastern Europe. A famous Jewish family, the ultra-rich Rothschilds, financed an endeavour to minimize Jewish immigration to Western Europe by diverting it to Palestine; thus the dire consequences of anti-Semitism were avoided and Jewry was aligned to the expansive imperialist interests in the Middle East in the post-Suez era.[9] A young Viennese Jew, a journalist by profession, named Theodor Herzl was to provide the political and organizational leadership of the new movement.

What converted Herzl from indifference to his Jewishness to active Zionism was the anti-Semitic Dreyfus Affair of 1894. In 1896 his *Der Judenstaat* (The Jewish State) aroused the interests of Jewish activists from various parts of the Western world. The book dealt with the situation of the Jews and argued that only through the attainment of statehood on a land purely their own could the Jewish Question be solved. In the following year Herzl was able to convene the First Zionist Congress at Basle (August, 1897) and form the World Zionist Organization. Herzl was elected president and its carefully worded program declared that the aim of Zionism was a "publicly recognized, legally secured homeland in Palestine," to be achieved through organization, colonization and negotiation under the umbrella of the imperialist powers.

It would be difficult to overstate the importance of Herzl's ideas and the effect his efforts had on the Zionist movement. As the founding father, he left his imprint on the entire mold of that movement and may be said to have influenced it more than any other leader. A reading of his works and the followup of his frame of mind and reference of action, as well as an analysis of the congress at Basle are most revealing particularly in the light of his meticulously and candidly recorded *Diaries*.[10] His ideas, strategies and methods were of tremendous impact on Zionist thought and action, even to the point of becoming characteristic of the movement.

Herzl's Zionism was an outcome of the Jewish Question and his vision of its solution within the framework of alliance with the dominant imperialist powers and as molded by the ideologies of nationalist-cum-racist European movements and societies. To Herzl these societies were permanently incapable of tolerating the Jew who was aliented by his apartness and nonconformism and this was the basis of anti-Semitism as well as of the rootlessness of the Jew. The solution could not possibly be the reform of these societies through such notions as freedom and equality, nor the loss of Jewish identity and apartness, but rather the realization of conformity on "a national basis" and the alignment of the proposed Jewish national-state, which was to be established on a purely Jewish land, with the European powers, whose umbrella and patronage was necessary for bringing about the state as well as protecting it thereafter, in return for services rendered against third parties.

The relationship between the European powers and the proposed Zionist settler-state was conceived on an imperialist-colonialist basis. This underlying fact notwithstanding, Zionist colonialism had nuances of its own, which in turn render it more anomalous or extreme. The first of these nuances was that while the European colonialists were an extension of an already established national identity and state, the Jewish colonialists sought to forge a nation or a national identity through the colonization act itself. Unlike the other nation-seeking movements this was to be based on religion, as they did not speak one language nor did they have social norms and continued historical experience in common.[11] In order to make it more viable to the European mind, Zionism claimed the racial unity of the Jews thus adding pseudo-scientificism to the anachronistic concept of building a religious nation state. Another characteristic was that, while endeavouring to secure the enthusiastic patronage of the most powerful or most interested of the Western powers, Zionism based itself on the consensus of Western and imperialist powers through and through. It sought and procured benefit from inter-imperialist competition in contradistinction with other colonial settler-states. The last of these nuances was an ideologically-powered one—namely that Zionism sought to expel the "natives" as their basic strategy called for a purely Jewish national state.

Any thorough examination of the writings and guiding lines of Zionist theory and action would reveal the overriding and dynamic impact of imperialist thought and modus operandi, as well as the dominant racist influence of nineteenth century Europe. To illustrate this it is proposed to establish Herzl's outlook and methods regarding the basic concepts and issues involved in the imperialist-Zionist alliance with occasional reference to his successors to point out the consistency and continuity of Zionist strategy and tactics. It should be noticed how influential and crucial were Palmerston's proposals and thoughts and subsequently the climate of British imperialist and European racist thought, on the subject of a Jewish settler-state in Palestine.

Outlook

The fundamental concepts underpinning Herzl's thought and Zionist outlook are in his *Der Judenstaat*: "Supposing His Majesty the Sultan were to give us Palestine, we could in return undertake to regulate the whole finances of Turkey. We should there form a portion of the rampart of Europe against Asia, an outpost of civilisation as opposed to barbarism. We should as a neutral State remain in contact with all Europe, which would have to guarantee our existence."[12] The same theme recurs, appropriately enough, in Herzl's address to the First Zionist Congress: "It is more and more to the interest of the civilised nations and of civilisation in general that a cultural station be established on the shortest road to Asia. Palestine is this station and we Jews are the bearers of culture who are ready to give our property and our lives to bring about its creation."[13]

Twenty-one years later, Herzl's prominent successor Chaim Weizmann was to explain to the British imperialist statesman most readily associated with Zionism, Arthur James Balfour, the contemplated Zionist plan: "a community of four to five million Jews in Palestine . . . . from which the Jews could radiate out into the Near East . . . . But all this pre-supposes free and unfettered development of the Jewish National Home in Palestine not mere facilities for colonisation."[14] This concept did not only echo Palmerston's proposal but also responded to the rising Western needs in the area after the opening of the Suez Canal, British occupation of Egypt and World War I. The gist of British strategic thought was spelled out in a memorandum by the General Staff at the War Office: "The creation of a buffer Jewish

State in Palestine, though this State will be weak in itself, is strategically desirable for Great Britain."[15]

Basic Strategy

The Basle Program, formulated by the First Zionist Congress determined that the "aim of Zionism is to create for the Jewish people a home in Palestine secured by public law." A reading of Herzl's *Diaries* as well as an examination of subsequent Zionist action would reveal that the term "public law" refers to the patronage of the imperialist powers. This patronage was deemed necessary in more ways than one. Herzl sought a colonial concession with explicit and public imperial backing as this would establish his own credibility among the Jews[16] as well as secure viability and protection to the venture. He envisaged that the European powers would back Zionism for one of three main motives: (1) imperialist self-interest; (2) ridding themselves of Jews and anti-Semitism (in West Europe's case avoiding the influx of Jewish immigrants from Eastern Europe) and (3) using organized Jewish influence to combat revolutionary movements and other internal factors.

Herzl first turned to the German Kaiser, the "one man who would understand my plan,"[17] not merely because of the German cultural influence within Zionist ranks but because Germany was bent on pushing its imperialist way toward the East:

> German policy has taken an Eastern course, and there is something symbolic about the Kaiser's Palestine journey in more than one sense. I am, therefore, more firmly convinced than ever that our movement will receive help whence I have patiently been expecting it for the past two years. By now it is clear that the settlement of the shortest route to Asia by a neutral (among Europeans) national element could also have a certain value for Germany's Oriental policy.[18]

In a draft letter to the Kaiser, Herzl later explained the Zionist aim and its use to Germany's Oriental policy, that the Jews were the only European colonialists ready and willing to settle Palestine as the land was poor, and that Palestine had to be settled as it occupied a strategic position. Europe, he added, "would more readily permit settlement to the Jews. Perhaps not so much because of the historic right guaranteed in the most sacred book of mankind, but because of the inclination, present in most places, to let the Jews go."[19]

This last argument was his passway to M. de Pleuwhe the anti-Semitic Russian Minister of Interior who in 1903 endorsed the Zionist idea.[20]

It was inevitable that London would become the center of gravity.[21] Britain was the imperialist power most interested in the future of Palestine as it had possessions in neighboring countries as well as an interest in the overland route to India. There Herzl approached the arch-imperialist Colonial Secretary Joseph Chamberlain, through the good offices of Lord Rothschild, whom Herzl described as "the greatest effective force that our people has had since its dispersion."[22] During the Chamberlain interview in October 1902, Herzl's voice trembled as he explained his proposal for an Anglo-Zionist partnership involving colonial concessions for the Jews in Cyprus, el Arish and the Sinai Peninsula to serve as a "rallying point for the Jewish people in the vicinity of Palestine."[23] (A later reference will be made to the imperialist-colonialist logic used by Herzl.) To Chamberlain and to Lord Lansdowne, the foreign secretary, Herzl explained that by patronizing the Zionist endeavour the British Empire would not only "be bigger by a rich colony" but that also ten million Jews:

> will all wear England in their hearts if through such a deed it becomes the protective power of the Jewish people. At one stroke England will get ten million secret but loyal subjects active in all walks of life all over the world. At a signal, all of them will place themselves at the service of the magnanimous nation that brings long-desired help .... England will get ten million agents for her greatness and her influence. And the effect of this sort of thing usually spreads from the political to the economic.[24]

Herein lies the Zionist quid pro quo: for the power that undertakes to be universal protector they offer the Jews as universal agents and the Jewish settler-state as a client-state.

Herzl's efforts in England included soliciting the backing of the major colonialist figures. Foremost among them was Cecil Rhodes and in a letter to Rhodes Herzl explained that although his project did not involve Africa but a piece of Asia Minor, "But had this been on your path, you would have done it yourself by now."[25] Why then did Herzl turn to him, the Zionist leader rhetorically asked; "Because it is something colonial" was the answer.[26] What Herzl sought was a Rhodes certificate for colonial viability and desirability — "I Rhodes, have examined this plan and found it correct and practicable" and quite good for England, for Greater Britain. Furthermore, there was profit for Rhodes and his associates if they joined in.

Rhodes died before Herzl got what he wanted from him. Fifteen years later Herzl's successor Weizmann obtained from the British imperialists what Herzl could not possibly have obtained from his British sympathizers, namely imperialist patronage protection for a Jewish National Home in the form of the Balfour Declaration of November 2, 1917. International endorsements (public law) followed from the other powers and the Declaration was incorporated in the Palestine Mandate against the will of the Arab Palestinian people who constituted the overwhelming majority of the population of Palestine.[27]

At a later stage the Zionists obtained U.S. patronage for statehood endorsed by "public law" in the form of the Palestine Partition Plan (1947) followed by the Tripartite Declaration (1950), the major imperialist powers (the United States, Britain and France) guaranteeing the expanded Zionist state. The U.N. Resolution of November, 1975 regarding Zionism as a form of racism is the beginning of rectifying this anomalous situation.

Basic Tactics

Zionism sought self-fulfillment through mobilizing the Jews, negotiations with the imperialist powers and colonization. The primary mobilizing force in favor of Zionism was anti-Semitism, which, as we have seen, attracted gentile politicians to the Zionist fold. Herzl explained: "No great exertion will be necessary to stimulate the immigration movement. The anti-Semites are already taking care of this for us."[28] Indeed a prominent "spiritual" Zionist — Ahad Ha'am — described Herzlian Zionism as being "the product of anti-Semitism and is dependent on anti-Semitism for its existence."[29] The Grand Duke of Baden told Herzl that "people regarded Zionism as a species of anti-Semitism"[30] and Herzl reported it without objecting. Wherever anti-Semitism was weak or nonexistent the Zionist movement sought to elicit "Jewish national feeling" by incitement and propaganda or by staging anti-Jewish violent acts through special agents as happened in Iraq after 1948.

Another means of mobilizing Jewish opinion was the appeal to Jewish complexes through certain Jewish notions, most notably that of the "chosen people." In the racist climate of nineteenth century Europe this was transformed to sound like the notion of the "white man's burden," and tied to the concept of the "Promised Land" and the promise of "return," despite the fact that the leading Zionists were either nonreligious or downright agnostics. Moses Hess maintained, "Every Jew has the makings of a Messiah, every Jewess that of a Mater

Dolorosa." Ahad Ha'am stated, "we feel ourselves to be the aristocracy of history." Herzl declared, "our race is more efficient in everything than most other peoples of the earth."[31] In 1957 Ben Gurion asserted the same notion, "I believe in our moral and intellectual superiority to serve as a model for the redemption of the human race."[32]

The second tactic — negotiations with the imperialists — involved stressing the common interests against third parties as the basis of partnership, and the use of deception and graft. During his negotiations with Chamberlain over Jewish colonization of Cyprus, Herzl betrayed his colonialist outlook and method: "Once we establish the Jewish Eastern Company, with five million pounds capital, for settling Sinai and El Arish, the Cypriots will begin to want that golden rain on their island, too. The Moslems will move away, the Greeks will gladly sell their lands at a good price and migrate to Athens or Crete."[33]

The colonization tactic was an even more telling feature of the nature of Zionism for it explains its colonial nature, its dependence on imperialism and its racist attitudes vis-à-vis the Arab natives as well as its intended reactionary role in the area. The names and purposes of the early colonization nation-building instruments tell something about the nature of the Zionist movement — The Jewish Colonial Trust (1898), the "colonization commission" (1898), the Palestine Land Development Company. From the start the Zionist colonists sought to acquire lands in strategic locations, evict the Arab peasants and boycott Arab labour; all this was closely related with the essence of Zionism, the creation of a Jewish nation on "purely" Jewish land, as Jewish as England was English to use their famous expression.[34] The same notion was clearly implied by Palmerston's concept of a Jewish barrier colonial-state.

These aspects of Zionism became more pronounced as the Zionist colonial invasion developed. Here again these Zionist traditions owe their origins to Herzl and his racist-colonial dominated mind: "The voluntary expropriation will be accomplished through our secret agents .... we shall then sell only to Jews, and all real estate will be traded only among Jews."[35]

What about the fate of the natives? "We shall try to spirit the penniless population across the border by procuring employment for it in the transit countries, while denying it any employment in our own country .... The property owners will come to our side. Both the process of expropriation and the removal of the poor must be carried out discreetly and circumspectly."[36]

But before spiriting them away Herzl had some work for them:

"If we move into a region where there are wild animals to which the Jews are not accustomed – big snakes, etc. . . . – I shall use the natives, prior to giving them employment in the transit countries, for the extermination of the animals."[37] When he later discovered that the Zionist colonies needed large-scale drainage operations he decided to use the Arabs, a fever attacked the workers and he did not want to expose the Zionists to such dangers.[38]

But what would happen if the Arabs refused to be spirited away from the country they naturally considered their own? Herzl could not have possibly ignored what all colonialists and colonial ventures possess as a precondition to their venture: "Out of this proletariat of intellectuals I shall form the general staff and the cadres of the army which is to seek, discover, and take over the land."[39] His projected army would comprise "one-tenth of the male population; less would not suffice internally."[40] Indeed life in his proposed Zionist state would have to be paramilitary: "Organize the labor battalions along military lines, as far as possible."[41]

No one can accuse Herzl of not realizing the logical conclusions of this plan: evicting the natives would be a formidable task and the unheard of ration of one-tenth of the male population for internal purposes is in order. Regimenting labor is a corollary to the garrison-state, the forward citadel of Western "civilization" in what Herzl considered the "filthy corners"[42] of the Orient.

Using force was what British imperialist bayonets had to perform in Palestine to enforce the Zionist Jewish National Home in the wake of the Anglo-Zionist unholy marriage declared on November 2, 1917. Weizmann lost no time in facing the British with the facts of imperialist life in Palestine as early as 1919: "Will the British apply self-determination in Palestine which is five hours from Egypt or not? If not it will have to be co-erced . . . . Yes or no: it amounts to that."[43] On this point as on many other issues Weizmann found himself on the same platform as the major British imperialist politicians.[44]

Zionist Expansionism

The annals of Zionist history are full of Zionist leaders outdoing other Zionist leaders on the importance of military power and the role of military action and terror in the building and safeguarding of the Zionist state: Joseph Trumpeldor, Vladimir Jabotinsky, Menahem Begin, Ben Gurion and all the generals-turned-politicians. In some of their writings and revelations the gods of the Zionist war machine assert that violence and coercion are the backbone of the plan to enforce the

Zionist program, in addition to its being an adulation of power in reaction to Jewish meekness in European history. This was necessarily so because the Zionists invaded the country, evicted the majority of the population, followed this up by further use of force and terrorism[45] and continued to carry out their expansionist schemes through wars and military occupation. The garrison-state had to expand the domain of the citadel as an inner mechanism (economic, political and psychological) as well as to intimidate the Arabs for the benefit of imperialist designs in the area.

Expansionism was not alien to Herzl, an admirer of German expansionists as well as British imperialists: "We ask for what we need — the more immigrants, the more land."[46]

The story of Zionist expansionism is a long one,[47] suffice it to read the above statement in the light of the Zionist aim of the in-gathering of *all* the Jews of the world and to remember the utterances of the major leaders of Israel in 1956 and 1967 which in essence reflected another of Herzl's mottoes: "Area: from the Brook of Egypt to the Euphrates."[48]

These attitudes are part and parcel of Zionism. Jay Gonen, an Israeli scholar, writes of "the Arab Problem": "From the very beginning of the Zionist endeavor most Zionists displayed a blind spot in their view of the Arabs, a blind spot that was a total lack of vision and later became distorted vision."[49] They called the Arabs derogatory racist names and were convinced "that the Arabs understood only the language of force, a bias that persisted for many years and became especially pronounced after the Holocaust."[50] The Israelis, furthermore, are convinced "that physical force is the only tangible political reality which carries weight and is significant in the affairs of nations ... current Israeli political vision is mostly conceptualized in terms of tanks, jets."[51]

The prevalence of the Massada complex or fortress Israel is not accidental. Nor was Golda Meir's absurd rhetoric of June 15, 1969 when she inquired assertively "The Palestinians ... where are they? there is no such thing."[52] The Koenig report[53] is merely the most recent manifestation, by no means the most extreme, of Zionist attitudes towards the Arabs of Palestine.

It would be both erroneous and dangerous, however, to think that Zionist racist-colonialist attitudes toward the Palestinian Arabs are divorced from the wide context of imperialist-Zionist attitude vis-à-vis Arab unity and the Arab future as a whole. On several occasions Herzl sought to present Zionism as the political meeting point between Christianity and Judaism in their common stance against

Islam and the "barbarism" of the Orient. A thorough reading of Herzl reveals that to him as well as to other imperialists the term "Islam" refers to the Arabs and to no other Islamic people. This became more evident when the Zionists allied themselves with the Ottoman Revolution of 1908 "in their common battle against the incipient Arab national movement and Arab independence."[54] In 1919, in a secret meeting attended by Weizmann and a number of high-ranking British officials the matter was very frankly discussed. Ormsby-Gore, who later became colonial secretary and therefore effective ruler of Palestine, was in favour of encouraging non-Moslems, Europeans and Jews, to develop and stabilize the Near East in view of the fact that Islam was the main danger. Since the Zionist Organization provided the required human element to man the Palestinian outpost in Europe's fight against Islam: "It is the interest of England to assist the Zionist Organization and any other organization which may cooperate with them in the practical development of Jewish colonization in Palestine".[55]

The idea of Balkanization was implemented in the post-World War I division of the Arab nation. Zionism, however, continued to work for the creation of smaller sectarian states, this time in cooperation with the French imperialists. During the thirties a Zionist rapprochement with the pro-French Maronite leaders in the Lebanon took place. In 1941, as the Zionists began to push for declaring their state, an associate of Ben Gurion, Berl Katznelson stated: "We should say to the Arab peoples: in us, Jews, you see an obstacle in your way toward independence and unification. We do not deny it."[56]

After 1948 the Zionist state worked on creating a "Druze nationality" through state legislation and segregation from the other sectors of the Arab population in Palestine. In 1965, the foremost Zionist spokesman, the then Foreign Minister Abba Eban wrote a major article in *Foreign Affairs*, which presented a polite sugar-coated version of Zionist thinking and strategy. Eban reiterated the Zionist opposition to Arab unity claiming that the area is a mosaic and that a Jewish state therefore is a natural part of the scene. More recently the Zionists have been very active in the Lebanese civil war. Their backing of the Maronite isolationists is no longer a secret.

From the imperialist point of view Zionist opposition to Arab unity is Israel's *raison d'être*, from the Zionist point of view it is a sine qua non. Viewed in the wider imperialist context Israel is essentially a tool, a bet, against Arab liberation, unity and progress. Historically, Zionism sought to ally Jews and imperialist gentiles against and at the expense of the Arabs. They sought to bring about Jewish conformism by adopting the same reactionary notions that aggravated the Jewish situation in Europe. Zionism accepted and emulated (elsewhere) the notions of the European enemies of the Jews: chauvinist nationalism, anti-Semitism and reactionary governments. With the help of the imperialist West they recreated the ghetto in the East in the form of an alien aggressive nation-state, and reincarnated the traditional role of being an agent for the feudal lord by becoming the agent of the dominant imperialist power, only this time they could play the role of the oppressor for a change. That is why Zionism viewed anti-Semitism as being one of its best friends for they constitute two faces of the same coin: Zionism represented an escapist reactionary movement, a negative verdict on human societies and their inability to tolerate the Jew merely because he is different.

Inasmuch as Israel is a regression to the idea of religion as a basis for a nation-state it is an anachronism. Inasmuch as it is an alien Western invasion of Arab land it is another Crusade doomed to failure. Inasmuch as it is a colonial-racist state it is an enemy of the spirit of the age of liberation and equality. Thus, the peoples of the Third World started to move in the direction of denying Zionism the international legitimacy it unjustly enjoyed since the declaration of its state. Inasmuch as it is naturally allied to the imperialist powers in their battle against Arab rights and the Arab future it will collapse with the defeat of imperialism in the Arab homeland as it was defeated elsewhere.

The verdict of history is clear: there is no place in the coming century for racism, Zionism and imperialism. The peoples of the Third World shall assert their rights and liberate themselves, thus ridding all societies of the burden of inequality and oppression.

Notes

1. Albert Hourani, "Ottoman Reform and the Politics of Notables," in *Beginning of Modernisation in the Middle East: The Nineteenth Century*, ed. William Polk and Richard Chambers (Chicago, 1968), pp. 41-68.

2. Albert Hyamson, *The British Consulate in Jerusalem in Relation to the Jews of Palestine, 1838-1914* (London, 1939-41) pt.1, p. xxxiv.

3. Viscount Palmerston to Viscount Ponsonby, August 2, 1840, F.O. 78/390 (No 134), Public Record Office.

4. *See* the excellent study by Richard Stevens, *Weizmann and Smuts* (Beirut, 1976).

5. *See* Philip Henderson, *The Life of Lawrence Oliphant, Traveller, Diplomat, and Mystic* (London, 1956).

6. Ben Halpern, *The Idea of a Jewish State* (Cambridge Mass., 1961), p. 107.

7. A. Taylor, *The Zionist Mind*, (Beirut, 1974).

8. Richard Stevens, *Zionism and Palestine Before the Mandate* (Beirut, 1972), p. 6.

9. The Rothschilds themselves were extremely involved in the Suez Canal. It was Disraeli, with money from the Rothschilds, who acquired the British share in the Suez holding company which later brought British invasion of Egypt.

10. Raphael Patai, ed. and Harry Zohn, trans., *Diaries of Theodor Herzl* (New York and London, 1960).

11. For a thorough discussion of the subject *see* Godfrey Jansen, *Zionism, Israel and Asian Nationalism* (Beirut, 1971), pp. 12-79.

12. Patai, ed., *Diaries* p. 213.

13. Quoted in Jansen, *Zionism*, p. 83.

14. "Note on the Interview with Mr. Balfour," December 4, 1918, F.O. 371/ 3385, PRO.

15. "The Strategic Importance of Syria to the British Empire," General Staff, War Office, December 9, 1918, F.O. 371/4178, PRO.

16. Patai, ed., *Diaries*, pp. 223, 240-41 and 445.

17. *Ibid.*, p. 187.

18. *Ibid.*, pp. 639-40.

19. *Ibid.*, p. 642.

20. *Ibid.*, p. 1535.

21. *Ibid.*, p. 276.

22. *Ibid.*, p. 1302.

23. *Ibid.*, p. 1362.

24. *Ibid.*, pp. 1365-66.

25. *Ibid.*, p. 1194.

26. *Ibid.*,

27. For a detailed history of Palestinian Arab resistence to Zionism and imperialism, *see* Abdul Wahhab Kayyali, *Tarikh Falastin al-Hadith* [Modern History of Palestine] (Beirut, 1970).

28. Patai, ed., *Diaries*, p. 152.

29. A. Hertzberg, *The Zionist Idea* (New York, 1959), p. 24.

30. Patai, ed., *Diaries*, p. 657.

31. Quoted in Jansen, *Zionism*, pp. 33-34.

32. *See* Patai, ed., *Diaries*, pp. 70, 322, 568 etc.

33. *Ibid.*, p. 1362.

34. *See* Kayyali, *Tarikh Falastin*.

35. Patai, ed., *Diaries*, p. 89.

36. *Ibid.*, p. 88.

37. *Ibid.*, p. 89.

38. *Ibid.*, p. 740-741.

39. *Ibid.*, p. 28.

40. *Ibid.*, p. 38.

41. *Ibid.*, p. 64.

42. *Ibid.*, p. 1449.

43. May 10, 1919, Central Zionist Archives, Z/16009.

44. *See* Balfour to Prime Minister, February 19, 1919, F.O. 371/4179.

45. For a detailed account of Zionist terrorism *see* Who Are the Terrorists, (Beirut, 1974).

46. Patai, ed., *Diaries*, p. 701.

47. For a detailed account *see* al-Matame al Sahhiyoniyyah al-Tawsu uyyah [Zionist Expansionism] (Beirut, 1966).

48. Patai, ed., *Diaries*, p. 711.

49. Jay Gonen, *A Psychohistory of Zionism* (New York, 1975), p. 182.

50. *Ibid.*, p. 180.

51. *Ibid.*, p. 181.
52. Zionist propaganda had previously circulated the totally deceptive motto "Land without people, people without land," in reference to Palestine and the Jews.
53. *Al Hamishmar*, September 7, 1976.
54. *See* Kayyali, *Tarikh Falastin*, chap. 2.
55. May 10, 1919, C.Z.A. Z/16009.
56. Gonen, *Psychohistory*, p. 186.

2 THE RACIAL MYTHS OF ZIONISM

Abdul Wahab Al-Massiri

Even though the Zionists do not accept a religious definition of the Jew, it should be pointed out that their anti-religious stance is neither necessary nor essential. The Zionists do not hesitate to make full use of mystic elements and to take full advantage of any religious sanction they can get. They form many government coalitions with the "religious" parties, and make many concessions to some of the formalities of orthodoxy. Their main target has been, and still is, the assimilated Jew, be he religious or non-religious. A religious definition of the Jew, placed within a "nationalist" context, is perfectly acceptable.

The 'Danger' of Assimilation

The assimilationist outlook views the Jew as a complex personality, belonging to whatever country he may be living in, contributing to whatever cultural tradition he may have evolved from, yet simultaneously interacting with his specific religious and cultural heritage. But Zionist theoreticians denounce assimilation and characterize it as a form of alienation from a hypothetically true and pure Jewish identity. Their writings are replete with references to assimilation as a poisonous and destructive force. Arthur Ruppin, a Zionist theoretician who was also in charge of a Zionist settlement in Palestine, described absorption as an "imminent danger"[1] threatening Jewish life. Klatzkin could characterize assimilation as a disease "infecting" the Jewish communities and "disfiguring" and "impoverishing" them,[2] and Chaim Weizmann had nothing but unqualified contempt and deep "hatred" for assimilated Jews,[3] even talking of the "assimilationist taint."[4]

In keeping with this anti-assimilationist Zionist outlook, the joint meeting of the Israeli Cabinet and the Zionist Executive, held on March 15, 1964, referred, in its official communiqué to "the danger of assimilation" as a major problem facing the Jewish people in the Diaspora. This fear of political freedom and assimilation as a "threat" to Jewish survival, even more detrimental to the Jews than "persecution, inquisition, pogroms and mass murder," was the theme of the 26th Zionist World Congress in 1965,[5] (a theme earlier harped on by Dr Goldmann in his speech to the World Jewish Congress Executive in 1958: "Our emancipation may become identical with our disappearance").[6] Rabbi

Moritz Guedemann of Theodor Herzl's home town Vienna pondered the question of assimilation and the Zionist attack mounted against it in the name of "race and nationhood"[7] and pure Jewishness. He then asked a moot question, in a pamphlet on Jewish nationalism: who is indeed more assimilated, the nationalist Jew who ignores the Sabbath and dietary laws, mistaking Judaism for the folk dances and ways of eastern European ghettos, or the believing and practicing Jew who takes himself to be a full citizen of his country?[8] It is a question to be put not only to Zionists, but also to "ethnic Jews" who, preferring the easy to the good life, follow the lure of consumerism, dissociating themselves from any oversubtle religious beliefs, and practice folk rituals devoid of any moral content.

As expected, the Zionist attack on assimilation in the name of a higher, autonomous Jewish nationalism is not always met with universal jubilation among the vast majority of the Jewish people in the Diaspora. In the hope of pacifying an indignant or embarrassed Diaspora, Zionist spokesmen at times make conciliatory statements which assure the Diaspora Jews of their autonomy. Such a statement was made by Ben Gurion on August 23, 1950, when he said that the state of Israel "represents and speaks only on behalf of its own citizens." He then drew a sharp distinction between "the people of (the state of) Israel," and the Jewish communities abroad. In no way, said Ben Gurion, did the Zionist state presume to represent or speak in the name of the Jews.[9] In its lead editorial of May 10, 1964, the *Jerusalem Post* asserted "the right of every Jew . . . to have as much or as little contact with Zionism and Israel as he personally pleases."[10] Such statements are duly quoted at the appropriate moment, but the more persistent underlying premise in Zionist thought and practice is one of universal pan-Jewish peoplehood. Ben Gurion's use of the phrase "the people of Israel" in reference to the Jewish citizens of Israel only, is neither representative of the Zionist use of that term nor of the meaning usually attached to it.

Zionism, always dissatisfied with a belief in complexities, ever intolerant of dialectics, advocated the concept of the abstract, quintessential Jew, or, to use Klatzkin's comic term, "the unhyphenated Jew"[11] who has a unique, separate, national identity. What constitutes this pure Jewishness of this peoplehood? What is the basis of this "new definition of Jewish identity," the new "secular definition?"[12] In attempting to answer this question a curious fact emerges: the anti-assimilationist Zionists wanted to reconstitute "the Jewish character and situation"[13] in such a way that they become a people *like any other*.

Instead of assimilation, what is suggested is a dissolution, a complete merging into the world at large, a trend quite consistent with their levelling godless pantheism.

The way to achieve that goal is to "normalize" the Jew,[14] deriving the norms not from the Jewish tradition but rather from the beautiful world of the gentiles the Zionists at times claim to hate so much. Nathan Birnbaum sarcastically notes in his moving essay "In Bondage to Our Fellow Jews," that Zionists try "to remold" the Jews "on the European model, 'to make men of us' . . . and to drag (our children) away from our holy teachings, from our Judaism . . . to 'their' teachings, to their world of license."[15] Describing Zionist vocational training, a speaker at a Histadrut convention referred to it as being "the self-preparation of the Jewish worker to become a gentile. . . . The Jewish village girl shall live like a gentile country lass.."[16]

To prove that this program for reform, this vision splendid, is not untenable, the Zionists tried to develop a theory of a national Jewish identity, separate from all others, yet not any different from them. The Jew, who is at the heart of the Zionist program, is at times biologically determined, at others the determination is cultural or even religious, but at all times he is determined by the one or two exclusively "Jewish elements" in his existence, which turn him into an immutable element or essence, existing above all gentile time and place and therefore, like all gentiles, he needs to be "ingathered" in his own Jewish Homeland, on his own soil.

Corporate Identity: A Racial Definition

The view of a biologically or racially determined Jewish identity was first advocated by Moses Hess, who, predicting that the race struggle was going to be the "primal one," subscribed zealously to the celebrated Semitic-Aryan racial dichotomy which was destined to serve as one of the main dichotomies of later theoreticians of European racialism.[17] Herzl, for a while at least, flirted with the idea of a corporate racial identity freely using terms and phrases such as "Jewish race" or the "uplifting of the Jewish race." Even though the term was then, as now, ambiguous, acquiring at times a biological, at others a cultural content, we know from his answer to an anxious Nordau about the anthropological fitness of the Jews to be a nation, that what Herzl had in mind was a biological determinism.[18] On his first visit to a synagogue in Paris, what attracted Herzl's attention was the racial "likeness" he claims to have noticed between the Viennese and Parisian Jews, "bold misshapen noses; furtive and cunning eyes."[19]

It appears that the ranks of the Zionists were buzzing with "scientists" interested in proving that the Jews were a distinct race, so that they could claim to be just like the gentiles. Klatzkin reported that some Zionists wanted to argue for "the impossibility of complete assimilation" on the basis of a "theory of race."[20] Karl Kautsky refers to one such Zionist thinker, Zollschan, who, while objecting to some of the ideas contained in Chamberlain's classic on race, *The Foundations of the Nineteenth Century*, nevertheless firmly subscribed to the central thesis of the book: that humanity is moving from a "politically conditioned racelessness to a *sharper and sharper definition of race.*" Zollschan, like others, tried to prove that the Jews constitute a pure race, to make the Zionist world ghetto "the necessary goal for all Jews."[21]

It seems that Zollschan, who is relatively unknown now, was an authority on the subject of the "Jewish race", for he is approvingly quoted several times by Ruppin, in his *The Jews of Today*, the most systematic Zionist effort at evolving a racial definition of Jewishness. The Jews, Ruppin argues, "have assimilated to a small extent certain foreign ethnical elements, though *in the mass*, as contrasted with the Central European nations, they represent a well characterized race."[22] The racial purity achieved instinctively throughout history should be perpetuated consciously now. Ruppin asserts that a "highly cultivated race deteriorates rapidly when its members mate with a less cultivated race, and the Jew naturally finds his equal and match most easily within the Jewish people."[23] He frowns on the whole process of "assimilation which begins in denationalization and ends in intermarriage" — the enemy of all racist thinkers.[24] Through "intermarriage, the race character is lost," and the descendants of such a marraige, are not the "most gifted." Since intermarriage is "detrimental to the preservation of the high qualities of the races, it follows that it is necessary to try to prevent it to preserve Jewish separation."[25]

Defense not only of Jewish racial purity but also of Jewish racial superiority runs through Ruppin's study as it does through the writing of many Zionists. Morris Cohen noticed that the Zionists fundamentally accept the racial ideology of the anti-Semite, but draw different conclusions: "Instead of the Teutons, it is the Jew that is the purer or superior race."[26] Ruppin is true to type, for on the basis of this alleged purity and superiority, he builds his ideological Jewish separatism. He argues that races "less numerous and infinitely less gifted than the Jews have a right to a separate national existence, so why not the superior Jews." He also quotes with obvious satisfaction Joseph Kohler, another racialist theoretician, who declared that the Jews are "one of the most gifted races mankind has produced." Ruppin accounts for the superiority on Darwinian grounds: "The Jews have not only preserved their great natural racial gifts, but through a long process of selection these gifts have become strengthened."[27]

Many Zionist theoreticians and functionaries, who did not consciously advance the racial definition, assumed it as a matter of fact in their statements. Norman Bentwitch, in an interview in 1909, claimed that a Jew could not be a full Englishman "born of English parents and descended from ancestors who have mingled their blood with other Englishmen for generations."[28] Judge Louis Brandeis defined Jewishness, in a 1915 speech, "as a matter of blood." This fact, he said, was accepted by the non-Jews who persecute those of the Jewish faith, and Jews themselves who take pride "when those of *Jewish blood* exhibit moral or intellectual superiority, genius, or special talent, even if they have abjured the faith like Spinoza, Marx, Disraeli, or Hume."[29] Nahum Sokolow "frequently referred to his people as a race," and, like the theoreticians of racialism, believed that there were no pure races; however, of those that existed, "the Jews were the purest."[30]

Dr. Eder, the acting chairman of the Zionist commission, argued in 1921 against the "equality in the partnership between Jews and Arabs," and called for "a Jewish predominance as soon as the numbers of that race are sufficiently increased."[31] In a 1920 speech at Heidelberg University, Nahum Goldmann asserted the eternal racial separateness of the Jews. According to his view, "the Jews are divided into two categories, those who admit that they belong to a race distinguished by a history thousands of years old and those who don't;" he characterized the latter group as open to the charge of dishonesty.[32]

Lord Balfour, a gentile Zionist, thought in racialist terms of the Jew. Perhaps it is not entirely without significance to recall that one of the earlier drafts of the Balfour Declaration talked of a "national home for the Jewish race,"[33] a phrase which, given the racialist outlook of the time, carried an unmistakable biological content and designation.

An Ethnic Definition

All these Zionist efforts notwithstanding, the argument for a racialist corporate identity had to be dropped. Theories of race and racial superiority and inferiority have always had a dubious validity and little scientific sanction. "By the 1930s, the intellectual climate had swung clearly away from racism and racism had lost its apparent scientific respectability."[34] Even though we still hear statements about the "Jewish race" among Zionists and racists, such statements were far more frequent before the 30s.

Simcha King observed that "having lived through the era when the word 'race' has become identified with cruelty and barbarism, most people shy away from using the word. Moreover, anthropology has shown that the term cannot be correctly applied to the Jews."[35] However, he pointed out that "it was *very common* to refer to the Jews as a race in pre-Hitler days and many believed that being a Jew was a matter of birth and physical relationship."[36]

Moreover, a tight racialist definition is simply too mythical and therefore readily challenged by reality. The Nazis, after evolving their "scientific" hierarchy of races, found themselves forming an alliance with the Asiatic Japanese, and therefore the Japanese were reappointed as "honorary Aryans," destroying the very biological determinism underlying the Nazi outlook. The South African apartheid regime has inherited the practice and Japanese businessmen are considered white. In other words, the mad biological determinism of the racialist outlook is always moderated by reality and the very complexity it tries to ignore or flatten.

Zionist determinism, being no different, found it impossible to continue to perpetuate a biological definition and the racialist typology of a Gobineau, Chamberlain, Zollschan and Ruppin, because biological apologetics proved too simple, especially in view of the fact that the Zionists had something the Nazis did not, a widely dispersed Diaspora, multiracial and mutli-cultural. The racial definition would have alienated the Diaspora which is clearly not genetically homogeneous; any one purely and strictly genetic definition would have had to exclude the majority. Herzl, the Austrian, already had his difficulties with one of the Zionist leaders. Israel Zangwill was a Jew who was of "the long-nosed Negroid type, with very wooly deep-black hair." Herzl said with good humour that so much as a glance at Zangwill or at himself would demolish the racialist argument.[37] Thus rather than seek the determination of history, the Zionists sought another definition of a corporate identity, one derived from ethnicity rather than heredity.

But even though the relatively complex formula of culture or ethnicity replaces the simplistic biological formula, the determinism is very much there, hardly moderated at all. The Jew is seen as eternally determined by a unique historical and cultural structure to which the Jew is reducible and outside which he has no healthy existence and over which he has no control. This is not peculiar. Many racialists see that culture itself is an expression of the *Weltanschauung* of a nation whose character is biologically determined. Race, nation and culture overlap to such a degree that Sokolow's biographer recommended that "when one reads the passages where Sokolow uses the word 'race,' one notices that he frequently uses it in the sense of nationality, in the sense of being born a member of a group with a great heritage."[38]

The biological determinism of culture and the correlation of nation and race in Zionist literature is such that any reader will not fail to see that the categories of "nation" or "culture" in a religious or ethnic sense, overlap with the category of race in the genetic sense. Moses Hess, as noted earlier, viewed world history as the arena for two world historic *races*, then he added that "the final aim of history is harmonious cooperation of all *nations*,"[39] that is, races. Ruppin also correlates the racial and cultural asserting that "a nation's *racial* and *cultural* values are its justification for a separate existence,"[40] and he talks of the Jew, a racial category according to his definition, as "a high type of human culture."[41]

The same correlation is implied by Rabbi Joachim Prinz when he called for the replacement of integration by "an acknowledgement of the Jewish nation and Jewish race."[42] Barnet Litvinoff described the Zionist view of brotherhood as founded "on a strictly *nationalist* or *racial* basis," for it "meant brotherhood with Jew, not with Arab."[43]

Unlike the French view of nationalism which grew out of the Enlightenment and considered all men equal, Zionism grew out of German idealism and romanticism with its emphasis on the "Volk" and its organic ties with the Fatherland. Dr. Hans Kohn points out that Zionism defined Jewish identity, borrowing organicist, determinist terms such as "blood, destiny and organic folk community" from nationalist German thought to describe the Zionist definition of Jewish nationhood. He says that some of his Zionist friends believed that "a man of Jewish ancestry and cultural heritage could never become or be a true German, Italian, Frenchman, or Dutchman. He is bound to remain alien everywhere except in his own 'ancestral' soil." Kohn finds this concept of nationhood, based on "biological determinism," counter to the spirit of the Enlightenment.[44]

The same point is made by Dr. Arendt in her celebrated essay "Zionism Reconsidered." Speaking of the "crazy isolationism" of the Zionists, she traces it back to an "uncritical acceptance of German-inspired nationalism." Summarizing the underlying premise, she finds it to be based on a belief in the nation as "an eternal organic body, the product of inevitable *growth* or *inherent* qualities." This view explains "peoples not in terms of political organization but in terms of biological superhuman personalities."[45]

When reading Zionist literature we perhaps ought to decode the phrase "Jewish people" into "Jewish race," or at least to remember that the terms "people" or "nation," given the organicist orientation of Zionist thought, imply a reductive determinism, almost biological. This Zionist-Germanic concept of the Jewish nation underlies many of the statements of Zionist spokesmen such as Ambassador Herzog, who pointed out that the Zionist ideal was based "on the unique and unbroken connection, extending for some 4,000 years, between the People of the Book and the Land of the Bible,"[46] a Germanic organicism of the purest and most elongated kind.

This denial of the concrete complexity and variety of the Jews, this assertion of permanence and fixity, are manifested in a variety of terms and concepts. The very use of the term "Israel" implies this idea of unbroken continuity and incessant self-duplication. Some refer to the Zionist state as the Third Commonwealth (Bayit sh'lishi), one link in a series that began with David, temporarily disappearing with the Roman conquest of Jerusalem, only to be revived in 1948 A.D. To restore faithfully that general museum atmosphere the Zionists pride themselves on, the Parliament is called a Knesset and the Israeli lira will be called shekel. Many Zionist historians and political scientists refer to the society of the Zionist settler-colonialists before 1948 as the new Yishuv to confuse it with the old religious Yishuv and to assert the unbroken settlement in Zion. To give an illusion of continuity some Israeli military commentators seriously compare David and Solomon's cavalry with the tanks of the Israeli army.

Ben Gurion is a prime example of this trend. In *Rebirth and Destiny*, he tried to understand the Middle Eastern realities of his time by referring them to what he consideres similar events in the past. Consequently with a straight face he could talk of the modern Arabs as Assyrians and Babylonian Iraqis, Phoenician Lebanese and Pharaonic Egyptians. Given his Zionist ahistorical continuity, he once told a newspaperman to challenge Nasser to speak in his native tongue — the language of the ancient Egyptians, as if one of the leading figures of Arab nationalism were not an Arab at all. His perception of reality and history in terms of his impossible Zionist continuity or repetitiveness sometimes provides comic relief. The Zionist leader talks of the "third return to Zion," i.e. Zionist settlement in Palestine, as distinct from the first two, not in terms of level of morality or depth of vision, but rather in terms of its geographical characteristic: the third commonwealth happily overlooks both the Atlantic and the Indian Ocean, a view of Zion that undoubtedly will leave the Redeemer, when he comes, at a loss. Ben Gurion then goes on to indicate that the third *aliyah* or ascent to Zion was by sea from the West, unlike the other two returns which were by land. Given the fact that the new Zion is surrounded by hostile Arab states (a detail which is not part of the divine scenario), this leaves the sea as the only way of communication between the third Zion and the Diaspora. And lo and behold! It is all prophesied in Isiah's splendid verses: "that made the depths of the sea a way for the redeemer to pass over,"[47] an exegesis that would shock the Creator Himself.

Nor is this firm commitment to the unbroken continuity confined to ideologues like Ben Gurion, but includes the academic circles. During the 1967 victories of the Israeli army, an Israeli professor of history at the Hebrew University, commenting on the outcome of the war, said that the Israeli soldiers saw the Red Sea for the first time again after 4,000 years of absence since that celebrated time when they had had to cross it with "General" Moses, (therefore General Dayan was referred to as Moshe II). Once an Israeli professor of International Law, in a debate at the Peace Academy in New York, in earnest compared the return of a Jew to Palestine to the return of an American to his homeland, the latter returning after a two or three year residence abroad, the former, the professor said, returning after a two or three thousand year trip. He was serious. What are two or three thousand years, after all, for a wolfish hegelian mind that can gobble up millennia with extraordinary matter of factness!

Good Hegelians as they are, the Zionists think in terms of hypothetical abstract beginnings of a unique Jewish history and they postulate the equally abstract happy endings of that history. Max Nordau summarized this Zionist Hegelianism when he suggested that "Palestine and Syria be restored to their original owners,"[48] with total disregard for the intervening two millennia of Diaspora existence and unfolding history in Palestine. What makes history shrink to these miniature proportions is the fixed cultural identity of the Jew.

The ethnic argument, like the racialist one, claims not only ethnic purity, but also ethnic superiority. Herzl boasted of "the human material we possess in our people! They divine what one would have to hammer into other people's heads."[49] Ruppin, in all humility, claims that other nations may have other points of superiority, but, he hastens to add, "in respect of intellectual gifts, the Jews can be scarcely surpassed by any nation."[50] Ambassador Herzog served the

United Nations a list of Jewish thinkers excelling in many fields, imply-
ing that their Jewishness, not their concrete cultural surroundings, was
the prime factor and the determining cause.[51]

A Religio-National Definition

The usual Zionist definitions and assumptions concerning the hypothetical Jewish identity are taken from the "normal" world of the
gentile. However, there is also a religious Zionist version which accepts
a strict, though formal and literal definition of the Jew. Like all such
religious Zionist definitions, it is deeply religio-national, with the first
element rhetorically emphasized.

The Zionist establishment does not find it at all difficult to cooperate with accommodating religious Zionist parties[52] because their
view of "the Jews," in its fundamentals, is not any different from the
Zionist outlook; the Jew is determined exclusively by his Jewish
tradition. They all agree on, and operate in terms of, the "Jewish
people," alien and unique and sacred, with the source of the sacred-
ness differing from one group to the other – divine for the religious
and selfbegotten for the nonreligious. This difference within identity
accounts for the agreement between the chief general and the chief
rabbi of Israel. When the godless Dayan said that if one has the Torah
and the people of the Torah, one should also have the land of the
Torah, the theocratic Rabbi Nissim sent him a cable congratulating him
on his deep understanding of the Torah. In the midst of this exegesis
and congratulations, what they forgot is the fact that a religion divorced from a moral commitmént and disrespectful of the existence of
others, is dangerous religiosity which bestows not only legitimacy but
also sanctity on one's prejudices.

The overlapping of the religio-national definition of Jewishness
with the ethnic racialist definitions is quite manifest in Golda Meir's
appeal to a Jew, who proved to be of Tartar descent, to "make a great
sacrifice for the state and convert to Judaism," thereby reconciling the
two apparently contradictory definitions.[53]

Double or Multiple Loyalties?

But whether a Jew by race, or cultural historical heritage, or national
religion, or even a combination of all these criteria, this Zionist construct of a "pure Jew," unrelated to the historical tradition of the
gentiles or their "soil," is the crux of Zionism. The Zionist controversy
surrounding the rationale of the claimed purity is quite marginal in
comparison. When Levi Eshkol advocates a "corporate Jewish life" that

aims at strengthening itself and Israel,[54] he does not dwell for long on
the source of this presumed unitary existence. Out of this concept of
pure Jewishness branch out a number of Zionist/anti-Semitic concepts
and themes such as Jewish power, Jewish block, Jewish vote, Jewish
genius, and Jewish interests. But implied in Eshkol's argument throughout is the premise that the pure and exclusive Jewish state is the cardinal
Zionist political channel for the fulfillment of pure Jewishness.

Ben Gurion emphatically stated that "only in a sovereign Israel is
there the full opportunity for moulding the life of the Jewish people
according to its own needs and values, faithful to its own character and
spirit, to its heritage of the past and its visions of the future."[55] If pure
Jewishness is bewildering and impossible when applied to a human
being, it veers toward the comic when applied to inanimate objects.
Ben Gurion talks of "the Jewish book, the Jewish laboratory and
scientific research . . . the Jewish field, the Jewish road, the Jewish
factory, the Jewish mine, and (naturally) the Jewish army."[56] Barnett
Litvinoff described the settlers as living "on Jewish bread, raised on
Jewish soil that was (naturally) protected by a Jewish rifle."[57]

The concept of the pure Jew underlies the Zionist schematic division
of the world into Jew and gentile. This division, common to Judaism
and other monotheistic religions, is sharpened by the Zionists, then
given a nonreligious content. The Israeli/Zionist tries tenaciously to
maintain an unalloyed purity in the state. Two non-Jewish Norwegian
sportsmen, who were invited to participate in the Maccabiah (a kind of
Zionist Olympiad) were prevented from participating after the American
delegation claimed that the Maccabiah was a strictly Jewish event,
for pure Jews only (gentiles need not apply).[58] In November, 1975, as
the U.N. was debating the Zionism/racism resolution, Jim Baatright,
the American basketball professional, had to convert to Judaism, not
for the sake of the state, but for the sake of sports. Baatright was so
cooperative that he discovered he had a Jewish grandmother back in
the Bronx, a discovery that speeded up the process of conversion at
the hands of one of Israel's chief rabbis.[59] The same polarity underlies
Israeli tinkering with the International Women's Year symbol. The
symbol was censored because it incorporates a cross, which happens
to be the scientifically accepted symbol for the female sex. A new
crossless sign was designed to be used in connection with local events,
one incorporating the star of David. This is not religious fanaticism,
but rather a form of deep chauvinism, or rather, a religious chauvinism.

The concept of the pure "Jewish national," the term now used in Israel to refer to Israeli citizens of the Jewish faith, implies a presumed loyalty on the part of Jews everywhere to their true Jewish homeland. This was undoubtedly Weizmann's belief, who, his close friend Crossman tells us, believed that every Jew was a potential Zionist and that those Jews "whose (Jewish) patriotism was qualified by any other national loyalty were to be pitied or despised,"[60] as mere traitors of their one and only homeland and God.

Klatzkin, the most radical of all Zionists, harping on the theme of Jewish national consciousness, warned the German people quite a few years before the publication of *Mein Kampf* that the boundaries of Germany could not in any way restrict the movement or loyalty of the Jewish people because Jewish unity is something that transcends national boundaries: "A loyal Jew can never be other than a Jewish patriot." Then, in language that anticipated Nazi propaganda, he said, "Not the slightest feeling of belonging can be found in the Jewish consciousness."[61]

Ben Gurion draws a chilling image of the purely Jewish lawyer in exile, "in Jewish duty bound to oppose the state and its ordinances." But in Israel this lawyer should "implant instincts of reverence and esteem for the state."[62] The Jewish lawyer, then, owes allegiance only to the Jewish state. As for the Jew who has the misfortune to live in the world of the gentiles, he will be influenced by gentile culture, even though he has "no roots" in it, and therefore he experiences "a constant duality in his life if he wants to preserve his purity."[63]

In the 1920s in Germany, Dr. Nahum Goldmann struck the Klatzkin theme of Jewish loyalty to the Jews' homeland. However, in New York City, on January 9, 1959, he moderated his statement, undoubtedly in the face of the resentment of the happily assimilated American Jews. He exhorted American Jews (and those of other countries) to gather courage and declare openly that they entertained a double loyalty. After dividing loyalty evenly between the country in which the Jews lived and the Jewish homeland, Goldmann went on to counsel them not to "succumb to patriotic talk that they owe alliance only to the country in which they live."[64]

Kallen presents a fantastic system of classification of Jews. Jews are not good or bad, nor ordinary, nor are they American, Arab or French or any such recognizable category. Rather they "may be distinguished as Undispersed and Ungathered, Dispersed and Ungathered, Undispersed and Ingathered, Dispersed and Ingathered, Dispersed, Undispersed and Ungatherable,"[65] a frightfully allegorical catalogue.

The Zionist definition of a corporate Jewish identity, be it racial, ethnic or religious, is a simple formula based on a simple determination; it is an encrustation corresponding to no concrete reality. All of us as individuals have multiple identities and, as a result, conflicting loyalties. The problems Jewish Americans encounter in secular society, based on the separation between church and state, are not radically different from those faced by a believing Christian who wants his children to believe in Christian values (or, for that matter, a believing Jew in the Jewish state). But the Zionist simplistic definition rejects the complexity of the assimilated Jew and sees it as a "duality" that would be better liquidated, (in the radical or Israeli/Zionist version), or mechanically maintained (in the schizophrenic Diaspora Zionist version, which implies the simultaneous centrality of Israel and the permanence of the Diaspora). If the monism or duality are replaced by complex dialectics, then the image which emerges would be that of the assimilated Diaspora Jew, for in a rich assimilationist context, there are not one or two loyalties, there are multiple loyalties which each individual, be he Jew or gentile, organizes according to his individual existentialist situation and moral commitment. In the context of a corporate national personality, we have the suffocating monism of one loyalty advocated by the Ben Gurions, or the schizophrenics, or the double loyalties of the Goldmanns (and anti-Semites)!

The Arabs are not so presumptuous as to engage in a definition of what constitutes Jewish identity, prescribing and proscribing, if such a matter were a completely subjective one, or if it lay completely outside their national interests. But this is not the case, and therefore the Arabs have to discuss this one Zionist definition of Jewish identity which encroaches on our lives and impinges on our destiny. Other definitions, however, are not part of our political consciousness or concern, and they remain a matter of purely intellectual or cultural interest. If a Jewish American decides to deepen his relationship with his religious tradition, rediscovers, revives, develops or abandons it, it is entirely his own choice; politics, at least Middle East politics, is not relevant to that level of analysis. But when the definition of Jewish identity nibbles at or engulfs Palestine, then it is a different matter. A good example of an issue relevant to Jewish American life but completely irrelevant to the Middle East, is the controversy raging around the hyphenation of the term of reference to "the Jew." The radical Zionist position is a complete rejection of the hyphen because Zionism considers "all the Jews of the world" as "one 'folk' in spite of their diverse political allegiances."[66] Klatzkin bluntly said, "We are not hyphenated Jews; we are Jews with no provisions, qualification or

reservation. We are simply aliens,"[67] a position remarkably similar to
the Nazi attitude which forced Jewish organizations in Germany to
change their names so that "they spoke for 'Jews in Germany' rather
than 'German Jews'!"[68]

Some "ethnic Jews" prefer to use the hyphen, because although
they feel they are full Americans, they still claim that they have a
Jewish national past which binds them together and sets them apart
from other ethnic minorities. Therefore, they are not Jewish Americans
but rather Jewish-Americans — an analogy with Irish-American and
Arab-American. Some Jews, like George Bagrash, the research director
of the American Council of Judaism, object, indicating that the said
process of hyphenation is erroneous since Judaism is neither "a national
culture nor a system of racial values." Hyphenation, Bagrash maintains,
misrepresents the religious identity of Americans of the Jewish faith,
and if an ethnic determinant be required, they should be called Italo-,
Greek-, Afro-, or Irish-Americans, after ascertaining their national or
racial origins.[69]

Nobody in the Arab world is inquisitive enough to have raised the
issue in any political platform. Many Arabs cannot even begin to understand the subject of the controversy concerning hyphenation, there
being no parallel in their historical experience; those who grasp it
might consider it of intellectual interest, yet it will remain of very little
political relevance to them as Arabs.

But when a definition of the self, be it religious or ethnic, be it based
on Judaism or Jewishness, spills over into a political program which
encroaches on the land and rights of others, then those others inevitably become involved and begin to engage in the process of definition
because it touches on their destinies and lifestyles. For example,
Aryan mythology was the exclusive domain of the anthropologist until
it began to serve as a base of Nazi ideology; it then ceased to be a
matter of pure academic interest or mere self-identification and became
the subject of international political controversy. When Shinto was
used as a means for the rationalization of Japanese militarism, the
whole world reacted and a religious sect in Japan was the subject of
wide discussion by people whose interest was primarily political. There
is no controversy in the Arab world concerning what constitutes
American-ness or Britishness, except perhaps among specialists who
have no particular political interests. But there is a political interest
in the definition of the limits of Jewishness and an attempt to distinguish between Judaism and Zionism, and between Jewishness and
Zionism because of the Zionist invasion of Palestine.

The Negation of the Diaspora

Zionist activism and militancy on behalf of Jewry is undoubtedly
motivated by a strong and probably sincere belief in the nationalist
ideology of pure Jewishness. However, the "nationalist," apparently
positive, assertions imply by definition negative aspersions on the not
so nationalist Diaspora. On a deep and latent level, one discovers that
Zionist ideology is predicated on the belief in the worthlessness of the
Diaspora. One can even argue that just as the conquest of the national
Eretz implies that the cultural life of the Palestinians is not worth
retaining, the conequest of the communities implies that the cultural
life of Diaspora Jewry is also not worth keeping. The nationalist Zionist
affirmation means the negation of the Diaspora.[70]

Ben Gurion described *galut* (exile) as mere dependence — a "rootless
alien people" depending on others.[71] Klatzkin saw it as nothing more
than "deterioration and degeneration" and "eternal impotence,"[72] an
abnormal and unnatural people. The abnormality, according to Zionist
ideology, is most evident in the occupational abnormality of the Jews,
heavy concentration in trade and the professions and little or no
presence in the ranks of the peasantry of the proletariat. Zionist education, to put an end to this state of affairs, tries to inculcate the negative
aspects of Diaspora existence, denying its achievements, presenting
Jewish contributions on "foreign soil" as a mere betrayal of the pure
Jewish spirit.[73] Levi Eshkol, in his official foreword to the 1965 *Israel
Government Year Book*, talks of Diaspora creativeness as drawing
"sustenance from alien soil and to that soil gives back its fruit."[74] The
presumed abnormality is always underscored and the Zionist happy
ending becomes inevitable with a Zionist Israel as a growing, normal
center and the Diaspora as a dying abnormal margin.

This negative description of the Diaspora is the essence of the
Zionist outlook, for if the life of Jewry in the Diaspora was presumed
to be any better, having its normal quota of human suffering and joy,
if it were a normal historical experience, why then the Zionist state?
Why Zionism at all? One can perhaps outline the Zionist strategy concerning world Jewry and the Jewish question as operating in terms of
two possible alternatives with no middle ground: settlement and Jewish
survival in the Jewish homeland or total assimilation and eventual disappearance for those who remain in exile. Both alternatives lead to the
liquidation of the Diaspora.[75]

The cornerstone of the Zionist program, according to Ben Gurion,
is a "radical break" with Diaspora dependence, "making an end of it."[76]

The "godless" Jewish communities willingly remaining in exile; these traitors to the divine Zionist state will merely serve as a bridge for the Zionists to cross over victoriously to the Promised Land. Diaspora Jewry from now on will serve as "a source of supply" for the national renaissance and any Zionist effort at delaying the total dismantling of the Diaspora edifice for a short while longer is simply a matter of expedience, giving the Zionists "the time to salvage some bricks" for the new national structure.[77] This approach defined the Zionist strategy vis-à-vis the Nazis; rather than organize the Jewish communities in Nazi-dominated Europe to join the resistance, the communities were seen as "a natural reservoir from which immigrants could be drawn to strengthen the key position of the Jewish community in Palestine."[78] In itself the Diaspora does not deserve to survive. "The transitional existence," Klatzkin says in no uncertain terms, "is of significance, precisely because it is transitional."[79]

Gordon, whose writings are largely a torrent of mystical epithets and nebulous nostalgic images referring to something vaguely infinite, draws a picture of a Jewish Palestine acting as the mother country of world Jewry "with the Jewish communities in the Diaspora as its colonies,"[80] a curiously mixed metaphor of a colonizing exploitative mother. Interestingly enough, a half century later, an American "Bundist," Chil Spiegel, found the metaphor of conquest and colonialism quite appropriate to describe Israel's "neo-colonial hold on world Jewry, drawing from it the material — dollars — to fuel her machinery."[81] Spiegel's metaphor, though apparently similar to Gordon's, is far more precise because there are no illusions about the motherhood of the extortionists.

The Zionist negation of the Diaspora was also a negation of Judaism and Jewry, because both have no concrete existence outside "exile." Almost all Jewish religious books and literature — from the Babylonian Talmud, that "portable homeland," to the *Shulhan Arukh*, to the Zohar, to Yiddish literature, to Philip Roth's novels and other Jewish-American novels — were produced by "exiled" Jews in the Diaspora. In that sense, the Zionist perception runs counter to the Jewish religious experience. It is also at variance with the Jewish historical experience itself. The Zionists could not understand or cope with the transcendence of the religion or the complexity of the historical experience.

Zionist Anti-Semitism

Zionism grew out of and was undoubtedly conditioned by one aspect of the historical experience of Jewry in the Diaspora: anti-Semitism. In

---

a real sense it should trace its genealogy back not to the positive assertions of the religious Jewish tradition, nor to the complexity of the Jewish historical experience, but rather to the negative aspersions of anti-Semitism. Herzl wrote that he and Nordau agreed that only anti-Semitism "had made Jews of us," and he specifically traced his recognition of Judaism or Jewishness (they overlap in Zionist literature) to the days when he read Duehring's anti-Semitic classic. The link between his sense of his own presumed Jewish identity and anti-Semitism is so deep and organic that in the first entry of the *Diaries*, written for posterity, he recorded that "anti-Semitism has grown and continues to grow — and so do I."[82]

Any reader of Zionist literature will not fail to notice that anti-Semitism is at the very center of the Zionist outlook of reality and at the heart of the Zionist view of history. Herzl's *The Jewish State* is premised on the simple view that wherever Jews live they are "persecuted in greater or lesser measure." There is a whole "sorry catalogue of Jewish hardships" which includes murder in Romania and exclusion from clubs in France (still a major grievance among Zionists in the United States). But regardless of time and place, "the fact of the matter is, everything tends to one and the same conclusion" — anti-Semitism — a breathtaking abridgement of history.[83] Weizmann felt that an assimilated Jew was an intellectual coward, unequipped with "a philosophy of history or of anti-Semitism"[84] in the manner of the nationalist Jews who largely focus on pogroms and rapes. If the Zionists do otherwise, they lose the legitimacy based on their highly partisan and critical view of the experience of Jewry.

The Zionists attribute to anti-Semitism a certain inevitability, eternity and centrality in the Jewish experience. Pinsker speaks of the hatred of the Jew as a "hereditary psychic aberration," a kind of "incurable . . . disease transmitted for two thousand years."[85] The comparison of anti-Semitism to organic phenomena is dramatically illustrated by one episode in the lifelong friendship between Weizmann and Crossman. When the Zionist leader asked Crossman whether or not he was an anti-Semite, the latter unhesitatingly replied, "Of course." Crossman's reply demonstrated to Weizmann his sincerity and honesty, for anti-Semitism, according to Weizmann, was "a bacillus which every gentile carries with him."[86]

The determinism of the bacillus metaphor betrays the narrow and infantile reductionism of the Zionist view of life. It dehumanizes the gentile, reducing him to the level of a racist assassin, actual or potential. It denies the efforts of all those gentiles who fought for the political and civil rights of the Jews and other minorities. But above all, it negates the great ages of Jewish creativity in the Diaspora. Zionism, however, cannot operate but in terms of abstractions: if the Jew is abstracted into a permanent victim or a permanent parasite, the gentile is equally abstracted into a permanent wolf.

If anti-Semitism has such permanence and persistence, if it is elevated to the status of an organic aspect of gentile human nature, then it necessarily follows that it is the most *natural* of phenomena. Pinsker and Herzl not only assumed the impossibility of assimilation, they also assumed the naturalness of anti-Semitism — "the inseparable companion" of Judaism throughout history, Pinsker said.[87] This assumption becomes a belief in its reasonableness, a belief which in point of fact makes the Jew responsible for anti-Semitic attacks. As a parallel to Weizmann's baccilus metaphor, one can refer to Nordau's equally pseudoscientific deterministic metaphor characterizing the Jews. The Jews, the Zionist leader said, are like a certain kind of microbe which is "perfectly harmless so long as they live in the open air, but become the cause of frightful disease when deprived of oxygen." Then this "scientific" racist goes on to warn governments and nations that the Jews might become just such a "source of danger."[88]

Klatzkin needed no metaphors. He bluntly declared that he could perfectly understand the legitimacy of anti-Semitism as "essentially a *defense* of the integrity of the nation in whose throat the Jews (another nation) are stuck," and therefore he candidly asked the Jews to admit the "rightfulness of anti-Semitism." In its denial is implied a denial of Jewish nationalism.[89]

Herzl, the gentle liberal, shared the same outlook, dissociating anti-Semitism from "the old religious intolerance," and characterizing it as "a movement among civilized nations (*sic*) whereby they try to exorcise a ghost from out of their own past." He also conceded that the Jewish state meant a victory for the anti-Semites, but this does not seem to bother him: "They will have turned out to be right because they *are* right." (Emphasis in the original.) This theme of the rightness of anti-Semitism is a cardinal one in the *Jewish State*. Herzl poses the question of all anti-Zionists: will not Zionism provide weapons for the anti-Semites? His answer is rather ambiguous but suggestive: "How so? Because I admit the truth? Because I do not maintain that there are none but excellent men among us." The anti-Semites, by expelling the Jews, were simply liberating themselves, ridding themselves of Jewish dominance. "They could not have let themselves be subjugated by us in the army, in government, in all of commerce. Many Jews objected to Zionism as anti-Semitic and even a friend of Herzl's, jokingly of course, told him that he would become "an honorary anti-Semite." But apparently the joke impressed Herzl so much that he took good care to record it in his diary.[90]

A famous anti-Semite of Herzl's days, who reviewed *The Jewish State*, heaved a sigh of relief that finally anti-Semitism had been correctly, and probably scientifically, understood by the Jews, and that the anti-Semites were perceived not as maniacs or fanatics but as "citizens who exercise the right of *self-defense*."[91] As if reciprocating, Nordau expressed his deep gratification "to see that honest anti-Semites applaud our proposed (nationalist) solution for the Jewish question."[92] From now on they would no longer have to defend themselves against the Jews but would simply play a positive role in transferring them, as Eichmann and other Nazi war criminals said.

The naturalness of anti-Semitism is predicated on a perception of the Jews' unnaturalness or abnormality, a basic premise of Zionism which has already been dealt with briefly. The Zionists, to establish the abnormality of the Diaspora, based their critique of the Jewish character "on a rationale of charges"[93] taken over from the literature of anti-Zionism in the Western world. Zionist literature is indeed replete with discussion of the ways and means to "productivize" the Jews in order to make them less parasitical, marginal or dependent. The Jew who emerges in Zionist literature is a usurer, a sick personality, living like "dogs and ants," accumulating money, following the values of the market place. The Zionist assumption is that Diaspora Jewry are leading an abnormal life and that Zionism will restore them to normalcy.

Brenner probably expressed himself in relatively extreme terms when he urged the Jews "to recognize and admit" their "meanness since the beginning of history to the present day," and then went on counselling them to negate all of that and make a fresh start, a push-button abstract revival.[94] His very extremeness puts in sharp focus an important aspect of the Zionist perception of the Jews. Sometimes the Zionist critique spills over into direct anti-Semitic caricature, for Klatzkin talked of a "rootless and restless" people, "living a false and perverted existence,[95] and the Jews, in Pinsker's words, are "everywhere a guest," "nowhere at home," moving like ghosts from one country to another, an alien body; they are half-dead, struck with the sickness of wandering.[96]

Yehezkel Kaufmann, in an article entitled "The Ruin of the Soul," culled his own collection from Zionist literature — Frishman: "Jewish life is a 'dog's life' that evokes disgust"; Berdishevski: "Not a nation, not a people, not human"; Brenner: "Gypsies, filthy dogs, inhuman, wounded dogs"; A. D. Gordon: "Parasites, people fundamantally use-less"; Schawadron: "Slaves, helots, the basest uncleanliness, worms, filth, rootless parasites."[97]

In *Davar*, the Histadrut newspaper, a headline referred to the "regeneration of a parastic people."[98] This is a theme at the very heart of the Zionist conception, recurrent in the works of the liberal Herzl as well as in the unliberal Brenner. If the latter spoke in rather extreme terms, Herzl too, used certain language and drew certain stereotypes which, if used by a gentile, would undoubtedly be characterized as racist. What could be more racist than Herzl's negotiating with a colon-ialist power, trading on world Jewish loyalty in exchange for colonial sponsorship. The words of the Zionist Chaim Kaplan reek of the worst variety of anti-Semitism: "Every nation in its time of misfortune has conspirators who do their work in secret. In our case an entire nation has been raised on conspiracy. With others the conspiracy is political; with us it is religious and national."[99] Kaplan has obviously taken over an anti-Semitic stereotype and applied it to himself and Jews at large. The identification with the oppressor and his view is a familiar pheno-menon in the history of man and oppression.

Thus the Zionists considered anti-Semitism a natural ally and posi-tive force in their nationalist struggle to liberate the Diaspora Jewry from their captivity. Rather than combat anti-Semitism, Herzl declared that "the anti-Semites will be our most dependable friends, the anti-Semitic countries our allies." From the very beginning he perceived the parallelism between Zionism and anti-Semitism and saw the potential for cooperation. In an 1895 blueprint for his future Zionist activities, the second step concerned publicity. He notes that it would "cost nothing, for the anti-Semites will rejoice," and will presumably give the Zionist idea free publicity. In another diary entry, he enumerated the elements of world public opinion he could mobilize in the fight against the imprisonment of the Jews, and he included the anti-Semites.[100] This hope for anti-Semitic militancy on behalf of Jews could not be expected unless there were an acceptance of a common anti-semitic/Zionist frame of reference and common interests.

The theme of a common Zionist/anti-Semitic outlook and dynamics is reiterated by later spokesmen. in 1925, Klatzkin proposed that "instead of establishing societies for defense against the anti-Semites, who want to reduce our rights, we should establish societies for defense against our friends who desire to defend our rights."[101] Nahum Goldman, in his heady radical Zionist days, lamented the thought of

the disappearance of anti-Semitism because even though it might benefit the Jewish communities politically and materially, it would have
"a very negative effect on our eternal life."[102]

Again this abnormal sentiment is no aberration but a theme inherent
in Zionist ideology and practice and harped on repeatedly and relentlessly. If the Zionist founding fathers were the first to propound it,
their descendents in Israel still perpetuate it with the same vigour. In
The End of the Jewish People? the Jewish French sociologist Georges
Friedman noticed that the Ashkenazim of Israel reacted negatively (and
sometimes aggressively) to any news indicating that Jews were leading
a normal life in any country of the Diaspora without being worried
or harassed by anti-Semitism. However, they showed a positive reaction on hearing "any piece of news indicating anti-Semitism anywhere
in the world."[103]

Anti-Semitism was so "positive" from the point of view of the
Zionist settler Yavneli that he believed it more or less "divinely
ordained,"[104] unconsciously echoing Herzl who claimed that "anti-
Semitism . . . probably contains the divine will to Good because it
forces us to close ranks."[105] In an exchange in the Hebrew press in
Palestine between Yavneli and Kaufmann, the former described himself as "an anti-Semitic Zionist," adding, "how could any Zionist
avoid a similar position?"[106] Kaufmann himself concurs. Zionist negation goes beyond Judaism and Jewry to reach to the "Jewish" remnants
in the Zionist soil, becoming a form of a negation of the Self, the ultimate form of alienation and surrender to the oppressor.

Notes

1. Arthur Ruppin, *The Jews of Today,* trans. Margery Bentwich (London:
G. Bell and Sons, 1913) p. 212.
2. *The Zionist Idea,* p. 321.
3. *A Nation Reborn,* p. 18.
4. Weizmann, *Trial and Error,* p. 346.
5. *Brief,* February 1965.
6. *Brief,* September 1958.
7. "Anti-Zionism," *Encyclopedia of Zionism and Israel,* I.
8. Stewart, *Theodor Herzl,* p. 247.
9. "Israel and the Diaspora," *Encyclopedia of Zionism and Israel,* I.
10. Cited by Elmer Berger. "After Talbot: Zionism on the Defensive," *Issues,*
Fall-Winter, 1964, p. 13.
11. Cited by Benyamin Matovu, "The Zionist Wish and the Nazi Deed",
Issue, Winter 1966-1967, p. 10.
12. *The Zionist Idea,* p. 319.

13. "Introduction," *Zionism Reconsidered*, p. xii.

14. *Ibid.*

15. *Ibid.*, p. 5.

16. Michael Selzer, "The Jewishness of Zionism: A Continuing Controversy", *Issues*, Autumn 1967, p. 17.

17. "Moses Hess," *Encyclopedia Judaica* (New York: The Macmillan Company, 1971), VIII.

18. Stewart, *Theodor Herzl*, p. 178.

19. *Diaries*, I, p. 1.

20. *The Zionist Idea*, p. 320.

21. Karl Kautsky, *Are The Jews a Race?* Translated from the second German edition (New York: International Publishers, 1926), pp. 217-220.

22. Ruppin, *The Jews of Today*, p. 216.

23. *Ibid.*, p. 220.

24. *Ibid.*, p. 228.

25. *Ibid.*

26. Morris R. Cohen, "Zionism: Tribalism or Liberalism," in *Zionism*, p. 50.

27. Ruppin, *The Jews of Today*, p. 217.

28. Tahseen Basheer, ed., *Edwin Montaqu and the Balfour Declaration* (New York: Arab League Office, n.d.), p. 20.

29. *A Collection of Addresses and Statements by Louis Brandeis*, with a foreword by Mr. Justice Felix Frankfurter (Washington: Zionist Organization of America, 1942), pp. 14-15.

30. Simcha King, *Nachum Sokolow: Servant of His People* (New York: Herzl Press, 1960), p. 177.

31. Esco Foundation for Palestine, *A Study of Jewish Arab and British Policies* (New Haven, Yale University Press, 1947), I, 272.

32. Agus, *The Meaning of Jewish History*, II, p. 427.

33. Leonard Stein, *The Balfour Declaration* (London: Vallentine, Mitchell, 1961), p. 541.

34. "Race", *The New Encyclopedia Britannica* (Chicago: William Benton, 1943-1973), V.

35. King, *Nachum Sokolow*, pp. 176-77.

36. *Ibid.*, p. 177.

37. Stewart, *Theodor Herzl*, p. 393.

38. King, *Nachum Sokolow*, p. 177.

39. "Moses Hess," *Encyclopedia Judaica*, VIII.

40. *The Jews of Today*, p. 229.

41. *Ibid.*, p. 228.

42. Cited by B. Matovu, "The Zionish Wish and the Nazi Deed," *Issues*, p. 12.

43. In *The Road to Jerusalem*, cited by Ibrahim Al-Abid, *127 Questions and Answers on the Arab Israeli Conflict* (Beirut: Palestine Research Center, 1973), p. 31. Henceforth referred to as *127 Questions*.

44. Hans Kohn, *Living in a World Revolution: My Encounter with History* (New York: Trident Press, 1964), p. 67.

45. *Zionism Reconsidered*, p. 241.

46. WCRP Report, p. 5.

47. David Ben Gurion, *Rebirth and Destiny of Israel* (New York: Philosophical Library, 1964), p. 310.

48. Bloch, "Notes on Zionism by Max Nordau," p. 34.

49. *Diaries*, I, 231.

50. *The Jews of Today*, p. 217.

51. WCRP Report, p. 18.

52. Nedava, "Herzl and Messianism", p. 20.

53. *The Shahak Papers,* p. 39.

54. Richard Korn, "Eshkol's Official Plan for Israel and the Diaspora," *Issues,* Winter 1965-1966, p. 16.

55. M. Pearlman, *Ben Gurion Looks Back,* p. 245.

56. *Ibid.,* p. 246.

57. Cited in *127 Questions,* p. 31.

58. A Haaretz despatch dated July 22, 1973, cited in *Viewpoint,* July 1973, p. 31.

59. Patrick Marnham, "Is Israel Racist," *Spectator,* March, 6, 1976.

60. *A Nation Reborn,* p. 19.

61. Cited by B. Matovu, *"The Zionist Wish and the Nazi Deed"* p. 10.

62. Ben Gurion, *Rebirth and Destiny of Israel,* p. 421.

63. M. Pearlman, *Ben Gurion Looks Back,* p. 244.

64. *Jewish Daily Forward,* January 9, 1959, cited in Lilienthal, *The Other Side of the Coin,* p. 81.

65. Kallen, *Utopians at Bay,* p. 44.

66. Agus, *The Meaning of Jewish History,* II, 412.

67. Cited by B. Matovu, "The Zionist Wish and the Nazi Deed", p. 10.

68. Lucy S. Dawidowicz, *The War Against the Jews, 1933-1945* (New York: Bantam Books, 1975), p. 260.

69. Letter to the *Richmond Times-Dispatch,* April 19, 1975, cited in *Brief,* Spring-Summer 1975.

70. *The Zionist Idea,* p. 325.

71. *Ibid.,* p. 609.

72. *Ibid.,* p. 325.

73. Cited by Michael Selzer, "Politics and Human Perfectibility: A Jewish Perspective," in *Zionism,* p. 298, n. 29.

74. Korn, "Eshkol's Official Plan for 'Israel and the Diaspora,' " p. 14.

75. Agus, *The Meaning of Jewish History,* II, 469.

76. *The Zionist Idea,* p. 609.

77. *Ibid.,* p. 324.

78. Jon and David Kimche, *The Secret Roads, The "Illegal" Migration of a People, 1938-1948* (London: Secker and Warburg, 1954), p. 27.

79. *The Zionist Idea,* p. 325.

80. *Ibid.,* p. 382.

81. Cited by Allan C. Brownfield, "American Jews: Doubts About Zionism," *Middle East International,* September 24, 19, p. 13.

82. *Diaries,* I, p. 7.

83. *The Zionist Idea,* p. 216.

84. *A Nation Reborn,* p. 18.

85. *The Zionist Idea,* p. 185.

86. *A Nation Reborn,* p. 21-22.

87. *The Zionist Idea,* p. 185.

88. Stewart, *Theodor Herzl,* p. 178.

89. Agus, *The Meaning of Jewish History,* II, 425.

90. *Diaries,* I, p. 266.

91. Stewart, *Theodor Herzl,* p. 251.

92. Bloch, "Notes on Zionism by Max Nordau," p. 29.

93. Yehezkel Kaufmann, "The Ruin of the Soul," *Zionism Reconsidered,* p. 121.

94. *The Zionist Idea,* p. 312.

95. *Ibid.,* p. 323.

96. *Ibid.,* p. 184.

97. Kaufmann, *Zionism Reconsidered,* p. 121, n. 7.

98. *Ibid.*

99. Kaplan, *The Scrolls of Agony* (New York: The Macmillan Company, 1965), p. 174.

100. *Diaries,* I, p. 51.

101. Agus, *The Meaning of Jewish History,* II, 425.

102. *Jewish Critics,* p. 27.

103. *Zionism,* p. 142.

104. Selzer, "The Jewishness of Zionism," *Issues,* Autumn 1967, p. 18.

105. *Diaries,* I, 231.

106. Selzer, "The Jewishness of Zionism," p. 18.

3 ZIONISM: A FORM OF RACISM AND RACIAL DISCRIMINATION

Fayez Sayegh

Much controversy and protracted debate preceded the adoption of the U.N. resolution which determined that Zionism is a form of racism and racial discrimination. During these debates not one of the defenders of the Zionist movement came out with any statement or advanced any evidence to the effect that Zionism is not a form of racism or that its practices do not constitute racial discrimination.

Two substantive points were raised from the pro-Zionist side. The representative of Barbados said that racism as he understood it referred to a matter of color, and that there could be no racism where the target of discrimination was not 'black'. This was immediately answered by envoking the International Convention on the elimination of all forms of racial discrimination. Article I of the Convention explicitly states that the word 'race' in the U.N. context is used not in the narrow biological genetic sense, but in the generic sense — subsuming under it the concept of 'race', 'color', 'descent', 'national origin' and 'ethnic origin'. If there is discrimination on any of these grounds it constitutes racial discrimination according to the Convention. The Convention had been adopted unanimously by every member of the United Nations including Israel, the United States, and Barbados, ten years earlier. The second argument of substance was raised by the U.S. ambassador, Daniel Moynihan, who simply said that if it were true that the United Nations had defined 'racial discrimination', it was certainly also true that the United Nations had not defined 'racism'. How could the General Assembly then determine that Zionism was a form of racism, when it did not have at hand a definition of racism, Moynihan continued.

The background of Moynihan's argument requires the interjection of a personal episode. I had been honoured by the twenty Arab delegation by being named the sole debator on the Arab side. Only four days before the vote, the U.S. Ambassador asked that we meet. At that meeting he requested my definition of racial discrimination. I replied that my definition was unimportant and quoted the U.N. definition in Article I of the International Convention. "I swear to God I have not heard of it," was the U.S. Ambassador's answer. The *New York Times* reported that a shaken Moynihan later spoke to the editor of *Commentary* who verified my statement adding, "but there is no definition of racism." At this, the article reported, Moynihan jumped to the ceiling saying, "Good . . . . Now I can get back at them."

In fact there is a U.N. definition of racism. The four essential components of racism are in the International Convention — interspersed and prohibited throughout its Articles:

1. The concept of racial supremacy and any discrimination or ideas based on racial supremacy is prohibited (Article IV).
2. Racial segregation is condemned and an undertaking is made to prohibit it (Article III).
3. Racial discrimination is the bulk of the Convention. It is defined (Article I) and there are undertakings to prohibit it (Article II, Parts 4, 5 6 and 7).
4. The advisability and desirability of racial harmony. Parties to the Convention undertake to promote organizations which foster racial harmony and tolerance (Article II) and to initiate educational programs to create, in the minds of the youth, ideas of racial harmony instead of racial intolerance (Article VII).

What is racism? Stripping it of all particulars, racism exists wherever there is a belief that racial identification is paramount and of decisive significance. Six ideas are subsumed under this general statement: two implications, two principles of faith and two principles of practice. The implications are (1) that mankind is divided into groups of ethnic or racial or color distinctiveness and these groups are distinct from one another and different from one another, and (2) belonging to any of these groups has an important — if not a decisive effect on the aptitude, qualities and capabilities of the persons who compose the group.

The principles of belief are (1) that some races, or at least one race, are superior and therefore the others are inferior. The superior races are entitled to privileges to which the inferior races are not entitled. (2) Races cannot live in harmony with one another; coexistence is precluded by the very nature of the relationship; racial incompatibility is an essential corollary to racial diversity. Two principles of practice follow: (1) since races cannot live with one another, since they are essentially diverse, they must be separated; racial segregation is an essential prerequisite of a healthy international existence. (2) Where races coexist, supremacy and discrimination by one race against another are the inevitable consequence.

Every racist movement in the world consciously or unconsciously subscribes to these premises, believes in these principles, and practices racial segregation and racial discrimination. Where you do not have all these ingredients together, you do not have a perfect racism. This century has witnessed three perfect racisms: Aryan or Nazi Racism, Zionist Racism and Apartheid Racism. Zionism while agreeing with all the others in the application of the theoretical and practical principles, nevertheless differs in the form of application.

The application of the concept of racial superiority is illustrative. To the Aryan, it was a matter of biological determination. To the proponent of Apartheid, it is color that makes the white man, in his own conviction and belief and practices, superior to the black or the colored in South Africa. What makes the Zionist believe that the Jew is superior? The answer is in the Biblical concept of the 'chosen people' which — like every other Biblical concept — the Zionist movement has assaulted, called out from its spiritual and religious context (in which it may or may not have been appropriate), secularized, and given a new political temporal meaning that was not implicit in the original Biblical spiritual connotation. The concept of the chosen people is at the root of the Zionist belief in the superiority of the Jew to the non-Jew and therefore in the necessity for the Jew to enjoy privileges which he denies to the non-Jew both in theory and in practice. This concept of the racial superiority of the Jew is rampant in Zionist literature. In November, 1972 *The Jewish Press* commented on the fact that three of the five American Nobel Prize winners were Jews — and it said that this percentage was certainly higher than the Jewish share of the U.S. population. That very same newspaper had castigated General Brown a few months earlier because he had said that Jews had greater influence in the press and in the banks and in the politics of America than is warranted by their numerical proportion. And that same newspaper castigated Congressman Stein of New York who disclosed a multimillion dollar nursing home scandal all of whose luminaries were Jews; the newspaper said: "People are going to say, all the people involved in this scandal are Jews, this is going to create anti-Semitism." Thus, it is fine for a Jewish newspaper to say, "We have more than our share of Nobel Prize winners." But it is not all right for any-one to say, "You have more than your share of influence in the press, or in the banks, or in politics, or in scandals." One is appropriate and expected and legitimate, the other is inappropriate. This is a manifestation of how the concept of superiority links into that of special privilege.

The second important principle is that of racial segregation. Under Nazism the important thing was to create Aryan purity, to remove those incompatible with that purity under Nazi jurisdiction and to extend that jurisdiction to wherever there were German ethnics in residence. The Nazis interpreted racial segregation in this manner: purify the Aryan land and extend it to incorporate all Aryans. The Apartheid regime understands segregation by putting people of different colors in separate residential areas, culminating now in the Bantustanization of Southern Africa.

Zionism's peculiar form of racial segregation is relocation of people throughout the world. Jews, wherever they are, must be separated and detached from their normal area to live on one piece of land from which the non-Jews must be ousted. It can be likened to a heartbeat: the heart of Zionism cannot beat until every non-Jew is 'pumped-out' of the coveted territory and every Jew is 'pumped-in' to create the Judenstaat. And the Judenstaat does not mean a Jewish state. Herzl protested when the title of his book was translated as "The Jewish State." He said "I am speaking of the State of Jews." The difference is that a Jewish state would be one characterized by Jewish law, governed by Jewish norms and manifesting the Jewish ethos, but a state of Jews is one whose population is made up of Jews. This exclusion is the heartbeat of Zionism. This is what Zionism means by racial segregation.

The fact of Zionist racial discrimination is written into the fundamental laws of Israel; the Jew has privileges which the non-Jew, the indigenous Palestinian Arab, does not have.

Finally, and most significantly, how does Zionism understand the principle of racial disharmony and racial incompatibility? The title for this concept, in Zionist literature, is the inevitability of anti-Semitism. In order to make Zionism possible, in order to make the Jew conscious of his distinct Jewishness, in order to make him want to immigrate and go to Palestine, in order to make him want not to assimilate and not to be integrated, anti-Semitism must be perpetuated. Zionism not only believes in the reality and eternity of anti-Semitism, but also in the need for anti-Semitism, for without it the Jew would be likely to lose his identity through assimilation.

It follows that where there is no anti-Semitism, the memories of past anti-Semitism must be recreated. According to Ben Gurion, that is why the Eichmann Trial was made, so that a generation which did not live with the experiences of Nazis would be able to know what the Nazis did to the Jews. If anti-Semitism does not exist, any slight hint of hatred to the Jew must be magnified into an international conspiracy. If anti-Semitism does not exist it must be simulated, as in Baghdad in the late 40s and early 50s when Zionist agents led Jews to believe that there was a conspiracy in order to expedite and accelerate their mass exodus.

Where anti-Semitism does not exist it must be, if need be, generated. The Zionists say, let us pretend, let us claim that any opposition to Zionism, any criticism of Israel, is anti-Semitism, directed at the entire Jewish people in order to make all Jews feel insecure. This was precisely the Zionist response to the U.N. Resolution. The moment the Resolution was adopted it was declared to be a declaration of war by the United Nations against the Jewish people and against Judaism. In full-page ads in the United States, Canada and in some places in Western Europe, the Zionist movement told Jews all over the world: "This Resolution is not against Zionism only, it is against the Jewish people, and against Judaism, because there is no distinction [the ad said] between Zionism, Judaism and world Jewry." The ultimate purpose is to keep the fear of self-determination alive in the heart of Jewry, because without it Zionism has no viability.

4 NON–JEWISH ZIONISM: ITS ROOTS AND ORIGINS IN ENGLAND IN RELATION TO BRITISH IMPERIALISM, 1600-1919

Regina Sharif

The phenomenon of non-Jewish Zionism has been little known and often only vaguely understood. It has been found and continues to exist in many countries, for example, the United States, West Germany and France. The Zionist idea itself has its organic roots deep within the European imperialist movement. Nowhere in Europe was support for Zionism as widespread and popular over the ages as in England.

Non-Jewish Zionism existed and flourished in England long before the birth of Jewish political Zionism. In fact, some of the most enthusiastic and ardent supporters of political Zionism were Englishmen who saw England's interests best served by the creation of a Jewish state in Palestine. The idea of Jewish restoration in Palestine became prominent in England where it developed into a doctrine that lasted well over three centuries.[1] Nahum Sokolow, the well-known Jewish historian of the Zionist movement, commented on this permanent connection between England and Zionism: "English Christians taught the underlying principles of Jewish nationality." He expressed his gratitude to the many "English thinkers, men of letters and poets throughout the ages," who championed the Zionist cause. "For nearly three centuries Zionism was a religious as well as a political idea which great Christians and Jews, chiefly in England, handed down to posterity."[2]

Chaim Weizmann thus very well knew why he chose England as the starting ground from which to labour to gain international diplomatic support and legal assurance for his Zionist political schemes.[3] He had early recognized the importance of non-Jewish support and had moved to England "on the conviction that the British were the most promising potential sympathizers of Zionism."[4] In his words: "The English Gentiles are the best Gentiles in the world. England has helped small nations to gain their independence. We should try and get Gentile support for Zionism."[5] Most credit for the issuance of the Balfour Declaration goes to Weizmann and his unbounded energy, determination and singleness of purpose. But such interpretation is too simple and just as inadequate as that given by Lloyd George in his *War Memoirs*, where he suggests that the Balfour Declaration was given to

Weizmann as a reward for his solution of the acetone shortage during World War I.[6] Weizmann's skills in international diplomacy and persuasion, however great they might have been, would have remained fruitless had not the English mind been conditioned to Zionism long before Herzl's or Weizmann's time and had not the seeds of Zionism been laid and cultivated in England by non-Jewish Zionists long before the appearance of Theodor Herzl's *Judenstaat* – the publication of which is often considered the birth of Jewish political Zionism.

The English Zionist Tradition: Biblical Beginnings – Puritan and Evangelical Zionism

England of the seventeenth century was, in Carlyle's own words, an England of "awful devout Puritanism."[7] Puritanism meant the invasion of Hebraism as transmitted through the Old Testament, but distorted by the effort to apply the ethics, laws and manners of the Old Testament Hebrew people, a people that lived in the Middle East more than two thousand years earlier, to post-Renaissance England.[8] William Cunningham described the Puritan society: "The general tendency of Puritanism was to discard Christian morality and to substitute Jewish habits in its stead."[9] They baptized their children by the names not of Christian saints but of Hebrew patriarchs or warriors. They "turned the weekly festival by which the church had from primitive time commemorated the resurrection of her Lord, into the Jewish Sabbath."[10]

The concept of Jewish race thus came to play a special role in English thought and understanding of the existing world order. The idea that Palestine had to be restored to its Hebrew ancestors had its beginnings here. Palestine had up until then been remembered as the Christian Holy Land, unfortunately lost to Islam. But in seventeenth century England it came to be regarded as the homeland of the Jews, whose return to Palestine was, according to Old Testament prophecies, inevitable for the coming of the Second Advent of Christ. Before long some Englishmen had organized a movement calling for the return of the Jews to Palestine. In 1649 a petition was sent to the English government: "That this Nation of England, with the inhabitants of the Netherlands, shall be the first and the readiest to transport Izraell's sons and daughters in their ships to the land promised to their forefathers, Abraham, Isaac and Jacob for an everlasting inheritance."[11] Its authors were Joanna and Ebenezer Cartwright, two English Puritans residing in Amsterdam.[12] They further requested that the Jews be allowed again into England from which they had been banned by Edward I 350 years earlier.

Reentry of the Jews was based on the Puritan belief that since Puritanism was in its doctrine very close to Judaism, the Jews, once in contact with it, would no longer resist conversion to Christianity. A similar request was made in 1650 by Manassah ben Israel, a rabbi of Amsterdam who wanted the extension of the Jewish Diaspora into England so that the worldwide Jewish dispersion might be complete, in order for the "ingathering of the exilees in Zion" to begin.

For the religious fanatic Oliver Cromwell these reasons were enough, but they were not decisive. As a statesman, Cromwell's motive was self-interest — the aid that he and many later statesmen believed the Jews could render in a critical situation. In the case of Cromwell it was commerical profit mixed with religious justification. Civil war had badly affected England's position as a trade and maritime power. The British business and commercial class, almost exclusively Puritan, was particularly jealous of the Dutch, who had seized the opportunity to gain control over the Near and Far Eastern trade routes. The Dutch Jews were especially active in the expansion of Dutch trade during the time of the English civil war. When Cromwell agreed to the readmission of Jews he was engaged in a series of trade wars with Portugal, the Netherlands and Spain. Each of these countries had a considerable Jewish community known for its wealth, commerical skills and international contacts. Thus the Jews "could be useful to him as intelligencers whose connections, threading across Europe, could bring him information on trade policies of rival countries and on royalist conspiracies abroad."[13] The large amounts of capital that Jews would bring with them was an added incentive.

On the religious level Cromwell showed more interest in the ingathering of the Jews in England than in Zion. But his England was not yet the British Empire and his interests were not yet imperial but merely commercial. With British overseas expansion during the following century the issue of Jewish restoration in Palestine became increasingly colored with imperial considerations. The Puritan tradition of Zionism contented itself merely with the hope that Jewish restoration in Palestine was imminent. It saw no political role for England in its realization. Nevertheless, the very idea of Jewish restoration in Palestine was cultivated as the prelude to the Second Coming of Christ. It continued to be the religious dogma of Protestant English thought and, especially during the nineteenth century, was used to cover up British imperial interests in Palestine.

At the beginning of the nineteenth century England experienced an evangelical revival: "Now the pendulum had swung back again, after the

Hellenic interlude of the eighteenth century, to the moral earnestness of another Hebraic period. Eighteenth century skepticism had given way to Victorian piety, eighteenth century rationalism was again surrendering to Revelation".[14] The English establishment, shocked by the French Revolution which they regarded as the result of rationalism, returned to the Bible and its revelations. Evangelicalism, often called the "Israel for Prophecy sake" school, dominated England until the beginning of this century. It even spread to the United States where it is called Fundamentalism. Its dogma rested on the literal acceptance of the Bible as God's word: "The Bible is God's word written from the very first syllable down to the very last and from the last back to the first."[15] These, the words of Lord Shaftesbury, who considered himself the "Evangelical of the Evangelicals."

Shaftesbury (1801-1885) had the vision of a Jewish state in Palestine and occupies a central place in the tradition of non-Jewish Zionism. His Zionism was based on biblical prophecies and their fulfillment but it was also justified by the political realities of Victorian England. Like Oliver Cromwell, he was interested in the Jews as a nation, but his work concentrated on bringing this nation to Palestine. Shaftesbury certainly was not an advocate of Jewish civil emancipation. He consistently opposed it as a violation of religious principle. True, the Emancipation Bill was passed by Parliament in 1858, but it was not the Evangelicals who favored admitting the Jews to full citizenship on equal terms, but the less pious Liberals!

Shaftesbury's constant preoccupation with the Jewish return to Palestine made him the plan's chief advocator with the British political and imperial establishment. Unlike Cromwell, he believed that he personally, and England as a nation, had to work for the great event of Jewish restoration in Palestine. He was convinced, much more so than the Puritans ever had been, that human instrumentality could bring about divine purposes, a principle unacceptable to the orthodox Jews of the time. Shaftesbury made it his task to convince his Christian fellow Englishmen that the Jews "though admittedly a stiff-necked, dark-hearted people, and sunk in moral degradation, obduracy, and ignorance of the Gospel were not only worthy of salvation but also vital to Christianity's hope of salvation."[16] He preached his idea at a politically opportune time, because apart from prophecy, benevolence and philosemitism, Jewish settlement in Palestine became a political desideratum for England. Three major British interests involving the area of Palestine commanded the attention of many British statesmen during the nineteenth century: the European balance of power; the security of India threatened by France and Russia; and the unimpaired transit and route of communication with India via Syria. Thus began what William Polk described as "the curious union of empire policy with a sort of paternalistic Christian Zionism which is evident in British policy in succeeding generations."[17]

Early British Imperial Zionism: Lord Palmerston and the Eastern Question

Lord Palmerston (1784-1865) was a very valuable political advocate for Shaftesbury's idea.[18] Although Palmerston did not know Moses from Abraham, he could be appealed to in terms of practical British self-interests. Shaftesbury was well aware of this and presented his appeal not in terms of biblical prophecies and their escatological fulfillment but in terms of contemporary political realities and power politics. Foreign Secretary Palmerston's major concern was the complex Eastern Question and he was particularly receptive to Shaftesbury's proposal to use the Jews as a British wedge within the Ottoman Empire.

The political situation in the Middle East after Mohammed Ali's defiance of his overlord, the Sultan, required that England do everything in its power to keep the Ottoman Empire intact. It was argued that England needed a protégé in the Near East to guard Britain's future interests. "France, as the leading Catholic power, had large numbers of ready-made clients in the Levant. Protestant England had next to none."[19] Even the Russians had been at various times recognized by the Sultan as the protectors of the Russian Orthodox Christians living within the Ottoman Empire. Both France and Russia were eagerly awaiting the death of "the sick man of Europe," hoping to receive their share of his empire. England, under Palmerston, was willing to do everything in its power to prevent the sudden disintegration of the Ottoman Empire, and the Jews were to represent a key element in bolstering the Sultan. On August 11, 1840, Palmerston sent a letter to his ambassador in Constantinople, M. Ponsonby, urging him to press the Sultan on the issue of Jewish settlement in Palestine. On September 4, 1840 Palmerston again reminded Ambassador Ponsonby:

> ... don't lose sight of my recommendation to the Porte to invite the Jews to return to Palestine. You can have no idea how much such a measure would tend to interest in the Sultan's cause all of the religious party in this country, and their influence is great and their

connexion extensive. The measure moreover in itself would be highly advantageous to the Sultan, by bringing into his dominion a great number of wealthy capitalists who would employ the people and enrich the Empire.'[20]

The issue of Jewish settlement in Palestine was further discussed in an article in the *Times* on August 17, 1840 which particularly commended Shaftesbury for his "practical and statesmanlike plan to plant the Jewish people in the land of their fathers."[21] It also stated that this plan was now under serious political consideration in the Foreign Ministry.

For Palmerston, a Jewish presence in Palestine was connected with two advantages that were to serve British interests, both directly and indirectly. A direct advantage was the presence of a pro-British partisan group in an area where Britain heretofore had none and which was becoming increasingly vital for British imperial interests abroad. Additionally, an indirect advantage was seen in the influx of Jewish capital urgently needed by the Sultan in order to prop up his almost bankrupt economic system and to make it easier for him to maintain the territorial integrity of his empire. But the Sultan showed no interest in the British proposals. He remained adamant in refusing to concede to England a special status in relation to the Jews. Despite the Sultan's refusal Palmerston continued in his course of policy. British involvement in the Jewish question and the Near East was no longer seen as a political option, but as a political necessity.

Palmerston was not alone. Contingency plans were made for future developments and various political as well as economic reasons were found to defend British policy vis-à-vis Jewish restoration in Palestine. E.L. Mitford appealed in 1845 to the British government to work for the "reestablishment of the Jewish nation in Palestine as a protected state, under the guardianship of Great Britain." He also referred to the "final establishment, as an independent state, whensoever the parent institutions shall have acquired sufficient force and vigor to allow of this tutelage being withdrawn, and the national character shall be sufficiently developed, and the national spirit sufficiently recovered from its depression to allow of their governing themselves."[22] Mitford saw some "advantages of incalculable importance:" a Jewish state would "place the management of our steam communication entirely in our hands and would place us in a commanding position in the Levant from whence to check the process of encroachment, to overawe open enemies and, if necessary, to repel their advance."[23] Colonel George Gawler, the former governor of South Australia, put forth similar justifications and proposals: "Divine providence has placed Syria and Egypt in the very gap between England and the the most important regions of her colonial and foreign trade, India, China, the Indian Archipelago and Australia . . . A foreign power . . . would soon endanger British trade . . . and it is now for England to set her hand to the renovation of Syria, through the only people whose energies will be extensively and permanently in the work — the real children of the soil, the sons of Israel."[24]

Charles Henry Churchill[25] was yet another Gentile Zionist during the Palmerston era. As a staff officer in the British expedition to Syria which had aided the Sultan in the overthrow of Mohammed Ali, Churchill had realized the strategic importance of Palestine for British interests. But he also was a critic of Palmerston's policy to keep the Ottoman Empire alive at all costs. Instead, Churchill advocated the early liberation of Syria and Palestine under British protection. He envisioned the Jews as colonizers and guardians. Unlike Palmerston, however, he had a much more realistic understanding of the Jewish condition in Europe at his time. He knew very well that there was no "strong notion among Europe's Jews to return to Palestine". But all his efforts were geared into this direction, namely, to create such a notion among Europe's Jews. In his correspondence with Montefiore, president of the Jewish Board of Deputies, on June 14, 1841 he wrote:

> I cannot conceal from you my most anxious desire to see your countrymen endeavour once more to resume their existence as a people. I consider the object to be perfectly obtainable. But two things are indispensably necessary: Firstly that the Jews themselves will take up the matter, universally and unanimously. Secondly that the European powers will aid them in their views.[26]

Surprisingly enough, it was Churchill, a non-Jew, who called upon the Jews to assert themselves as a nation, forty years before Leo Pinsker, in his *Auto-Emancipation,* proclaimed to his Jewish co-religionists: "We must reestablish ourselves as a living nation."

The Jewish and Non-Jewish Zionist Collusion

After the 1860s, England had officially become an empire. Its entrenchment in the Middle East began in 1875 with Disraeli's purchase from the Khedive of Egypt's shares in the Suez Canal Company. In 1878 came the British occupation of Cyprus to be followed by the occupation of Egypt in 1882.[27] By the end of the nineteenth century, the changed geographical realities called for a revision in England's Eastern policy. With its concern now centered on Egypt and its protection, there was ample reason for the British government to deviate from its traditional policy of maintaining the territorial integrity of the Ottoman Empire in order to annex part of it.

The new significance of Palestine in the British imperial scheme came to lie primarily in its proximity to Egypt, Lord Kitchener, one major proponent of the new Eastern policy, called upon his government to "secure Palestine as a bulwark to the British position in Egypt as well as an overland link with the East."[28]

The changed political realities in the Near East also brought forth a new generation of non-Jewish Zionists. They were still possessed with the curious amalgamation of religious and imperial motives. But gone were the apocalyptic slogans and the Shaftesbury-type religious verities. These new generation Zionists were empire builders, fully aware of the strategic advantages to be gained from a British sphere of influence in the Middle East. Pro-Zionist literature written by non-Jews during the 1870s created a wave of public sympathy, and the idea of a British annexation of Palestine, through the medium of a British-sponsored restoration of Israel, began to appeal to many heretofore indifferent.[29]

At the same time, the Jews themselves began to actively take part in the gradual reopening of the Jewish path to Palestine. Shaftesbury, Palmerston and the others had been premature in their Zionist policy. Their estimate of the Jews as a people had been based on a total ignorance of Jewish history and aspirations. Only during the 1890s did Zionism begin to assert itself as a minority movement among European Jews.

Jewish Zionists actively lobbied among non-Jews, and even Herzl, after having failed with the Kaiser and the Sultan, had in 1900 turned to England. During the 4th Zionist Congress, held in London during 1900, he proclaimed: "From this place the Zionist movement will take a higher and higher flight. . . . England the great, England the free, England with her eyes fixed on the seven seas, will understand us."[30] Herzl also set high hopes in the Anglo-Jewish community itself. But British non-Jews were much more receptive to Herzl's proposals than were their Anglo-Jewish contemporaries. The latter generally refused to be associated with the Zionist movement.[31]

Joseph Chamberlain, the colonial secretary, and Arthur Balfour, the prime minister, in many ways personified the new type of non-Jewish Zionist. Chamberlain's first concern was the British empire. Biblical prophecy was of no concern to him; neither was he moved by humanitarian considerations or a sense of moral debt to "God's ancient people." But like Palmerston he recognized that Zionist prognostications presented legitimate opportunities for extending the British Empire. "He saw the Jews as a ready-made group of European colonizers available to settle, develop and hold all but empty land under the British aegis."[32] Chamberlain, in his efforts to extend the empire, was in continuous search for colonizers and settlers to bring civilization to the "lesser breeds" that lived without the law. His Zionism was not a philosophical one but a very practical one. Thus, when he offered Herzl Al Arish on the Sinai for Jewish settlement, he did not mind compromising on a major axiom of Zionism, namely that Zionism can only accept Palestine as the territory for the Jewish homeland.[33] There is some disagreement among scholars as to why Chamberlain decided to be a Zionist. His biographer, Julian Amery, first suggested humanitarian motivations and only later recognized that a "Jewish colony in Sinai might prove a useful instrument for extending British influence in Palestine proper when the time came for the inevitable dismemberment of the Ottoman empire."[34] Christopher Sykes paints another picture of Chamberlain's Zionism:

> In Chamberlain's enthusiasm for Zionism, and it was a passionate thing with him, we must not suppose that we see another manifestation of the Millennial tradition. Here was no successor of Lord Shaftesbury, no spiritual brother of Hechler and Sibthrop. Chamberlain's interest in Jewish fortunes was financial.[35]

If Chamberlain had any humanitarian concern for the Jews it was not a very serious concern, especially when it came to have unpleasant repercussions in England. During Chamberlain's time as colonial secretary, England's chief domestic problem was unwanted immigration, mostly Jews from Eastern Europe. Together with other Zionists, Jews and non-Jews alike, Chamberlain was very much in favor of restricting Jewish immigration created by the pogroms in Eastern Europe. His major fear was that of cheap labor competition and other social problems.[36]

Chamberlain's efforts were supported by Lord Balfour, who was prime minister (1902-1905) and later foreign secretary (1916-1919) under the premiership of another Zionist, Lloyd George. As prime minister, Balfour did his best to support the El Arish project even though be believed that Chamberlain's proposal had one major defect, "it was not Zionism".[37] Lloyd George, as a member of Parliament in

1904, was employed as legal counsel by Greenberg and Herzl to draw up the Uganda proposal in 1904.

Both Balfour and Lloyd George were self-confessed Zionists, ardent and united in their support for the Zionist cause. Balfour was a Conservative and Lloyd George a Liberal Party member. Balfour's Zionism had biblical roots. "Though he was the reverse of Shaftesbury, not ardent but a skeptic, not a religious enthusiast but a philosophical pessimist, he was nevertheless strongly infused, like the Evangelicals and the Puritans, with the Hebraism of the Bible."[38] His biographer and niece, Blanche Dugdale, herself a devout Zionist, describes Balfour as deeply religious, strongly believing that "Christian religion and civilisation owes to Judaism an unmeasurable debt, shamefully ill repaid."[39]

Lloyd George, too, hints at his early religious upbringing as the reason why he was drawn to Zionism. The memories of his childhood in Wales include the prophecies which foretold the restoration of the Jews to Palestine. "I was taught far more about the History of the Jews than about the History of my own people."[40] Chaim Weizmann, too, recalled that the "Lloyd George advocacy of the Jewish homeland long predated his succession to the Premiership."[41] In his own memoirs, Lloyd George gives most of the credit for his conversion to Zionism to Weizmann. His now famous phrase, "I am his proselyte . . . acetone converted me to Zionism"[42] also implies that the Balfour Declaration was given as a reward for Weizmann's acetone process. Yet, however great Weizmann's skills in chemistry and persuasion might have been, Lloyd George was certainly predisposed to be receptive to Weizmann's arguments in favor of a Jewish national home in Palestine.

Weizmann's first personal acquaintance with Lloyd George was in January 1915. But Lloyd George advocated Zionist goals before that meeting. On November 9, 1914, he had met with Herbert Samuel, a member of the Asquith cabinet and a Jew, and had told him that he "was very keen to see a Jewish state established in Palestine." When Samuel, in January, 1915, circulated his memorandum on the Future of Palestine, Lloyd George, as minister of munitions, together with Edward Grey, the foreign secretary, were the only cabinet members in favor of Samuel's proposal to combine British annexation of Palestine with British support for Zionist aspirations.[43] Prime Minister Asquith, however, single-mindedly rejected Samuel's "dithyrambic memorandum" and describes Lloyd George as "the only other partisan of this proposal . . . who I need not say does not care a damn for the Jews or their past or their future, but thinks it will be an outrage to let the Holy Places pass into the possession or under the protectorate of agnostic, atheistic France."[44]

Lloyd George's responsibility for the Balfour Declaration was far greater than that of Balfour. The *Zionist Review,* a semi-official organ of the Zionist Movement, assigned to him "the foremost place inside the Cabinet among the architects of this great decision."[45] When Lloyd George ascended to the premiership in December 1916, the British government began to seriously consider a public statement of policy on Palestine and opened official talks with the Zionists. By then the Palestine question had become part and parcel of the war's most complicated, entangled and mutually conflicting diplomatic maneuvers. But with Lloyd George at the wheel, Zionism had nothing to fear. Balfour was foreign secretary. Other Zionists like Mark Sykes, Leopold Amery, Lord Milner, Robert Cecil, Col. R. Meinertzhagen, Harold Nicolson, General Smuts and C.P. Scott also held important positions from which to work in the interest of Zionism.

In the controversy of how to conduct the war, Lloyd George chose to support those who saw the Near East as the major theater of English war effort after the deadlock on the Western front. According to Scott, Lloyd George regarded the Palestine campaign as "the one really interesting part of the war."[46] Lloyd George's fears were centered not only on the German-Turkish alliance but also on the threat of future French influence in the area. "The French will have to accept our protectorate; we shall be there by conquest and shall remain."[47] It became clearer than at any other time before, that British and Zionist interests coincided and were complementary. The Jewish Zionists, Weizmann in particular, did their part in identifying their own interests with those of Britain. For England, the acquisition of Palestine had become an irreducible strategic requirement. But a claim based on military conquest alone could not be reconciled with the principle of non-acquistion of territory by war, as advocated by U.S. President Woodrow Wilson, and would have alienated world opinion. Thus, open annexation was out of the question. The only course open to England was to link its own war aims with the principle of self-determination. The Jewish Zionists fitted very well in such a plan. For Balfour the Zionists were "the guardians of a continuity of religious and racial traditions . . . they were a great conservative force in world politics,"[48] and therefore could be relied upon. British non-Jewish Zionism found it appropriate to enter Palestine as a trustee for its Old Testament proprietors. It not only quieted the British conscience but left the door open for future British interests in the region. Mark Sykes once wrote to Lord Robert Cecil: "We should so order our policy that, without in any way showing any desire to annex Palestine or to establish a Protectorate over it, when the time comes to choose a mandatory power for its control, by the consensus of opinion and desire of its inhabitants, we shall be the most likely candidate."[49] The Balfour Declaration provided the effective moral attitude, the good cause. When the Peace Conference turned to the Mandate issue, the British mandate for Palestine was no more than the inevitable recognition of an already accomplished fact.

Gentile Zionism and Anti-Semitism

Non-Jewish Zionism is not derived from philosemitism. In fact, most non-Jewish Zionists felt the same prejudices as their anti-Semite contemporaries. It was not love for the Jews that motivated their Zionism, but their own selfish interests, be they religious fulfillment of prophecies or imperial expansion. Christian Zionists favoured Jewish Zionism as a step leading not to the perpetuation but to the disappearance of the Jews. In this respect the old Lord Shaftesbury-type religious Zionists advocated Jewish restoration in Palestine only to hasten the event of the Second Advent. Any deep analysis of early Puritan Zionism suggest that it was not for the sake of the Jews, but for the sake of the promise made to them according to Puritan biblical teachings. For most Puritans, the Jews were not a people but a mass Error that had to be brought to a belief in Christ in order that the whole chain of reaction leading to the Second Coming and the redemption of mankind might be set in motion.

Arnold Toynbee, in his *Study of History*, touches on the subject of Gentile Zionism and suggests that the pro-Zionist inclinations of non-Jews are generally derived from a sense of guilt arising out of a subconscious anti-Semitism.[50] He intimately relates Zionism and anti-Semitism. In theory, as well as in praxis, Zionism and anti-Semitism operate on the same plane, they are complementary to each other. One reinforces the other. Recent studies on Nazi-Zionist collaboration, for example, clearly bring to light such a relationship. Jewish emigration to a Jewish state served the cause of both the Nazi anti-Semite elite, who wanted to free Germany from its "Jewish yoke," and the Zionists who were in desperate need of increased Jewish immigration in order to create their Jewish state.

When Jews in England were working toward the goal of their complete civil emancipation, they most often were opposed by non-Jewish Zionists. Lord Shaftesbury spoke against the 1858 Emancipation Act and in 1905, Balfour introduced and fought for the Aliens Bill which restricted Jewish immigration from Eastern Europe to England, because of the "undoubted evils that had fallen upon the country from an immigration which was largely Jewish."

Much more vulgar were the remarks of other Gentile Zionists, such as Richard Meinertzhagen or Mark Sykes. The former, a chief political officer for Palestine in the British Foreign Office, turned to Zionism because "the Jews are virile, brave, determined and intelligent" as a race. The Arabs, on the other hand, he described as "decadent, stupid, dishonest and producing little beyond eccentrics influenced by the romance and silence of the desert". That his Zionism was most likely a cover-up for the latent anti-Semitism shows in the following statement: "But if the Jews are going to gain a predominant influence in this country (England) in profession, in trades, in universities and museum, in finance and as landowners, then of course we shall have to act against them."[51] Sykes, who in 1915 was appointed assistant secretary to the War Cabinet, was known for his anti-Semitic slogans, but most of all because he was before his conversion to Zionism a true anti-Semite, immovable in his prejudices.

Non-Jewish Zionists look at nations and people in terms of belonging to certain races. The Jewish race was praised but only came second to the English one which Chamberlain called "the greatest of governing races the world has ever seen."[52]

Notes

1. F. Kobler, *The Vision was There* (London, 1956), p.7.
2. Nahum Sokolow, *History of Zionism, 1600-1918,* 2 vols. (London, 1919), 1: xxvi-vii.
3. Chaim Weizmann, *Trial and Error* (New York, 1949), p. 258. At that time the main office of the Zionist organization was still in Vienna. Its intellectual center was mainly in Berlin, Germany, while its manpower was in Russia. But, as Weizmann rightly assumed, the movment's political importance could only be found in England in conjunction with British imperial schemes and ambitions. Such thinking was not commonly accepted by other leading Zionists during the early years of the movement. Moses Hess, the German Zionist Jew, speculated that "France will undoubtedly lend a hand to the founding of Jewish colonies in the land of their ancestors." *See* Moses Hess, *Rome and Jerusalem* (New York, 1918, 1945), pp. 129-130. About half a century later, Theodor Herzl himself thought his best allies to be Germany and Turkey. *See* ESCO Foundation for Palestine, Inc., *Palestine, A Study of Jewish, Arab and British Policies,* (New Haven, 1947), 1:43. Only after he had failed to obtain the legalization for Jewish colonization in Palestine from Germany and Turkey, did he then concentrate his efforts on England. *See* Sokolow, *History of Zionism,* 1:295.
4. Alan R. Taylor, *Prelude to Israel, An Analysis of Zionist Diplomacy, 1897-1947* (Beirut, 1970), p. 10.

5. M. Weizgal & J. Carmichael, eds., *Chaim Weizmann: A Biography by Several Hands* (New York, 1963), p. 92.

6. Lloyd George, *War Memoirs*, 3 vols. (New York, 1933), 1:50. Lloyd George is supposed to have asked Weizmann: "Is there nothing we can do as recognition of your valuable assistance to the country?" Weizmann answered: "Yes, I would like you to do something for my people". This, remarks Lloyd George was the "fount and origin" of the Balfour Declaration.

7. Thomas Carlyle, *Oliver Cromwell's Letters and Speeches* (Boston, 1884), 1:32;

8. In the words of Matthew Arnold, "Puritanism was a revival of the Hebraic spirit in reaction to the Hellenic spirit that had animated the immediately preceding period of the Renaissance." *See* Matthew Arnold, *Culture and Anarchy* (London, 1869), chap. 4.

9. William Cunningham, *Growth of English Industry and Commerce*, 3 vols. (Cambridge, 1892).

10. T.B. Macaulay, *History of England*, 5 vols. (Philadelphia, 1861), 1:71.

11. As quoted by Don Patenkin, "Mercantilism and the Readmission of the Jews to England," *Jewish Social Studies,* July 1946.

12. Amsterdam had become the refuge for Puritans, while they were still persecuted by Chalres I (1625-1649), as well as for Jews driven out of Spain and Portugal by the Inquisition.

13. Barbara Tuchman, *Bible and Sword* (London, 1956), p. 89. It is interesting to note that Cromwell sent Manasseh ben Israel a passport to come to England to plead his cause one day after he had passed the Navigation Act which gave rise to the war with the Netherlands.

14. *Ibid.*, p. 115.

15. Edwin Hodder, *Life and Works of the 7th Earl of Shaftesbury*, 3 vols., (London, 1886), vol. 1, chap. 6.

16. W.T. Gidney, *The History of the London Society for the Propagation of Christianity among the Jews* (London, 1908).

17. William R. Polk, *Backdrop to Tragedy* (Boston, 1957), p. 40.

18. Palmerston, a member of the Liberal Party, was British Foreign Secretary between 1830 and 1841 and again from 1846 until 1851. He then was appointed Prime Minister in 1855 and held that office until 1865. He also was Lord Shaftesbury's stepfather-in-law.

19. Leonard Stein, *The Balfour Declaration* (New York, 1961), p. 8.

20. Charles Webster, *The Foreign Policy of Palmerston* (London, 1951), p. 762.

21. As quoted in Tuchman, *Bible and Sword,* p. 113.

22. Albert Hyamson, *British Projects for the Restoration of Jews to Palestine* (Philadelphia, 1918).

23. Israel Cohen, *The Zionist Movement* (New York, 1946), p. 52. The advent of steam navigation during the 1840s made the Near East important in the route to India. Steamships required frequent recoaling and therefore the British ships used the Mediterranean-Red Sea route with transhipment at Suez rather than the long Cape road.

24. Hyamson, *British Projects,* p. 37; Cohen, *The Zionist Movement,* p. 52.

25. Charles Henry Churchill was a grandson of the Duke of Marlborough and therefore an antecedent of Winston Churchill.

26. Cohen, *The Zionist Movement,* p. 51.

27. Strangely enough, Britain's eastward expansion in the latter nineteenth century was under the guidance of Disraeli, England's first prime minister of Jewish descent. Disraeli, although baptized in the Anglican church, still had kept his pride in his race. For a complete and detailed analysis of British penetration into the sphere of influence of the Sultan, *see* James A. Marriott, *The Eastern*

Question, An Historical Study (Oxford, 1940), and John Marlowe, *A History of Modern Egypt and Anglo-Egyptian Relations, 1800-1893* (New York, 1954).

28. George Antonious, *The Arab Awakening* (London, 1938), pp. 261-62.

29. To mention here only George Eliot and her novel *Daniel Deronda*, published in 1876. Through her hero Daniel, the author advocates Jewish nationhood: "The idea that I am possessed with is that of restoring a political existence to my people, making them a nation again, giving them a national center." *See* also Tuchman, *Bible and Sword*, pp. 150-52.

30. Alex Bein, *Theodor Herzl*, (Philadelphia, 1954), p. 346.

31. In 1880 there were about 60,000 Jews in England, many of them British born and nearly all of them more of less anglicized. But between 1880 and 1905 about 100,000 Jews came to settle in England from Eastern Europe. Most Jewish Englishmen were very adament in their opposition to Zionism, which they believed threatened their status and recognition just recently gained. *See* Leon Simon, *The Case of the Anti-Zionists* (London, 1917), p. 9.

32. Tuchman, *Bible and Sword*, p. 189.

33. This Sinai offer, made in 1902, did not materialize; it was rejected by Lord Cromer as politically unfeasible for England and Egypt and many Jewish Zionists believed El Arish to be economically unsuitable for Jewish settlement.

34. Julian Amery, *The Life of Joseph Chamberlain*, 4 vols., (London, 1951), 4:261.

35. Christopher Sykes, *Two Studies in Virtue* (London, 1953) p. 162. Most Zionist financial institutions were located in London: the Jewish National Fund, The Jewish Colonial Trust and the Anglo-Palestine Company.

36. In 1905, Balfour, as prime minister, signed the Aliens Bill into law, restricting immigration from Eastern Europe. Balfour himself fought for the passage of the Bill in Parliament on the grounds that every country has the right to choose its immigrants and because "undoubted evils had fallen upon the country from an immigration which was largely Jewish." *See* House of Commons, July 10, 1905, Official Record, Col. 155 and House of Commons, May 2, 1905, Official Record, Col. 795. *See* also V.D. Lipman, *Social History of the Jews in England, 1850-1950* (London, 1954), pp. 141 ff.

37. Sokolow, *History of Zionism*, Introduction.

38. Tuchman, *Bible and Sword*, pp. 198-99.

39. Blanche E.C. Dugdale, *Arthur Balfour, First Earl Balfour,* 2 vols. (New York, 1937), 1:324.

40. Philip Guedalla, *Napoleon and Palestine* (London, 1925), p. 48.

41. Weizmann, *Trial and Error*, p. 192.

42. Guedalla, *Napoleon and Palestine*, pp. 49-51.

43. Viscount Samuel, *Memoirs* (London, 1954), pp. 139 ff.

44. Earl of Oxford and Asquith, *Memories and Reflections*, vol. 2 (London, 1928), p. 65.

45. *Zionist Review*, December 1917, p. 214.

46. C.P. Scott's *Journals*, as quoted by Stein, *The Balfour Declaration*, p. 145.

47. *The Diary of Lord Bertie of Thame* (London, 1924), vol. 2, p. 122. Lord Bertie was British ambassador to France.

48. Dugdale, *Arthur Balfour*, vol. 2, p. 158.

49. Leslie Shane, *Mark Sykes: His Life and Letters* (New York, 1923).

50. Arnold J. Toynbee, *A Study of History* (London, 1953), p. 308.

51. Richard Meinertzhagen, *Middle East Diary, 1917-1956* (Paris, 1967).

52. S.H. Jeyes, *Joseph Chamberlian* (London, 1896), p. 245.

5 ZIONISM: RACISM OR LIBERATION?*

Abdeen Jabara

The nineteenth century witnessed a development in the relationships among human beings and the political organization of society more important than that of any other single epoch in human history: the concrete emergence of the proposition that all citizens of a state were equal, vis-à-vis the laws and institutions of the state. Further certain rights, privileges and duties which were defined and secured by law were attached by definition to citizenship in the state. Chief among these rights was the expectation of treatment equal to that accorded any other citizen.

This idea inspired the French and American revolutions. It was a vast departure from the preceding periods in that the legal structures sought to codify the proposition. That it has not been possible in the succeeding century and a half to achieve operative equality in systems based upon the accumulation of private capital does not detract from the basic ideal which Western liberal democracy sought to enshrine in its codes.

Indeed, it was this ideal which the black struggle in the United States in the 60s sought to enforce thereby leading to a renewal of interest in equal protection clause of the U.S. Constitution and the passage of the Civil Rights Act of 1964. Internationally, the existence of a colonial system under which the principal of equality was not extended beyond the political boundaries of Western liberal democracies made millions in the developing nations acutely aware of the gap between the ideal and its practice. The insistence by the large majority of the peoples of the earth that equality was indivisible was manifest. Liberation movements and popular democratic struggles were active throughout the globe. The newly independent nations likewise sought to codify the principles of universal human rights and the equality of man in numerous international conventions such as the International Convention on Racial Discrimination of 1965.

Two notable aberrations stood in stark contrast to the movement: the sytems of Apartheid and Zionism. Both were to emerge at a time when the old order of privilege was crumbling. Both went beyond the passing physical domination represented by the colonial system. The

* Portions of this essay have been published previously.

ideological precedents of Zionism and Apartheid were the settler regimes of the sixteenth and seventeenth centuries.

The vote in the U.N. General Assembly on November 10, 1975, in which Zionism was designated a form of racial discrimination was perhaps one of the most momentous decisions of that body since its Partition of Palestine some twenty-eight years previously. One could witness the momentum for the vote building up when on November 9, the *New York Times* dutifully reported two separate statements condemning the Resolution being circulated by "black intellectuals" and "Christian clergy." The pressure brought to bear by the United States and its West European allies on Third World countries which had voted for the Resolution in Committee was described by one participant as being no less than the pressures exerted by the United States on behalf of the partitioning of Palestine in 1947.

The United States strategy was clear — split black Africa from the Arabs. The vehicle was the threat to withhold Western support for the U.N. Decade to Combat Racism. Not only did this strategy fail, but its failure demonstrated the vast changes which have occurred in international politics over the three decades of U.N. existence. The most notable change is the decline of American power.

The cries of moral outrage and indignation which went up had an unreal quality to them. In none of the commentaries in the Western corporate media — the editorials, the news columnists, the television commentators — was one substantive fact presented about the nature of Zionism as a political philosophy and the fashion in which that philosophy is concretized in the laws and institutions of the state of Israel.

A *New York Times* article of December 7, 1975, throws a great deal of light on some of the behind-the-scenes mechanics of the U.S. position on the Resolution. Tom Buckley, a close friend of the U.S. ambassador to the United Nations, Daniel Patrick Moynihan, wrote:

> With Moynihan that night at the Waldorf Towers, listening to his shouts, his groans, his rhetorical flourishes, were Suzi Weaver, who is on leave from the Yale University faculty to serve as his special assistant, and Norman Podhoretz, the editor of *Commentary,* which is published by the American Jewish Committee. Podhoretz is an old friend and fellow old leftist or neoconservative, depending on how you look at it.
>
> When it came to the politics of the Middle East, an area in which he has never set foot, Moynihan was happy to take his direction

from the State Department, he had told me, but when it came to Zionism, Jewish history, anti-Semitism and related topics, Podhoretz is Moynihan's maven.

Thus, Moynihan revealed that, at best, his sources of information on "Zionism, Jewish history, anti-Semitism and related topics" were ones with a particular political persuasion. The article continued:

"I think we've got them another way," he went on. The resolution doesn't define what racism is. And we looked through all the documents and we couldn't find any place where the United Nations had defined what racism is. The closest thing to a definition, and Suzi found it, dated from debate in 1968. The Soviet Union – the Soviet Union, mind you – said that racism and Nazism were the same thing! Identical! So if Zionism is racism it means that Zionism is Nazism, and if that isn't lunacy, I don't know what is."

Obviously Moynihan was not aware of, or didn't want to deal with, the International Convention on Racial Discrimination which *does* define racism.

Moynihan's ignorance was to be the basis of his defense at the United Nations. Israel and Zionism, he claimed, fit no known definition of racism:

Now I should wish to be understood that I am here making one point, and one point only, which is that whatever else Zionism may be, it is not and cannot be 'a form of racism.' In logic, the State of Israel could be or could become, many things, theoretically including many things undesirable, but it could be and could not become racist unless it ceased to be Zionist.

The action of the U.N. General Assembly was predicated on the duties and obligations imposed by the International Convention of Racial Discrimination. Since Israel is not a signatory to this Convention, it is not bound by it in the sense of a treaty obligation, even though many of the provisions in the Convention codify or have acquired the force of customary law. Accordingly, the Convention may provide a juridical basis for alleged human rights violations even though the state whose conduct is the subject of a complaint has not undertaken to implement the measures of the Convention.

The report filed in 1971 by the Syrian government with the Committee on the Elimination of Racial Discrimination illustrates this. The parties to the Convention are required to submit reports on "the legislative, juridical, administrative or other measures" which they have adopted to give effect to its provisions. Syria's 1971 report stated that since Israel's occupation of the Golan Heights in the 1967 June War, some 110,000 Syrians had been subject to "discriminatory and racist policies and practices" in violation of Article 5. The report concluded by calling upon the parties to the Convention to take action to eliminate these practices. The Committee, while noting that Israel was not a party to the Convention, issued a decision stating that: (1) it took note of information "to the effect that racial discrimination is being practiced in that part of Syrian territory which is known as the Golan Heights and which is under Israeli occupation," and (2) it wished to draw the attention of the General Assembly to the situation.

Zionism Vis-à-vis the International Convention

The International Convention on Racial Discrimination defines racial discrimination as:

> any distinction, exclusion, restriction or preference based on race, color, descent, or national or ethnic origin, which has the purpose or effect of nullifying or impairing the recognition, enjoyment or exercise, on an equal footing, of human rights and fundamental freedoms in the political, economic, social, cultural or any other field of public life.

Article 5 specifies a number of rights which the parties to the Convention undertake to guarantee "without distinction as to race, color, or national or ethnic origin." The right to equal treatment before judicial tribunals, to freedom of movement and residence, to return to one's country, to form and join trade unions, to housing and to education are among those guaranteed.

Thus, the definition of racial discrimination is clearly set forth as an international legal norm. There are essentially four requirements contained in this definition before an idea may be designated a legally impermissible practice of racism: (1) There must be a distinction, exclusion, restriction or preference; (2) These distinctions, exclusion, restrictions, or preferences must be based on race, color, descent or national or ethnic origin; (3) These distinctions, exclusions, restrictions or preferences must have either (a) the purpose or (b) the effect of impairing the equal exercise of human rights and fundamental freedoms;

(4) The freedoms which are impaired must be in the political, economic, social or cultural field.

It is against these criteria that Zionism must be judged.

Zionism is a nationalist political movement. It was organized as such in a visible manner in 1897 in the creation of the World Zionist Organization. It claims that all people who are Jews are members of a single nation, and that this nation has first by virtue of being a "nation dispersed" and second by virtue of certain international agreements, political rights in Palestine. Zionism arose out of two fears: (1) fear of anti-Semitism which Zionism states is an ineradicable element in non-Jewish societies and (2) fear of assimilation — that Jewish survival as a civilization or culture could only be assured through an independent national state. Further, safety for Jews, or a solution to what was seen as a specifically Jewish problem, could only be had in a society in which Jews constituted the majority.

In 1897 the founders of Zionism set out to gain international recognition and support for their program and to secure acceptance by Jews in the various countries of the world of the "Jewish People" concept. Anthropologists are generally agreed that Jews are not a separate race and there has been a great deal of confusion among Jews and non-Jews alike as to whether to use the term race, religion, nation or culture to clarify the nature of Jewish identity. This question has not been resolved in Israel today. The legal test of citizenship, for instance, under the Law of Return is a religious one while the identity cards of Jewish Israelis designates Jewish as being a nationality description.

Receiving the support of a Great Power in 1917 in the Balfour Declaration, the World Zionist Organization (WZO) was prepared for the colonizing effort after World War I. The object was British control over Palestine while unlimited Jewish emigration would lay the groundwork for the creation of a Jewish state. Indeed, in its early days the Zionist movement had no difficulty in seeing itself as a colonizing movement when it called its first bank the Colonial Trust Company and its settlement department the Department of Colonization. With British control of Palestine accorded the license of the League of Nations after the war the vehicle for the creation of a closed Jewish settlement in Palestine (Yishuv) was the Jewish Agency, an alter ego of the World Zionist Organization. The Agency's three slogans were: conquering the land, conquering the work, and purchase Jewish goods.

In practice this meant that the native Arab population, both Christain and Muslim, were to be excluded from any participation in the political, social, economic, or cultural life of the Jewish settlement.

This exclusion was obtained through an official boycott of Arab goods, labor, mixed government schools and local governing bodies.

A concrete example of this exclusion is the Jewish National Fund (JNF) set up in 1901 at the Fifth Zionist Congress to purchase land in Palestine. Its first purchases were in 1905, but the extensive acquisitions and development of a land policy occurred only after the British mandate came into being. Under the terms of the Charter of the JNF, land purchased by it was to be held in perpetuity "as the inalienable property of the entire Jewish people." During the mandate the JNF became the largest private landowner in Palestine.

Use of the land was organized under a system of long-term leasing for specified purposes for periods of up to ninety-eight years. These leases, with JNF approval, could be sublet, sold, mortgaged, bequeathed or given as a gift subject to one overriding condition: the lessee must be Jewish. Non-Jews could not be employed on the land or even in work connected with cultivation of land. Violation of this term of the lease made the lessee liable to damages and cancellation of the lease without compensation. As John Hope Simpson noted in 1930 as one of the causes of Palestinian Arab unrest: "The land has been extra-territorialized. It ceases to be land from which the Arab can gain any advantage either now or any time in the future."

The fate of two Christian Arab villages in northern Israel illustrates the manner of Zionist "principle." In 1948 the population of the villages of Birem and Ikrit were moved out by the Israeli army with the promise that they would be allowed to return after hostilities. The land was turned over without compensation to the JNF. The Supreme Court of Israel upheld their right to return to their villages but the military immediately declared the people to be a security risk and the Cabinet voted that they should never be allowed to return to their land although they were citizens of Israel. Golda Meir said that to return the land to the Arab Israelis would constitute an erosion of the Zionist principle — that once Jews own land, it can never be alienated to anyone who is a non-Jew.

This extra-territorialization of land ownership meant that the rights of ownership rested not just in the Jews or Jewish settlement in Palestine, but in all Jews everywhere which the World Zionist Organization, and its arm in Palestine, the Jewish Agency, claimed to represent. After the state of Israel came into being in 1948, the heads of various departments of the Jewish Agency became the heads of the various ministries of the state. The World Zionist Organization and the Jewish Agency were charged in the Status Law of 1952 with being the "authorized agency" which would continue to operate in Israel for: (1) "the development and settlement of the country," (2) "the absorption of immigrants from the Diaspora," and (3) "the coordination of the activities in Israel of Jewish institutions and organizations active in those fields." Section 5 of the law states that "the ingathering of the exiles" is the "central task of the State of Israel and the Zionist Movement in our days."

The JNF, after the creation of the state, continued under the control of the WZO although a separate governmental body, the Israel Lands Authority, was created. The most significant consequence of the agreement between the JNF and the government was that the restrictive policies regarding the sale and leasing of land were applied to all state lands, which, together with JNF lands, today constitute 94.5 percent of the land in Israel.

In 1948, not more than 6½ percent of the land in Palestine was owned by Jews. The great majority of Arab-owned land was transferred to the state through the enactment and enforcement of a series of laws. These were, *inter alia*, the Law of Emergency Articles for the Exploitation of Uncultivated Lands (1948); the Law for the Requisition of Land in Times of Emergency (1949); the Law for the Acquisition of Land (1953); and the Law on the Acquisition of Absentees' Property (1950).

More recent legislation has reinforced the intention of these laws. Through the Agricultural Settlement Law passed by the Knesset on August 1, 1967, the use of state land by a lessee for a "non-conforming use" subjects the lessee to termination of his rights in the land and the water allocated for it. A nonconforming use includes vesting any rights in the land or its crops in a tenant. The real effect of the law is to prevent Jewish lessees from sharing their land in *any* manner with the local Arab inhabitants.

The English language *Jerusalem Post* reported on August 18, 1975 a new government plan to expropriate thousands of acres of additional land in the Galilee region for the purpose of establishing new Jewish settlements. It reported that "small towns and settlements in Galilee can no longer grow because of a land shortage." The Jewish population in Galilee has declined during the past 15 years from 58 to 52 percent and the plan is now to arrest the trend by more intensive settlement. Earlier, in July, the Israeli Finance Minister Yehoushua Rabinowitz had stated that the government planned to channel 32 percent of the new settlements to Galilee and that this would necessitate the expropriating of land.

The work of the World Zionist Organization/Jewish Agency in Israel today is contained in periodic reports of its activity and of the Zionist Congresses held every four years. These reports consistently refer to the work being done on behalf of Jewish housing, Jewish agriculture, Jewish fishing and these are either public institutions or quasipublic institutions where Jews are advantaged as against those who cannot qualify as members of the Jewish people.

A recent piece of legislation demonstrates the exclusionary principles which are logically attendant to Zionist philosophy. The Discharged Soldiers Law of 1970, as amended, provides a family subsidization plan to increase the Jewish population in Israel. Since 99 percent of Arabs in Israel may not serve in the defense forces and since only discharged soldiers and their families are entitled to family allowances, the Arab population of Israel is barred from family allowances even though it is the most economically disadvantaged.

The principal law relating to citizenship in Israel is the Law of Return of 1920, as amended. This law established the "right" of every Jew to immigrate to the state of Israel. No person other than a Jew has this right. Amendment No. 2 of 1970, Paragraph 4 (b) states that: "For the purposes of this law 'Jew' means a person who was born of a Jewish mother or has become converted to Judaism and is not a member of another religion." As for the Palestinian Arabs in Israel, their citizenship rights are controlled by the Nationality Law of 1952. For a Palestinian Arab to be considered an Israeli citizen, regardless of whether he was born in Israel or has lived there most of his life, it must be established that (1) he or she was registered as a resident of Israel on March 1, 1952, by virtue of the Population Registration Law of 1949; (2) he or she was a resident in Israel on April 1, 1952; and (3) he or she was, from the date of the establishment of the state and until April 1, 1952, in Israel or in an area that was attached to it after the establishment of the state, or had entered Israel legally during that period. Because of the provisions of this law, there are several tens of thousands of Arabs residing in Israel who are forever barred from citizenship and this statelessness is inherited by the individuals' children and children's children. The only recourse is to apply for citizenship between the 18th and 21st years of age. Such persons are not encouraged by any program of notice regarding citizenship rights.

Essentially, then, Zionism and its legal framework in Israel can be defined as being based on the principle of exclusion. A necessary and immutable germ of Zionism was the idea that it could realize its objective only through a process of exclusion. The process was one which had occurred numerous times previously in the history of the world — that of colonization, settling a land. The land may or may not be inhabited by other people. If the land is inhabited by persons other than the colonizer, the colonizer has three options to deal with the indigenous population: (1) eliminate by genocide all or part of the indigenous populace, (2) subjugate the indigenous populace in a defined system of inclusions and exclusions, or (3) the colonizer may push the indigenous populace outside the parameters of the area.

It was the latter two of these which were central to Zionism: pushing the bulk of the population out and subjecting the remainder to a system of inclusions and exclusions. It was, as Jacques Berque wrote, "a total colonialism" because the native Palestinian Arab could derive no benefit from it.

If Zionism was to succeed in pushing the bulk of the indigenous population out and subjugating the remnants, it was essential to have laws to facilitate this subjugation. These were provided in the adoption *in toto* of the draconian Emergency Laws of the British Mandatory Authorities. These "security" measures which the British administration instituted to deal with the Palestinian Arab rebellion of 1936 and later Zionist guerilla activity against the British took the matter of state security out of civil jurisdiction and placed it in the hands of the military.

As soon as the Zionists in Palestine proclaimed the creation of the state of Israel, the British Emergency Laws were the new state. The Palestinians were divided into three regions, each under a military commander. The military governor had the power to declare an area closed and restrict entrance and exit to it (Article 125). Passes were required for movement into and out of these areas. The governor was empowered to issue an administrative order for police supervision of any person. The individual under such an order may be restricted in his movements; his contacts with other persons may be rigorously controlled; his professional work may be supervised and restricted; he must inform the police of his whereabouts at all times, appear at the nearest police station when so required, and remain indoors between sunset and sunrise; the police have access to his home at any hour of the day or night (Articles 109 and 110). Article 111 allows the administrative detention of anyone whom the military government may decide to detain, for any reason whatsoever, *for an unlimited period without trial and without charge*. The military government may confiscate or destroy a person's property if the military government suspects that a shot has been fired or a bomb thrown from such property (article 119).

Moreover, the military government may expel a person from the country (Article 112) or confiscate a person's property (Article 120). A total or partial curfew may be imposed in any village or area (Article 124).

The public school systems which exist in Israel today demonstrate how completely the tenets of Zionism are applied. There is one system of primary and secondary schools for Arabs and another system for Jewish Israelis. Jewish Israelis are completely prohibited from attending Arab schools while an Arab Israeli may attend a Jewish school only by special state authorization.

All Israeli government ministries or departments have special sub-departments on Arab affairs to which an Arab Israeli must apply in any dealing with the ministry. For instance, the Israeli Ministry of Health has a general health office for Jews only while a subdepartment exists for minorities.

All municipal governmental units receive subsidies from the national government. The official figures reveal that those towns whose population is Arab receive substantially less per capita than those whose population is Jewish. A table compiled by a member of the Knesset and published in one of Israel's largest circulation Hebrew dailies, *Yediot Ahronot*, on October 10, 1975, shows the extent of this discrimination: the Jewish towns received 1,220-3,100 IL per capita, while the per capita subsidy to the Arab towns was 140-235 IL.

It is important to remember that the discrimination in Israel between Jewish and non-Jewish Israelis is not only sanctioned by the state and may not be challenged in a court of law but that it is a fundamental precept upon which the state is founded. It is incorporated as an integral part of the law of the land. In the examination of any society, one must distinguish between discrimination as it exists between individual citizens or private parties, on the one hand, and discrimination as a part of public policy or state action, discrimination contained not just in the way the laws are applied but in the terms of the law itself. This distinction reveals the basis upon which the state is organized. In the United States there may and does exist discriminatory application of the laws and in many instances the laws themselves may in their terms discriminate between citizens without a reasonable basis. The law of the land, however, is that all citizens will receive equal protection of the laws and where the laws are not equally applied or there is an invidious discrimination in the terms of the law, the citizen may challenge it in a court. The goal of constructing and maintaining a Jewish state made the "national" discrimination a necessary part of the state itself.

Zionism's Defense

The two principal defenses of Zionism raised by Israeli Ambassador Yosef Tekoah in the United Nations debate were that Zionism was (1) an anti-imperialist movement, and (2) the national liberation movement of the Jewish people. It seems likely that they will constitute the thrust of the movement that is under way to defend Zionism.

As for the defense that Zionism is an anti-imperialist movement little commentary is required. Zionism as a movement is neither imperialist nor anti-imperialist. That it could realize itself and continues to through a complete alliance with the major imperialist powers does not make it imperialism. It would be more correct to state that there exists an organic and symbiotic relationship between Zionism and imperialism. It can be stated categorically, however, that Zionism is not anti-imperialist and it is inconceivable, given its foundations as a political philosophy, that it would become anti-imperialist in the future. The nature of Zionism as being directed at a land populated by a non-Jewish people compels this conclusion.

With regard to the claim that Zionism is the national liberation movement of Jews, there is a much debated question as to whether Jews constitute a nation. A nation has been generally defined as a historically involved, stable community of language, territory and psychological makeup manifested in a community of culture. As conceived by its founders, Zionism was seen as a movement of liberation of Jews from the dangers of anti-Semitism and assimilation.

One can easily accept that Jews are a "nation" or a "people" without in any way detracting from the proposition that Zionism is a form of racism. It would be important, however, to seek to clarify the question of Jewish identity within the context of a discussion on the national question and the questions relating to national integration and self-determination. With regard to the question of Jewish identity one principle can be stated without condition or reservation: no person or group of persons may define the identity of other persons. According to this rule, both the statement by Golda Meir that "There are no Palestinians" and the statement that "Jews are not a people or nation" are equally invalid. Only Jews and Palestinians may define their respective national, cultural, or religious identities. Zionism was an attempt by a group of Jews to define Jewish identity. It states that Jews constitute a people or nation in the psychic and cultural sense. One may subscribe to this claim by Zionists and at the same time posit that

Zionism is a form of racism.

Zionism, as a nationalist movement, can be viewed from several perspectives. On the one hand, one might adopt a position frequently espoused by Western liberals and intellectuals and even some radicals that nationalism is regressive and narrow and something to be disdained. Despite their "intellectualism" these practical internationalists are unable to distinguish between the aggressive and often brutal nationalism of an oppressor nation and the nationalism of an oppressed nation. The nationalist of an oppressed nation loves his people and is pained by their suffering or indignities. These liberal intellectuals see no difference between predatory and exploitative nationalism and defensive nationalism. As Lenin wrote, "whoever does not recognize and champion the equality of nations and languages, and does not fight against all national oppression or inequality, is not a Marxist; he is not even a democrat."

Obviously the question of Jewish identity has not been resolved among Jews. The numerous cases before the Israeli Supreme Court on the question of "who is a Jew", the conflicts in the Law of Return, and the failure of Israeli and Zionist leaders to create that one resource which Zionism needs most, immigration, is indicative that this question is still unresolved.

Whether one accepts the Zionist contention of a Jewish nation or people, one can enunciate the application of the rights of national minorities to Jews. A democratic Marxist position was set forth by Lenin, "Guaranteeing the rights of a national minority is inseparably linked up with the principle of complete equality . . . . that decision demands 'the incorporation in the constitution of a fundamental law which shall declare null and void all privileges enjoyed by any one nation and all infringements of the rights of a national minority' ".

"Don't Jews have the right to self-determination?" This serious question is frequently raised and many persons who oppose Zionism have either carelessly glossed over its answer or studiously avoided it for fear that it would legitimize Zionist colonization in Palestine. The question and its answer are vitally related to the Zionism-Racism issue for if Jews were merely exercising a right to self-determination through the colonization of Palestine, that movement could not properly be called a form of racism. Self-determination of nations means the political separation of these nations from alien national bodies and the formation of an independent national state. In other words, it is the secession from one body politic and the creation of a new body politic.

Before the question of Jewish self-determination can be answered, another must be raised. Is there an absolute and unconditional right of self-determination for an oppressed nation? Marxist-Leninists propound the right to be absolute. But they also said that it was "a right to free political separation *from the oppressor nation*" (Emphasis added). It cannot be realized, for it would be a contradiction in terms, at the expense of another nation or people. Marxist-Leninists saw the exercise of the right of self-determination as being led by the proletariat and advancing the cause of international socialism. But this unconditional right could be exercised only by an *oppressed* nation. Accordingly, members of a nation in a multinational society who were not oppressed would not have a right of secession from the body politic of which they are a part.

Likewise, a further qualification on the right of self-determination was the necessity for a struggle by an oppressed nation for full democratic freedom and a constitutional and economic system that would ensure that equality. Here the differences between the Zionist reaction to persecution of Jews and a revolutionary Jewish socialist reaction in Eastern Europe during the political turmoils in the later part of the nineteenth and early twentieth century is most apparent. The Zionist solution was secession and colonization without participating in the social and political struggles of societies in which Jews lived. For the Zionist such struggle was futile and made no difference for the security of Jews. But the many Jewish partisans of the socialist revolutions posited the idea that it was possible to construct a nonexploitative and nondiscriminatory system under the guidance of Marxist-Leninist principles.

Historically, movements of colonization have been undertaken by minorities who desired to retain the particular characteristics of their groups rather than forego them or for group safety. Does the desire to maintain group identity or safety and the organizing of the group with a program to maintain that identity or ensure its safety qualify as a liberation movement?

First, there can be no doubt that any group or members of that group should not be obliged to relinquish its particularism, religion, culture, language or expression of self where those characteristics do not violate the rights of others. The Jews or any other national or religio-ethnic group should be free to maintain their specific expressions of their individual or collective consciousness of existence. To the extent that Jews or any other people are prevented or prohibited through discriminatory legal structures from doing so, they have the right to resist and rebel. They have the right to undertake a struggle for change of the system which denies them equal rights.

There is only one unconditional rule attached to the right of national liberation. *No man or people may achieve national liberation at the expense of another people.* Given this fact, any movement including Zionism which seeks to solve the national problem of one people at the expense of another may not properly be called a movement of national liberation.

Far from being the national liberation movement of Jews, Zionism might better be seen as a death trap for Jews in Israel today. Rather than leading to greater security for Jews, Zionism has isolated Jews in the Middle East and the world community. Rather than bringing peace and security to Jews in Israel it has brought them interminable conflict and war without any foreseeable conclusion. Rather than giving Jews in Europe, the Soviet Union, the United States and Latin America greater hope for the future of successful communal existence on a multi-national basis, it has sought to polarize them in support of a movement that alienates Jews from the social and political struggles of their societies.

In this connection it is interesting to note the recent statement of Morris Amitay, head of the American Israel Public Affairs Committee, the principal Zionist lobby in the United States, that AIPAC's success stems "from the fact that we are single-issued." This is in conformity with the Zionist dogma that Jewish security can only be had in self-segregation as an obscene caricature of the eastern European ghetto. More recently the Anti-Defamation League of B'nai Brith charged that pro-Palestinian information in the United States was "not only a dagger pointed at the heart of Isreal," but *"likewise poses a threat to the security of the American Jewish community and Jewish communities everywhere"* (emphasis added).

In 1968 after the jubilation and euphoria in Israel from its stunning June 1967 victory, Moshe Dayan, in a speech before an officers' school, quoted several passages from Arthur Rupin, the grandfather of Zionist colonization in Palestine:

We are aiming at relations (between the Zionist colonists and the Palestinians) which we will be able to defend against our own consciences and against the League of Nations as a just solution without renouncing the fundamentals of Zionism.

It became clear to me how hard it is to realize Zionism in a way compatible with the demands of universal ethics.

What is interesting about Dayan's use of these quotations is that they were made after a stunning military victory and that they were made before an officers' school. The intensity of the moral conflict between Zionism and the universal ethics was revealed a half century after Zionism had achieved so many of its objectives. Even the state machinery designed to mold a strong Zionist national consciousness created a plaque of self-doubt and questioning.

Zionism has consistently sought to rationalize itself in the name of "universal human justice" but to be able to do this required its conciliation with an immoral phenomenon, the inherent discrimination against and oppression of national minorities. This is a permanent phenomenon of human society since it is inseparable from human nature. Anti-Semitism or persecution of minorities is not a problem for humanity as a whole involving scientific investigation into its social, economic, cultural and political causes, but an exclusively Jewish problem. In its attempts to "normalize" Jews in a "society like other societies" Zionism takes on the problem of minority oppression as a normal condition.

Conclusion

The headline on November 11, 1975, of a major metropolitan newspaper in a populous midwestern city read "U.N. Declares Zionism is Racism." The U.S. Congress threatened retaliatory action against the United Nations and the United States contribution to the U.N. Budget was decreased. Moreover, the United States announced that it would not participate in the U.N. Decade to Combat Racism. In New York City, the City Council sought to change the name of the U.N. Plaza to Zion Square. Israel quickly moved to take measures to counteract its growing isolation. An emergency meeting of world Zionist leaders was called in Jerusalem to discuss a plan of action. Israel strengthened and made public its previously covert ties with the Union of South Africa. A hundred thousand Jewish Americans were reported to have marched in New York City in denunciation of the U.N. resolution. They were housewives, factory workers, students, retirees, shopkeepers, businessmen who were hurt and angry and who wanted to defend *their* movement of salvation. What was it that had gone wrong with their dreams? What had happened to the sacrifices on behalf of Jewish victims less fortunate than themselves? What had so changed the world from their childhoods when they were in idealistic Zionist youth movements or saved their coins in the boxes marked "Jewish National Fund?" How they asked, could the majority of the world turn on the

Jewish movement for salvation and national liberation?

The one flaw in what had, until the emergence of the Palestinian resistance, been a record of success for Zionism was that the Palestinians refused to acquiesce in their national oppression and obliteration. This is hardly surprising. And it was because of their refusal and the mounting of their struggle for national liberation that the issue of the nature of Zionism was thrust upon the peoples of the world.

6 ZIONISM AS A RACIST IDEOLOGY

Sayed Yassin

The Resolution passed by the U.N. General Assembly considering Zionism a form of racism has evoked worldwide repercussions. This decision underlines the importance of an in-depth analysis of the Zionist phenomenon which formed the basis of colonial settlement in Palestine. In focusing on Zionism as a racist ideology a definition of both ideology and racism is appropriate.[1]

Ideology

There are various trends in defining the concept of "ideology."[2] According to Adam Schaff,[3] these definitions may be generally divided into three categories: genetic, structural and functional: The genetic definition underlines the environmental factors leading to and accompanying the emergence of an ideology. The structural definition springs from the features distinguishing one ideology from another from the viewpoint of logic and epistemology; in other words, the judgements and propositions that set one ideology apart from other ideologies on the one hand, and from other intellectual structures, such as scientific theories, on the other. Finally, the functional definition focuses on, and draws attention to, the functions of ideology vis-à-vis society, social groups and individuals.

Adam Schaff tended to adopt the functional definition of ideology, regarding it as the most descriptive and neutral. As such, this definition might prove to be the most acceptable to different points of view. In this light, Schaff suggests the following definitions: "Ideology is a pattern of ideas which, by being based on a specific set of values, serves to delineate the orientations and conduct of men in relation to the development of society, social groups or individuals."

Though this functional definition might be acceptable in general terms, in that it is applicable to Zionism as well as to other ideologies, Adam Schaff's exclusion of genetic and structural definitions is not acceptable, for it is not sufficient to solely indicate the function or functions of a given ideology. Rather, it becomes necessary, particularly in a critical context, to define the genetic origins of the ideology under discussion. The basic intellectual components must also be considered. This applies in particular to Zionism. The functions of Zionism in relation to Zionist groups cannot be understood without determining its origins and internal structure.

Racism

Racism is based on the central idea that a certain race of people are naturally superior to others.[4] The distinguishing characteristics of the chosen group are usually defined on physical bases, or on purely cultural bases. In addition, there exists a number of attributes and values which are often regarded as marks of superiority and distinction: like military ingenuity, technological superiority or, as the Zionists claim, divine predestination, leading them to regard themselves as God's chosen people. The racists, more often than not, claim that the race to which they belong is superior from the biological viewpoint, which superiority shall continue forever.

Nazism, one of the most prominent racist ideologies of modern times, set itself the task of achieving a world peace, "based on the victorious sword of a race of masters which shall put the world in the service of a superior civilization.[5] Japan, before its defeat in World War II, also based its extreme nationalism and expansionist policy on a nationalist-racist myth.

Africa is a further example of the manner in which racism is attempting to create unbridgeable gulfs between the white colonial rulers and the indigenous black population. Sarah Millen, writing on South Africa in the 20s, declared that "the gap between black and white had become too wide to be filled."[6] Similar ideas may also be found among ultra-Zionist thinkers who believe that there are basic differences between Jews and Gentiles, hence the predominant psychological attitude among the Jews and their mistrust of anyone or anything non-Jewish.

Racism has been employed to justify a diverse range of economic, political and social situations. In reading of the early days of American colonialism, for example, one may discern that the American society, which was dominated by powerful religious tendencies at the time, had to search for a justification for the sytem of slavery imposed on Negroes, particularly after the latter's conversion to Christianity. As the Christian faith does not allow one Christian to possess and enslave another, racism became a handy justification of enslavement on the premise that Negroes were a race inferior to the whites, which renders enslavement justifiable; and, as someone stated with formidable candor that property is property, and it is therefore in no need of protection by reasonable pretexts. It is worth noting in this context that German racists had often spoken badly of the Japanese in their mention of the

"Yellow Danger" describing them as "trained monkeys". But when political expediencies made it necessary to include Japan in the axis-group, German anthropologists unabashedly stepped forward to say that the Japanese belonged, after all, to the Aryan race.

Modern racist ideology derives its origins from the writings of the French author, Count De Gobineau, who, in 1855, published a famous work entitled *"Essai sur l'Inégalité des Races Humaines."*[7] Gobineau's racist theory saw the real causes of the rise and fall of societies and human civilization not in economic, political, religious or social circumstances, but only in racial factors. Gobineau also held that the human race could only be classified into superior and inferior. Whereas the former was capable of progress, the latter was condemned to eternal backwardness.

Gobineau's theory was taken up by some other writers and researchers, chief among whom were Chamberlain in his *The Foundation of the 19th Century*, the French anthropologist and biologist V. de la Bouge, and the German anthroplogist Otto Amun.[8]

The fact that modern racism emanated from Gobineau's ideas in the nineteenth century is by no means a coincidence. The social sciences have shown that ideas do not crop up, develop and mature in a vacuum. They have to be linked to the specific historical moment as well as to the type of social structure prevailing in the society. The development of racist ideology corresponds to the emergence and expansion of international imperialism based on the colonialization of the Third World. The need arose to contrive a cover-up for justifying this colonial system. Hence the claims like "the white man's burden" to civilize backward nations and similar formulas were meant as an ideological support for the colonial process.

Considering the close association between racism and colonialism it is small wonder that Zionism, as a racist ideology, was the moving political force for settler-colonialism in Palestine.

Zionism and the Formation of Racist Israeli Society

The Formation of Jewish Society in Palestine

The appearance and development of Jewish society in Palestine resulted from the efforts of Zionist groups which were forming in East and Central Europe towards the end of the nineteenth century. These groups operated under the slogan that "no proper Jewish life could be led in any society outside Palestine." Zionism held that life in the shadow of modern European societies could lead the Jews to be split between spiritual and cultural oppression (resulting from the disappearance of their traditional and social way of life, under the yoke of modern political and economic systems) and physical extinction through "absolute assimilation" in society. It further claimed that only in Palestine could appear a modern Jewish society, through a blending of Judaism and human civilisation at large, or by a mixture of tradition and modernity.

Jewish society in Palestine adopted a well-rounded ideology, consisting of a set pattern of coherent ideas, and molded them into one overall guiding norm. The "pioneering ideology" spurred on the pioneers, who were in reality the spearhead of colonial-settlement in Palestine. Zionism went to great lengths to present an ideal image of the pioneer as an example of the ideal Jew. Thus, early Zionist leaders took special pains to emphasize that early settlers be in their conduct and tendencies an example of the pioneer, especially in sacrifice. The pioneer was described as a man willing to suffer deprivations, forsake the pleasures of life and renounce material gains. He is capable of rigid self-discipline and a life of austerity, not for its own sake – though this later became a predominant tendency – but for the sake of pioneer objectives of creating a Jewish community in Palestine. Another attribute of the pioneer is his readiness to work alone, since exploiting labor is prohibited. This has its influence on the type of activities pursued in the creation of a Jewish socity in Palestine. Non-exploiting labor was emphasized in agricultural and manual fields, on the assumption that, in this manner, it was possible to regenerate the youth of "the Jewish Nation" and create the new Jew.

The 'pioneering' ideology centered on two basic points: self-sufficiency and self-defense. An analysis of this ideology which, through its principles, values and strategies, was the main force motivating the early Zionist settlers in Palestine, may throw light on the beginnings of racists ideas, which were later to give birth to the Zionist movement. This may be discerned in the goals which Zionism pursued in its efforts to create a Jewish society in Palestine, in the way the Zionists regarded the Arabs, the indigenous population of Palestine, and, finally, in the settlement policies, the most prominent of which were the usurpation of land, labor, self-defense and production:

1. Zionism's first claim was that it intended to take upon itself the onerous message of "civilizing and modernizing" Palestine. Such a claim dovetailed perfectly with the nineteenth century racist orientations of European capitalism, which sought a cultural justification through the claim that it was "colonizing backward nations" with the

purpose of 'civilizing' and 'preparing' them for self-rule. The Zionist thinker Moses Hess put it this way: The mission of the Jewish nation and of the Jewish state in Palestine is to stand guard over "the area of intersection between three continents." Elaborating on this mission, Hess says: "Your capital will bring back life to this arid land. Your efforts and labour will once more turn this ancient land into fertile valleys after you have saved it from the clutches of the desert sands. The world will present you once more with allegiance and respect." Theodor Herzl, amplifying the same idea, wrote: "Over there, we shall be the barrier protecting Europe in Asia. We shall pose as an outpost of civilization in the face of savagery. As a neutral state, we must maintain our contact with Europe which must under-write our existence." Max Nordeau elaborated this point further: "We shall, in the Middle East, endeavour to do what the British did in India, namely undertake cultural activities and not foster domination. We are going to Palestine as an expedition on behalf of civilization. Ours is the mission of spreading Europe's ethical code out to the Euphrates." In brief, Zionism based itself from the beginning on European racist ideology, in order to justify its colonization of Palestine. The 'Jews' were regarded as a race superior to the Arabs, who had failed to cultivate their own land. The Jews, with their unique skills, had come to lead them along the road of advancement and social progress.

2. This racist view, which set the stage for colonial settlement in Palestine, entailed a negative attitude toward the native Arabs. This finds its expression not only in the Zionist indifference as regards the Arabs' fate, but also in the belief in the necessity of exterminating or driving them out of the country if they were to resist colonial settlement operations.

Zionist settler-colonialism pursued this policy relentlessly both before and after the creation of the Jewish state. This is evidenced by the campaigns of terror planned and executed by Israeli leaders in order to expel as many Palestinians as possible from their homes in 1948. There is much evidence to refute the Zionist claim that the exodus of the Palestinian Arabs was instigated by Arab leaders. Israeli settler-colonialism continued to expand, particularly in the aftermath of the 1967 June War. Since then, the world has been standing witness to the seizure of the Palestinians' land, the dynamiting of their houses, their expulsion from their villages and the prevention of their return. These are the policies pursued by racist colonial-settlement systems.

3. Racism is also manifested in the policies of colonial-settlement, formulated and practiced by early Zionists. The most significant

aspects of these policies were the usurpation of land, of labor, of self-defense and of production facilities.[9]

The usurpation of land was paramount in the Zionist settlement pro-gramme. This specifically meant the seizure of Palestinian land, in order to exploit it and wrest it from the control of the Gentiles, namely the Arabs. The Zionist leadership strove to give this principle a psycho-logical as well as an economic connotation. By conquering the land, the Jew purified himself, relinquishing the parasitic behaviour to which he had become so accustomed in the Diaspora, as a result of separation for many generations from agriculture, industry and various productive activities. Yet, it is quite important to emphasize the terroristic aspect of the conquest of Arab land. The land was not purchased from its owners, nor was it acquired by deceptive means. It was forcibly taken from the Palestinians by the Hagana. Thus, in 1948, 76 per cent of the whole area of Palestine was seized in less than one year.

Zionist colonialism in Palestine was not only of the settler-type, but also a substituting one. In other words, this type of colonialism aspired to replace the Arabs of Palestine with Jews. Conquest of land was there-fore not sufficient and had to be supplemented by the monopolization of the labor market. This was the racist economic facet of Zionist settler-colonialism, camouflaged with an ideological mask. Some of the advocates of this line, in particular the Zionist thinker Jordan, held that the Jewish worker should work for work's own sake. Agri-cultural and other types of manual labor, would have the effect of fostering ties between the Jew and the land, a bond the Jew had been deprived of for many generations as a result of the parasitical activities which he was forced to take up in the Diaspora. Apart from all these abstract ideas about the purity and indispensability of work in reviving a Jew's personality, the principle of manual labor revealed itself as a racist one in that it entailed, on the one hand, the introversion of the Jews and, on the other, denial of work to the Arabs and forcing them out of the labor market.

Conquest of land and monopolization of the labor market meant wresting Arab land from its owners, thus weakening their economic position in the labor market. This obviously entailed the possibility of provoking the Arab's resistance. Hence, the takeover of self-defence. The Arabs must not be trusted with the defense of Zionist settlements or Zionist enterprises. Only Zionist guards should take on this vital job.

After land, labor and self-defense, there comes in a natural sequence, the principle of monopolizing production. This meant boycotting Arab products and banning any dealings with Arabs. The Histadrut played a prominent role in imposing the principle of Jewish labor, of boycotting Arab products and of purchasing only Jewish products.

Racism in Israeli Society after the Creation of the State in 1948

The first wave of Jewish settlers, who succeeded in building a Jewish society in Palestine, were aided by diverse historical circumstances. The most important of these were the encouragement received by world colonialism (personified by the major powers, particularly Britain), the support of European capitalist Jewry and, finally, the Arab inability, at that stage, to offer organized and effective resistance. Almost all Arab states were then under foreign control. The Jewish settlers' successful efforts were intensified through the establishment of various institutions and organizations, which subsequently became the nucleus of the state.

With the creation of Israel, many of the specific problems and ideas associated with the early stages of settlement disappeared. But problems of a new kind appeared in their stead.

The creation of the Jewish state was linked to three major events: a new inflow of immigrants, the appearance of disparities within the economic and social structure and the conversion of the "pioneer" elite into a ruling elite. These combined to leave an indelible imprint on the ideological identity of the Israeli society, the heir of the former Jewish community in Palestine. One of the most important consequences might be seen in the disintegration of the pioneer ideology during the process of transformation from a basically agrarian into an industrial society. This transformation was marked by the predominance of the private sector, which has remained at the helm of the economy, despite the claim about the socialism of the Israeli society.

Without delving into details concerning the process of ideological disintegration accompanying the social decomposition of Israeli society, it must be pointed out that one essential change following the creation of the state was the Israeli leadership's realization of the necessity of working out a social strategy for the education of new generations of Israelis, to enable them to adapt to the new environment. The creation of Israel meant the emergence of disparities among the nationals of the new state on the one hand, and among the Jews in general, on the other. This gave rise to complicated problems concerning the new Israeli identity and the extent to which this identity was attached to, or detached from, the traditional Jewish identity.

What are the psychological and social features of the strategy worked out by the Israeli ruling elite to fulfill its ambitions regarding the process of social education of the Israeli society? This strategy, in the words of the Israeli psychologist George Tamarin, led to "the Israeli dilemma."[10] Tamarin outlined the main characteristics of this dilemma as consisting of the contradictions in social and spiritual realities in Israel. On the one hand was the "Israeli ideology," which called for the creation of a democratic, progressive and enlightened society, in which equality reigned supreme — and which Israeli propaganda claims has already been realized — and, on the other, the theocratic-racist laws, the bigotry-saturated atmosphere, the narrow-minded culture and the repressive measures carried out by the Israeli authorities.

This dilemma reflects, in reality, the failure of Zionism to realize its declared program, which claims that the creation of the state of Israel was the fulfillment of the Zionist dream of gathering the Jews together, for the first time in their history, to live in an environment marked by the absence of anti-Semitism. In such an environment, God's chosen people, which had been exposed to all kinds of dangers throughout their history, would at long last settle down together. Tamarin puts his finger on the root of the problem when he says that the conflict within the Israeli society is betrayed through the basic contradictions between those who advocate an Israeli society in the form of a "ghetto" in the physical and spiritual sense of the word, and the others, who are striving to build an open and free society. This fundamental contradiction, in addition to the advocates of an open versus an isolated society, is at the root of what has come to be called the "Israeli problem." In Tamarin's opinion, the solution of this problem will not only define the basic social and cultural features of the state, but, more important, will prove decisive in determining its political future.

To summarize Tamarin's view, which is fairly accurate: the plan worked out by the Israeli ruling elite to make of Israel a fortified military bastion in the face of its Arab neighbors, contributed greatly to Israel's cultural isolation and to its conversion into a "big ghetto" marked by isolationist and reactionary cultural trends. This in turn constitutes the appropriate environment for the development of racist ideas and the spreading of racist policies which are directed against the Arabs.

The Isolation of Israeli Society

Contact between Israeli youth and the outside world has been severed, except through conservative educational program and local sources of information. This is a result of the fear that the values, which the Israeli authorities have been pounding into the minds of the Israeli youth, might be undermined if the latter should have the chance of comparison on a wider scale. By propagating the fear of the assimilation of Israelis into other societies or the needs of security measures, imposed by the military situation with the Arab countries, a cultural blockade has in fact been set up around the Israeli youth. Nonetheless, quite a few have managed to slip out to go abroad and settle, particularly in the United States.

This cultural blockade has led to an aversion against any criticism of political and social practices, to xenophobia, to ideological fanaticism as well as to wide discrepancies between theory and practice in the enforcement of the law. These phenomena resulted in fanaticism and racial discrimination. As Tamarin puts it, a legal basis was laid for the practice of fanaticism and racism. It is worth noting that the manifestations were not only directed against the Arab population inside Israel. They were also expressed in the Israeli treatment of Oriental Jews as well as certain segments of Western Jews.

The understanding of the many aspects of racism in Israeli society requires an in-depth analysis of the multitude of ideas, ideologies and social norms prevailing in this society. This study however will be confined to the discussion of the manner in which the type of racism prevailing in Israeli society affects the attitudes of Israelis toward the Arabs, as well as the legal foundations, on which this fanaticism and racism depend.

Racism and Israeli Attitudes toward the Arabs

The racist character of Israeli society has markedly influenced the attitude adopted by the Israelis toward the Arabs. Although this aggressive attitude remained unchanged over a long period of time, there are discernible signs of certain changes, particularly in the aftermath of the war of June 1967, which brought about an increase of contact between the Arabs of the West Bank and the Israelis, and also as a result of the policy of "open bridges". Change here must not be construed to mean that the Israelis have become less aggressive towards the Arabs. Rather the Israelis came into contact with segments of an Arab population differing to some extent from the Arabs in Israel, whom the Israeli authorities had physically confined to an existence under military rule.

The most dangerous of all trends, however, is the one which has taken root in the minds of Israeli youth, as a result of a systematic racist strategy, which uses school, army and mass media to propagate

negative ideas about the Arabs. A study by Tamarin managed to uncover all these negative trends. His aim was the examination of certain
impacts fanaticism has had on the ethical code, from two points of
view: (1) fanaticism in the ideology of the youth population; and (2)
the uncritical teaching of the Torah, and its effects in terms of encouraging fanatical trends, including the doctrine of the "chosen people",
of propagating the superiority of the Mosaic law and the citing of mass
extermination as practiced by biblical heroes.

Tamarin chose to concentrate on the most extreme form of fanaticism, namely the stories of mass extermination of the enemy. He prepared 1066 questionnaire forms which were distributed to students of
various age groups. The questionnaire, which was anwered in writing by
563 boys and 503 girls, referred to the Book of Joshua, taught in
Israeli schools from the 4th to the 8th grades.

The form ran as follows: You are well-familiar with the following
excerpts from the Book of Joshua:

'So the people shouted when the priests blew with the trumpets: and
it came to pass, when the people heard the sound of the trumpet,
and the people shouted with a great shout, that the wall fell down
flat, so that the people went up into the city, every man straight
before him, and they took the city'.
'And they utterly destroyed all that was in the city, both man and
woman, young and old, and ox, and sheep, and ass, with the edge of
the sword'. *Joshua VI, 20-1.*
'And that day Joshua took Mak-kë-däh and smote it with the edge of
the sword, and the king thereof he utterly destroyed them, all the
souls that were therein; he let none remain: and he did to the king
of Mak-kë-däh as he did unto the king of Jericho.'
'Then Joshua passed from Mak-kë-däh, and all Israel with him, unto
Lile-nah, and fought against Lilé-nah':
'and the Lord delivered it also, and the king thereof, into the hand
of Israel; and he smote it with the edge of the sword, and all the
souls that were therein; he let none remain in it; but did unto the
king thereof as he did unto the king of Jericho'. *Joshua X, 28-30.*

Two questions were put to the students:
1. In your opinion, did Joshua and the Israelis act right or were they
wrong? Amplify your view on this matter.
2. Suppose the Israeli army captured an Arab village in the war, is it
right or wrong for the army to behave in the like manner with the

population of the village as Joshua did with the population of Jericho?

Although the Torah contains many examples of mass extermination, Tamarin chose the Book of Joshua in particular because of the special significance it is given in Israeli school curricula.

The students who answered the questionnaire were from Tel Aviv, a village near Ramleh, the town of Sharon and the Mochet settlement.

A student from Sharon answered the first question: "The aim of the war was the capture of land for the sake of the Israelis. Therefore the Israelis did the right thing in capturing towns and killing its inhabitants. It is undesirable to have foreign elements inside Israel, as people of other religions might have untoward influences on the Israeli society." A girl from the Mochet settlement wrote: "Joshua was right in killing the whole of the people of Jericho. As it was necessary to occupy all the country, he had little time to waste on captives." Similar answers formed 66-95 percent of the replies depending on the school, settlement or town.

Thirty per cent of the students replied in a categorical affirmative to the question regarding contemporary Israel. A seventh-grade student replied: "Everything, I believe, was done in the right way. What we are after is to vanquish our enemies and expand our frontiers. Like Joshua and the Israelites, we also have killed Arabs." A student of the eighth grade wrote: "In my opinion, our army should do to Arab villages what Joshua did to Jericho. This is because the Arabs are our enemies and will, even in captivity, look for ways to harm us."

As Tamarin rightly puts it, the answers received from such a psycho-sociological fieldwork imply a complete indictment of the Israeli educational system which, in collaboration with other social institutions in Israel, has sought to implant racist and fanatical ideas in the minds of Israeli youth.

When first published, the results of Tamarin's research caused an uproar in Israel, simply because they unmasked, in a scientific and objective way, the racist character of the Israeli society. Tamarin paid the price of his moral courage. He lost his job as professor at the University of Tel Aviv. Nevertheless, his study gained popularity and came to be known as the "Tamarin Affair."

The Legal Foundations of Racism and Fanaticism in Israel.

It is an established fact in social psychology that fanaticism, as a social phenomenon, may be found in many societies. It is the result of the interaction between various social systems and different political practices. Nevertheless, in Israeli society, one is faced with a peculiar situation, one which may be defined as "legalised fanaticism." For the Israeli legal system clearly tends to encourage racial discrimination inside Israel and, as such, may be regarded as a faithful replica of Zionist racist ideology.

In a study on this subject, Tamarin explains that the danger of such legal texts lies in the effect they have on people's minds. People tend to respect the inherent values and to believe in the validity of these laws despite their racist and reactionary values.

Discriminatory practices in Israel which have legal bases may be grouped under three main headings: (1) the denial of some basic human rights by discriminatory legislations; (2) the violation of the freedom of belief by means of religious coercion; and (3) legislations containing racial discrimination against the Arab minority.

In Tamarin's view, the most dangerous, undemocratic and reactionary of these laws is the one providing for the recreation of rabbinical courts. Promulgated in 1953, it is a modified version of the legislation of the days under the British Mandate. Under this law, all matters relating to personal status are judged in accordance with Judaic laws. It can be considered the most reactionary for several reasons:

1. The law encourages racism by prohibiting mixed marriages between Jews and non-Jews, as well as between Jews and certain other Jewish groups. As such, it constitutes a glaring violation of Paragraph 2 of the U.N. Declaration on Human Rights. From a socio-psychological point of view, this law constitutes a source for fanaticism. It also influences the nonreligious segments of the Israeli society by fostering an aversion towards Gentiles.

2. The law allows the formation of an independent group of theocratic judges not bound by the laws of the state. At the same time it discriminates against women by disqualifying them from becoming judges. It also discriminates between two groups of lawyers: those who can practice their profession in religious courts and those who cannot.

3. The law suspects the authenticity of marriages and divorces contracted under civil law outside Israel. In this way it also violates the established rules of International Private Law.

4. The law asserts the principle of inequality between Jews and non-Jews, as the latter are disqualified from appearing as witnesses before religious courts.

5. The law violates the freedom of belief by obliging the areligious to marry or divorce in accordance with the traditional religious rites. Sometimes, such persons are asked to renounce their own belief in order to be allowed to marry.
6. The Israeli Supreme Court is denied its right to legalize a marriage which is prohibited by religious law.

Tamarin attributes the difficulty of changing this law (in which a racist and reactionary judgement of non-Jews is implicit), to the dogmatic mentality of the elder generation among the ruling elite.This elder generation, which continues to cling to the principles of Zionism, still holds that the encouragement of religion will foster the ties among those Jews who are members of the Israeli society.

When one adds to the above-mentioned law the iniquitous laws that have been, and still are, applied against Palestinian Arabs in Israel, the kind of treatment meted out by Israeli society to the Arabs, who at one time formed the majority of Palestine's indigenous population, becomes apparent.

A Political Analysis of the Israeli Racist Personality

The Basic Features of the Israeli Personality

A racist ideology, such as Zionism, which has an illusionary and fictitious basis, cannot but leave its imprint on the social group formed during the development of settler-colonialism. Thus, the enforcement and encouragement of a racist and reactionary social strategy culminated in an Israeli personality deeply influenced by the racist roots of Zionism.[11]

A careful analysis of the collective Israeli personality will show that there is a nascent Israeli identity, differing in varying degrees from the predominant Jewish identity in the various Jewish communities of the Western world. A number of questions arise concerning the political implications of the characteristics of this Jewish identity, as well as the plans pursued by the ruling elite to link the traditional Jewish identity with the emerging Israeli one. Such questions cannot be answered without a political analysis of the Israeli personality. An in-depth study of this personality is indispensable for a genuine assessment of Zionism. It is also vitally important to analyse the impact of this type of personality on the Arab-Israeli conflict, from a social as well as a political point of view.

Problems of the Formation of Israeli Identity

A number of scholars have tried to specify the problems related to the formation of the present Israeli identity. Foremost among these problems is the transformation of "traditional Jewish characteristics" into the "emerging Israeli identity". In the opinion of certain psychoanalysts, these characteristics, which may be derived from the analysis of Jewish history, are linked to the self-image of the Jews as a persecuted minority. They include anxiety, a feeling of inferiority and suspicion and mistrust of non-Jews.

Some American psychoanalysts believe that some of these characteristics have been transmitted to present-day Israeli society. They noticed the prevalence of suspicion, which on the one hand is based on their feelings of uniqueness and superiority, and, on the other, is the result of their subjection to periodical persecutions. However, the feeling of inferiority has been transformed into a feeling of Israeli superiority towards the rest of the world. This superiority is illustrated through the laws favoring the Israelis, which go against the established principles of international law. The Israeli Law of Return, which gives every Jew the right to immigrate to Israel, thereby automatically qualifying him for Israeli citizenship, is a pertinent example.

In his remarks concerning the Jewish personality, the Jewish psychologist Rubenstein stresses the fact that the Israelis, both as a society and as individuals, are marked by a deep suspicion of others. In his opinion, these suspicions have left their mark on their interpersonal relationships. They come particularly to the foreground during any contact with the outside world. According to Rubenstein, this suspicion and rejection manifests itself in three different directions: against the Arabs, against non-Jews and against international systems and organizations. Rubenstein concludes that the Israeli personality is characterized by an extreme form of paranoia, emanating from the traditional mistrust which Jews bear toward Gentiles.

The decisive factor affecting social relationships within Israeli society is closely associated with the problem of identity. Researchers differentiate here between the "traditional Jewish" and the "emerging Israeli" identities. As the American scholar Margret Main said in her *Israel and the Problems of Identity*, "the preservation of Jewish identity has always depended upon the existence of non-Jewish groups." The only thing that is absolutely necessary to distinguish a Jewish group is the existence of some Gentiles. Main pointed out that Israelis are very much preoccupied with, and highly sensitive about, matters relating to their identity. They are also very concerned with the special mission of Israel, as well as the situation of its people, which is distinguished from other societies. All this corresponds to the characteristics of the racist ideologies mentioned previously.

In his study on the Israeli identity, the Jewish sociologist S.N. Herman[12] arrived at conclusions similar to those Main had propagated in the 50s. He wrote that the division of the world between Jews and non-Jews was one of the essential elements of the Jewish identity. The image of the non-Jew occupies a central position in the mind of the Jew. The barriers between these two worlds have an immense importance in Israel.

A discussion of the emerging Israeli identity must pay due attention to the diffierent generations to which the Israelis belong. Researchers focus particularly on the Sabra generation (those born in Israel), in the attempt to uncover their personality structure. The researcher's interest is motivated by the qualitative differences between the social and psychological experiences of immigrant Jews as compared to the Sabras. In the opinion of a number of researchers, the Sabras may be characterized by the following: (1) their clustering around Israel (in the sense of time and place); (2) their non-concern with modern Jewish history, even that relating to their fathers; (3) their ambition to attain material security and a comfortable living standard; and (4) their solid attachment to their country. In addition to differences between the generations, Herman points out other factors which have a far-reaching effect on the emerging Israeli identity, the most important of which is the question of lineal descent (being an Oriental or an Occidental Jew) and the degree of religiosity (religious versus secular Jew).

What influence does the emerging Israeli identity have on the Arab-Israeli conflict and to what extent is it influenced by this conflict?

It should be noted that the Israeli ruling elite employs a coherent psychosocial strategy in order to form a prototype Israeli identity, so as to carry out its military and economic policies effectively, precisely and pragmatically. It can be argued that the psychological characteristics of the Israeli masses, their suspicion, rejection and aggressiveness is not necessarily characteristic of the Israeli ruling elite in the same manner as it is of the Israeli public. Granting the fact that each nation has its distinctive characteristics, it does not follow that the ruling elite would necessarily share these characteristics. Even if this should be the case, the elite's decisions are generally the result of their personal effective power in addition to geographical, historical and economic considerations. This is best illustrated by the Eichmann Trial.

The Political Significance of Eichmann's Trial

The Eichmann Trial illustrates the gap between the Israeli elite strategy for the formation of an Israeli identity and the psychological state of Israelis who, for many reasons, are no longer much interested in fostering ties with Jews living outside Israel.

In her *Eichmann in Israel*, which provoked the wrath of the Israeli ruling elite, the well-known Jewish researcher, Hannah Arndt, maintained that the ruling elite put on trial not Eichmann the individual, but Eichmann the symbol. This is revealed by Ben Gurion's declaration on the eve of Eichmann's trial: "The person who fell into the trap and is about to face a historic trial is not a mere individual, nor even the incarnation of the Nazi system. What is now on trial is the anti-Semitic ideology throughout the history of the world."

Daniel Bell, in his "ABC of Justice," disagreed with Arndt. He listed a number of motives behind the Eichmann trial: (1) The world should be a witness to the fate of the Jews; (2) The Israeli elite wanted to arouse in the nations of the world a sense of guilt, thereby impelling them to come to the defense of Israeli interests; (3) They further meant to give the Israeli Jews a proof of the kind of life led by the Jews in the Diaspora, as a result of being a minority group; (4) Finally, they intended to prove to the Israelis the soundness of the Zionist solution of the Jewish problem.

Arndt reported that Ben Gurion had mapped out the whole trial from beginning to end, well before it started. He betrayed his objectives in a series of articles published in the Israeli newspaper '*Davar*', one of which asserted that "contemporary Israelis were in danger of losing their ties with the Jewish people, and thus with their history. They therefore needed to be reminded of what had befallen the Jewish people."

The planning of the trial by the ruling elite reveals how this elite is systematically striving to form an Israeli personality conforming to a racist prototype which is characterized by mistrust and rejection of Gentiles, as well as aggressiveness toward the Arabs. This is all based on the fundamental racist theory that the Jews are God's chosen people and, therefore, superior among races.

The Racist Components of the Israeli Personality

Israeli social and psychological field studies display how the reactionary strategy employed by the ruling elite succeeded in throwing light upon the basic implicit and explicit racist tendencies of the Israeli personality.

These tendencies are confirmed in a number of field studies carried out by the Israeli psychologist Simon Hermann, published in his *Israelis and Jews*. The importance of these studies may be attributed to the fact that the sample involved students in the 16-17 age group, including some first-year university students. Hermann carried out the main part of his research in 1965; it was completed by the end of 1968.

For the second part of his study, Hermann prepared a questionnaire which was distributed to secondary school students in Jerusalem and Haifa. The questionnaire was addressed to three different groups: the devout, who regularly observe religious rites; the traditionalists, who do not regularly practice their religion and finally, those who are non-religious. Hermann's theoretical standpoint is revealed by the type of questions he formulated, questions which contained basic racist slogans implicit in Zionism.

Thirteen questions were formualted and covered the following subjects: The Israelis as a continuation of the Jewish people. The Israeli state as a continuation of Jewish history. The negative aspects of Jewish conduct at the time of the Jewish massacres in Germany. The positive aspects of Jewish conduct at the time of the massacres. Sympathizers with long suffering Jews during the massacres. Sympathizers with Jews subjected to persecution in Islamic countries. The possibility of a recurrence of these massacres. The duty of the Jews to consider themselves the survivors of the massacres. The abstract definition of Zionism. The self-image of Jews as Zionists. The extent of their affinity regarding those American Jews willing and unwilling to immigrate to Israel. The prospects of rooting out anti-Semitic trends. Anti-Semiticism in relation to Jewish characteristics and behavior.

A comprehensive look at the result of this research points out the fundamental racist elements of Zionism: (1) The emphasis on the continuity and the uniqueness of the Jewish people throughout history; (2) The emphasis on the persecution which the Jews faced in Western societies; (3) The emphasis on alleged persecution of Jews in Islamic countries; (4) Keeping alive the fear of the danger that anti-Jewish pogroms might recur; (5) The emphasis on the continuing anti-Semitism in the world.

The Israeli ruling elite succeeded in implanting these crucial ideas in the minds of the Israelis, which led to the latter's pathological attitudes. This strategy also led to a clearly authoritarian Israeli personality, as Tamarin has confirmed. The formation of this racist Israeli personality was encouraged by the consolidation of values advocating violence and aggression against the Arabs, both those who remained in

Israel after 1948 and those now living in the Arab States bordering Israel. This is revealed in Ben Gurion's dissuasive policy during the 50s, a policy which was based on the assumption that the Arabs "understand nothing but force." It is easy to prove that this judgement is identical with those propagated by all racist systems, which discriminate between a superior race (the colonialists) and an inferior or degenerate race (the indigenous population). This racial discrimination is presented as a justification of the practise of violence and terrorism against the native population. It happened in Algeria and is being currently practised in South Africa and Israel.

Conclusion

The racist character which marked Zionism since its appearance in the nineteenth century has led — after the creation of Israel in 1948 — to the emergence of a racist society in every sense of the word. The publication of *The Racism of the State of Israel* (by the Israel scholar Yesrael Schahak, chairman of the Israeli Committee on Human Rights) came as a shock to many cultural quarters in the West that have long been misled by claims of socialism, democracy and a society of equality in Israel. The field studies of the Israeli psychologist George Tamarin, published in his *The Israeli Dilemma*, which caused his discharge as a professor at Tel Aviv University, prove beyond doubt that racist Zionist ideologies and enforced policies have all led to the formation of an Israeli personality which is aggressive, domineering, fanatical and narrow-minded.

It is useful to note that these qualities are common among a great number of settler-colonial systems. Hence the special importance of comparative studies of these systems, since these studies both reveal the basic political structure and underline the components of settler mentality.[13] The conclusions of comparative studies may be of vital importance to policymakers in the countries which resist these colonial systems. In the light of these studies it will be possible to draw counter-revolutionary policies and it will be possible — in the long run — to disperse these imperial illusions by means of intellectual activity, and political and military struggle.

Notes

1. *See* Sayed Yassin, Aladdin Hilal et al., *Zionist Settler-Colonialism in Palestine*, (Cairo, 1975).

2. For a detailed discussion, see Sayed Yassin, "Ideology and Technology," *Al-Katib*, no. 101 (August 1969), pp. 7-20.

3. Adam Schaff, "La Definition Fonctionnelle de l'Idéologie et le Problème de 'la Fin du Siécle de l'Idéologie,' *L'Homme et la Société*, no. 4 (1976).

4. D. Felman, *Twentieth Century Political Thought*, ed. Joseph S. Roucek (New York, 1946), pp. 105-131; O.C. Cox, *Caste, Class and Race* (New York, 1959).

5. Adolf Hitler in *Mein Kampf*, as quoted by D. Felman *Twentieth Century*, *op. cit.*, p. 106.

6. *Ibid.*, p. 107.

7. Count De Gobineau, *Essai sur l'inégalité des Races Humaines*, (Paris, n.d.).

8. For an accurate and critical analysis of these racial theories *see* T.A. Sorokin, *Contemporary Sociological Theories* (New York, 1967), pp. 219-51.

9. For a definition of these concepts, *see* Abdul Wahab Al-Masiri and Sawsan Hussain, *The Encyclopedia of Zionist Concepts and Terms: A Critical View* (Cairo, 1975).

10. G. Tamarin, *The Israeli Dilemma: Essays on a Warfare State* (Rotterdam, 1973).

11. A.R. Taylor, *The Zionist Mind* (Beirut, 1974). See also Sayed Yassin, "A Political Analysis of the Israeli Personality," *Al-Ahram*.

12. S.N. Hermann, *Israelis and Jews* (New York, 1970).

13. I. Abu-Lughod and B. Abu-Laban, eds., *Settler Regimes in Africa and the Arab World: The Illusion of Endurance* (Wilmette, Illinois, 1974).

Part Two

THE APPLICATION AND EFFECTS OF ZIONISM IN PALESTINE

7 THE RIGHT TO NATIONALITY IN THE STATE OF ISRAEL

Anis F. Kassim

I am certain that the world will judge the Jewish State by what it will do with the Arabs. — Chaim Weizmann, 1949

The General Assembly. . . . Determines that Zionism is a form of racism and racial discrimination. — November 10, 1975.

In the Israeli law books there are, in fact, two nationality laws; one deals with persons who are 'Jews' and the other is concerned with 'non-Jews'. This distinction is codified in Israel's Nationality Law of 1952.[1] The first section of the Law provides that Israeli nationality is acquired: (1) by return (section 2); (2) by residence in Israel (section 3); (3) by birth (section 4); or (4) by naturalization (sections 5-9). A study of this law with reference to the U.N. Resolution must focus on nationality by 'return' and by residence. The two other means of obtaining nationality are, under Israeli practice, almost void of legal significance.

Nationality by Return

For proper understanding of this means of nationality, it is imperative to refer to its politico-legal background. On July 5, 1950 the Knesset passed the famous Law of Return,[2] the first section of which proclaims that "Every Jew has the right to come to this country as an *'oleh'*." This alleged 'right' of a 'Jew' to immigrate to Palestine is, in the words of Israeli Prime Minister David Ben Gurion, "inherent in him from the very fact of his being a Jew; the State does not grant the right of return to the Jews of the diaspora. This right preceded the State; its source is to be found in the historic and never-broken connection between the Jewish people and the homeland."[3]

Once a 'Jew' 'returns' to the claimed 'homeland', the Nationality Law provides him with immediate and automatic citizenship. Section 2(a) of the Law provides that "Every *'oleh* under the Law of Return shall become an Israel national."

The Legal Procedures

Since the Law provides every 'Jew' with the 'right' to 'return', such a Jew is not under any legal obligation to initiate any procedure in the course of obtaining Israeli citizenship. He is neither required to 'apply' for citizenship, nor is he supposed to 'reside' for a certain period of time before he becomes eligible. No oath of allegiance, as traditionally required by other countries, is a prerequisite. The Law does not even demand the 'returning' Jew to declare his desire or intention of becoming an Israeli citizen, and he is not asked to renounce his original citizenship. According to a prominent Israeli lawyer, an immigrating Jew becomes an Israeli citizen "without there being any element of will on his part or any discretionary act on the part of the (Israeli) administration."[4]

Conversely, any 'Jew' coming to Israel is required by the Law to *express* his renunciation of Israel's citizenship before an Israeli official if he does not wish to be clothed with such citizenship. The subtle wording of the Nationality Law is indicative: Section 2 (c) (2) provides that nationality by Return "does not apply . . . to a person of full age who *immediately* . . . . declares that he does not desire to become an Israel national;" (emphasis added).

Since nationality by return is exclusively concerned with 'Jews' without any regard to their respective citizenship, the issues that may be promptly posed are, what effects might the applicability of this rule have on Jews who come to Israel, and, more significantly, who is a Jew to start with.

Status of Jews coming to Israel. Every "Jew" coming to Israel shall be "immediately" and "automatically" clothed with Israeli citizenship, unless he expressly opts out. This means of acquiring nationality has created legal problems for those Jews who do not desire to become citizens of Israel but do not know, or are not fully aware of Israel's nationality by return. It also created legal responsibility for foreign governments toward their nationals who happen to be of the Jewish faith. In particular, the problem is sharper when the nationality law of the country of origin is strict regarding dual nationality.

When Israel's Nationality Law was passed, several foreign governments took a hard look at that legislation. The reaction of the U.S. Government, for example, was evidenced by its official instructions to American Jews living in Israel to file a declaration opting out of Israeli nationality if they did not want to lose their American citizenship. And the U.S. State Department used to provide American Jews going to Israel with instructions to declare immediately, at the Israeli port of arrival, that they did not wish to become Israeli citizens, unless they otherwise desired.

The Netherlands' Foreign Office took a similar position. It instructed Dutch nationals of Jewish faith that they would not lose their Dutch nationality if they opted out of Israeli citizenship at the port of arrival in Israel.[5]

This is not as yet the end of the complexities. According to the Law, a 'Jew' born in Israel shall immediately become an Israeli citizen from the day of his birth. Such a child does not acquire Israeli citizenship by virtue of birth, but by virtue of "return," for Section (4) of the Law of Return deemed "every Jew who was born in this country" an *'oleh*. The consequential application of this provision is that "all Jewish children born in Israel will *prima facie* be Israel nationals regardless of the nationality of their parents."[6] Should the child's parents opt out of Israeli nationality their opting out would not necessarily include the child, unless they expressly include him in their declaration.[7]

Who is a Jew? One of the major issues that has plagued the Zionist-Israeli establishment is the definition of a Jew. The answer appears, quite often, as a jungle of religious mystiques of "legal acrobatics." The crux of the issue is found in the fundamental Zionist doctrine of the "Jewish people."[8] To Zionism, members of the Jewish faith, regardless of their place of residence or citizenship, constitute one distinct and separate entity called the "Jewish people." Zionism agrees with the Judaic teachings that a Jew may be defined as a person born to a Jewish mother or converted to Judaism. But the difference between Zionism and Jewish religious law becomes sharper and more crucial if the issue is put in the form of a negative question: "who is the non-Jew?" In Jewish religious law, if a Jew becomes a convert to another religion he is still regarded as a Jew,[9] while Zionism does not consider him so, for he has severed his relationship with the "Jewish people."

The definition of a Jew in Zionist–Israeli jurisprudence was put in perspective in the authoritative judgement of Israel's Supreme Court in the famous Daniel Case. Oswald Refeisen was born in Poland to a Jewish mother but later on he was voluntarily baptized and became Father Daniel of the Catholic Carmelite Order. When he immigrated to Israel in 1958, he, considering himself a Jew, requested the minister of interior to grant him the status of an *'oleh* under the Law of Return.

His request was denied, so he brought his case to the Supreme Court.

The Court decided by a majority of 4 to 1 that Father Daniel was not a Jew for the purposes of the Law of Return. All of the Supreme Court justices held that the concept of Jew in the Law of Return should not be confused with the concept of a Jew in religious law. Based on that premise, Justice Silberg, presiding, held that "a Jew who becomes a Christian *cannot* be called a Jew" (emphasis original). Justice Landau, tracing the genesis of the Law of Return in Zionsim and the philosophy of its founders, concluded that: "The Ministry of Interior correctly drew the line dividing Jew from non-Jew, within the meaning of the Law of Return, at the point of change of religion." The 'legal' reasoning for that conclusion is that a Jew who is a convert to another religion would necessarily dissociate himself from the Jewish people. Justice Landua aptly said: "A Jew who cuts himself off from the heritage of the national past of his (Jewish) people, by changing his religion, accordingly ceases to be a Jew in that *national sense* which found expression in the Law of Return" (emphasis added).[10]

The emphasis of the Court on the nexus between the "Jew" and the "Jewish people" is the central theme of the definition of who is a Jew. A "Jew" in Zionist–Israeli jurisprudence is the "national" of the so-claimed "Jewish people." The identity of such a 'national' is not determined by his religion; but rather by not being a convert to another religion. This concept has finally been established by a 1970 amendment to the Law of Return. The Amendment reads: "For the purpose of this Law, a "Jew" means a person born to a Jewish mother or converted to Judaism and who is not a member of another religion."

Nationality by Residence

All means of nationality other than that of return deal with non-Jews. Nationality by residence is particularly concerned with Palestinian natives who remained in Palestine after the state of Israel came into existence. The Law sets up certain legal procedures for native Palestinians to apply for Israeli citizenship.

Legal Procedures

Section 3 (a) of the Law reads:

> A person who, immediately before the establishment of the State was a Palestinian citizen and who does not become an Israeli national under Section 2 (by return) shall become an Israel national . . . if

(1) he was registered on the 4th Adar, 5712 (1st March 1952) an inhabitant under the Registration of Inhabitants Ordinance, 5709 – 1949; and

(2) he is an inhabitant of Israel on the day of the coming into force of this Law; and

(3) he was in Israel, or in an area which became Israel territory after the establishment of the State, or entered Israel legally during that period.

These conditions "were in practice very difficult to fulfill." Professor Don Peretz, at the time very sympathetic to Israel, recorded that most Palestinian citizens "had no proof of Palestine citizenship, which could be established only by possession of a Palestine passport or identity card." Peretz added "Large numbers of Arabs who had possessed identity cards either lost them or surrendered them to the Israeli army during, or immediately after, the war." In addition, many Palestinians were excluded from the Registration of Inhabitants because often there was a "deliberate attempt not to register many (Palestinian) villages."[11]

A Palestinian who was fortunate to pass these obstacles still had to establish that he was an inhabitant of Israel or in Israeli territory between the day of the establishment of Israel and the day of the coming into force. Considering the war situation and the terror that plagued Palestine before and after May 14, 1948, it was almost impossible for many Palestinians to determine whether they were in an Israeli territory or a nonoccupied territory. A further problem was the continuous territorial expansion of Israel between May 14, 1948 and the Armistice Agreements of Rhodes (1949).[12]

The Applicability of Nationality by Residence

Palestine citizenship was regulated by the Order-in-Council of 1925 as enacted by the mandatory power. When the state of Israel passed its Nationality Law, it first repealed the Palestinian Citizenship Order retroactively "from the day of the establishment of the State."[13] Palestinians henceforth became legally 'stateless' – a principle which was maintained by several Israeli tribunals including the Supreme Court.

The 'stateless' status of the majority of native Palestinians continued to prevail after the coming into force of the Law. The stringent conditions stipulated in Section 3 (a), resulted in the creation of a 'stateless' class of Palestinians living in Israel, for those who could not prove that they were Palestinian citizens, and not registered in the Registration of Inhabitants, and inhabitants of Israel at the day of its establishment, were not eligible for Israeli citizenship.

The most traumatic legal repercussion of this situation is that such "stateless" Palestinians still, to the present time, breed stateless children. A careful analysis of section 3 (b) of the Law reveals this fact:

> A person born after the establishment of the State who is an inhabitant of Israel on the day of the coming into force of this Law, and whose father or mother becomes an Israel national under subsection 3 (a), shall become an Israel national with effect from the day of his birth.

The preceding text should not be confused with the traditional right of nationality by birth. The text is tied up with subsection 3 (a) quoted above. If subsection (b) is read carefully it becomes obvious that a Palestinian born in Israel to a father or mother who could not become an Israeli citizen under subsection 3 (a), cannot accordingly become an Israeli citizen.

A Juridical Appraisal of the Nationality Law of Israel under the International Nationality Law Criteria[14]

It is an established doctrine in public international law that every state is subject to certain procedural limitations in the course of regulating its nationality law. These limitations are well defined by international nationality law. A nationality law of a given state in order to be honored by other states, should observe these legal limitations.

Limitations upon Conferment of Nationality at Birth

Customary international law has sanctioned two means of conferring nationality by a state upon a person at his birth: *jus soli* and *jus sanguinis*. As to the former, a person will acquire the nationality of the state within whose territory he was born and regardless of the nationality of his parents. The latter means of nationality provides that a person will acquire the nationality of his parents, or one of them, regardless of the territory in which he was born. Every state in the world adopts one or both of these means of nationality.

Israeli nationality by return conforms to neither *jus soli* nor *jus sanguinis*. It was correctly described by an Israeli scholar as a "unique" means of obtaining nationality.[15] For a person born in Israel becomes an Israeli citizen only if his parents are of the Jewish faith, but native Palestinians were "legally" denationalized and still give birth to stateless children born in Israel. Put differently, the internationally accepted means of nationality has been "legally" qualified in Zionist-Israeli jurisprudence by adding "Jewish" to both *jus soli* and *jus sanguinis*.

Limitations upon the Conferment of Nationality by Naturalization

Naturalization is a means of acquiring nationality by an individual subsequent to his birth. Nationality by naturalization may be obtained directly by an adult or indirectly by the children of an applicant. International nationality law provides for certain legal procedures. One of the major legal limitations is that there must be a "genuine link" between the naturalizing state and the applicant seeking its citizenship. This link can be manifested in the fact that the applicant has established his residency in the naturalizing state.

Israeli nationality by return does not conform to this limitation. The 'link' required by the Law is that the person be a Jew. Therefore, his religious identification rather than his residency is the only "legal" prerequisite. In contrast, the residency requirement was instituted in four of the six requirements for applicants who are not Jews.[16]

Limitations upon the Conferment of Nationality on a Discriminatory Basis

Under public law any discrimination, distinction, exclusion, restriction or preference based on race, color, descent or national or ethnic origin is prohibited. Among the major civil rights that public law protects against discrimination is the right to nationality. This principle was finally codified in the International Convention on the Elimination of All Forms of Racial Discrimination.

The Harvard Research in International Law explained in its Draft Convention on Nationality that "if State A should attempt to naturalize all persons in the world holding a particular *political or religious faith* or belonging to a particular race," it would appear that such a state had gone beyond the limits set by international law.[17] Conforming to the same principle of nondiscrimination in regulating nationality claims, many sovereign states did not honor the Nazi nationality laws which discriminated between Aryans and non-Aryans. Professor E. Lauterpacht noted that because those legislations were based on racial discrimination, "it is not surprising that they should have been among the first selected for repeal" by the Allied Military and Occupation Authorities.[18] Following the same principle, the Swiss Federal Court declined to give effect to the Nazi laws, because "to the extent that the German legislation makes a distinction between 'Jews' and 'Aryans' on the ground of race, it is contrary to Swiss public policy ... [and]

to the principle of equality of men . . ."[19]

The Nationality Law of Israel has set up the legal criteria to regulate Israel's nationality claims along discriminatory lines between Jews and non-Jews. M.D. Gouldman, first assistant attorney of Israel, did not challenge discriminatory character. He wrote: "There can thus be no doubt that it is easier for a Jew than a non-Jew to acquire Israel nationality, and the Nationality Law is therefore open to the charge that it discriminates on ethnic grounds, in favor of Jews." In attempting to defend it, Gouldman unwittingly fell on the very central source of discrimination. He said that "The Law cannot be divorced from its historic context. It is easier for a Jew to acquire Israel nationality for the *simple reason* that Israel is primarily a State for the Jewish people" (emphasis added). He reasoned that it "could be alleged that the essence of the Law of Return is selective in that it deals with Jews and their families; but then Israel is a 'Jewish State'.[20]

Conclusion

Racial discrimination has become "legally" institutionalized in the state of Israel. The Nationality Law, and particularly, the doctrine of return, gives hard evidence of Israel's discriminatory and racist policies. The Law considered here was not accidentally enacted. It is, rather, an integral part of the Zionist policy consistently pursued ever since the Zionist colonization processes began in Palestine.

Palestine was envisaged by the Zionist movement to be "as Jewish as England is English." It necessarily follows that all shaping and sharing of values have to be conducted along the exclusive line of "Jewishness." All rights and obligations have been predicated on the premise of 'Jewishness'. The Zionist elite's approach throughout the colonization era, has been based on three principles: Jewish land, Jewish labor and Jewish product. There is Jewish land, exclusively owned by Jews or in the name of the Jewish people; there is Jewish labor that can be exclusively hired by Jewish employers and should only be hired to till the Jewish land; and there is Jewish product that only Jews should buy and consume. One may add, consistently, that there are Jewish rights of nationality, Jewish rights of immigration and Jewish rights in every aspect. By this comprehensive Judaization of all community social processes, Palestine could ultimately become "as Jewish as England is English."

Racial discrimination is inherent to Zionism. In a State of Jews those who are "nationals" of the "Jewish people" cannot be equal with those who are not, and should they become equal, the *raison d'être* of having a State of Jews would vanish.

Notes

1. 6 LSI, 50 (1952). There were two amendments, one in 1958 and the other in 1968, both of which were incorporated in the text of the Law as reproduced in M.D. Gouldmann, *Israel Nationality Law* (Jerusalem, 1970), p. 133.

2. 4 LSI, 114 (1950). There were two amendments, one in 1954 and the other in 1970, incorporated in the text of the Law and reproduced in *Ibid.*, p. 141.

3. Quoted in *Ibid.*, pp. 19-20.

4. Rosenne, "The Israel Nationality Law 5712-1952 and the Law of Return 5710-1950," 81 J.D. Int. 5, 19 (1954).

5. Boasson, "Some Theoretical and Practical Considerations of the Israel Nationality Law," 2 N.T. Int'l.R., 375 at 377, 380 (1955). Boasson was the Legal Adviser to the Netherlands Legation in Israel.

6. Rosenne, "The Israel Nationality Law," p. 37.

7. *See* the Nationality Law, Section 2 (c) (3).

8. For a Zionist legal analysis of this concept *see* Feinberg, "The Recognition of the Jewish People in International Law," *Jewish Yearbook of International Law* (1948). For an objective legal analysis of this concept see Mallison, "The Zionist-Israel Juridical Claims to Constitute 'The Jewish People' Nationality Entity and to Confer Membership in it: Appraisal in Public International Law," 32 Geo. Wash. L. Ref. 983 (1964).

9. *See* the testimony given by the Chief Rabbi, Dr. Herzog, before the U.N. Special Committee on Palestine in 1947, A/364, Add. 2, Vol. III, 130 (N.Y. 1947).

10. "The Oswald Rufeisen (Brother Daniel) Case," *Midstream*, March, 1963.

11. Don Peretz, *Israel and the Palestine Arabs* (Washington D.C., 1958), p. 123.

12. Palestinians who lived in the Triangle suffered most because that area was ceded to Israel as a result of the Armistice Agreements.

13. Section 18 (a).

14. The following section is based on Anis F. Kassim, *The Law of Return and the Nationality Law of the State of Israel: A Study of International and Municipal Law* (Beirut, 1972) (in Arabic), chaps. 4 and 5.

15. Gouldmann, *Israel Nationality*, p. 18.

16. Section 5 (a) (1-4).

17. 23 Am. J. Int'l. L. Supp., 26. (emphasis added)

18. E. Lautherpacht, "The Nationality of the Denationalized Persons," *Jewish Yearbook of International Law*.

19. Cited in *Ibid.* and Silving, "Nationality in Comparative Law," 5 Am. J. Com. 410, ft. 36, at pp. 418-19.

20. Gouldmann, *Israel Nationality* pp. 19, 67.

8 ISRAEL'S TREATMENT OF THE ARABS IN THE OCCUPIED AREAS

Michael Adams

Even today the world remains woefully ignorant about the situation of the Palestinians living under Israeli occupation. But increased awareness of the injustice suffered by the Palestinians, and of its results in terms of discrimination and spiritual and material hardship, has been an important factor in bringing about a reappraisal of international attitudes toward the Arab-Israeli conflict and the proper solution to it.

Early Zionist Attitudes Toward the Palestinian Arabs

The basic problem which the early Zionists largely ignored, and whose importance their successors have consistently tried to belittle, was and remains the native Arab population. When they conceived their ambition of establishing in Palestine a Jewish homeland or commonwealth, all but the most perceptive among them left out of account the fact that Palestine already had a population – a population which could not be expected to share the enthusiasm of the Zionists for their wholly Jewish vision.

From the beginning there were among the Zionists those who were aware of the facts, and who tried to warn their colleagues against the dangers of implanting a Jewish national entity on Arab soil. One was Asher Ginzberg, a Russian Jew who became interested in Zionism toward the end of the nineteenth century and who visited Palestine in 1891 to assess the prospects for Jewish settlement. Finding the country already had a settled population and that it was "difficult, except on sand dunes or stony hills, to find untilled soil in Palestine," he warned his fellow Zionists in an article entitled "Truth from Palestine" (signed with his pen name of Ahad Ha'Am) that Jewish settlers must be very careful to win the goodwill of the local population. If they wanted to find a secure foothold, he said, they must treat the Palestinians with friendliness and respect.

'Yet what do our brethren do in Palestine? Just the very opposite! Serfs they were in the lands of the Diaspora and suddenly they find themselves in unrestricted freedom and this change has awakened in them an inclination to despotism. They treat the Arabs with hostility and cruelty, deprive them of their rights, offend them without cause and even boast of these deeds; and nobody among us opposes this despicable and dangerous inclination.[1]

Unhappily, the warning of Asher Ginzberg went unheeded, as did the warnings of those in the next generation of Zionists who shared his humanity and his realism, men like Martin Buber and Judan Magnes. To such men, no action could be justified which failed to take account of the principle that you should "do nothing to your neighbor that you would not have him do unto you." But it was not they who were to control the destiny of the Zionist movement. Instead, a group of men gained the upper hand who either knew nothing of the Arab presence in Palestine or believed that it could be elbowed aside by force. This was a tragedy both for the Palestinians and for the future Israelis; and it was all the more tragic because these activists were successful — in the short run.

To Zionist eyes, their success was even greater than they had expected. Few of them considered the price that had been paid by the Palestinian Arabs; and those who did tended to dismiss it as one of those inevitable historical tragedies whose victims had no option but to learn to live with their fate. This was a short-sighted view. Whether or not it had been a mistake in the first place to try to establish a Jewish presence in Palestine, there can be no doubt that it was a mistake to do so by force and without Palestinian consent — and the success of the undertaking only made matters worse. That same Asher Ginzberg observed that "a mistake that succeeds is still a mistake."

It is important to be clear about the nature of that mistake on the part of the early Zionists, for it has dictated the policy of their successors toward the Arab world, and it lies at the root of the failure of the Israelis to achieve their goal of a secure national existence.

In the Balfour Declaration, the British government had expressed its support for the idea of establishing in Palestine a Jewish "national home" and this idea was also written into the terms of the Mandate by which the League of Nations authorized Britain to rule Palestine. But both before and after accepting the Mandate, the British government expressly ruled out the suggestion that a national home meant a Jewish *state*. The condition stated in the Balfour Declaration, that "nothing shall be done to prejudice the civil and religious rights of existing non-Jewish communities in Palestine," should have ruled out such a suggestion in any case. But because there were doubts about the true intention, the British government published a policy statement in

1922 which contained the following categorical assurance:

> 'His Majesty's Government therefore now declare unequivocally that it is not part of their policy that Palestine should become a Jewish State. They would indeed regard it as contrary to their obligations to the Arabs under the Mandate, as well as to the assurances which have been given to the Arab people in the past, that the Arab population of Palestine should be made the subjects of a Jewish State against their will'.

This was clear as far as the British government was concerned. But the British could not speak for the Zionists and it is also clear now (and should have been then) that the Zionists were aiming at the establishment of Jewish state. It was also clear from the beginning that such a state could only be achieved by violating the rights of the Palestinian Arabs. This must be clearly recognized in order to understand the attitude of the Zionists toward the Palestinians, both in the early stage of the Zionist enterprise and at every subsequent stage of its development. The Zionists had set their sights on a goal which necessarily involved the violation of the rights of the Palestinians. They were prepared to use every means, including force, to achieve that goal. It is not surprising, therefore, that once they had gained control of most of Palestine in 1948 (or when they went on in 1967 to gain control of all of it), they felt no compunction about infringing still further what few rights were left to the Palestinians. Indeed, it can be argued that by starting out on the wrong foot, using violence and political manipulation to gain their ends, they left themselves no alternative, once they were in control of the situation in Palestine, but to continue on the same course. This explains the otherwise inexplicable heartlessness with which the Israeli government has continued to persecute a people to whom it has already done such irreparable injury.

No amount of sophistry can disguise the extent of that original injury. It found its full expression in the dispersion of the Palestinian people in 1948 and the forcible seizure of their lands and property. But long before that it was implicit in several aspects of Zionist policy during the British Mandate. In particular, the creation of the Jewish Agency and other specifically Jewish organizations (the embryonic infrastructure of the future state) established a form of apartheid, which excluded native Palestinians from participation in important areas of social, economic and political life in their own homeland.

The policies adopted by the Israelis toward the Palestinian Arabs after the establishment of the Jewish state followed logically — and, indeed, inevitably — from the attitudes of the Zionist "pioneers" in the pre-state period. Zionism as it developed in the 1930s and 40s was an essentially undemocratic movement, because it favored one section of the community in Palestine at the expense of another. Those of the Zionists who pointed out this failing and the implicit dangers were disregarded by the majority, who refused to face the fact that there was a basic conflict between Zionism and democracy.

Zionism in Practice in the State of Israel, 1948-67

The conflict made itself felt the moment the Jewish state came into being. Those who signed Israel's Declaration of Independence, dated May 14, 1948, described themselves as the representatives of "the Jewish people in the Land of Israel and the Zionist Movement." They proclaimed "the establishment of a Jewish State" and declared that the new state would be "open to Jewish immigration and the ingathering of exiles." Yet the Declaration went on to say that it would maintain "complete equality of social and political rights for all its citizens, without distinction of creed, race or sex"; and it called on "the sons of the Arab people dwelling in Israel to keep the peace and to play their part in building the state on the basis of full and equal citizenship."

The hollowness of the promise was exposed as soon as the question arose of who was entitled to live in the new state. Its boundaries had been extended far beyond those envisaged in the U.N. partition plan and the great majority of the Palestinians whose homes were within those boundaries fled into exile, some out of a simple instinct for self-preservation, others because they had been forcibly expelled by the Israelis. The U.N. General Assembly, in one of its earliest attempts to limit the scope of the tragedy that had overtaken Palestine, called for their return. The General Assembly had acted on the advice of U.N. Chief Meditator Count Folke Bernadotte who had urged in his September 1948 report:

> It would be an offence against the principles of elemental justice if these victims of the conflict were denied the right to return to their homes while Jewish immigrants flow into Palestine, and indeed offer at least the threat of permanent replacement of the Arab refugees who have been rooted in the land for centuries.

This recommendation aroused grave apprehension in the minds of the

Israelis, who had seen their task of taking over Palestine "miraculously" simplified by the flight of so much of the indigenous population. Faced with the possibility that the United Nations would insist on their return, Israel's new prime minister, David Ben-Gurion, said, "We must do everything to ensure they never do return."[2] Nor, to their shame, did any influential Israelis raise their voices in support of Bernadotte's principle of "elemental justice" for the refugees. Indeed, it was probably Bernadotte's insistence on the right of the refugees to return which contributed as much as anything to the hostility he aroused among the Israelis. The day after completing his report, Bernadotte was murdered by Jewish terrorists in Jerusalem; and the danger he foresaw, that the refugees would be replaced in their ancestral homeland by Jewish immigrants became a fact, with terrible consequences for both sides.

The consequences were most immediate and most devastating for the Palestinian refugees, dispossessed and condemned to a life of exile and misery. In the end, however, the consequences may prove even more far-reaching for the Israelis and their supporters, for the Arab refugees were to become, as the Jewish-American journalist I.F. Stone was later to remark, "the moral millstone about the neck of world Jewry." By throwing Israel open to unlimited Jewish immigration while excluding several hundred thousand Palestinians whose homes lay within its de facto boundaries, the Zionists gave the lie to their own claim that Arabs and Jews would be treated with "complete equality" in the new state. They also created a fearful reservoir of bitter and justified resentment.

Discrimination against the Arabs in Israel

The Arab refugees who lost their homes in 1948 numbered about 750,000. Some 140,000 Palestinian Arabs remained within the area of Palestine under Israeli control, according to official Israeli statistics.[3] Under the terms of the Declaration of Independence, these "Israeli Arabs" should have enjoyed exactly the same rights and privileges as the Jewish citizens of Israel. In fact they were subjected to a strict regime of discrimination which governed every aspect of their daily lives.

This discrimination was automatic and inevitable. As Arabs in an avowedly Jewish state, they could not hope to share on equal terms the benefits of a state structure which was consciously and explicitly designed to further the interests of the Jewish population. But the inequality and the material and spiritual disadvantages which they suffered were reinforced by a series of discriminatory laws expressly designed to limit their participation in society. These laws were inherited from the British Mandatory Government. Entitled the Defence Laws (State of Emergency) 1945, they were originally designed by the British administration to control the activities of both Jewish and Arab organizations and individuals opposed to British rule. They incorporated emergency regulations which the British had used to subdue the Arab rebellion between 1936 and 1939; in their revised form they were used after 1945 against the Jewish terrorist organizations, Etzel (the Irgun Zvai Leumi) and Lehi (generally known as the Stern Gang).

When they were introduced, the Defence Laws were violently criticised by representatives of the Jewish community in Palestine. A conference of the Jewish Lawyers' Association held in Tel Aviv in February, 1946 heard a future justice of the Israeli Supreme Court say:

> These laws . . . contradict the most fundamental principles of law, justice and jurisprudence. They give the administrative and military authorities the power to impose penalties which, even had they been ratified by a legislative body, could only be regarded as anarchical and irregular. The Defence Laws abolish the rights of the individual and grant unlimited power to the administration.

The representative of the Jewish Agency, Dr. Bernard Joseph, who was later to become Israel's minister of justice, went even further:

> With regard to the Defence Laws themselves, the question is: Are we all to become the victims of officially licensed terrorism, or will the freedom of the individual prevail? Is the administration to be allowed to interfere in the life of each individual without any safeguards for us? There is nothing to prevent a citizen from being imprisoned all his life without trial. There is no safeguard for the rights of the individual. There is no possibility of appeal against the decision of the Military Commander, no possibility of resort to the Supreme Court, and the administration has unrestricted freedom to banish any citizen at any moment.

Even more emphatic was the future Israeli attorney-general Ya'acov Shimshon Shapiro, who also served as minister of justice:

> The system established in Palestine since the issue of the Defence

Laws is unparalleled in any civilised country; there were no such laws even in Nazi Germany. They try to pacify us by saying that these laws are only directed against malefactors, not against honest citizens. But the Nazi Governor of occupied Oslo also announced that no harm would come to citizens who minded their own business. It is our duty to tell the whole world that the Defence Laws passed by the British Mandatory Government of Palestine destroy the very foundations of justice in this land.[4]

The conference of Jewish Lawyers adopted a number of resolutions which stated, among other things, that the Defence Laws "deprive the Palestinian citizen (in the Land of Israel) of the fundamental rights of man" and that they "establish a rule of violence without any judicial control." It might have been expected that as soon as the state of Israel achieved its independence two years later, these same eminent Jewish lawyers would have clamored for the repeal of laws so brutal and so unjustified. Instead, in their new roles as legal officers and judges, they forgot their criticisms and turned these same laws against the Palestinian Arabs. The Declaration of Independence might have promised that in the Jewish state there would be "complete equality of social and political rights for all its citizens" but the reality was very different.

The Legal Structure of Discrimination

The Defence Laws (State of Emergency) 1945 constituted a complex body of legislation. One hundred and seventy articles, divided into fifteen sections, described an elaborate network of detailed regulations whereby the movments and activities of the Arab population in Israel could be controlled. There were restrictions on freedom of speech and the press and restrictions on freedom of movement, both from one area of the country to another and within each area. The minister of defense was empowered to appoint military governors in any area who were then authorized to enforce, at their own discretion, all the regulations contained in the Defence Laws. They could restrict movement into and out of the areas they controlled, or close those areas to movement altogether. They could, by simple administrative order, subject an individual to police supervision, refuse him access to his own property, control his professional life (this power was used especially against journalists and writers) and his contacts with other people, detain him without explanation for any length of time, deport him from the country, and in certain circumstances confiscate or destroy his property (if the military governor *suspected* that a shot had been fired or a bomb thrown from it).

The powers of the military governors were, in short, absolute, being subject to no administrative control of any kind and to no judicial control except the formal right of appeal to the Supreme Court. Even this right was virtually meaningless, since the military governor could always invoke the justification of "security reasons" for any decision, however arbitrary. An English writer, himself Jewish, who published a study on the situation of the Arab minority ten years after the establishment of the Israeli state, summed up the impotence and the frustration experienced by the victims of this comprehensive system of repression when he quoted an Arab from Galilee:

> 'They take our land. Why? For security reasons! They take our jobs. Why? For security reasons! And when we ask them how it happens that we, our lands and our jobs threaten the security of the State, they do not tell us. Why? For security reasons!'[5]

Theoretically, the Defence Laws were applicable to Jews as well. In practice, they were only enforced against the Arabs; indeed, they were only maintained in the statute book of the new state as a means of exercising strict control over the Palestinian Arab population. In 1959, when the legitimacy of the Defence Laws – in particular Article 125, which restricted freedom of movement – was challenged, the state controller examined the position and published a report which contained the following passage:

> If an area is declared closed by the Military Governor, this order is, in theory, applicable to all citizens, whether male or female, without exception, whether they live inside or outside those areas. Thus anyone who enters or leaves a closed area without a written permit from the Military Governor is, in fact, committing a criminal offence. In practice, Jews are not expected to have such permits and, in general, criminal actions are not brought against Jews when they offend against the provisions of Article 125. There *is something improper about this law, which was drafted with the intention of its being applicable to all the inhabitants of the country, whereas in fact it is only enforced against some of them.* [6]

Expropriation of Arab Land

An additional series of laws, which were enforced in conjunction with the Defence Laws, had an even more far-reaching effect on the lives of the indigenous Palestinian Arabs. These laws were passed between 1948 and 1958 with the express aim of taking land away from its Arab owners and cultivators and transferring it to Jewish control.

The acquisition of land in Palestine had always been a central objective of the Zionist movement. During the period of the British Mandate, land had been acquired wherever possible by purchase, mainly from absentee landlords. The area of land involved was small, but even so the process aroused widespread resentment, especially because the new Jewish owners at once dispossessed the Arab tenant farmers who were actually working the land and who thereby lost their livelihood. The Mandatory Government, aware of the injustices that resulted from these transfers of land, tried to control them and finally put a stop to them in some areas and severely restricted them in others under the terms of the White Paper of 1939.

In 1948, their success on the battlefield left the Zionists in control of wide areas of Palestine which were Arab-owned and situated for the most part in the territory allocated under the U.N. Partition Plan for an Arab state. Where the Palestinian population had fled before or during the fighting of 1948, these areas were simply seized in accordance with a plan of action drawn up by the significantly-named "Transfer Committee" in the strictest secrecy and with the approval of Ben-Gurion and his colleagues in the new Israeli government.[7] Where the Arab inhabitants had not fled, the Zionists faced a dilemma, which they resolved in a number of cases by expelling the Palestinians themselves, either to other areas under Israeli control or across the armistice lines into the neighboring Arab countries. But such summary methods ran the risk of alienating international opinion, which was already concerned over the injustice to which the Palestinian Arabs had been subjected. The Israeli government saw the need to give some legal cover to the process of expropriation.[8]

A series of laws were promulgated during the first decade of Israel's existence, whose combined effect was to strip the Palestinian Arabs of an estimated one million dunams of land.[9] Two principles were invoked of "security," which the Israeli authorities interpreted to mean that Arabs should not be left in possession of lands close to the de facto borders of the new state, and that of the need to cultivate all available land. Arabs living in what were designated as "security areas" were ordered to leave and forbidden to return without permission (which of course was not granted). Once Palestinian-owned land was left uncultivated, it was expropriated under the "Emergency Articles for the Exploitation of Uncultivated Lands" published in the *Official*

Gazette in October 1948. There were numerous other laws and articles
designed to close any possible loopholes in the system, such as the
"Law for the Requisitioning of Land in Times of Emergency" published in November, 1949. Another was the "Law of Prescription"
published as late as April, 1958 and stipulating that anyone (in practice
this meant "any Arab") claiming ownership of a piece of land must
prove that he had controlled and cultivated this land for fifteen years
— something which many cultivators were unable to prove because the
ownership of the land had not been registered in the days of the British
Mandate.

But these are details. The important fact is that, in open disregard of
the promise in the Declaration of Independence, the Israeli authorities
embarked at once in 1948 on a program of legalized spoliation of its
Arab citizens. What was in effect the straightforward theft of vast areas
of land, whose true ownership was not in doubt, was given a spurious
legal cover by means of legislation expressly aimed against one section
of the population. It was a shameful process — and its harmful effect on
the structure of Israeli society is most evident today. The rioting which
took place on the "Day of the Land" in parts of Israel in March,
1976, after the announcement that further land expropriations were to
be carried out, demonstrated the depth of feeling after nearly thirty
years among the Palestinian Arab victims. What was most shameful of
all about the original process was the lack of public protest on the part
of a community — the Jewish community of Israel — ostensibly
devoted to the principles of justice and nondiscrimination.

To their credit, a few Israelis did raise their voices in protest. One
was Azriel Karlibach, who wrote an article published in the Israeli newspaper *Maariv* on December 25, 1953. In the article, an Israeli describes
to his nine-year old daughter the stratagems by which so many of the
Arabs in Galilee were dispossessed of their lands. He observes sadly that
the Jews, who have known so much persecution at the hands of others
who were stronger than themselves, must also expect to be judged by
the way they behave toward a weaker minority in their midst. If the
Zionists, he says, are called before "the throne of History" to account
for their behavior toward the Arab world, they will be able to offer
some sort of justification for some of the things they have done. But
if they are asked "Did you have to desecrate all law and all justice —
in order to steal a few thousand dunams from a handful of miserable
Arab villagers?" then they will not be able to hold up their heads.[10]

Results of Israeli Policy toward the Palestinians before 1967

By refusing to allow the return of the Palestinian refugees and by expropriating their lands and much of the land belonging to those who remained in Israel after 1948, the Zionists confirmed the pattern of their relationship with the Palestinian people. They set no bounds to their own ambitions, accepted no restraints on their freedom of action, showed no mercy toward those whom they had injured. Instead, when any Palestinian tried to recover even a portion of what he had lost, the Zionist authorities treated him as an outlaw, a criminal. If they could catch him, they killed him; if not, they practiced a policy of retaliation by which others were made to pay the penalty for his offence. A special unit of the Israeli army (Unit 101) was formed to mount reprisal raids against border villages from which any attempt at infiltration might be made by the dispossessed Palestinians.

The brutality of Unit 101 brought repeated condemnations down on the Israeli government. In the raid on the Jordanian village of Qibya in October, 1953, a uniformed Israeli task force attacked without warning and blew up thirty houses over the heads of their inhabitants, killing more than fifty men, women and children. The Israelis justified such actions by arguing that only a demonstration of force could deter Palestinian attempts to undermine Israel's security. No such excuse could be used to explain the relentless repression practiced against the Palestinian Arabs inside Israel, a small and impotent minority which had lived in a state of shock since 1948 and which was in any case rigorously controlled by the pattern of military government and emergency legislation. Yet in 1956, on the eve of the Israeli attack on Egypt, Israeli security forces carried out a punitive action at the village of Kafr Qassem which vividly illustrates the state of mind of the Zionist authorities. This time forty-nine Palestinian villagers, citizens of Israel, were shot in cold blood by Israeli border guards, who were enforcing a curfew of which the villagers had been given no previous warning. A public enquiry was held after the Israeli press uncovered the story, but it failed to discover who had authorized the atrocity. But for Jewish and Arab Israelis alike, its message was clear. The Palestinians in Israel were a community apart who could in no circumstances expect to be treated on a basis of equality with their Jewish compatriots. They must be held in subjection, their every movement supervised and controlled, and now and then, to remind them of their situation, they must be taught a bloody lesson. The underlying contradiction between Zionism and democracy remained as sharp and as clear-cut as ever.

Israeli Policy and Practices in the Occupied Territories since 1967

During the nineteen years from 1948 to 1967, the Zionist authorities, now represented by the government of Israel, consolidated earlier gains by settling Jewish immigrants on the lands vacated by the Arabs and by subjecting those Arabs who remained in the areas under Israeli control to the most rigorous controls. The fiction that Israel was a democratic society was maintained, but in practice the Arab citizens of the Jewish state were subjected at every turn to an elaborate pattern of officially sponsored discrimination. Zionism further revealed itself as a straightforward movement of colonialism and settlement, whose objective could only be achieved by destroying the concepts of Palestinian nationhood. Acceptance of the Palestinian right to exist as a nation on Palestinian soil would call into question what the Zionists had already achieved and would render impossible the further expansion to which they aspired.

The opportunity for that further expansion came in 1967, when, in a swift and meticulously prepared military operation, the Israelis occupied the remainer of Palestine, as well as large areas of Egyptian and Syrian territory. Theoretically, the victory also provided an opportunity for the Israelis to propose a comprehensive settlement of the Palestine problem, one which would take account of the claims of both sides and attempt to resolve on the basis of justice and humanity a dispute which had already caused so much bitterness and bloodshed. But to do this would have involved facing the fact that the Palestinians had rights, both as individuals and as a people, which were incompatible with the full achievement of the Zionist goal. It was probably inevitable, in the light of their past policies and attitudes, that the Israeli authorities would turn away from such a course and would seize instead what seemed to them a golden opportunity to establish their dominion over the whole of Palestine and to dispose once and for all of the Palestinian claim to nationhood.

The Israelis were motivated, at this crucial turning point in the Arab-Israeli conflict, by the two considerations which are a recurrent theme in the history of the Zionist struggle to gain possession of Palestine: the appetite for land and the preoccupation with national security. The two, of course, were closely linked; the more they could extend their territorial occupation, the more the Zionists believed they would be able to make themselves secure against a possible counterattack. And since every further extension of their occupation of Palestine sharpened Palestinian resentment and desire for revenge, the Israeli preoccupation with security was a real one. Precisely because they knew they had deeply injured the Palestinians, the Israelis realized that they must face the danger of Palestinian counteraction; and the more the injury was compounded, as it was in 1967, the greater that danger would become — unless the Israelis could destroy the Palestinian sense of nationhood and tear out at the roots any incipient movement of Palestinian resistance. It was on this dual aim that the Israelis based their policy toward the occupied territories after June, 1967.

In the initial stage of the occupation of the West Bank and the Gaza Strip, Israeli methods closely followed the precedents established in 1948. By psychological pressures, intimidation and straightforward expulsion, Palestinians were encouraged to leave these areas and to cross the borders into the neighboring Arab countries. Those remaining were subjected to a strict regime of military government which enforced rigorous penalties against anyone showing the slightest sign of insubordination. In particular areas along the old armistice lines (e.g. in the neighborhood of Latrun and Qalqilya) Arab villages were destroyed and their inhabitants forcibly expelled. It should be noted that these measures were not taken in response to military necessities and that they contravened specific provisions of the Fourth Geneva Convention, of which Israel was signatory.

Establishment of Jewish Settlements in the Occupied Territories

Apart from East Jerusalem, which the Israeli government incorporated into the state of Israel by special legislation at the end of June, 1967, the territories were not annexed by Israel. But official Israeli intentions were indicated by the establishment in July, 1967 of the first of a series of Jewish settlements. Within a program of colonization which was rapidly extended during the next six years, more than forty such settlements were established before the next Arab-Israeli war in October, 1973 checked Israel's self-confident territorial expansion throughout the occupied territories. Once the shock of that war had been digested, the colonization program was resumed and even accelerated. The total number of settlements in the occupied territories today amounts to seventy, of which more than half are in the West Bank and the Gaza Strip. In almost all cases they were established initially under the auspices of the Israeli army, as paramilitary outposts; later, most of them were turned over to civilian occupation. Clearly the underlying intention is to plant Jewish communities in all parts of the occupied Arab lands, with a view to incorporating these areas in a "Greater Israel" when the time is ripe.

Under international law, East Jerusalem constituted occupied territory just like any of the other areas occupied in 1967, but the Israeli government claimed it as part of the Israeli state. Essentially the same technique of settlement and colonization was followed there but it provoked more international criticism. Starting in January, 1968, the Israeli authorities expropriated substantial areas of Arab-owned land within the municipal boundaries and constructed housing projects for Jewish settlers. By their location, these housing estates, consisting for the most part of multi-story apartment blocks (many of them clearly designed for military use in emergency), were distributed in such a way as to form a ring of Jewish settlement around the remaining areas of Palestinian Arab inhabitation. Their importance as an element in the Israeli attempt to make the annexation of Jerusalem a fait accompli, in defiance of a succession of U.N. resolutions can hardly be exaggerated. Nor could there be any clearer symbol of the official Israeli policy of racial discrimination than this concrete ring of buildings, set on Arab land in "united Jerusalem" – but open only to Jews.

Israel's Use of Arab Labor from the Occupied Territories

The 1967 Israeli victory attracted a huge amount of financial support from Jewish communities throughout the world, especially from the United States. During the succeeding years until 1973, an economic boom in Israel, with the construction industry playing a leading part, brought about a shortage of labor. In the newly occupied territories, on the other hand, there was a surplus of unemployed or under-employed labor among the Arab population. The Israeli authorities perceived a double advantage in offering employment inside Israel to Arab laborers from the occupied territories: to resolve their own labor shortage and at the same time offer workers material benefits (in the shape of regular employment with relatively high wages) which would distract them from the spiritual and psychological disadvantages of life under occupation and ultimately reconcile them to Israeli rule.

Until 1973 these expectations were largely realized. The population of the occupied territories met the needs of the Israeli labor market. (Arab labor was largely responsible for building the Jewish settlements in and around Jerusalem and Hebron.) The wages enabled these Arab workers to enjoy a higher standard of living than they had previously known. But the cost to both sides was considerable. Among the Arabs, the knowledge that their labor was helping the Zionists to reach their objective caused recriminations and a sense of humiliation. (It was argued that the Arab laborers had no alternative if they were to avoid destitution.) Among the Israelis, especially those who remembered the early Zionist ideals of socialism and self-help, it was painful to see their society evolving into a form of capitalism with racialist overtones, in that the managerial class consisted of Jews while the manual work was performed by a captive Arab labor force.

Despite these objections, the system was maintained, even after the 1973 October War brought the boom to an end and prompted widespread misgivings among Israelis about their government's policy concerning the occupied territories. Again it was probably inevitable that the relationship between Israeli Jews and Palestinian Arabs should continue to be based on discrimination and prejudice. After half a century in which the Jewish citizens of the Zionist state had been conditioned to think of the Palestinians as human obstacles in the way of the Zionist objective, to be pushed aside if possible and otherwise simply held in subjection, it was not easy to suddenly adopt a different attitude. So long as the Arabs remained submissive, there was little incentive to change the prevailing attitude, which remained at best patronizing and at worst openly racist.

By this combination of the stick and the carrot — repressive military government and the offer of relatively well-paid employment, though in degrading conditions — the Israelis maintained their grip. The system depended on two factors for its success. First, the Arab population must remain submissive and without hope of liberation from outside. Second, the Israelis must succeed in persuading the outside world that the subject population in the occupied territories was content with its lot under their generally benevolent rule. Before 1973, the first condition was satisfied: Israel's military supremacy was apparently so overwhelming that there seemed to be no hope of salvation from outside, either from the armies of the Arab states or from the divided factions of the Palestine Liberation Organization (PLO). As for the second condition, the Israeli success, even before 1973, was only qualified. By means of intensive propaganda, which was uncritically accepted by much (though not all) of the Western press and information media, Zionist agencies managed to disseminate the legend of the "benevolent occupation" and to disguise from all but the most persistent enquirers the nature and scale of the repressive measures by which Israeli rule was maintained. But enough gaps appeared in this curtain of misinformation for the outside world gradually to acquire a more realistic picture of the Israeli occupation regime. Zionist pressures, taking advantage of the extreme sensitivity of public figures in the Western world to the charge of anti-Semitism, ensured that the resulting criticisms of Israeli policies and actions would be carefully restrained, especially so long as the Arab governments appeared to be without political or economic influence. As soon as the events of October, 1973 demonstrated that, on the contrary, the Arabs possessed a collective influence — when they chose to exercise it in unison — which the world could not afford to neglect, the international community suddenly showed itself aware of the rights of the Palestinians and of the grave infringements of these rights which were being regularly practiced by the Israeli authorities, both inside Israel and on the international plane.

The Specifics of Israeli Repression in the Occupied Territories

The techniques of Israeli repression in the occupied territories after 1967 followed the same broad pattern used against the Palestinians inside Israel after 1948 — but with one significant difference. The occupied territories did not form part of the state of Israel, so that not even in theory were their inhabitants considered the equals of Israeli citizens in the eyes of the law. As a result, Palestinians in the occupied territories have enjoyed no rights and no representative institutions since 1967. There is no authority to which they can appeal, no protection which they can invoke. Their every movement and action is subject to the arbitrary authority of the Israeli military governor. They can be detained, imprisoned, deported, without the intervention of any tribunal. Their houses and property may be destroyed, their lands confiscated, their crops burned and their trees cut down.

This state of affairs has continued for almost ten years, despite numerous attempts to find a remedy. Amnesty International, the International Red Cross, private organizations and individuals, even the formally constituted U.N. Special Committee to Investigate Israeli Practices in the Occupied Territories have met with no cooperation. The Israeli government actually refused admission to the U.N. Special Committee and then slandered its witnesses. It has also refused, despite representations from the International Committee of the Red Cross, to acknowledge that the Fourth Geneva Convention (for the Protection of Civilians in Time of War) is applicable to the inhabitants of the occupied territories.

The evidence of Israeli ill-treatment of the inhabitants of the occupied territories has therefore been unusually difficult to gather, especially because the great majority of the journalists working in Israel as correspondents for the international press are themselves Jewish (and frequently Israeli) and therefore feel a sense of loyalty to the Jewish state. Nevertheless, thanks to the investigations of a number of journalists not subject to such inhibitions and other individuals and organizations which have devoted themselves to disclosing the truth about the Israeli occupation, a comprehensive picture has emerged. In summarizing the details of this pattern of officially sponsored repression, it is appropriate to draw attention to the outstanding work of Israeli individuals and organizations in uncovering and giving publicity to some of the worst excesses of the occupation authorities. Such individuals and organizations have inevitably drawn down upon themselves the particular animosity of the Israeli authorities and public opinion.

Techniques of Repression

1. Detention without trial: Any individual inhabitant of the occupied territories is liable to detention without trial and without explanation. This detention may last indefinitely. For example, Tayseer Arouri of Ramallah, employed as a teacher of physics at Bir Zeit College, served a three-year prison sentence for a "security offense." He was released in 1974 but immediately rearrested and has been under administrative detention ever since. In another case reported by the *Jerusalem Post* on May 26, 1976, Zuhair Amira from Nablus, who also served a three-year sentence for a "security offense" between 1971 and 1974, was rearrested after his release from prison and detained for a further year without charge. When this year was over, he was again detained and was still in prison in May, 1976.[11]

2. Destruction of houses: Any individual in the occupied territories who is suspected by the Israeli authorities of having committed a "security offense" is liable, in addition to other penalties, to have his house destroyed even before a preliminary enquiry is carried out. When this happens, the other persons living in the house will be evicted, whether or not they are suspected of complicity in the offense. Moreover, the house may be destroyed even if it is not the property of the suspect. Upwards of 15,000 houses have been destroyed in this way since June, 1967.

3. Punitive curfews: A favorite method of intimidation, whereby a village, refugee camp or the whole of a major town is kept under curfew for a period of days as a punishment for some offense committed by an individual or group of individuals, or else as a warning against some particular course of action. In the Gaza Strip in January 1968, curfews were imposed on refugee camps after minor "security offenses" by individuals. One such curfew, at the Shati camp, lasted for five days and nights and caused severe suffering to the inmates, who were without adequate supplies of food or water. The same method of collective punishment was still being employed in the summer of 1976, when curfews lasting several days were imposed at Nablus and Ramallah. Again, inmates of refugee camps in the curfew area suffered particular hardship and officials of UNRWA were prevented by the Israeli authorities from carrying out relief work.

4. Deportations: Arbitrary deportations have been employed especially against those who provided leadership in their communities. Deportations are normally carried out by the Israelis during the night, without warning and without even the semblance of legal action or pretext. They have also been carried out in brutal circumstances, the victims being taken blindfold to the border and turned loose, often in very difficult country (e.g. in the Wadi Araba) and without food or means of transport, sometimes with shots fired over their heads. For example, Dr. Walid Kamhawi of Nablus, Abdel-Jawad Saleh, (mayor of El Bireh), and Dr. Hanna Nasir, (president of Bir Zeit College) were summarily deported — all were outstanding figures in their local communities.

5. Expropriation of land: Jewish settlements established in the occupied territories have, for the most part, been established on uninhabited land, but where the land has been inhabited, its Arab population has been dispossessed, often violently and sometimes brutally. A case in point is the area of northeastern Sinai adjoining the Gaza Strip, where the Israeli authorities have created a complex of settlements including the nucleus of the future city of Yamit. The area had a substantial population of Bedouins and the Israeli journalist Amnon Kapeliouk reported in *Le Monde* on May 15 1975 that three years earlier Israeli soldiers "drove off some ten thousand farmers and Bedouin, bulldozed or dynamited their houses, pulled down their tents, destroyed their crops and filled in their wells."

In employing these methods and in denying the Palestinian refugees the right to return, the Israeli government is in breach of its obligations as a member of the United Nations and as a signatory of the Geneva Conventions. Israel was admitted to U.N. membership in 1949 after giving a specific assurance that it would abide by the terms of General Assembly Resolution 194 (iii) of December, 1948 which called for the return of the Palestinian refugees. The Fourth Geneva Convention (relating to the treatment of civilians in occupied territory) outlaws collective punishments in general. Article 49 states that:

> Individual or mass forcible transfers, as well as deportations of protected persons from occupied territory to the territory of the Occupying Power or to that of any other country, occupied or not, are prohibited, regardless of their motive . . . . The Occupying Power shall not deport or transfer parts of its own civilian population into the territory it occupies.

Article 53 of the same Convention states that:

> Any destruction by the Occupying Power of real or personal property belonging individually or collectively to private persons, or to the State, or to other public authorities, or to social or cooperative organizations, is prohibited.

The use of these practices by the Israeli Government and of measures of intimidation including the torture of suspects, have been repeatedly denounced by individuals and organizations in Israel, notably by the Israeli League for Human and Civil Rights and the Committee for Peace and Justice in the Middle East.

Notes

1. *See* Hans Kohn "Zion and the Jewish National Idea," in *Zionism Reconsidered* (New York, 1970).

2. Michael bar-Zohar, *The Unarmed Prophet* (London, 1967).

3. *Israeli Year Book 1952.*

4. *See* Sabri Jiryis, *The Arabs in Israel,* (Beirut, 1969) for an outstanding study of how the Israeli legal system infringes the rights of the Palestinians.

5. Walter Schwartz, *The Arabs in Israel* (London, 1958).

6. The Defence Laws remained in force until 1966.

7. *See* Yossef Weitz, *My Diary and Letter to the Children*, (Tel Aviv, 1965) and Michael Adams and Christopher Mayhew, *Publish it not . . .* (London, 1975), pp. 153-6.

8. For a detailed account *see* Jiryis, *The Arabs in Israel.*

9. Dr. Amnon Kapeliouk, Jerusalem correspondent of *Le Monde*, puts the figure at 150,000 hectares. *See Middle East International*, July, 1976, p. 11.

10. The article was reprinted in full by *Middle East International*, December, 1973.

11. A leading authority on the treatment by the occupation authorities of Palestinian political prisoners is the Israeli lawyer Felicia Langer. See her *With My Own Eyes* (Tel Aviv, 1974). An English translation was published by Ithaca Press (London, 1975).

9 CONSEQUENCES OF ZIONISM FOR PALESTINIAN CLASS STRUCTURE

Elia T. Zureik

Ideological Dimensions

No other social movement in this century has had a greater affect on Arab-Jewish relations than Zionism. Yet, it is significant to note that the question of Jewish-Arab relations assumed a minor role in the writings of key modern Zionist ideologists.[1]

Like any other doctrine, it is difficult to place Zionism within one simple ideological construct. Existing writings suggest four possible meanings and interpretations of Zionism.

First, there are those writers[2] who see Zionism as embracing two oppositionary trends, a conservative and a liberal one, or a "fundamentalist" and "universalist."[3] It is acknowledged that as events unfolded in Palestine, the universalist ideologists of so-called labor-Zionism[4] moved gradually toward adopting and implementing fundamentalist principles, while on the surface espousing liberal and secular values calling for accommodation with the Arabs. It is also argued that the adoption of fundamentalist beliefs regarding the Arab question is the outcome of miscalculation, misunderstanding and confusion on the part of the pragmatists.

A second group of writers argues that Zionism is essentially a by-product of ultranationalist and exclusivist ideology which is bound to have produced the existing chauvinist and racist structures in Israeli society. On a more specific level, this group argues that Zionism is essentially an offshoot of Western colonialism and nineteenth century imperialism. The only viable solution to the Palestinian-Israeli conflict is the establishment of either a bi-national secular state in all of Palestine, or at least the setting up of an independent Palestinian state in post-1967 occupied Palestine.

In-between these groups, it is possible to isolate a third group[5] of writers which typifies the bulk of Western and liberal Israeli social scientists. The view adhered to here is that the Zionist venture in Palestine would have benefited Arabs and Jews alike had it not been for the intransigence of the Palestinian Arabs and, later, the neighboring Arab states. The flaw, according to this popular interpretation, is not with the original premises and tenets of Zionism, which were basically

137

egalitarian, but with the Arab reaction. The disadvantaged status of the Arab minority in Israel is due, in the eyes of this group, to the state of war existing between Israel and its neighbors. The Arab-Jewish problem is thus an attitudinal problem rooted in irrationality and misunderstanding, and not in an institutionalized form of racism. More importantly, the Arab-Jewish problem is essentially a problem between states, with the Palestinian component playing a peripheral role.

Finally, a fourth group[6] argues that Zionism is essentially a messianic movement, and the culmination of modern Israel is only one step toward realizing the final goal: the Return to Eretz Israel. Relying on peculiar and ideosyncratic biblical interpretations, non-Jews living in any part of the ancient land of Israel, i.e. the Arabs, are viewed as temporary occupants or guardians of the land. It should be apparent that to the advocates of this fundamentalist philosophy, the essence of the problem is the Arabs, their presence in Eretz Israel. Once the Arabs are removed from Palestine either through expulsion or so-called population transfer and exchange the issue will be automatically resolved.

If one examines the types of policies and developments in pre- as well as post-1948 Palestine, there is no doubt that a quasi form of ultranationalistic and fundamentalist Zionism has prevailed. Zionist occupation was accompanied by marginalization of the Palestinian proletariat, destruction of Arab village life and further seizure of Arab land — all accomplished through the expansionist policies of successive Zionist governments. The impact of these policies upon the Arabs of Palestine will be dealt with along three main fronts: (1) demography, (2) colonization, and (3) proletarianization.

Demography

One of the main dilemmas facing any settler group, especially when this group is more urbanized and technologically advanced, is how to maintain a favorable demographic balance in the midst of a traditional indigenous population with a high birth rate. This dilemma was, and continues to be, the central issue facing Zionist leaders in Israel. Concentrated efforts toward facilitating Jewish immigration are the main mechanism by which Israel hopes to insure the continuity of the present Jewish numerical superiority. This policy has not proceeded without serious problems, as the relatively small number of Jewish immigrants from Western Europe and North America to Israel shows.[7] It is this trickling of North American immigrants which at one point prompted Ben-Gurion to attack North American Jews, who, in his view, had a duty to settle in Israel to prove their allegiance to Zionism.

In spite of the organized Zionist campaign encouraging worldwide Jewish immigration, only twenty percent of world Jewry currently reside in Israel.[8]

In addition to the recent decline in Jewish immigration (according to S. Rosen, minister of absorption, 32,000 immigrants came to Israel in 1974, compared to 55,000 in 1973),[9] a more alarming phenomenon as far as the Israeli government is concerned has been the increasing number of Jewish emigrants, or as they are labelled in Israel, *Yordim*, meaning "those who go down". According to N. Chomsky "Immigration has fallen sharply, by about 50% in the first half of 1975. Specifically, Russian immigration is turning elsewhere. At the same time . . . emigration is rapidly increasing, including long-term residents. Emigration in 1974 was almost triple the average of the 1967-1973 period." Specifically, from 1968-1973, 7,500 Israeli Jews emigrated annually; nearly 12,000 in 1973; 21,000 in 1974, while 6,000 immigrated in the first five months of 1975.[10]

With around 200,000 Israeli Jews residing overseas by 1972 (defined by the Israeli Central Bureau of Statistics as those who have not returned after two years of departure), attention of the Jewish Agency and the Israeli government turned toward inducing emigrants to return. This emigration had proved to be costly in terms of loss of high-level manpower to the Jewish state, since most of the *Yordim* are professional people of Western origin, including a sizeable number of *Sabra* emigrants. According to D. Elizur's study for the Jewish Agency, of a sample of 500 Israeli Jews residing in France and the United States, "the largest groups consist of persons from Europe and America (51 percent) and those born in Israel (38 percent). Persons from Asia and Africa make up only 7 percent."[11] While *attitudinal* responses to questions dealing with intentions to return should be interpreted with great reservation (due to the stigma attached to those leaving Israel),[12] Elizur's study shows that only a minority of 22 percent had definite plans to return.

A study carried out in 1974 by the Israeli Institute of Applied Social Research on a sample of 2,000 Israeli Jews sheds further light on reasons behind emigration: 31 percent mentioned taxes; 28 percent, the cost of living; 22 percent, the system of government; 21 percent, the future of children; 16 percent, the military security and guerrilla activities; 18 percent, the gap in socioeconomic conditions; 16 percent, conditions of employment; and 19 percent, military service. Furthermore, there was a positive relationship between military service as a cause for emigration, and the age of the respondent.

In May, 1968, the government enacted a scheme of inducements by which Jewish returnees would receive economic benefits, e.g. travel expenses, housing, business loans, and custom-free privileges. This system caused a great deal of resentment among other residents who could not qualify for similar benefits and was not renewed. More importantly, the system of incentives had no effect whatsoever on increasing the number of returnees. On the average, the mean percentage of those returning after one year was 67.6 percent, and 87 percent during the first two years of emigration. Of those who stayed for more than five years (nearly 13 percent of the total emigrants), only 1 percent returned.[13] Israeli Arab emigration is less substantial. Between 1949 and 1970, the official number is 5,508 (not including the substantial number of West Bank emigrants), although admittedly, like the Jews, not all Arabs declare their emigration intentions upon leaving Israel.[14]

Arab-Jewish Pattern

The establishment of the state meant a drastic numerical transformation in the size of the Palestinian Arabs, from being a majority to becoming a minority. In 1914 the ratio of Arabs to Jews in Palestine was estimated at 13:1, with Jewish settlers then numbering around 85,000. With the influx of Zionist settlers and organized immigration, illegal and otherwise, the ratio declined to 2:1 at the eve of the 1948 war, which culminated in the dispersion of the native Arab population.[15] Within a few weeks after the war the Palestinians became a minority in their own country. From 1948, when the ratio stood at 7:1 in favor of the Jewish population, up to the present time, the Palestinian Arab percentage of the total population ranged from 11 to 15 percent. In 1974, there were 506,900 Israeli Arabs, comprising 15.1 percent of the population. In terms of religious composition, the Moslem community continues to be the majority.

One of the most persistent problems facing the Zionist authorities has been how to prevent the continued existence of an all-Arab concentration in any of Israel's six geographic districts. In 1948, the Northern and Southern Districts were predominantly Arab. The status of the Southern District was altered within a short period after 1948 through concentrated efforts of Jewish immigration and the building of new settlements. By 1961, the Arab population amounted to 11 percent of the total population in the Southern District and it declined to 9 percent by 1971.[16]

Israeli efforts in recent years have turned to the "Judaization of the

Galilee." In 1973 the Jewish Agency prepared a detailed plan for Jewish settlements to be carried out in the next decades.[17] In the Southern District the Bedouins have been fighting a losing battle to prevent further confiscation of their land through official claims that lands in the South are State Lands;[18] but the situation is more complex in the Galilee. Close to one-half of the Arab population lives in the northern part of the country, where most of the Arab land is neither so-called State Land nor Absentee Arab Property. Nevertheless, expropriation and confiscation of Arab land have taken place, as the cases of Iqrit and Kafr-Birim, two northern villages, testify.[19] Indeed, the shooting in April, 1976 of Israeli Arab citizens by Israeli soldiers was in reaction to their protests at Arab land expropriation and confiscation in the Galilee.

While such practices are not perceived as discriminatory by the Israeli government, since it claims that compensation is usually paid, and whenever possible exchange of land is suggested, the fact remains that such land is being taken away against the will of an indigenous national group to accommodate another settler group. Equally important is the fact that the law does not allow Arabs to engage in reciprocal practices, either through buying or leasing land intended for all-Jewish settlements, as happened in the case of Upper Nazareth.[20]

Until recently, there has been little change in the proportion of Arabs living in mixed settlements, ranging from 16 percent in 1955 to 18 percent in 1971. The 1973 figures are somewhat high (25 percent) due to the inclusion of East Jerusalem's Arab population.[21] Still, more than 75 percent of Israel's Arabs live in segregated cities and villages. Even in the mixed cities, it would be misleading to interpret these figures as reflecting integration in any meaningful sense. There is little interpersonal contact on an equal basis between Arabs and Jews. Residential and educational segregation and socio-cultural and political exclusiveness prevail. This pattern is not exclusive to the relationship between Arabs and Jews. Within the Jewish communities, there exists a salient form of ethnic segregation. In towns such as Tel-Aviv, Haifa and Jerusalem, the Oriental and European Jews live in separate communities.[22]

At the center of the demographic debate is the future development of the Arab-Jewish population structures. Demographic projections vary, depending on the assumptions adopted. Appraising the demographic balance in Israel for the year 2000, in the light of various policy options emanating from the 1967 war, Friedlander and Goldscheider offer four possibilities: (1) if Israel were to adopt a minimalist stand in terms of its inflow of immigrants (40,000 annually) and retention of occupied territories (annexing East Jerusalem and the Golan Heights only), together with a decline of Jewish immigration and fertility rate, the proportion of Jews in Israel in the year 2000 would amount to 78 percent of the total population. The minimalist demographic assumption applied to the Arab population assumes a yearly Net Total in-migration of 100,000 Arabs into the occupied territories from neighboring Arab countries and constant high fertility rate. (2) With the same demographic minimalist position, but with maximum territories, the proportion of the Jewish population would decline to 47 percent in a quarter of a century. (3) If Jewish immigration were not to be curtailed at a rate of 40,000 per year, with minimum territorial assumptions, then in the year 2000 the Jewish population will attain its maximum growth rate of 86 percent. (4) Keeping the demographic and territorial assumptions at maximum levels, the proportion of Jewish population will amount to 66 percent.[23]

The projections of Friedlander and Goldscheider estimate the total population in Israel for the year 2000 at seven million. Using the minimalist assumption and the usual rate of natural increase, U. Schmelz estimates that in 1990 the Jewish population will amount to 4,191,300, while the Arabs in Israel will number one million.[24] Bustani's estimates for 1990, based on 2.8 percent rate of natural increase and 40,000 yearly Jewish immigrants, were 4,684,900 for the Jewish population; with a yearly rate of natural increase of 3.4 percent among the Arab population, the latter will approximate 860,000 in the year 1990.[25]

The main reason that the Palestinian Arabs have managed to retain their overall relative size in Israel during the last 25 years in the face of organized Jewish immigration is their high rate of natural increase. As early as 1922, it was noted that the Palestinian Arabs, particularly its Moslem segment, exhibited one of the highest known birthrates in the world.[26] Between 1922-1944 the Moslem community nearly doubled its population through natural increase whereas the Christians increased by 72 percent and the Jews by 28 percent.[27] This trend continued after the establishment of Israel, with the 1970 Arab population showing more than twice the rate of natural increase and almost double the rate of live births as the Jewish population.[28]

Leonard Singerman, in speaking of "the (demographic) threat within,"[29] reflects the concern of many Israeli officials. They suggest that the Israeli government should adopt an "anti-natalistic" policy to reduce the rate of Arab natural increase and prevent what they see as an eventual Arab majority in Israel within a century. Reducing the current Arab and Jewish crude birthrates by one-half, out of a total population of 4.7 million by the end of this century, the Jews will be three and one-half times larger than the Arab population.

While the trend toward reducing the infant mortality rate continued, the lag of the Arabs, compared to the Jews, persists. Between 1955 and 1973 infant mortality among Jews was reduced by 50 percent, from 32.4 to 18.1 per thousand; among the Arabs it declined from 62.5 to 37.1 per thousand.[30] Infant mortality is higher among Arabs in mixed cities than in other places, illustrating that while medical care is more prevalent in mixed cities than in all-Arab centres, it does not necessarily follow that such care is available or that it is being utilized to the same extent by Arabs as it is by Jews.[31]

Colonization[32]

An important and, to a very large extent, unexpected outcome of the process of colonization in Palestine has been the failure of the settlers to dispossess through normal purchase means the native Palestinian peasantry of their land. This is in spite of the fact that a purchase agency, the Keren Kayemet Le Israel Company, was set up at the turn of the century specifically for this purpose. Not more than six to seven percent of the total area of Palestine was sold voluntarily to the agency.[33] And, more importantly, the sale was not initiated by Palestinian peasantry; rather it was absentee landlords and local landowners, in addition to foreign interests, who cooperated primarily with the settlers.

This outcome must have come as a great disappointment to those believing in Jewish "redemption" of land, as was clearly expressed by Hertzel in 1895:

The private lands in the territories granted to us we must gradually take out of the hands of the owners. The poorer amongst the population we try to transfer quietly outside our borders by providing them with work in the transit countries, but in our country we deny them all work. Those with property will join us. The transfer of land and the displacement of the poor must be done gently and carefully. Let the landowners believe that they are exploiting us by getting overvalued prices. But no lands shall be sold back to their owners.[34]

In the light of the failure through legitimate and voluntary means, it became essential that new ways be devised to expand the Zionist hold on Arab land. This was facilitated by the dispersion of the Palestinian

Arabs during the 1948 war.[35] Laws were immediately instituted to seize and confiscate "absentee" Arab land and property. The seizure of Arab land was not confined to the "refugees" only; Arabs who remained inside Israel were also affected by the laws and many lost their property through a peculiar definition of "absenteeism." If, for example, an Arab changed his residence due to the circumstances of the war, and yet remained inside Israel, he still could be considered an absentee.[36]

> Every Arab in Palestine who had left his town or village after November 29, 1947, was liable to be classified as an absentee under the regulations. All Arabs who held property in the New City of Acre, regardless of the fact that they may never have travelled farther than the few meters to the Old City, were classified as absentees. The 30,000 Arabs who fled from one place to another within Israel, but who never left the country were also liable to have their property declared absentees. Any individual who may have gone to Beirut or Bethlehem for a one-day visit during the latter days of the (British) mandate was automatically an absentee.[37]

Another unanticipated feature of Zionist colonization has been the failure of the Zionist authorities to attract settlers who are committed to till the land, land which was handed over to them for a small amount of remuneration in the hope of "saving" it from idleness. It became apparent in the mid-sixties that many settlers were gravitating to urban centers for more profitable employment. This phenomenon alarmed the Zionist leaders, especially when it became known that they were leasing land to Arabs. The arrangement was that Palestinian peasants would cultivate the land (which originally might have belonged to them, but was later confiscated by the authorities) in return for a payment or a portion of the crops's yield. By no means was this an easy task for the Palestinian Arabs, since it involved uprootedness and in many instances the migration of whole families to live in shanty towns near the fields. It involved continual work with no holiday for pay amounting to one-half, or even less, of the crop's yield. This propelled the authorities to pass the Agricultural Settlement law in 1967 to halt the danger of Palestinian Arab repossession of their land. In the words of the minister of agriculture at the time of the submission of the bill:

> It is clear that in different parts of the country there are many instances of individual settlers not cultivating the land which was left in their occupancy and not themselves exploiting the quotas of water

allocated to them, but transferring to others the right to cultivate and the right to exploit the water by means of leases, partnerships, or in other ways. There are many instances in which it is clear that the settler himself is engaged in work other than agriculture and obtains an income — sometimes a large income — from leasing his land and transferring his water rights obtained from the exploitation of State properties which are entrusted to him with the clear intention that he should exploit the land himself.[38]

Although very few expressed negative reactions to this law, Uri Avenery, an independent opposition member of the Knesset, said:

There are two conflicting trends to this law; it is a Dr. Jekyll and Mr. Hyde law. To all appearances what we have is a law with an extremely positive social aim; the landlords, who, through various kinds of favouritism, have succeeded in obtaining from the Israel Land Authority State Land on cheap and easy terms, are to be compelled to return that land to the Israel Land Authority if they transfer their right to cultivate it to others. That is to say that the proposers of the law approve of the principle that the land should be in the hands of those who cultivate it, not in the hands of those who have friends at court or other parasites — the new class of party *effendis*. What they really aim at are the Jewish *effendis* and the Arab cultivators. What is meant is the land that was confiscated from the Arabs and handed over through favouritism to Jews who then leased it back to the Arabs who have thus become its cultivators.[39]

Citing related evidence, Chomsky remarks:

Ten settlements were recently fined 700,000 Israeli pounds "for illegally leasing agricultural lands to Arabs." The Minister of Agriculture warned that "anyone caught leasing land to Arabs will be punished" giving the estimate that 10,000 dunums have been leased to Arabs, "a very serious phenomenon which must be fought in every way possible." The Director of the Galilee region of the Jewish Agency announced "that his office has sent circulars to all (Jewish) settlements in which they are warned that leasing of national lands for cultivation by Arab lessees or rental of orchards for fruit picking and marketing by Arabs is in violation of law, regulations of the settlement authorities, and the settlement movement." The Ministry of Agriculture is reportedly undertaking an "energetic campaign" to eliminate the "plague" of leasing land to Arabs.[40]

It is estimated that less than ten percent[41] of the land in Israel is currently either owned by or accessible to the Arabs. The bulk of the land, including the vast area of the Negev where the Bedouins lost large tracts, is classified as State Land. Zionist writers, and their sympathizers,[42] do not hesitate to point out that the practise of State Land is not a Zionist invention, but was practiced by the British Mandate and the Turks before them. However, the definition of State Land under the Turkish regime implied usage and transfer by inheritance, as long as the occupant tilled the ground. Under Israel's rule, the definition is quite different, one built on racist and national criteria.

> As the Courts have repeatedly held, Israel is not the state of its citizens, in the Western sense, but rather the "sovereign State of the Jewish people." The legal and institutional structure of the state, as well as administrative practice, reflect this fundamental commitment to discrimination — what we would call "racism" in discussing any other society. For the Jewish majority, Israel is indeed a democracy on the Western model, but Arabs are second-class citizens at best, in principle. Furthermore, apart from a few courageous individuals, there is little protest in Israel over the basic commitment to Jewish dominance, that is repression of the Arab minority.[43]

In 1960, the Knesset enacted Basic Law: Israel Lands[44] which meant that State Land is defined under the principle of the Jewish National Fund.

> Two principles of Zionist colonization, both incorporated in the constitution of the Jewish Agency, are especially resented by the Arabs. These are: (i) the principle that Jewish property is inalienable; no Zionist settler may dispose of his lease to any one but a Jew, (ii) the principle carefully safeguarded by the powerful Jewish Federation of Labour, that only Jewish labour may be employed in Zionist colonies. The net result is that, when the Jewish National Fund makes a purchase the Arabs lose not only the land itself but also any chance of being employed on this land.[45]

A major portion of Arab land was acquired by the state through the application of a series of laws designed to dispossess Palestinian refugees. According to the 1950 Absentee Property Law, the property of the refugees was transferred to a "custodian" who would negotiate with the government concerning transaction of the land. In 1953 a Development Authority assumed "ownership" of the property, which was gradually turned over to the state for the sake of accommodating Jewish immigrants. Other laws of a similar nature had their origins in the legal framework enforced by the British to counter Palestinian Arab rebellion from 1936 to 1939. These emergency regulations, passed in 1945 by the British, approved the appointment of military governors in various districts, specifically in regions with Arab concentrations. Using the same regulations, the Israeli government through its military governors classified many regions in Palestine as "closed" areas for security reasons — the land could not be used by the original inhabitants, and most of it was eventually confiscated. Later, new Jewish settlements were set up on the same expropriated land.

The intentions behind these laws were clear from the outset. Concerning the emergency laws, in 1962, Shimon Peres, the minister of defense, remarked that "the use of Regulation 125, which served to a great extent as the basis of the military regime (in the Arab regions) is the direct continuation of the struggle for Jewish immigration." Ben-Gurion remarked in the Knesset that "the military regime exists for the defense of the right of Jewish settlement everywhere."[46]

Significantly, although the civil rights of the Arabs in Israel were blatantly violated through a system of "passess" practiced by the military regime, the voice of protest from the Jewish legal profession was not heard. Yet in 1946 when the same measures were applied by the British against Jewish settlers, the Hebrew Lawyers' Union said, "The powers given to the ruling authority in the emergency regulations deny the inhabitants of Palestine their basic human rights. These regulations undermine the foundation of law and justice, they constitute a series of dangers to individual freedom and they institute a regime of arbitrariness without any judicial supervision."[47]

One cannot attribute the abolition of the military regime in 1966 to the few voices of opposition coming from a handful of concerned citizenry. Similarly, one cannot attribute it to the altruistic motives of the government. Serious pragmatic considerations were involved. First, the concerted attack on the military government emanated from Jewish political parties, prompted by revelations that the military governor was engaged in vote-stacking among the Arab community in behalf of the ruling parties. Second, there was an increase in demand from the Jewish market for unskilled Arab labor. However, it is conceded that this relaxation of geographic mobility of the Arabs was done with little consideration for the eventual socioeconomic integration of Arabs in the Jewish sector.

Another law, passed in 1949 and not declared invalid until 1972, enabled the minister of defense to declare with the approval of the Knesset's Foreign Affairs and Security Committee all or part of the "protected area" — a zone stretching 10 kilometers north and 25 kilometers south of the 31st parallel along the whole frontier — to be a "security zone." In this manner hearly half of the Arab Galilee area was declared a security zone.[48]

Finally, in 1949 the minister of agriculture was empowered by law to assume control of "waste" (i.e. uncultivated) land if he is not satisfied with the way the land is managed. A simultaneous law, the Emergency Land Regulation Law of 1949, was designed to seize Arab property located in urban centres if, as article 2 of the law put it, "the defense of the State, public security, the maintenance of essential supplies and essential public services, the absorption of immigrants or the rehabilitation of ex-soldiers or war invalids"[49] required the land.

Two additional laws were enacted which aimed at defining citizenship in the state along theocratic lines. The Israeli Nationality Act, enacted in 1952, preceeded by the Law of Return of 1950, gave any Jew anywhere in the world the right to Israeli citizenship.[50] Palestinian Arabs, on the other hand, who had been residing in the country for generations and whose ancestors had been there for centuries were denied this automatic right of citizenship granted to Jewish settlers. Another law related to the "demographic battle" which Israel has been waging since 1948 is the 1953 National Insurance Law.[51] On the surface, this law intended to encourage families to have as many children as possible by awarding twenty Israeli pounds per child until the offspring reached the age of eighteen. When it became apparent that Arabs — who were contributing toward the scheme in taxes and insurance — were benefitting disproportionately due to large size families, and since the latent intentions of the law were to encourage Jewish families to have many children, the law was abolished. In its place, the government applied the existing Discharged Soldiers Law; Jewish families are likely to benefit most from this family allowance since most Arabs do not serve in the armed forces. In protesting against these measures, a Jewish member of the opposition in the Knesset remarked, "the intention (of this law) is to encourage births among one part of the population of Israel and to effect the opposite among the other part, to pay grants to the hungry children of one part of the population and withold them from the hungry children of another part. . . ."[52]

The implications of land dispossession and demographic structure on the Israeli Arabs, can be best illustrated in an analysis of Arab class structure and its transformation from peasantry to proletariat.

The Proletarianization of Palestinian Arabs

Occupation and Income

A central, important factor in the transformation of class structure among the Palestinian Arabs is the emergence of a large stratum of rural proletariat, manifesting the features of migrant laborers encountered in the metropoles of colonial societies, or more recently in advanced Western industrial societies, such as Western Europe and the United States.

According to the 1931 British census of Palestine, close to 80 percent of the Palestinian Arabs lived in rural areas.[53] Immediately before the end of the British Mandate in 1948, about 30 percent (of a total of 1,300,000 Arabs) were living in cities. At the end of the war in 1948, out of approximately 170,000 Arabs who remained in Israel, 27 percent were urban, with the majority being classified as rural or Bedouin. The Arabs under Israeli rule constituted the remainder of close to 900,000 Palestinians who used to live in the territories held by Israel. Thus, close to 700,000 Palestinian Arabs were displaced in what used to be Palestine within current pre-1967 Israel borders.[54]

As late as 1963, the proportion of rural Arabs in Israel was 75 percent.[55] The 1973 census shows 56 percent of the Palestinian Arabs to be residing in urban settlements (settlements of 5,000 or more) and towns.[56] While in terms of absolute numbers the majority of the Arabs in Israel are not considered rural, the qualitative aspects of this shift and the accompanying changes in social structure are most noteworthy.

Had this transformation reflected a natural shift from ruralism to urbanism, one can hardly be justified in singling out this aspect as an important factor in the sociological study of Palestinians. After all, many of contemporary urban societies were still in the rural stage forty to fifty years ago. However, what makes the Palestinian case of special significance is that this transformation took place, and continues to do so, in the context of colonization with strict patterns of domination and dependency. The urban character of the settlers, their acquisition of native land for colonization purposes, the contrasting occupational characteristics differentiating the settlers from the native population, all these factors explain the continued separate development in the social and economic spheres among the two groups, and the subsequent distortion of the original social structure of the Palestinian Arabs.

Contrary to the popular belief that what attracts the Zionist settler to Palestine is his attachment to the land and rural life, as early as the twenties, the Zionists tended to cluster in urban centers. In 1931, 74 percent lived in urban areas; in 1948 the proportion increased to 84 percent.[57] Today the proportion of Jews living in towns and urban settlements reaches 90 percent.[58]

Similarly, as early as 1931, the occupational structure showed a preponderance among the Zionists of individuals employed in nonagricultural pursuits. By 1963 only 38 percent of the Arabs were employed in agriculture, and in 1973 the percentage declined to 20 percent, around one-third of the 57 percent figure shown in 1931. This decline is accompanied by a significant increase in the proportion of unskilled workers, mainly those employed in construction and unskilled service industries. An examination of the 1973 figures shows that approximately one-fifth of the Arabs in the Israeli labor force are employed in construction.[59] A survey of the construction industry in Haifa showed it to be comprised of 36.5 percent Israeli Jews, 42.9 percent Israeli Arabs and 20.5 percent Arabs from the West Bank.[60] There has hardly been any improvement in the situation of professional and managerial strata; if anything, the divergence has increased between the two groups over the last decade.[61]

The same pattern applies in a study of the labor force in terms of sector of industry, rather than occupation per se. In 1944, 51 percent of the Palestinian Arabs worked in the agricultural, forestry and fishery sectors. In 1955 and 1961 the percentages of Arabs in these sectors were 50.4 and 41.5, respectively. Among the Jewish population the corresponding percentages were 15 and 12.8. By 1973, 6.8 percent of the Jews were employed in the agricultural sectors, against 17.4 percent of the Arabs. Here, too, the rising proportion of Palestinian Arabs channelled into construction and unskilled jobs is apparent. Between 1950 and 1973 the proportion of Arab workers in the construction sector rose from 6 to 25.5 percent.[62] It is important to note that while the share of Arabs in the Israeli labor force was only 9.8 percent in 1973,[63] they provided at least one-half of the total unskilled and semi-skilled workers. It is also significant to note the decline in the proportion of Arabs employed in the commercial, banking and public and personal services sectors:

In 1931 the percentage of those (Arabs) employed in those industries was 24.0 percent of all Arab earners; in 1944 it reached 33 percent; while in 1950 the percentage went down to 28 percent, in 1955 to 18.9 percent, and in 1959 to 16.7 percent . . . rising slightly in 1968 to 17.1 percent. There is a noticeable decline in the percentage employed in commerce and personal services and in the percentage employed in public services (from 11.0 percent in 1944 to 8.2 percent in 1963).[64]

In 1973, the Arab share of the commerce sector was 9.9 percent. It is this phenomenon of unnatural class structure which prompted Yosef Waschitz to conclude that while the Jewish occupational structure in the Diaspora used to be an inverted pyramid, "the Arab-Israeli pyramid is a truncated one."[65]

It is difficult to infer from the census the sociological significance of the employer/employee status of the Arabs in Israel. Waschitz remarks that "in 1973, Arabs constituted 4.5 percent of all self-employed in Israel."[66] S. Geraisy, in his 1969 study of Um-El-Fahm, an Arab settlement of around 11,000, notes that out of 116 villagers working in Jewish metropoles, 92 percent occupied subordinate occupational positions, only 8 percent were in supervisory roles and "for 95.8 percent of the respondents, the supervisors were Jewish, while for 5.4 percent they were Arabs."[67] The extent of wage differentials between Jews and Arabs doing the same kind of work is also difficult to determine. Ben-Porath claims that the differential narrowed down during the mid-sixties, though differences still persist. Between 1949 and 1952, "Arab wages were roughly 35 to 70 percent of Jewish wages for similar work. The smallest gap is between Jewish and Arab skilled workers,"[68] however, very few of the employed Arabs fall in the professional or skilled category. In the case of agriculture, the discrepency in wages existed as early as 1936 when a Jewish worker's income per annum amounted to L34, while that of an Arab was L7;[69] a 1960 study conducted estimated that Arabs working in agriculture earn one-half as much as Jews working in similar jobs.[70] It is important to note that Arab agricultural workers comprise the majority of workers in "Jewish agriculture." A study for the ministry of agriculture showed the ratio of Arab to Jewish workers in "Jewish agriculture" as six to ten.[71]

It is difficult to verify the optimistic claims regarding the narrowing of income gaps. The income distribution between the two groups is shown in Table 1. The gross annual income of Arab and Jewish urban employees has followed an erratic pattern. In 1973, the percentage ratio of Arab to Jewish income was 84; in 1971, 66; in 1967, 74. These figures are an improvement over those of 1963 in which the average annual income of an Arab amounted to 45 percent of that of a Jewish earner.[72] Data concerning rural employees are lacking, however, the gap would probably be much greater." The susceptibility of the Arab worker to the whims of the Jewish market is evident from the unemployment rates displayed in Table 2. During economic recessions such as those in 1961 and again in 1967, the unemployment rate among the Arabs is twice that in the Jewish sector.

Table 1: Gross Annual Income of Arab and Jewish Urban Employees (in Israeli Pounds)

Year	Jews	Arabs	Ratio of Arab/Jewish Income (%)
1967	9,400	7,000	74
1968	9,600	7,000	73
1969	10,500	8,400	70
1970	11,900	8,100	67
1971	12,900	8,600	66
1972	15,500	11,200	72
1973	17,600	14,900	84

Source: *Statistical Abstracts of Israel*, 1974.

Table 2: Unemployment Rates for Arab and Jewish Urban Employees, 1960-70

Year	Jews	Arabs
1960	3.6	13.9
1967	9.0	19.4
1969	3.6	5.0
1970	3.4	3.2

Source: Ben-Porath, "Short Term Fluctuations in Fertility and Economic Activity in Israel," *Demography* 10, no. 2 (1973): 185-204.

Table 3 shows the per capita income for the two groups taking into account family size and unemployment rates. The gap has not narrowed at all: in each case the per capita income of a Jew was 2.5 times that of an Arab. It is significant to note that, on the basis of these calculations, there has been little change in the relative position of the two groups from 1944 to 1970. In 1944, with rising prices during the war period, the average income per capita for the Arab population was L27, while corresponding Jewish per capita income reached L63.[73]

Table 3: Per Capita Income in Israeli Pounds, 1967-70

Year	Average Family Size		Adjusted Gross Annual Income*		Per Capita Income+	
	Jews	Arabs	Jews	Arabs	Jews	Arabs
1967	4.0	6.2	8,500	5,600	2,100	900
1969	3.9	6.3	10,100	8,000	2,600	1,300
1970	3.9	6.4	11,500	7,800	3,000	1,200

*Derived by rmultiplying the (Gross Annual Income) x (100 —% Unemployment rates).
+Derived by dividing the (Adjusted Gross Annual Income) / (Average Family Size).

Living Standards

One indicator of the economic well-being of a population is spending and consumption patterns. Up-to-date figures distinguishing between Arab and Jewish spending patterns are not available. However, the results of a 1956/1957 survey on family expenditures reveal that the "average monthly expenditure per individual member in an Arab family was about half the expenditure in the Jewish family, being L39 Israeli and L76 Israeli respectively."[74] Sixty percent of the Arab spending was devoted to food and shelter (50 percent on food alone), whereas among the Jewish population the spending on food and shelter amounted to 49 percent of the total.

Living conditions, measured in terms of number of persons per room, reveal the lopsided nature of the contrast between the Arab and Jewish population. In 1973 while 25 percent of the Arab population lived four or more persons in one room, the corresponding figure for the Jewish population was 1.5 percent.[75] Similarly, while close to 50 percent of the Jewish population were distributed on the average of one person or less per room, among the Arab population it was 15.4 percent. If these figures are compared to those of 1968, a marked improvement in the situation of the Jewish population is evident. But there has been hardly any such improvement among the Arab population. In 1968, 75 percent of the Arab population lived two persons or more per room, compared to 71 percent in 1973. The respective percentages for the Jewish population were 29 and 21.[76] Even when compared to the 1961 figures, as far as the Palestinian Arabs are concerned, the picture did not change that much. In 1961, 30 percent of urban Arabs lived, on the average, less than two persons per room, while the corresponding proportion among urban Jews reached 62 percent. Among rural Jews and Arabs the respective figures were 51 and 13 percent.[77]

Another accepted comparative indicator of the standard of living is the ownership of durable goods. Except for ownership of radios which extends to 80 percent of the Arab and 90 percent of the Jewish population, the comparison across the remaining consumption items shows a striking lag. Table 4 shows that the proportion of Jews to Arabs in terms of ownership of various commodities ranged from 10:1 in the case of telephones; 4:1 in the case of electric refrigerators; 5:1 in the case of private cars and so on.

Table 4: Ownership of Durable Goods by Jews and Arabs (1970)

	Jews (%)	Arabs (%)
Telephones	38.1	3.4
Private Cars	16.7	3.1
Television	53.4	14.3
Electric Refrigerators	95.5	26.8
Washing Machines	46.1	11.8
Gas Ranges	88.5	60.7

Source: *Statistical Abstracts of Israel*, 1971.

Marginalization

The transformation of Palestinian peasantry into a stratum of marginal proletariat has had two serious consequences. First, the Palestinian Arabs were uprooted from traditional village life. As early as 1961, approximately 50 percent of Arab workers were geographically mobile and worked in areas outside their residence. For 1970, the figure for migratory male Arab workers is about 59 percent, with the overwhelming majority coming from rural regions.[78] In 1961, for example, 21.5 percent of commuting workers in the Arab labor force came from urban centres, while 78.5 percent came from rural areas.[79] And of those employed in the construction industry, close to 77 percent worked away from home.[80] According to a governmental survey conducted in 1965, those who were considered to be transient workers amounted to

"27,000; i.e. one-half of the Arab workers, which included 23,500 males; 69 percent of these mobile workers came from rural areas, 13 percent from Nazareth and Shfaa'mer, 10 percent were Bedouins and the remaining 8 percent lived in cities."[81] At the initiative of the government, plans were drafted in 1963 to organize residential living for these village proletariat who worked in the cities. However, a referendum carried out among 116 Arab village workers in 1964 showed that very few were prepared to make the move away from the village,[82] and, as a consequence, a parliamentary committee looking into the matter concluded in 1968 that the initial idea of government subsidy to build such residences was not a viable one. Instead, the government promised to look into securing cheaper transportation rates for commuters. Current estimates state that around 90 percent of Arab village workers commute each day to Jewish towns and cities.[83] Geraisy gives a somewhat lower estimate (70 percent) although among the 15-25 age-group it reaches 90 percent.[84] "Such a situation makes Arabs vulnerable to any contraction of employment; the 'non-local' Arab villager will be the first to be fired (e.g. in the Haifa port, this year)."[85] These findings put into question a statement by Toledano, the advisor to the prime minister on Arab affairs, who cited official census figures showing that close to 50,000 Arab workers (i.e. one-half of the officially registered Arab labor force) are engaged in Jewish enterprises located in the Jewish sector.[86]

In the early seventies two separate studies, one conducted at the Hebrew University and the other at the Technion, came up with results similar to those discovered almost a decade ago by Rosenfeld. They concluded that: (1) The Arab village is very quickly losing its traditional character; (2) Toward the end of the British Mandate, the Arab village was more developed than today; (3) The Arab agricultural workers suffer from the lack of a permanent place of work; (4) As to work relations between Arabs and Jews in cities, the Arab attaches importance to them while, in most cases, the Jew does not; (5) By the age of 40 to 45, the Arab villager who works in construction or in the different service industries is found to be an "old man," after having spent 25 years working; (6) Out of 94 villages sampled in the Technion study, only 20 had an acceptable level of modernization.[87]

The second aspect of the distortion of social structure among the native Palestinian Arabs is a function of the depletion in the size of agricultural land as well as in the transformation of the Arab village into an economically stagnant unit. Writing more than a decade ago, Ben-Porath commented, "The present structure of the Arab sector is such that it generates only limited demand for educated manpower and the potential source of demand is the Government and the Jewish sector."[88]

All the evidence shows that Ben-Porath's observation still holds true. In commenting on the underdevelopment of the Arab region and the deterioration in its economic position relative to pre-1948, Fred Gottheil comments:

> Although it is clear that Arab incomes and consumption have increased considerably since the formation of the state, it is also clear that the Arab region, as a producing region, has declined relative to the rest of the economy. Arabs are increasingly leaving their villages for employment opportunities in the Jewish sector, and although their consumption of houses, automobiles, refrigerators, televisions, food and clothes has increased, construction of factories, expansion of agricultural acreage and the development of local services in the Arab regions have not. This circumstance, incidentally, contrasts with the experience of the Mandate Period. While the Jewish economy during 1922-1931 was expanding rapidly. . . ., the development of the Arab economy in Palestine was also substantial. The extent of Arab participation in the industrialization process is reflected in the growth, from 1918 to 1928, of 1,373 new Arab-owned enterprises. Although clearly of smaller scale than the Jewish enterprise, they nonetheless represented over 70 percent of the total Arab enterprises. But since 1948 disparity between the Jewish and Arab regions in Israel has increased rather than diminished.[89]

An additional factor which would account for the economic lag of the Arab village has been analysed by Lustick, who focuses on the tremendous gap of inflow of capital in the form of government subsidies to Arab villages as an important factor in slowing down, or even preventing, their industrialization. Out of 105 Arab villages, only 43 are supplied with electricity, with 20 other villages still in the planning stage, thus leaving slightly less than one-half of the Arab villages with no immediate or future plans to acquire electricity. While Jewish villages and settlements have access to funds from the government as well as the Jewish Agency, Arab villages, if they embark on programs of improving social services, have to take out loans with added interest to meet the costs. For example, since the total budget for an Arab village council amounts to slightly more than IL500,000 (Israeli Pounds), it becomes next to impossible to try and install an electric network when the connection to the nearest grid could cost anywhere from IL500,000 to 3,000,000. It is estimated that since 1948, more than U.S. $1,200,000,000 were granted by the Jewish Agency alone toward the development of Jewish settlements. It is unlikely that such an inflow of capital will ever be channeled into Arab villages. Within the last fifteen years, with an overall government budget totalling into billions of Israeli Pounds, a meager sum of IL15,000,000, has been spent in improving Arab villages.[90] Bayadsi, an Israeli Arab, confirms this picture:

A Ministry of Interior report on Municipalities in Israel during 1971/1972 reveals that the total grants allocated by the Ministry to local authorities amounted to IL158,580,000, of which the Arab sector received a total of IL1,785,000 or 1.1 percent of the total, while the population included within the Arab local authorities is as much as 11 percent of the entire population governed by local authorities in Israel. In the matter of loans, the Arab minority's share is minute. Again, the Interior Ministry's report for 1971/72 shows that the Ministry made loans to cover deficits in local authorities' budgets to an amount of IL50,185,500. The Arab villages had no share at all of these loans. The Ministry of the Interior also granted loans for the repayment of indebtedness to an amount of IL60,897,000 to Jewish local authorities, while Arab local authorities received nothing for this purpose.[91]

Table 5: Arab and Jewish Localities with No Local Councils*
(1958-1971)

Year	Number of Cities Villages and Settlements		% Cities, Villages and Settlements with No Local Councils	
	Jewish	Arab	Jewish	Arab
1953	742	112	12.5	79.5
1957	802	111	5.0	73.0
1960	780	112	2.9	59.8
1966	774	103	1.7	44.7
1971	781	104	1.1	28.8

Source: Sabri Jiryis, *The Arabs in Israel* (Beirut, 1973) Table 13.
*Excluding Arabs in East Jerusalem.

The economic well-being of the Jewish and Arab sectors is a function of the extent to which each sector is politically organized, in particular on the local level. Here too the Arab and Jewish villages have developed in separate directions. As late as 1963, about 70 Arab villages, i.e. more than one-half of the entire Arab villages, had no local councils. As shown in Table 5, about 29 percent of the Arab localities in 1971 had no local councils.[92] In contrasting the two sectors, it must be borne in mind that the patterns of development are not a new phenomenon. They existed prior to 1948 where the Jewish sector had already included the development of local councils in its pockets of Zionist settlements. After all, the idea of local councils is a Western concept of political and social participation, which was imported into the region on large scale by the Zionist settlers. Within the Arab sector, there were two localities that had municipal councils as early as 1948, Nazareth and Shfa'amer.

The most drastic change has occurred in the magnitude of decline in the number of Arab villages and settlements in the area now constituting Israel. In 1945, there were 863 villages, compared to the present 104 villages and settlements. The Zionist takeover and destruction of Arab villages has been greatly facilitated by the mass exodus of the Palestinians. Peretz points out that "of the 370 new Jewish settlements established between 1948 and the beginning of 1953, 350 were on absentee property."[93]

In contrast to the Jewish villages, it is claimed, Arab villages were run according to clan and family units, or the *hamulas*, and had in them many of the traditional structures which prevented industrialization and the development of mass-based participation in local affairs. Family feuds and traditional value systems are usually cited by the Israeli authorities and social scientists alike as the main reasons for the economic backwardness of the Arab sector. Several studies[94] make it clear that if an adequate explanation is sought concerning social structures of Arab villages, one must study the role of political economy, and move away from current approaches fashionable in socio-anthropological writings which emphasize the centrality of values and kinship systems.

In this context it is difficult to ignore the role of the Israeli government, including the dominant political parties, who have capitalized on, and even perpetuated, the presence of the *hamula* phenomenon to the detriment of the economic development of Arab villages. Contrary to Abner Cohen's conclusions regarding *hamula* revival under Israeli rule,[95] it is plausible to argue that the *hamula* phenomenon existed all along side by side with social class cleavages, and that its continued existence is due to governmental policies. Lustick stated:

> Perhaps the single most important factor explaining the political
> longevity of the traditional hamula framework is the support that
> hamula leaders have received from the government, specifically
> from the military government, the office of the advisor to the
> Prime Minister on Arab Affairs, and politicos in the Mapai-Labour
> Party and in the Histradrut's Arab Department.[96]

Sabri Jiryis demonstrates in detail the extent of manipulation of local
leaders in Arab villages by the ruling parties. The introduction of
"whole scale democracy" in Arab villages has had debilitating effects
on the efficiency levels of the various councils. For example, in 1965
and 1969 a total of 252 and 195 voting lists were included in local
elections, respectively. In 1965, 154 lists won and in 1969, 151. In
other words, the average number of lists for each village totalled five,
which made it impossible to conduct the affairs of the councils with
any efficiency. Instead of (and maybe in addition to) family feuds, the
Israelis have managed to introduce political party feuds; in both cases,
the results are similar in their overall effect. In some instances the communist parties have formed coalitions with Arab nationalist elements in
order to confront Zionist-based political parties. In such cases, the
ministry of interior would interfere and upset the political balance by
reclassifying the status of the village so as to justify the election of
additional members, thus annulling the existing balance. In one such
case, the local council of Kufer Yassif village which was led by an Arab
nationalist-communist coalition appealed its case to the Israeli Supreme
Court for governmental interference in the political affairs of the
village by deposing the elected mayor, and won its case.[97]

In Jiryis' view another reason for the government's reluctance to
take definite steps in increasing the scope and number of local councils
in the Arab sector is due to the fact that the setting up of local councils
implies recognition of the existence and legitimacy of that particular
village. This has implications concerning the size of the land holdings by
the village inhabitants and the extent of the local council's jurisdiction.
Such final steps might impede future government designs to confiscate
land and relocate villagers. Bayadsi comments:

> In spite of the Planning and Construction Act in 1965, and its prac-
> tical implementation as of 1966, local town-planning committees
> have yet to be established in a number of Arab villages. Most Arab

villages have no approved zoning plan and no status has been accorded to any local zoning committee in any Arab local council, in spite of the fact that in most large local councils in the Jewish sector the authority has also been designated as a local zoning committee.[98]

As of 1971, only three Arab villages had been land-surveyed; 49 other villages are still in the planning stages, while the rest have not even been considered. In those villages which have not been land-surveyed and incorporated into the municipal or local council government structure, the day-to-day disadvantages for the inhabitants are obvious. It is difficult in the absence of clear-cut zoning and ordinance laws to secure licenses to build and develop village land. In those instances when the villagers "violated" nonexistent zoning regulations they discovered, to their sorrow, that their houses could be — and were in fact — demolished. Toledano, the adviser to the prime minister on Arab affairs, confirmed the existence of these measures, admitting that not too long ago eighteen houses were demolished in one Arab village due to the violation of zoning laws.[99]

The economic lag of the Arab sector is not confined to income differential or to distorted occupational structure, but also to a highly marginalized agricultural sector, which traditionally has been the backbone of the Palestinian Arab economy. Although by far a larger proportion of Arabs live in rural areas, compared to Jews, neither the size of land nor the productivity of cultivated land show the same pattern. Table 6 clearly shows the infinitesimal size of Arab cultivated land, when compared to Jewish land. Between 1951 and 1971 the average cultivated land in the Jewish sector exceeded that found in the Arab agricultural sector by more than 400 percent. Similarly, the agricultural yield in the Jewish sector exceeded that of the Arab sector an average of 289 percent for a two decade period, 1951-1971. In 1971 the disparity reached 368 percent.

Even in tobacco growing, traditionally one of the most successful agricultural pursuits among the Palestinian Arabs, although in terms of tonnage the Arabs produced more than the Jews, in terms of price per ton the situation of the Arabs deteriorated during the last two decades. In 1961, the difference in the price of a ton of tobacco was IL685 in favor of the Jewish farmer. In 1971 the disparity rose to IL1,444.[100]

Not surprisingly in the light of the previous discussion, the actual consumption of water for irrigation purposes differs drastically in the two sectors. In fact between 1961 and 1970 the proportion of Arab

Table 6: Jewish and Arab Cultivated Land and Value of Agricultural
Output (1950-71)

Year	Cultivated Land*		Value of Agric. Output**		Value per Dunum***		% Difference
	Jewish	Arab	Jewish	Arab	Jewish	Arab	Jewish/Arab
1950-1951	2705	645	65172	5798	24.09	8.99	186
1954-1955	2965	625	353237	24168	119.13	38.67	208
1958-1959	3350	755	671245	41767	200.36	55.32	262
1962-1963	3185	820	1102997	58330	346.31	71.13	387
1966-1967	3273	865	1516272	98563	464.27	113.95	307
1970-1971	3387	774	2393200	116700	706.58	150.97	368

* In thousands of Dunums.
** In thousands of Israeli Pounds.
*** In Israeli Pounds.
Source: Sabri Jiryis, *The Arabs in Israel* (Beirut, 1973) Table 12.

consumption of water for agricultural purposes remained around one
percent of the total water consumption in Israel.[101]

Conclusions

In spite of the historical neglect of the Arab place in the Zionist
scheme, contemporary writers and supporters of Zionism do not hesitate to blame the Arabs for standing in the way of the Zionist experiment in Palestine. "Zionism which set out to 'normalize' Jewish conditions," writes the Israeli writer Amos Elon, "and to establish a 'safe'
haven, cannot now be considered a 'success' by any so-called normal
standards. Perhaps the opposite is true." Like most writers in this
genre, Elon perceives the problem to lie solely with the Arab reaction
to Israel. "In Israel," he goes on to say, "the former pariah people
live in a pariah state, paradoxically perhaps the only place left where
the Jews are in moral danger precisely because they are Jews."[102]

Bernard Avishai expounded his views on the "myth" of Zionist
colonialism by advancing a similar argument levelling the blame for
Israel's colonialist tendencies on Arab intransigence:

War, not Zionism, is driving Israel step by step, expediency by
expendiency, to particular colonialist policies. But Jewish (rather
than Zionist) colonialisation is still a distant nightmare and will not
materialize except as the self-fulfilled prophecy of Palestinian
maximalists who still resist the very concept of Jewish national
life.[103]

Thus, in Avishai's scheme Israel mainly reacts and responds to external stimuli, and whenever she responds in a negative fashion it is because she is compelled to do so by Arab extremists. One can hardly attempt to account for the discrminatory legal structure in Israel, the systematic seizure and expropriation of Arab land for Jewish settlement, the racist attitude with which the majority of adult and young Jewish citizens perceive the Arabs in general,[104] not to mention the glaring truncated class structure of the Arabs in Israel which is the direct outcome of the colonized status of the Arab minority, solely in terms of Arab irrationality and "maximalism." How blatantly untrue in the light of the evidence is Avishai's statement that "the intended result of Zionist policies has been substantially achieved and class domination of one people by the other avoided."[105]

For various complex reasons the Jewish problem is becoming increasingly interconnected with the Palestinian problem, irrespective of whether or not doctrinaire Zionists perceive and define it to be so. Redefining the Palestinian issue in a way which suits the expansionist policies of the Israeli government, i.e. by relegating the Palestinian problem to either "refugee" or "international" status is to show an unlimited capacity to misperceive the lesson of recent history. Doctrinaire Zionists and various pressure groups, academic and otherwise, are equally at fault for attempting to popularize in the West the official Israeli view which advocates appending the Palestinian problem to other Arab problems, in particular to the dispute between Jordan and Israel. The upshot of this solution is the substitution of Israeli colonialism by a Jordanian one – or more appropriately restoring the old Hashemite colonialist dominance over the Palestinians: it is old wine in new bottles and is bound to fail as it did in the past.

If the solution of the perennial "Jewish problem" has not been accomplished through the creation of Israel, it is too simplistic to attribute this failure solely to Arab reaction to Zionism. It is in the way Zionism set out to "normalize" the Jewish condition by means of colonization and the mechanisms it used to achieve this goal that must be studied, before the Arab reaction can be understood.

Notes

1. Although Palestinian Arab hostile reaction to Zionism was evidenced as early as the latter part of the last century, Zionist attitude to the indigenous Palestinians was oblivious and characterized by indifference. *See* Neville Mandel, "Turks, Arabs and Jewish Immigration into Palestine, 1882-1914," *St. Antony's*

Papers, no. 17 (London, 1965), pp. 77-108. A notable exception in this regard is the spiritual Zionist, Ahad Ha-Am who, after taking a trip to Palestine in 1891, warned against accepting the Hertzlian slogan, "land without people to people without a land." One should also note the minority movement of Zionist bi-nationalists who foresaw the outcome of doctrinaire Zionists as revealed in the Arab rebellion of 1936-1939, and advocated recognition of the Arab factor. The defeat of this movement was reflected in the triumph of the labor-Zionists who asserted the hegemony of "Jewish labour," "Jewish products," and "Jewish con-quest of the land," thus giving rise to Jewish exclusivist institutions.

2. See, for example, Noah Lucas, *The Modern History of Israel* (London, 1974).

3. Teodor Shanin, "The Price of Suspension," in *Israel and the Palestinians,* ed. Uri Davis, Andrew Mack and Nira Yuval-Davis (London, 1975), pp. 24-56.

4. Labor-Zionism is associated with the ideas of Ber Borochov (1881-1917) and A.D. Gordon (1856-1922), both of whom provided the bases for the applica-tion of socialist doctrines in the Zionist colonization of Palestine. The stress was placed upon the "normalization" of Jewish occupational and class structure through the development of a Jewish proletarian base. Conventional Zionist writers emphasize the "marxist" and "socialist" aspects of labor-Zionism. A con-trary view is provided by Alan Taylor, *The Zionist Mind* (Beirut, 1974). Taylor places Gordon's philosophy within "the imperial episodes of the time." For a critique of Borochov's writings, see "Borochovism," in *The Other Israel,* ed. Arie Bober (N.Y., 1972), pp. 145-58.

5. *See* Bernard Avishai, "Zionist 'Colonialism': Myth and Dilemma," *Dissent,* Spring 1975, pp. 125-134; Saul Friedlander and Mahmoud Hussein, *Arabs and Israelis* (New York, 1975).

6. *See* the articles by Israel Eldad and Shraga Gafni in *Documents From Israel,* ed. Uri Davis and Norton Mezvinsky (London, 1975), pp. 183-99. Gush Emunim, the ultra-right religious movement in Israel which calls for Jewish occupation and settlement of the West Bank is a concrete embodiment of Eldad's ideas. As Beit-Hallahmi demonstrates the influence of religious ideas on the Israeli political culture is not confined to religious fanatics and fundamentalists but is also found to permeate the rhetoric and ideologies of the secular and socialist leadership in Israel, ("Some roles of Religion in the Arab-Israeli Conflict," mimeographed, University of Michigan, 1972).

7. It is difficult to reach a precise assessment of the size of North American Jews immigrating to Israel, since the Israeli census does not separate European from North American immigrants in its data. Overall, the most optimistic claims put the total number of North American Jewish immigrants prior to the 1967 war in the vicinity of 20,000. Leonard Weller estimates that since 1967 the average annual immigration of North American Jews has risen to between 6,000 to 8,000. *See* his *Sociology in Israel* (Westport, Connecticut, 1974, pp. 29-35. These estimates are slightly inflated, compared to those reported in the Israeli press. In 1973, 4,393 American Jews immigrated, compared to 2,693 in 1974. For the same years, 1,300 and 800 French and British Jews immigrated to Israel per year, *Yedioth Aharenoth,* 6 Jan. 1975, cited in the *Bulletin of the Institute for Palestine Studies* 5, no. 1 (1975): 44. It is also interesting to note that the West, rather than Israel, is becoming an increasingly attractive place for Russian Jewish emigrants. According to Noam Chomsky, "It is safe to assume that the emigration of Russian Jews, if permitted by the Soviet authorities, will turn towards the West. Already in December 1974, 35 percent of the Russian Jews reaching Vienna chose to go to the West, as compared to 4 percent in 1973 . . . " in "Reflections on the Arab-Israeli Conflict," *Journal of Contemporary Asia* 5, no. 3 (1975): 337-44. The general director of the immigration division of the Jewish Agency cites the figure of 30 percent of Russian Jews who decide to

remain in reception centres in Vienna, see *Davar*, 2 Sept. 1975, cited in the
Bulletin of the Institute for Palestine Studies 5, no. 18 (1975): 500.

8. U.O. Schmelz, "The Demographic Development in Israel since 1967,"
Gesher, nos. 3-4 (1972): 118-39.

9. *Al-Hamishmar*, 13 February 1975, cited in the *Bulletin of the Institute
for Palestine Studies* 7, no. 7 (1975): 217.

10. "The Interim Agreement," *New Politics* 11 (1976): 4-33.

11. D. Elizur, "Attitudes and Intentions of Israelis Residing in the U.S.
towards Returning to Israel," *International Migration* 2, nos. 1-2 (1973): 3-14.

12. *See* Georges R. Tamarin in *The Israeli Dilemma* (Rotterdam Univ. Press,
1973).

13. Nina Toren, "The Effect of Economic Incentives on Return Migration,"
Interntional Migration 13 (1975): 134-44.

14. Yahiel Harari, *The Arabs in Israel: Facts and Figures*, no. 4 (Givat Haviva,
1974).

15. The figures up to 1948 were based on data cited by Edward Hagopian and
A.B. Zahlan, "Palestine's Arab Population: The Demography of the Palestinians,"
Journal of Palestine Studies 3, no. 4 (1974): 32-73; data for 1948 were obtained
from *Statistical Abstracts of Israel* (Jerusalem, 1971), p. 21.

16. M.F. Bustani, "Population in Israel: Analysis and Estimates for 1990,"
Supplement to the Bulletin of the Institute for Palestine Studies 3, no. 2 (1973):
389-400. Data for 1948 and 1961 are taken from Sabri Jiryis, *The Arabs in Israel*,
(Beirut, 1973), p. 17. For 1968 and 1973 from Harari, *The Arabs*, p. 6.

17. Chomsky, "Interim," p. 26.

18. Yosef Waschitz, "The Plight of the Bedouin," *New Outlook* 18, (1975):
62-6. Jiryis' discussion of the Bedouin predicament remains the most comprehensive, *see* chap. 2, "Liberation of the Land," in *Arabs in Israel*, pp. 175-230.

19. Joseph L. Ryan, "Refugees within Israel: The Case of the Villages of Kafr
Birim and Iqrit," *Journal of Palestine Studies* 2, no. 4 (1973): 55-81.

20. There is little research on the implictations of the legal system for land
ownership in Israel. Israel Shahak comments on further confiscation of Arab land:
(1) Most of the confiscated land belongs to Arabs. (2) the 'displaced owners'
cannot choose their compensation: they must take what is offered to them.
(3) The cash offered is not 'market value', but according to the estimates of a
governmental 'appraiser', whose valuations are usually 5-20 percent of the market
value. (4) The land which is offered as a compensation, although nominally state
land, really belongs to Arab refugees. (5) The plan for the 'Judaization' of Galilee
was strongly opposed in 1966, especially round the town of Carmiel built at that
date. Many joint Arab-Jewish demonstrations were held, and broken by stiff
prison sentences . . . . Finally, for what purpose is the land confiscated, both from
Arabs and from Jews? So long as it is private, the owner can discriminate on it or
not, as he pleases. Once it becomes 'Judaised,' it becomes apartheid country, on
which Israeli citizens who are not Jews have no right to live" *The Economist*,
10 April 1976, p. 6.

21. Data for 1955, 1961 and 1971 are taken from Niryis, *Arabs in Israel*, p.
18; for 1973 from Harari, *The Arabs*, p. 9.

22. Vivian Z. Klaff, "Ethnic Segregation in Urban Israel," *Demography*
10, no. 2 (1973): 161-84.

23. Dov Friedlander and Calvin Goldscheider, "Peace and the Demographic
Future of Israel," *Journal of Conflict Resolution* 18, no. 3 (1974): 486-501.

24. Schmelz, "The Demographic Development".

25. *Ibid*.

26. Nathan Weinstock, "The Impact of Zionist Colonization of Palestine
Society before 1948," *Journal of Palestine Studies* 2, no. 2 (1973): 50-63.

27. Hagopian and Zahlan, "Palestine's Arab Population," Table 2, p. 43.

28. Data from 1922-45 are taken from *ibid.*, Table 3, p. 43; for 1951-1970, from *Statistical Abstracts of Israel*, 1971, Tables c/2, c/3, pp. 60-61; for 1973, from Harari, *The Arabs*, p. 4.

29. Leonard J. Singerman, Joel A. Singerman and Janice Singerman, *The Threat Within: Israel and Population Policy* (N.Y., 1975).

30. Data for 1955 and 1965 were taken from *Statistical Abstracts of Israel*, 1971, pp. 60, 61; for 1972 from I. Lustick, "Israeli Arabs: Built-In Inequality," *New Outlook* 17, no. 6 (1974); 32-40, Table 5, p. 36.

31. Chomsky, "Israel and" note 40, p. 137.

32. One could say with absolute certainty that every practicing Israeli social scientist, and most of the liberal Western social scientists, reject categorically the labelling of the Zionist experiment in Palestine as colonialism; rather, for them, it is colonization. *See*, for example, Avishai, "Zionist 'Colonialism' " pp. 125-34. It is not our intention to deal with the theoretical aspect of this debate in this paper. What we are attempting to do is establish the sociological features of Israel, being a settler state. What the state was intended to be and how it actually developed need not be identical, and it is the latter which is our concern in this study, i.e. actions and not attitudes and ideologies. *See* the relevant comments made by Henry Pachter on the nature of Zionism, "Who are the Palestinians?" *Dissent* 22 (1976): 387-94, and the correspondence arising out of his article in the subsequent issue (vol. 23 (1976): 107). I shall use the term Zionist colonization and colonialism interchangeably in this paper.

33. Sabri Jiryis, "Recent Knesset Legislation and the Arabs in Israel," *Journal of Palestine Studies* 1, no. 1 (1971): 53-67.

34. Cited in Haim Hanegbi, Moshe Machover and Akiva Orr, "The Class Nature of Israeli Society," *New Left Review*, Jan-Feb. 1971, pp. 3-26.

35. Concerning the conditions surrounding the exodus of Palestinian Arabs in 1948, *see* Don Peretz, *Israel and the Palestine Arabs* (Washington, D.C., 1958), p. 152; and Walid Khalidi, "Plan Dalet: The Zionist Blueprint for the Conquest of Palestine," *Middle East Forum* 37, no. 9 (1961): 22-8.

36. According to Simha Flapan, "Integrating the Arab Village," *New Outlook* 7, no. 9 (1964); 24-36, "there are still nearly 20,000 Arab 'absentees' living in Israel, who enjoy all the rights granted to all citizens except one: to regain their former possessions," p. 25.

37. Peretz, *Israel and*, p. 152.

38. Cited in Jiyris, "Recent Knesset," p. 54.

39. *Ibid.*, p. 61.

40. Chomsky "The Interim" pp. 24-5.

41. Because of the application of JNF principles to State Lands, Uzzi Ornan of the Hebrew University estimates that 95 percent of the land within the pre-1967 borders are classified as State Land. Cited in Chomsky, "Israel and", note 49, pp. 138-9.

42. For a recent attempt to falsify Palestinian history through "academic" documentation regarding land and demography issues, *see* the collection of papers edited by Michael Curtis, Joseph Neyer, Chaim L. Waxman and Allen Pollack, *The Palestinians, People, History and Politics* (N.J., 1975).

43. Chomsky, "The Interim," p. 24.

44. For a discussion of the implications of this law, see Walter Lehn, *op. cit.*

45. *Great Britain and Palestine: 1915-1945*, Royal Institute for International Affairs Information Paper no. 20 (London and N.Y., 1946), p. 36.

46. Cited in Emmanuel Dror, "The Emergency Regulations," in *The Other Israel* ed. Arie Bober (N.Y., 1972), pp. 134-44.

47. Cited in *ibid.*, p. 134.

48. Jiryis, "Expropriation of Arab Land in Israel," *Journal of Palestine Studies* 2, no. 4 (1973): 82-107.

49. *Ibid.*, p. 98.

50. *See* Jiryis' discussion of this and related laws in "Recent Knesset"; also Tamarin, *Israeli Dilemma.*

51. Jiryis, *Ibid.*

52. Cited in *ibid.*, p. 66.

53. Y. Porath, *The Emergence of the Palestinian-Arab National Movement, 1918-1929* (London, 1974), p. 19.

54. *See* Don Peretz, *Israel and*, p. 95; Janet Abu-Lughod, "The Demographic Transformation of Palestine," in *The Transformation of Palestine*, ed. Ibrahim Abu-Lughod (Evanston, Ill., 1971), p. 161.

55. *Israel Statistical Abstracts*, 1963, p. 25.

56. Harari, *The Arabs in Israel*, pp. 9-10.

57. Arieh Tartakower, *The Jewish Society*, (Tel-Aviv/Jerusalem, 1959).

58. *See* Schmelz, "The Demographic Development," p. 122; Harari, *The Arabs in Israel*, p. 6.

59. Data for 1931 were obtained from Y. Porath, *The Emergence*, p. 19; for 1963, Y. Ben-Porath, *The Arab Labour Force in Israel* (Jerusalem, 1966), Table 2-1, p. 22; for 1972, Harari, *The Arabs in Israel*, p. 21.

60. Waschitz, "Plight of the Bedouin," p. 46 and "Commuters and Entrepreneurs", *New Outlook* 18, (1975): 45-53. We are excluding the large proportion of 47 per cent of Palestinian Arabs from the occupied territories who, out of more than 50,000 Arab transient workers in 1972, are employed in construction primarily. See *Middle East Research and Information Reports* No. 24, (1974) reprinted in *Journal of Palestine Studies* 3, no. 4 (1974): 171-84.

61. Lustick, "Israeli Arabs," pp. 34-5.

62. Harari, *The Arabs in Israel*, p. 20.

63. Waschitz "Plight of the Bedouin," p. 47.

64. Shaul Zarhi and A. Achiezra, *The Economic Conditions of the Arab Minority in Israel*, no. 1 (Givat Haviva, 1966), pp. 4-5.

65. Waschitz, pp. 46-7.

66. *Ibid.*, p. 47.

67. S. Geraisy, "Arab Village Youth in Jewish Urban Centres: A Study of Youth from Um-El-Fahm Working in the Tel-Aviv Metropolitan Area" (Unpublished Ph.D. thesis, Brandeis University, 1971), pp. 96-7.

68. Ben-Porath, *Arab Labour*, p. 70.

69. Doreen Warriner, *Land and Poverty in the Middle East* (London and N.Y., 1948), pp. 61-2.

70. Zarhi and Achiezra, *Economic Conditions*, p. 12.

71. Waschitz, "Plight of the Bedouin," p. 48.

72. Lustick, "Israeli Arabs."

73. Warriner, *Land and Poverty*, pp. 61-2.

74. Zarhi and Achiezra, *Economic Conditions*, p. 16.

75. *Statistical Abstracts of Israel*, 1973, p. 283.

76. *Ibid.*

77. Aharon, *op. cit.*, p. 504.

78. *Statistical Abstract of Israel*, 1971, p. 285; for 1972, the "official" figure is 52 percent who work outside their residence in Harari, p. 22. However, as Harari remarks these official figures are based on questionnaire surveys and as such suffer from the usual defects of sampling and survey research. As shown in the above text, the official figures are at variance with data offered by other researchers, such as Geraisy's case-study of Arab villages. The official figures seem to inflate the number of Arabs who work in their residence.

79. Ben-Porath, *Arab Labour*, p. 70.

80. Zarhia and Achiezra, *Economic Conditions*, p. 19.

81. Jiryis, *The Arabs* p. 386.

82. Jacob M. Landau, *The Arabs in Israel: A Political Study* (Oxford, 1969), p. 20. Geraisy, "Arab Village Youth," reaches similar conclusions. Of the respondents living in the city "5.95 percent (five persons) preferred their city dwelling, 5.95 percent (five persons) thought that they were equal, while 88.10 percent (seventy-four persons) preferred their village dwelling," p. 103. Furthermore, Geraisy points out (pp. 89-91) that the main reason behind leaving the village is not because of dreary village life, but because of economic necessity. Eighty-eight percent of his respondents could not find work in the village.

83. Lustick "Israeli Arabs," p. 33.

84. Cited in Waschitz, "Plight of the Bedouin."

85. *Ibid.*, p. 46.

86. *Yediot Aharonoth*, 1 September 1972.

87. The main points summarized in the text are taken from press coverage of both studies: *Al-Hamishmar*, 22 March 1970 and *Maariv*, 22 March 1970.

88. Ben Porath, *Arab Labour*, p. 34.

89. Fred M. Gottheil "On the Economic Development of the Arab Region in Israel," in *Israel; Social Structure and Change*, eds. M. Curtis and M.S. Chertoff (N.J., 1973), pp. 327-248.

90. See also the statement made by an Arab Member of Knesset (Mapam Party) in which he charged that not more than one percent of the funds devoted to local developments are spent in the Arab sector, *Davar*, 3 September 1973; Simha Flapan, writing a decade earlier, cites an identical figure of one and a half percent of the total government expenditure as being channelled to the Arab sector "National Inequality in Israel," *New Outlook* 7, no. 9 (1964): 24-36.

91. "The Arab Local Authorities: Achievements and Problems," *New Outlook* 18 (1975): 58-62.

92. It is also worth noting that the majority of Arab rural settlements are characterized by their small size which renders them unviable economically, especially when they have to compete against more efficient Jewish agriculture. In 1961, the proportion of "large" size Arab rural settlements was about 20 percent; in 1970 it rose to 42 percent; in the Jewish sector out of 708 settlements in 1961, only 57, i.e. slightly more than 10 percent, were classified as "small" size settlements; in 1971, the figure declined to 50, *Statistical Abstracts of Israel*, 1971, pp. 30-31. Flapan, "National Inequality" says with regard to Jewish settlements "these settlements are only called rural because their main occupation is farming. In all other respects they can hardly be called rural in the usual sense." When placed in an historical context it could be seen that the initial Zionist pattern of settlements has eventually led to a more viable agricultural sector. By 1943, "only 19.7 percent of the Jews lived in the hill districts (as opposed to the fertile plains), compared to 56.7 percent of the Arabs" in Weinstock, "Impact of Zionism," p. 57.

93. Peretz *Israel and*, p. 143. A detailed study by Jiryis in *The Arabs*, p. 225, shows that of 1,080,984 dunums belonging to Arabs in 1945, more than one million dunums were confiscated, seized or declared 'State Land' by the Zionist authorities. *See* also the systematic accounting by Israel Shahak of the names and locations of villages in pre-1948 Israel and those remaining now. Out of 475 villages, 385 could not be accounted for, "Arab Villages Destroyed in Israel," in *Documents from Israel, 1967-1973*, eds. Uri Davis and Norton Mezvinsky (London, 1975), pp. 43-54.

94. *See* Asad's study, *op. cit.* Of Rosenfeld's numerous publications about Palestinian Arab proletariat, *see* "The Arab Village Proletariat," *New Outlook* 13, no. 5 (1962): 7-26; "An Overview and Critique of the Literature on Rural

Politics and Social Change," in *Rural Politics and Social Change in the Middle East,* eds R. Antoun and I. Harik (Bloomington, Indiana, 1972), pp. 45-74; and K. Nakhleh, "The Direction of Local-level Conflict in two Arab Villages in Israel," *American Ethnologist* 2, no. 2 (1975): 497-516.

95. Abner Cohen, *Arab Border Villages in Israel* (Manchester, England, 1965).

96. "Israeli Arabs," p. 38.

97. *The Arabs* pp. 396-7.

98. "The Arab Local Authorities; Achievements and Problems," *New Outlook* 18 (1975): 58-61.

99. *Ha-Mishmar,* 1 September 1972.

100. In Jiryis, *The Arabs,* p. 370.

101. *Statistical Abstracts of Israel,* 1971, p. 354.

102. "Review of the Origins of Zionism," *Commentary,* June 1976, p. 68.

103. Avishai, "Zionist 'Colonialism'," p. 133.

104. *See* E. Zureik, "Arab Youth in Israel: Their Situation and Status Perceptions," *Journal of Palestine Studies* 3, no. 3 (1974), 97-108; Tamarin, *Israeli Dilemma*; and Seymour Lipset, "Education and Equality: Israel and the United States Compared," *Society* 2, no. 3 (1974): 56-66.

105. Avishai, "Zionist 'Colonialism'," p. 131.

10 THE COLONIAL EXPLOITATION OF OCCUPIED PALESTINE: A STUDY OF THE TRANSFORMATION OF THE ECONOMIES OF THE WEST BANK AND GAZA

Sheila Ryan

Since 1967, Israel has been enveloped in a cacophony of debate about the Arab areas which the Israeli army seized in the June war. From time to time some basic economic questions have pierced through the din of political and social argument: what about the tens of thousands of Palestinians who leave the occupied areas each morning to do the most menial work in a state where the slogan "Hebrew labor" has an aura of the sancrosanct? Are the effects of occupation positive or negative for the Israeli economy? What form should the economic relations between Israel and the occupied areas take?

This economic debate, despite the confused fashion in which it is conducted, goes to the heart of the dilemma which Israel has faced since 1967. Until that time, Zionism had, in the main, sought to build an exclusively Jewish settler society in Palestine, so exclusively Jewish, in fact, that the indigenous people were often prohibited even from wage labor on the soil of their homeland. After June 1967, the prospect of hiring Palestinian workers from the West Bank and Gaza at half the wage for which an Israeli worker could be hired proved irresistable to Israeli capital; within a few years important sectors of Israeli production were heavily dependent upon labor from the occupied areas.

It is true, of course, that the initial Zionist settlers in Palestine, the "First Aliyah," who arrived beginning in the 1880s, farmed their citrus groves, vineyards and fields in a manner not dissimilar to that of their counterparts on plantations in Rhodesia and Algeria: they hired indigenous workers at low wages to do the manual work and assumed for themselves the role of managers. The next wave of settlers, the "Second Aliyah" (1904-14) were horrified to see that the "rebuilding of Zion" of which they had dreamed was in fact being done by Arab hands; the settlers of the Second Aliyah initiated a campaign for a "kibbush 'avoda," the conquest of labor, or, in other words, for a boycott of Palestinian labor. The insistence of these settlers that only Jews work on land and in enterprises owned by Jews led to very bitter division in the Jewish community in Palestine. By the 1930s, however, "Hebrew labor" had won out.

This slogan, whatever the mysticism with which it was sometime masked, indicated a long-range political strategy: in order to build an entity with a Jewish majority, the immediate economic benefits of exploitation of cheap Arab labor would have to be waived. As David Ben-Gurion wrote decades later, "The reason that 'Hebrew labor' won out during the Second Aliyah and Mandate period is that every loyal Zionist understood that without Jewish labor there would be no Jewish state."[1]

The campaign for "Hebrew labor" led to the process, well documented elsewhere, by which the Palestinian peasantry evicted from extensive tracts of land when the Jewish National Fund (JNF) "bought' 'it from absentee landlords, was permanently denied employment on the land where once they lived. Infamous clauses in the leases which the JNF conferred upon settlers stipulated that "the lessee undertakes to execute all works connected with the cultivation of the holding only with Jewish labor."[2]

During the Mandate period the Zionist movement created a separate Jewish economy in Palestine, insulated from the Palestinian Arab economy by a complex system of quasi-public landholding in the name of "the Jewish people," restrictive clauses in leases, boycotts of Arab produce and labor, and upholding of "the Jewish product" and "Hebrew labor." In 1948 this exclusivity was given political expression in the establishment of a Jewish state and the expulsion of three-quarters of a million Palestinians from their homes. The property seized swelled the Zionist economy, and the remant of the Palestinian population which remained in the Zionist state was not large enough to seriously disturb the image of Jewish exclusivity.[3]

The Arab boycott of Israel, instituted after the establishment of the Zionist state enforced, however, a greater degree of separation between Zionist and Arab economies than the Zionist leadership had envisaged. Israel's first president, Chaim Weizmann, "talks of Israel's becoming 'the new Switzerland,' supplying consumer goods to the untapped markets of the Middle East," *Fortune* magazine reported in 1950.[4] Apparently sharing Weizmann's belief that the Arab boycott was a transient phenomenon, a number of major U.S. corporations, including Kaiser-Frazier, Philco and General Tire and Rubber rushed to build plants in Israel; these corporations, and a number of British, Dutch and South African capitalists, invested in Israel "not out of compassion, but in the expectation of profits" from sales in Middle Eastern and other markets," *Fortune* stated.[5]

The pattern of trade which Israel was seeking was outlined in a speech by Abba Eban at the United Nations in 1952: if the Arab boycott were lifted and peace established, he predicted, raw materials from the Arab countries — agricultural produce from Syria, Lebanon and Jordan, meat from Iraq and cotton from Egypt — would flow to Israel, which would, in turn export manufactured goods to the Arab countries. This exchange of manufactured goods for raw materials is, of course, typical of the pattern of trade between a metropolitan country and a colony, a pattern which, over the last centuries, has been a major factor in impoverishing great areas of the earth and delaying the economic development of their peoples. Abba Ebban called for a replication of this old pattern in the Middle East when he declared at the United Nations that Israel aspired to a relationship with the Arab countries "akin to the relationship between the United States and the Latin American countries."[6]

The persistence of the Arab boycott prevented the imposition of this pattern between 1948 and 1967. Cut off from the lucrative Arab markets and requiring large outlays for military expenditures against the Arabs and consumer goods for its settler society, the Israeli economy was kept alive by massive infusions of foreign capital, particularly U.S. capital. Most of this capital was not invested in the expectation of profit, but either donated for philanthropic reasons by individuals or for reasons of geopolitical interest by the U.S. government.[7]

Israel's conquests in the 1967 June War, though they hardly ended Israel's dependence on foreign capital, "radically modified" the isolation of Israel which the Arab boycott had imposed, in the words of David Horowitz, former governor of the Bank of Israel.[8] Two basic Zionist positions emerged on the question of exploitation of the occupied areas, a possibility opened up by the aggression of June 1967. (In addition, of course, there was the opposition of the small but struggling anti-Zionist forces in Israel.) The clearest Zionist opponent of exploitation of the occupied areas has been the secretary general of the Histadrut, Yitzhak Ben Aharon. In February, 1973 he shocked a Labor Party Secretariat meeting by declaring:

I do not know whether the territories that we hold are bargaining cards or perhaps embers burning away our foundations. Without being an extreme Marxist, I must say it's very sweet building Zionism with Arab labor, to build cities of our economy and enjoy it. We shall soon hear that anyone who does not want to get rich on the work of the Arabs from the territories questions the realization of Zionism and holds back redemption and development.[9]

Ben Aharon, defending "the basic values of labour Zionism" and opposing exploitation of the occupied areas, reflects a certain tendency in his economic base, the public and 'labor' sectors of the economy. These sectors have developed not on the basis of profitability but of transfer of foreign capital to Israel, and the labor bureaucracy, because of the economic basis of its historical development, is heavily imbued with the ideology of 'Hebrew labor.' The adherents of exploitation of the occupied areas are rooted particularly in the private sector, with the obvious appeal that cheap labor and the markets of minimally industrialized areas would have for capital. Ben Aharon has coupled his attacks on the exploitation of the occupied areas with a critique of the Israeli government's economic policies, which have led to the growth of private capital since 1967 and to the emergence of a new class of millionaires.[10]

Ben Aharon's most influential opponent has been Moshe Dayan. Even though Dayan had to leave the government in the aftermath of the 1973 war, the policies he developed for the military administration of the occupied areas are still being implemented. Dayan put forth the concept of the "economic integration" of the occupied areas[11] and advocated the free entrance of workers from the occupied areas to the labor markets of Israel, as well as the establishment of a virtual "common market" between Israel and the occupied areas, in which the West Bank and Gaza would export labor power and certain crops and industrial products for the use of Israeli manufacturers and consumers, and would, in turn, with customs barriers and regulations limiting imports from countries other than Israel, provide Israeli manufacturers with an important and conveniently located market.

As the Israeli Ministry of Defense declared in a report on the occupation: "The areas are a supplementary market for Israeli goods on the one hand, and a source of factors of production, especially unskilled labor, on the other."[12]

In examining Israeli colonial exploitation of the West Bank and Gaza, the expropriation of land and settlement by Israelis will not be discussed. This process has, of course, some economic effects, but at least at this time, it is primarily a political, social and military factor. By policy these settlements eschew exploitation of Palestinian labor, in order to better accomplish their political and military purposes.

This study will first examine the effects of Israeli occupation on the foreign trade of the occupied areas, then on labor, on the development of agriculture and industry, and finally on various economic classes in the West Bank and Gaza.

Foreign Trade

The occupied areas, if present trends continue, may soon be Israel's principal foreign market. In 1974 they absorbed $304.4 million of Israeli exports, only marginally less than the United States, historically the largest single foreign market for Israeli products, which purchased $305.6 million of Israeli exports.[13] Israel's exports to the occupied areas have been increasing each year since 1967, not only in absolute terms, but also relative to Israel's total exports. (See Table 1.)

Table 1: Israeli Exports to the Occupied Areas in Relation to Total Israeli Exports, 1967-74
(in $U.S. thousand current prices)

Year	Total Exports	Exports to Occupied Areas	Occupied Areas % of Total
1967	569,000	14,547	3
1968	690,062	50,843	7
1969	797,240	67,930	9
1970	852,587	73,852	9
1971	1,059,982	102,373	10
1972	1,282,020	137,048	10
1973	1,647,490	188,500	11
1974	2,129,214	304,355	14

Source: Computed from statistics in Israel Central Bureau of Statistics, *Statistical Abstract of Israel*, 1975.

The occupied areas thus help to alleviate one of Israel's most pressing economic problems — and one very much contingent upon the special nature of the Zionist state — its negative balance of trade. In 1974, for example, Israel's imports exceeded its exports by $2.5 billion (not including trade with the occupied areas), for a balance of trade deficit of $732 per capita; trade with the occupied areas decreased this deficit by $200 million, or 8 percent, to $672 per capita.[14] Israel's balance of trade problem stems primarily from the massive import of arms, which it requires to maintain itself in contradiction to the interests of the people of the region. It also derives from the import of great quantities of consumer goods, important to Israel's efforts to maintain a high standard of living for part of the population so as to attract and retain immigrants, and from the recession in the world capitalist economy, the fluctuations in which affect Israel quite acutely because of the intimate links between Zionism and imperialism.[15]

In the years since the onset of occupaton, Israel has dominated the foreign trade of the occupied areas to an ever-increasing extent, as Tables 2 and 3 show. Whereas only a decade ago the Arab boycott kept the occupied areas isolated from Israel, today 90 per cent of the imports to the occupied areas come from Israel and two-thirds of its exports are marketed in Israel.

In 1974 the occupied areas exported IL 454 million worth of goods to Israel, over 80 percent of its industrial products. These industrial exports, including construction materials, textiles, clothing and furniture, according to a study by the Bank of Israel "consist largely of sub-contracted processed goods."[16] Such exports do not represent the production of independent industry, but rather the completion of certain phases of the process of production in the occupied areas by workshops subordinate to Israeli industry.

Agricultural exports to Israel include crops for Israeli industry, like tobacco, sesame, sugar beets, grapes and other produce for Israeli canneries, as well as vegetables and fruits out of season in Israel for consumers. The production of crops for Israeli industry required changes in the agricultural production of the West Bank, which was one of the aims of the military government. Between 1967 and 1971, sale of produce from the West Bank and Gaza was restricted in Israeli markets; Israeli supervision teams at checkpoints permitted only those amounts of produce to cross the green line which were judged not to create surpluses and harm the interests of Israeli producers. In 1971, however, most restrictions were lifted: those on grapes, dates and sardines from Gaza are still in force.

Imports from Israel, which are about triple the volume of exports of goods to Israel, have flooded the markets of the West Bank and Gaza. Israel has protected its export market in the occupied areas by imposing regular Israeli customs duties on all imports to the West Bank and Gaza from all countries except Israel. Moreover, some industrial products are forbidden to be imported via Jordan, allegedly because they are difficult to examine at the border for security purposes.[17] The imports from Israel are predominantly industrial products, including basic foodstuffs, like flour, sugar and rice which were previously imported through Jordan, as well as textiles, electrical appliances and vehicles. (The possession of consumer goods has increased significantly: in 1967, for example, 3.3 percent of the households in Gaza owned televisions, and 1.8 percent of the households in the West Bank. By 1974, the figures had risen to 19.1 percent and 20.5 percent respectively.)[18]

The occupied areas also import from Israel a large quantity of

Table 2: Imports and Exports of the Occupied Areas
(in IL millions, current prices)

	1968	1969	1970	1971	1972	1973	1974
IMPORTS							
From Israel							
Agricultural produce	49.1	38.2	58.1	65.7	92.6	143.6	199.8
Industrial products	138.3	216.6	232.8	318.8	488.3	659.4	1,139.6
Total	187.4	254.8	290.9	383.9	580.9	803.0	1,339.4
From Jordan							
Agricultural produce	13.3	17.0	5.2	5.0	4.0	4.2	3.4
Industrial products	4.9	7.9	7.7	9.0	15.1	12.6	18.6
Total	18.2	24.9	12.9	14.0	19.1	16.8	22.0
From other countries							
Agricultural produce	23.7	26.8	30.9	31.3	22.7	17.0	19.8
Industrial products	15.4	10.9	13.6	34.2	60.9	56.1	116.2
Total	39.1	37.7	44.5	71.5	83.6	73.1	136.0
TOTAL IMPORTS	244.7	317.4	348.3	469.6	683.6	829.9	1,497.4
EXPORTS							
To Israel							
Agricultural produce	19.2	11.4	16.9	21.1	26.4	65.3	81.9
Industrial products	34.4	40.9	56.3	92.6	144.6	214.9	372.0
Total	53.6	52.3	73.2	113.7	171.0	280.2	453.9
To Jordan							
Agricultural produce	26.3	29.7	31.6	29.6	59.5	44.5	84.8
Industrial products	28.0	39.3	28.6	51.0	61.6	40.8	85.0
Total	54.3	69.0	60.2	80.6	121.1	85.3	169.8
To other countries							
Agricultural produce	15.4	20.8	23.5	54.6	57.1	57.5	56.9
Industrial products	0.9	1.3	1.4	2.0	1.9	1.8	2.8
Total	16.3	22.1	24.9	56.0	59.0	59.3	59.7
TOTAL EXPORTS	124.2	143.4	158.3	250.9	351.1	424.8	683.4

Sources: Israel Central Bureau of Statistics, *Quarterly Statistics of the Administered Areas* (December 1974) and *Statistical Abstract of Israel 1975.*

Table 3: Imports and Exports of the Occupied Areas By Origin and Destination, 1968-74 (% of Total)

	1968	1969	1970	1971	1972	1973	1974
IMPORTS							
from Israel	75.7	80.0	83.6	81.7	85.0	89.9	89.2
from Jordan	7.7	8.4	3.7	3.0	2.8	1.9	1.5
from other countries	16.6	11.6	12.7	15.2	15.2	8.2	9.1
EXPORTS							
to Israel	42.2	33.9	43.3	45.2	48.7	66.0	66.4
to Jordan	43.1	50.1	40.0	32.1	34.4	20.1	24.8
to other countries	14.6	15.9	19.5	22.5	16.8	13.8	8.7

agricultural produce, including grains, fruit and vegetables, and are now actually less self-sufficient in food supply, despite the increase in agricultural production, than they were in 1967, an obvious effect of Israeli efforts to tailor the production of farms in the West Bank and Gaza to the needs of the Israeli market rather than to the food requirements of the people of the regions.

The deficit in the occupied areas' balance of trade with Israel amounted to IL885.5 million in 1974. This huge deficit is financed by the sale of the labor power of the Palestinian residents of the occupied areas in Israel; the wages earned by the West Bank and Gaza residents in Israel have now become the dominant element in the credits of the occupied areas in the balance of payments with Israel, 60 percent in 1973. These wages are increasing in absolute terms, and relative to the gross national product of the occupied areas (see Table 4), an indication of how heavily the total economy of the West Bank and Gaza now depends on the workers who are employed in Israel.

Table 4: Wages Earned in Israel by Residents of the Occupied Territories in Relation to the Gross National Product of These Territories, 1968-73 (In IL millions)

Year	Wages Earned In Israel	GNP*	Wages as % of GNP
1968	12	556	2
1969	52	680	8
1970	111	687	16
1971	210	1005	21
1972	406	1582	25
1973	609		30+

*GNP at factor prices.
+estimated.
Sources: Arie Bregman, *Economic Growth in the Administered Areas*, (Bank of Israel, Research Department), p. 91; *Statistical Abstract of Israel*, various years.

While trade with Israel dominated the market of the West Bank and Gaza, trade with Jordan, via the "open bridges" is very significant. The occupied areas export agricultural produce, particularly citrus, and industrial products, mostly processed agricultural goods like olive oil and dairy products. It imports far smaller quantities of goods from Jordan in return. The "open bridges" policy, under which Israel allows the movement of goods and people across the Jordan River bridges, began informally as a means of providing a market for West Bank agriculture without eroding the prices in Israel, where products from the West Bank would have undersold Israeli produce by approximately 25 percent in 1967.[19] This policy achieves three basic benefits for the Israeli government. First, it weakens the Arab boycott, by using the West Bank as an entrepot in which Israeli and Arab trade can furtively mix. Second, it maintains economic links between the West Bank, especially some of the notables who are major exporters, and Jordan, and supports political relations between that class and the Hashemite regime. Third, it aids Israel economically, by providing a source of hard currency, the Jordanian dinar.

The Israeli government offers export incentives to exporters of industrial products who convert their Jordanian dinars into Israeli pounds; rates announced in August, 1970, for example, offered incentives of about 23 cents to the dollar for export of shortening; and for soap, candles, alcoholic beverages and plastic, about 30 cents to the dollar.[20] These incentives increase the number of dinars in the hands of the Israeli government. From exports, transfers by the Jordanian government to civil servants and others, the spending of summer visitors (who are said to average $250 each)[21] and private transfers, the Israeli government obtains significant amounts of dinars. Official conversions between 1968 and 1973 reached JD 23 million.[22]

Labor

The occupied areas have become a source of scores of thousands of workers for the most menial, miserable and poorly paid jobs in Israel. Each morning these workers leave their homes in Gaza and the West Bank to face a day of hard work and racial discrimination; their labor goes not to build a national economy of their own, but to augment the economy of the colonial power which oppresses them — this is the central fact of the economics of occupation.

The number of residents of the occupied areas working in Israel grew from 5,000 in September, 1968 to 68,700 in 1974. This figure represented about a quarter of all the residents of the occupied areas employed in work and, as Table 5 shows, some 35 percent of employees from the occupied areas. (The statistics for "employees" give a clearer indication of the working class, since "employed persons" includes those engaged in work for profit as well as for wages, such as tens of thousands of farmers and shopkeepers. According to the most recent figures available, there may now be a downward trend in employment of workers from the occupied areas in Israel, due to greater economic activity in the West Bank and Gaza, and to the recession in Israel.[23]

Table 5: Location of Employment of West Bank and Gaza Employees,
1970-74 (in thousands)

	1970	1971	1972	1973	1974
West Bank Employees					
in West Bank	56.5	63.8	71.8	72.9	78.4
in Israel	14.0	25.0	33.4	36.8	40.8
% in Israel	19.8	28.1	31.8	33.6	34.3
Gaza Employees					
in Gaza Strip	35.2	36.4	42.9	46.1	48.1
in Israel	5.8	8.1	17.4	22.5	25.7
% in Israel	14.1	18.2	28.8	32.7	34.8
Total Employees **from Occupied Areas**					
in Occupied Areas	91.7	100.2	114.7	119.0	126.5
in Israel	19.8	33.1	50.8	59.3	66.5
% in Israel	17.7	24.9	30.6	33.3	34.5

Source: Based on *Statistical Abstract of Israel, 1975*, tables xxvi/22 and 23.

The channeling of workers from the occupied areas into Israel is a matter of policy of the military government. The Israeli Ministry of Labor operates Labor Exchanges throughout the occupied areas. When the offices opened in December, 1968, they sent 44 percent of the workers who applied to them for jobs to relief and other work in the West Bank and Gaza themselves, but now virtually all of the placements are for work in Israel. The government describes the purpose of the Labor Exchanges as "mainly for the care and organization of the work of the inhabitants in Israel."[24] The Labor Exchanges, according to official estimates, arrange for the employment of about two-thirds of the residents of the West Bank and Gaza who work in Israel. In addition to this employment, called "organized work," there is the "unorganized work" of those who find jobs in Israel through personal initiative or through labor contractors. In "unorganized work," income taxes can be evaded by the employee and, more significantly, the employer can avoid payment of contributions to a number of official social and health benefit funds, which can amount to over 33 percent of the labor costs.[25] Workers in this "unorganized" sector are, of course, vulnerable to the most severe exploitation.

Many people, including some officials of the military government, believe that the estimate of one-third of all workers from the occupied areas in Israel being in "unorganized work" is actually too low: many of these workers cross into Israel by foot, and they have a motive to deny their illegal employment to Israeli censustakers. If this suspicion is correct, all figures for employment in Israel are downwardly biased.

In addition to Labor Exchanges, the Israeli military government uses "vocational training centers" to channel workers from the occupied areas into Israel. These centers offer training, often rather cursory (the construction course is only three months long) in the kinds of work in demand in Israel. In 1973 the Israeli Ministry of Labor reported that of 55,000 workers from the occupied areas then employed in Israel, 15,000 (or 27 percent) were graduates of these Israeli training centers,[26] and many trainees are known to leave the centers for work before graduation. The trainees receive a daily stipend: IL 1.75 for most courses and IL 2.50 for construction (the kind of workers most in demand in Israel, according to the 1971 rates) and a food ration from CARE, a U.S. relief agency which distributes surplus U.S. foods. In 1971/72, 70,000 of these monthly rations were distributed.[27]

Workers from the occupied areas, while constituting about 6 percent of all employed persons in Israel in 1973, played a much more critical role in the construction industry, where they numbered 26 percent of the work force, and in agriculture, where they made up 13 percent of the workers. As Table 6 points out, Palestinian Arab workers in Israel, including both those from the areas occupied in 1967 and those living within the territory seized in 1948, make up a very important segment of the work force in construction, where they hold 44 percent of the jobs, and in agriculture, where they are 29 percent of the workers. Other branches of the Israeli economy, such as public and personal services and banking and finance, rely on workers from the occupied areas to a minimal extent or not at all.

The workers from the occupied areas have played a very important role in the development of the Israeli economy since occupation, allowing the Israeli economy to expand very rapidly during the "boom years," unfettered by a labor shortage in Israel, and proving flexibility for the Israeli economy in the hard times which came in the wake of the October war. The Bank of Israel observed that workers from the occupied areas did not lose their jobs after the October war, as might have been expected of the most oppressed laborers in a contracting economy. The employment figure did decline in the fourth quarter of

1973, to 49,600 from the previous quarter's level of 68,500, but this was temporary; by the second quarter of 1974, the figure had reached a new high of 69,800.)[28] The Bank of Israel's *Annual Report* commented:

> It is precisely a definite deceleration in activity and uncertainty as to developments in the future that makes it more worthwhile to employ workers from the administered areas at low pay and without social benefits or work rights. This, so long as the deceleration in employment does not require the dismissal of workers in significant volume (the increase in employment from the administered areas in Israel occurred in unorganized work; in the number of man-hours per employed there was a decline). Moreover, in contrast to previous years, the rate of the rise of wages of workers from the administered areas (28.5 percent) was lower than it was for Israelis. It transpires that in unskilled, difficult and poorly paid jobs the workers from the administered areas managed to oust marginal Israeli workers (including Israeli Arabs), particularly in view of the fact that, as already mentioned above, some of these found alternative employment and income in the form of army service. Such a "conquest" of a branch involving the ousting of Israelis is particularly striking in the construction branch, in which most of the temporary employment is unorganized. Things have reached such a pass that unskilled jobs have come to be considered the preserve of workers from the administered areas.[29]

Table 6: Composition of Employed Persons in Israel by Branch, 1973

Branch	Total of Employees	% Palestinians from Areas Occupied ...	
		In 1948	In 1967
Construction	131,200	18	26
Industry	281,200	7	4
Agriculture	92,500	16	13
Other	645,000	8	1
TOTAL	1,149,900	9	6

Source: Based on statistics in *Statistical Abstract of Israel 1974* and Bank of Israel, *Annual Report 1973*, table ix/4.

The effects of occupation on the employment of women are not easy to assess. The participation of women in the West Bank and Gaza in work other than unpaid family labor is low. One analyst notes the movement of women in the West Bank into sewing and into packing and cannery jobs formerly held by men.[30] However, the rate of women's participation in the labor force, after rising in 1968-70, fell between 1970 and 1973, and rose again in 1974. The most likely explanation is that between 1970 and 1973, when the statistics were showing a decline in the number of persons employed in agriculture, some women were refraining from work in paid jobs and taking the place of male family members who had left work on their farms for jobs in Israel; probably these unpaid women workers on farms were, through statistical error, not enumerated. In 1974, the number of persons employed in agriculture rose in the statistics, at which point the number of women in the labor force also rose, and their rate of participation as well.[31]

Educated people in Gaza and the West Bank seem to have been especially adversely affected by the impact of occupation employment. The possibilities for employment for educated people are severely limited: Israel takes advantage of the pool of labor in the occupied areas to satisfy its need for unskilled labor, but it does not permit Palestinians from the West Bank and Gaza to compete with Israelis for skilled or professional work. A Bank of Israel study observed that

An analysis of employment rates in correlation with education levels indicates that, unlike the situation among the Jewish population of Israel, the employment rate in the administered areas goes down as the level of education (measured in years of schooling) rises. This may be attributed to the paucity of suitable jobs for educated workers. A similar problem exists among educated non-Jews in Israel [i.e., Palestinians] who have a relatively high unemployment rate.[32]

Workers in Israel from the occupied areas earn, on the average, about half the gross wages earned by Israelis.[33] (These figures refer to employment through the Labor Exchange; some employees in "unorganized work" are even more severely exploited.) In fact, the disparity between wages for Israeli workers and those from the occupied areas is even greater than this figure indicates, because a deduction of approximately 15 percent is made from their wages for various kinds of social and health insurance. For a number of years the government "froze" these deductions in a special account, from which it drew for the expenses of administration in the West Bank and Gaza.[34] Later the employees from the occupied areas were supposed to receive certain health, accident and social benefits but apparently they still do not in fact draw the same benefits available to Israelis.[35] Approximately one-third of the workers, those engaged in "unorganized work," receive no health and social benefits at all. Income tax is also deducted from the wages of those in "organized work," and any others who comply with the law, and paid to the Israeli government.

Furthermore, they have no protection through unions: the unions existing before the 1967 war were banned, and the Histadrut does not accept workers from the occupied areas as members. Even in a workplace with a majority of workers from the West Bank and Gaza, therefore, these workers will not be formally represented in the union committee.

The laborers from the occupied areas, especially agricultural workers from Gaza, are often forced to reside temporarily in Israel, illegally and in inhuman conditions, because the time and cost of transportation to their own residence is excessive. Moshe Dayan has admitted that "In Tel Aviv during the past five years Arabs [working in Israel] have been sleeping in the gutters – why evade this?"[36] The Israeli police have been instructed to take firm measures against "workers from the territories [who] sleep overnight near their work place in cellars of buildings under construction, in the kitchens of restaurants, in orchards and other agricultural areas."[37] Reports in the Israeli press describe "entire families [from Gaza] including children and toddlers sleeping overnight in the chicken houses of Jewish farmers."[38] Some employers lock their employees from the West Bank and Gaza in at night, lest they be found in the streets by the police, and the employer fined heavily. In March 1976, three workers were sleeping in a warehouse at night when a fire broke out; trapped behind lock doors, they died.[39]

No aspect of the economic changes brought about by the occupation has caused greater cultural confusion within Israel than the influx of Palestinian workers. For example, in 1975, the Haifa Labor Council organized a photo competition on the theme of "Man and his work" in which 130 photographers participated. The plan, according to *Maariv*, was to "exhibit the results at a large number of plants during the Hanukkah holiday. Over 1000 photographs were presented by the participants to the selection committee, but, to the great embarrassment of the committee, it appeared that over 70 percent of them showed the Arab laborer at work. Only 300 immortalized the Jewish worker. One of the committee members said, "The only work left for Jewish people to do is to photograph Arab labor in Israel."[40]

The cultural conflict is not merely between racism and humanitarianism, but between two different forms of racism: that which holds that Arabs are not fit to do the work of building Zionism, and only Hebrew labor ought to be employed, and that which maintains that Arabs are in fact precisely fitted to do the hard and dirty work of Zionist society. An interesting example of this conflict on a popular level is the contrast between two letters which appeared in the Israeli press. The first writer expressed his objections in the early days of occupation to Prime Minister Golda Meir's hesitation to permit workers from the West Bank and Gaza to be employed in Israel:

> If Mrs. Meir wants to see Hebrew workers sweating away on hot summer days, if it gives her pleasure, this is her own business. But it cannot become the national criterion on which to convince the public that we should not integrate the economy of the West Bank . . .
>
> Every Jewish mother wants her son to finish high school and university and to become a chemist, technician, engineer, or at least a trained plumber. Who is training the young people of today for the simple tasks, carrying buckets of cement or asphalt for road making? In the course of time we shall in any case need Arab workers for building agriculture and even industry. Immigrants are more and more people whose professions are far from these simple tasks.[41]

The second letter was written by a worried woman to Moshe Dayan, then published in the press:

> Both I and my husband were born in a moshav in the center of the country. Up until the Six Day War we lived comfortably, worked hard and made an honorable living. Since that war, however, things have changed dramatically, for my husband, a capable man, has become a farm-work contractor.
>
> His work involves no problems: labor is cheap and there is a ready market. Today we have five Arab workers and we have reached the point where no one on the moshav lifts a finger. Nowadays my eldest son refuses even to mow the lawn. "Let Mohammed do it," he says. And to ask him to shift the irrigation pipes or do any manual labor is simply out of the question. My children and the other children of the moshav are, before my very eyes, becoming rich men's sons of a base and disreputable kind, whose work is done by

servants. They do not know how to drive the tractor standing in our yard and they behave as if farm work is beneath their dignity.[42]

Agriculture

The Israeli occupation has had two main effects on the agriculture of the occupied areas: a decline in the number of persons employed in agriculture and a movement away from crops which would contribute to self-sufficiency in food or to export of food to the surrounding Arab region — and toward production of crops for the Israeli market and especially for Israeli industry.

The shift away from employment in the agricultural sector is occuring on the West Bank, where many farmers and agricultural workers have left the land for jobs in Israel. From an estimated 60,000 to 100,000 employed in agriculture before the 1967 war,[43] the number declined to 33,400 in 1973, and rose somewhat to 40,500 in 1974. About 90 percent of the farm land on the West Bank is owned by the farmers themselves, but there are agricultural workers available for hire: the figures for these employees show an especially sharp decline, from 12,200 in 1969 to 7,900 in 1974. (See Tables 7 and 8.)

Table 7: Persons Employed in Agriculture, Number and Percent of Total Persons Employed, 1969-74

	1969	1970	1971	1972	1973	1974
West Bank						
Number*	47.0	45.0	39.9	38.5	33.4	40.5
%	47.0	39,1	34.1	30.7	26.4	29.6
Gaza Strip						
Number*	11.0	19.2	20.2	19.4	20.0	20.2
%	33.0	32.0	33.0	30.5	29.3	27.7

*In thousands of employed.
Source: *Statistical Abstract of Israel*, 1970 and 1975.

Even the Israeli government admits that the increase in employment in Israel has been responsible for the decrease of certain kinds of agricultural production in the West Bank. A report by the Ministry of Defense for 1971/72, for example, states that, "The growth in number of those employed in Israel was among the causes for the liquidation of many herds of sheep and the decrease in production of lamb and goat

Table 8: Employees in Agriculture in the West Bank, Number and
Percent of Total Employees, 1969-74

	1969	1970	1971	1972	1973	1974
Number*	12.2	11.2	10.0	9.8	7.3	7.9
%	24.4	19.8	15.6	13.0	10.0	10.1

*In thousands.
Source: *Statistical Abstract of Israel, 1975*

meat. Similarly milk production was reduced by 6 percent."[44] Moreover, one critic of the Israeli occupation writes that the economic
deformations brought about by the occupation have led to a neglect
of olive culture, one of the most important forms of agriculture on the
West Bank.[45]

The Israeli Ministry of Agriculture, operating under the auspices of
the military government of the occupied areas, has played an active role
in transforming the kinds of crops grown in the West Bank. In 1968-69,
the Ministry of Agriculture drew up guidelines for the West Bank,[46]
which called for the reduction of dependence on trade with Jordan (the
East Bank); although the Israeli government wanted to maintain economic links between the West Bank and Amman via the "open bridges,"
it did not want trade with the East Bank to be crucial to the West
Bank's economy, for then Hussein would have great leverage if he
threatened to close the bridges. To replace certain crops which had
been important in export to the East Bank and surrounding Arab countries, the Ministry of Agriculture planned new crops which would com-
plement Israeli agriculture and be suitable for processing in Israel or
export to Europe.[47]

The Ministry of Agriculture uses a network of agricultural councils,
agronomists and agricultural training agents, and incentives of seeds
and partial subsidies of costs to encourage farmers to plant the new
approved crops rather than the traditional crops.[48] An excellent example
of the effect of this process is the melon crop: before the 1967 war, the
West Bank produced three times as many melons as it consumed,
exporting the rest to the East Bank and other Arab countries. In
1967/68, the West Bank grew 60,000 tons of melons; by 1973/74, the
figure had dropped to 4,200. In fact, in 1973/74, the West Bank was
importing 83 percent of its melons, most of them from Israel and a
small number from the Gaza Strip.[49]

The crops which have increased most are vegetables and potatoes and field crops. Thirty-two percent of the West Bank's vegetable and potato crop is exported, mostly to Israel,[50] either for canning or consumption. The West Bank now grows a significant amount of the cucumbers and tomatoes consumed in Israel. The opening of the Israeli market to West Bank produce in 1971/72 helped to cause a sharp rise in the prices of vegetables in the West Bank itself: the consumer price index for vegetables and fruit leapt to 142.1 in 1971, while the general index was 125.9; and to 177.3 in 1972, while the general index was 148.1. (Base: average July 1968 to June 1969 is 100.0.)[51] Field crops have also expanded, principally because of the expansion of industrial crops for export to Israel, including tobacco, sesame and sugar beets.[52]

The production of mutton, beef and poultry has been hampered by the occupation. The Israeli military administration halted the import of sheep from Jordan, for the stated reason of preventing contagion from sheep disease in Jordan. At the same time, Israeli officials were noting "the trend of many herders to kill off their herds once they shift to working in Israel."[53] Producers of beef and poultry were adversely affected by competition from Israel, where the poultry industry enjoys government subsidies.[54] In the words of a Bank of Israel study: Attempts were made [by Israeli authorities in the occupied areas] to change consumption habits from mutton to turkey and chicken meat through subsidies and price reductions. A high proportion of livestock products — such as chicken and turkey meat, eggs and milk products — is imported from Israel.[55]

Gaza's exports of agricultural produce have been expanding. In 1973/74 Gaza exported 197,000 tons of citrus, 73,000 tons to Jordan and the remainder to Eastern Europe, Western Europe and Israeli industry.[56] In addition Gaza vegetables, some produced under plastic cover in a joint enterprise by an Israeli entrepreneur and a Gaza landowner, are exported.[57]

There has been some increase in technology in the agriculture of the West Bank during the period of occupation: the number of tractors has risen from 147 in 1967 to 1,013 in November 1974.[58]

Industry

Industry in the West Bank and Gaza has not developed significantly during the nine years of occupation. There seem to have been modest increases in the number of persons employed in industry and in the industrial product, but it is difficult to make a statistical comparison with the prewar years because of a lack of data. The structure of industry has remained basically unchanged: small workshops, 90 percent of them employing 10 or fewer workers, 66 percent employing 5 or fewer, using labor intensive methods and concentrated in the processing of agricultural products.[59]

The occupation has had three basic effects on industry: (1) by direct investment; (2) by subcontracting, and (3) by placing constraints on the development of industry.

In October 1972, the Israeli government's Ministerial Economic Committee extended the Law for the Encouragement of Capital Investment to the occupied areas, giving Israeli investors there the same privileges awarded to investors in the "A" priority development areas in Israel itself: low-interest loans, grants and tax exemptions, delays and abatements.[60] In fact, however, Israeli capitalists have been reluctant to take advantage of these opportunities and invest in the West Bank and Gaza because of the political uncertainty and the danger that they would lose their enterprise if the West Bank and Gaza were liberated. An exception to this reluctance is the industrial zone near the Eretz checkpoint between Gaza and Israel. There Israeli entrepreneurs have invested IL 10 million, and employ 500 Gaza residents to produce metal goods, textiles and items of wood and rubber.[61] The owners are reported to be large Israeli corporations, like Koor, and former Israeli military officers and bank managers who served in the occupied areas.[62] On the West Bank an Israeli investor is involved in a joint enterprise in a packing house in Jericho. In general, however, investment is not extensive.

The major way that Israeli industrialists are benefitting from the industrial capacity of the occupied areas is through subcontracting: a large portion of industrial exports of the occupied areas to Israel are actually goods subcontracted by Israeli industry.[63] These subcontracted exports are a disguised form of Israel's quest for cheap labor: produced with high labor intensity, these articles of sewn and knitted clothing, textiles, furniture, mattresses, candy, building blocks for construction and floor tiles are produced to the order of Israeli manufacturers. Usually the work involves only part of the entire process of production. Using this indirect method, Israeli manufacturers can lower the costs of production significantly, since the wage rates in the West Bank and Gaza are even lower than in Israeli factories employing workers from the occupied areas. For example, in 1974 an industrial worker from the West Bank averaged (net) IL23.0 per day if he worked on the West Bank, but IL27.2 in Israel; and an industrial worker from Gaza earned (net) IL27.2 if he worked in Gaza, but IL31.2 if he worked in Israel.[64] In addition, employers in Israel of "organized" labor from the occupied

areas have additional labor costs of contributions to various government health and social funds which amount to about 50 percent of
the employee's net wages.[65]

The subcontracted work does not contribute to the growth of
national industry in the occupied areas. A Bank of Israel study noted
that, "replacement of subcontracting jobs with the full production of
the same products ... would most probably call for measures to
protect at least part of the administered areas' domestic production
from competition by Israeli products — as is common for infant industries."[66] Israel, of course, would not be willing to impose tariffs to
protect the industries of its colonies against competition from Israeli
manufacturers.

This subcontracting could, in the long run, if the occupation and
present economic trends were to continue, have a marked effect on the
composition of products produced by industry in the occupied areas.
The most rapidly growing sectors of industry are those in which subcontracting is extensive: clothing production in the West Bank had a
real annual growth rate of 32 percent (1969-1972), well above the
real annual growth rate of industry in general in that period in the
West Bank (15 percent); and nonmetallic minerals production (which
includes production for Israeli manufacturers of textiles and building
materials) had a real annual growth rate of 40 percent. However, these
branches are both quite small, accounting for only 3 percent and 2
percent respectively of total industrial production in the West Bank.
Food, beverage and tobacco production, the largest sector of industrial production on the West Bank, accounting for 38 percent of production in 1972, had a comparatively small rate of real annual growth, only
8 percent. Olive oil presses, the second largest sector of industrial
production in the region, recorded an annual real growth rate of 22
percent in that period.[67] (The significance of this figure is difficult to
assess: the olive crop is both cyclical in nature, alternating between
good and bad years, and very vulnerable to weather conditions. In that
period in question, olive oil production, which is directly dependent
on the olive crop, is "rising" from a low point at which the immediate
disruptive effects of the June war were still very much a factor, and at
which olive production was disastrously affected by drought.)

It appears then, that the Israeli occupation is tending to push industry in the West Bank away from processing its own agricultural products and toward the completion of certain phases of industrial production for Israeli manufacturers, relying on the import of raw materials or
partially completed goods from Israel, and the export of the materials

back to Israel after the addition of labor to the material.

Certain manufacturers receive subsidies involving significant sums for their exports to Jordan, as mentioned previously. In 1970-1971, nearly three-quarters of these subsidies were awarded to exporters of shortening, soap and oils from Nablus. (See Table 9.)

Table 9: Payments of Incentives for Exports, April 1970-March 1971

District	Product	Amount
Bethlehem	Plastic	IL 187,000
	Beauty Products	170,000
	Alcoholic Beverages	6,000
Ramallah	Paper	210,000
	Chocolate	53,000
	Soap	47,000
Hebron	Scales	1,357
	Steel Wool	1,887
Nablus	Shortening	1,194,000
	Matches	177,000
	Oils	11,000
	Soap	1,146,000
TOTAL		3,215,244

Source: Coordinator of Government Operations in the Administered Territories, Israel Ministry of Defense, *Four Years of Military Administration 1967-1971: Data on Civilian Activities in Judea and Samaria, the Gaza Strip and Northern Sinai,* p. 56.

These export incentives are a subsidy to a small class of industrialists, designed to encourage the maintenance of links with the Hashemite regime and to attempt to win their support of passive acceptance of occupation. However, whatever privileges awarded to this class by the occupying power, there has not been a significant increase in investment in industrial production or in the infrastructure of industry in the area.

The constraints which occupation places on industrialization of the occupied areas are illustrated by the experiences of two concerns: the United Company for Fodder Ltd. in Nablus and the National Textile Company in Beit Jala:

The directors of both enterprises emphasize the sharp competition of the Israeli industries who are technically more advanced and well provided with credits, raw materials and Government support, and noted, in effect, that they are living on borrowed time.

The director-owners of the first enterprise remarked that the raw materials allocated to his company were meagre and they have to buy their needs in the black market. Further he noted that the company has to pay high electricity rates because the occupation authorities collect high fuel prices from the municipality which does not receive any subsidies like those received by the municipalities or enterprises in Israel.

The owner-director of the second enterprise stated that his company buys raw material in Israel and added – in case Israeli industries consume the locally produced cotton then we shall have no raw material. It would be difficult for this company to import raw material from the outside.[68]

Effects on the Population

The people of the occupied areas have withstood the occupation without relatively massive emigration (except for the departure of refugees in 1967 and 1968); the population of the West Bank appears to be increasing at a more rapid rate than during the period of its annexation to Jordan. Population figures still give indications, of course, of emigration of men of working age, presumably for employment abroad, but the Palestinians under occupation are increasing in number, and the West Bank and Gaza are not being depopulated.

It is difficult to compare income, consumption and product with prewar levels, but in general the population of the occupied areas appears to have experienced a rise in standard of living from 1969 to 1973.[69] The sharpest increases in income seem to have been among the big exporters,[70] and workers employed in Israel earned more than those who remained in Gaza or the West Bank. Moreover, some sectors of the economy, notably tourism, never recovered their prewar position.

The economic recession which hit Israel after the 1973 war had a serious impact on the occupied areas. Inflation was very high, reaching 256.5 on the consumer price index (see Table 10). In 1973 and 1974, the residents of the occupied areas experienced a decline in their standard of living.

The most serious effect of the occupation has been the subordination of the economies of the West Bank and Gaza to that of Israel.

Table 10: Consumer Price Index of the Occupied Areas,* 1968-74

Year	Index
1968	100.0
1969	102.0
1970	106.4
1971	120.4
1972	148.1
1973	179.9
1974	256.5

*Base: Average 6/68 to 7/69 is 100.0.
Source: Israel Central Bureau of Statistics.

There is no doubt that when the Israelis entered the West Bank and Gaza Strip they found that the events of the previous twenty years had made their economies vulnerable to colonization. Gaza had been placed in an economically impossible position in 1948: refugees packed the narrow strip far beyond the capacity of its natural resources. The West Bank had suffered economically not only from the effects of the loss of part of Palestine to Zionism, but also from the bias of the Hashemite regime, which discouraged industrialization in the West Bank and favored it in the East Bank.

The principal effect of the occupation on the class structure of the West Bank has been to force a quarter of its employed people into the Israeli proletariat. Many thousands of farmers, artisans, small shopkeepers and herders have left the peasantry and petit bourgeoisie for the working class. The working class now has some 35 percent of its members going daily to jobs in Israel, facing severe racial discrimination. For professionals and educated people, employment opportunities are very limited. In Gaza, where the population is predominantly refugees, the people have found themselves not returning to the land and villages in Palestine, but going by truck and bus each day to do the most menial work of the Zionist economy.

The occupation has had mixed effects on the industrial bourgeoisie of the West Bank, a small class which controls a rather limited and under-developed means of production. The military government has sought to appease certain sectors of this class, especially those with established economic links to the Hashemite Kingdom, by the payment of "export incentives." However, competition from Israeli industry, which raises wages and reduces marketing possibilities, has made the growth of new independent industry all but impossible.

In sum, the occupation has cast the West Bank and Gaza into the form of classical colonies.

Notes

1. David Ben-Gurion, *Israel a Personal History* (New York, 1971), p. 845.

2. Quoted in Sir John Hope Simpson, *Palestine: Report on Immigration, Land Settlement and Development*, British Colonial Office cmd. 3836 (October 1930), p. 53.

3. For a description of the value of the seized property, *see* Don Peretz, *Israel and the Palestine Arabs* (Washington, 1956). For an analysis of the way the labor power of the Palestinians who remained in the Zionist state was used by the Israeli economy – in significant ways a forerunner of the exploitation of the people of the West Bank and Gaza – *see* Yoram Ben-Porath, *The Arab Labor Force in Israel* (Jerusalem, 1966).

4. "U.S. Capital in Socialist Israel," *Fortune*, June 1950, p. 5.

5. *Ibid.*

6. Abba Eban, *Voice of Israel* (New York, 1957), pp. 76 and 111.

7. Sheila Ryan, "Israeli Economic Policy in the Occupied Areas: Foundations of a New Imperialism," *MERIP Reports*, no. 24 (January 1974).

8. David Horowitz, *The Enigma of Economic Growth: A Case Study of Israel* (New York, 1972), p. 20.

9. *Ma'ariv* 2 February 1973, translated in *Israleft News Service*, 15 February 1973.

10. *Davar*, 7 March 1973, translated in *Israleft News Service* (3 April 1973). For a sense of the economic debate in Israel, *see* "The Demographic Problem," *Israel Economist* (September-October 1972). "The Credo of Mr. Ben Aharon," and "An Answer to Ben Aharon's Challenge," *Israel Economist* (December 1972), pp. 298-300.

11. *New York Times*, 3 June, 1969, p. 11; and Abraham S. Becker, *Israel and the Palestinian Occupied Territories: Military-Political Issues in the Debate* (Rand, 1971).

12. Unit for Coordination of Activity in the Administered Areas, Israel Ministry of Defense, *Development and Economic Situation in Judea, Samaria, the Gaza Strip and North Sinai: 1967-1969, A Summary*, October 1970, unpaged.

13. Israel Central Bureau of Statistics, *Foreign Trade Statistics Monthly* 26, no. 12 (December 1975).

14. *Israel Central Bureau of Statistics,* Statistical Abstract of Israel, *1975, pp. 188-9.*

15. *See* the Bank of Israel, *Annual Report*, 1974 (Jerusalem, 1975), p. 4 ff.

16. Arie Bregman, Bank of Israel Research Department, *Economic Growth in the Administered Areas 1968-1973* (Jerusalem, 1975), p. 85.

17. *Ibid.,* p. 88.

18. *Statistical Abstract of Israel 1968*, p. 602, and *Statistical Abstract of Israel 1975*, table xxvi/17.

19. Ann Mosley Lesch, *Israel's Occupation of the West Bank: The First Two Years* (Master's Thesis, Columbia University, 1969).

20. Coordinator of Government Operations in the Administered Territories, Israel Ministry of Defense, *Four Years of Military Administration, 1967-1971: Data on Civilian Activities in Judea and Samaria, the Gaza Strip and Northern*

194   *The Colonial Exploitation of Occupied Palestine*

Sinai p. 56.

21. Bank of Israel, Research Department, *The Economy of the Administered Areas*, 1970 (Jerusalem, 1971), p. 31.

22. Bregman, *Economic Growth*, p. 13.

23. *Israeli Economist*, June 1976, p. 20.

24. Coordinator of Government Operations in the Adminsitered Territories, Israel Ministry of Defense, *The Administered Territories 1971/72: Data on Civilian Activities in Judea and Samaria, the Gaza Strip and Northern Sinai*, p. 97.

25. Bregman, *Economic Growth*, p. 39 and elsewhere.

26. *Israel Economist*, 1973, p. 262.

27. Ryan, "Israeli Economic Policy," pp. 13 and 19.

28. Israel Central Bureau of Statistics, *Quarterly Statistics of the Administered Areas*, December 1974, p. 34.

29. Bank of Israel, *Annual Report 1974*, pp. 300-301.

30. Vivian A. Bull, *The West Bank: Is It Viable?* (Lexington, Mass. 1975) p. 124.

31. *Statistical Abstract of Israel 1975*, table xxvi/18.

32. Bregman, *Economic Growth*, pp. 34-5.

33. *Statistical Abstract, 1975*.

34. *Israel Economist*, January 1973, pp. 13-14; Bull, *West Bank*, p. 122.

35. *Maariv*, 1 June 1973, translated in *Israel Mirror* 14 July 1973.

36. *Haaretz*, 30 July 1972, translated in *Israleft*, 13 September 1972.

37. *Haaretz*, 3 August 1972, translated in *Israleft*, 13 September 1972.

38. *Yediot Aharonot*, 9 August 1972, translated in *Israleft*, 13 September 1972.

39. *Yediot Aharonot*, March 1976.

40. *Maariv*, 10 October 1975, translated in *Israel Mirror*, 28 November 1975.

41. *Haaretz*, 15 May 1969, translated in ISRACA, no. 2 (June-July 1969), p. 9.

42. *Yediot Aharonot*, 6 October 1972, translated in *Israleft*, 6 November 1972.

43. Bregman, *Economic Growth*, p. 58.

44. Israel Ministry of Defense, *Administered Areas 1971/71*, p. 5.

45. Emile Touma, "The Question of the Economic Viability of the Palestine State," *Information Bulletin*, Communist Party of Israel, (October-November 1974), pp. 93-94.

46. Israeli Ministry of Agriculture, *Judea and Samaria: Agricultural Development Plans for 1969-1970*, (no date).

47. *Ibid.*

48. Ryan, "Israeli Economic Policy," p. 14.

49. Coordinator of Government Operations in the Administered Territories, Israel Ministry of Defense, *Three Years of Military Government 1967-1970: Civilian Activities in Judea, Samaria, the Gaza Strip and Norther Sinai*, (June 1970), p. 15; *Statistical Abstract of Israel 1975*, tables xxvi, 26 and 27.

50. *Statistical Abstract of Isreal 1975*, table xxvi/27.

51. *Statistical Abstract of Israel 1975*, table xxvi/13.

52. Bregman, *Economic Growth*, p. 55.

53. Bank of Israel, Research Department, *The Economy of the Administered Areas* 1971, p. 27.

54. *Ibid.*

55. Bregman, *Economic Growth*, p. 57.

56. *Statistical Abstract of Israel 1975*, table xxvi/27.

57. Eliyahu Kanovsky, *The Economic Impact of the Six Day War* (New York, 1970), p. 180.

58. Bull, *West Bank*, p. 65; *Quarterly Statistics of the Administered Areas*, December 1974, Table 1/5.

59. Bregman, *Economic Growth*, p. 53.

60. *Haaretz*, 9 October 1972, translated in *Israleft*, 18 October 1972, p. 8.

61. *Israel Economist*, September 1973, p. 249.

62. *Haaretz*, 16 June 1972, translated in *Know*, 31 August 1972, p. 5.

63. Bregman, *Economic Growth*, p. 85.

64. *Statistical Abstract of Israel 1975*.

65. Bregman, *Economic Growth*, p. 39.

66. *Ibid.*, p. 85.

67. *Ibid.*, p. 64.

68. Touma, "Economic Viability," p. 93. (He cites *Al Fajr*, 28 August 1974 and 4 September 1974).

69. *Statistical Abstract of Israel 1975*, table xxvi/8.

70. Bank of Israel, *Economy of the Administered Areas 1971*, p. 15.

Part Three

ZIONISM AND THE ARAB WORLD

11 THE JEWS OF IRAQ IN THE NINETEENTH CENTURY: A CASE STUDY OF SOCIAL HARMONY

Walid Khadduri

It has become a popular notion in Western literature to point out the Jewish communities in the Arab countries as an example of an alienated minority, suffering both socially and economically. A careful study of the historical record shows, however, that the situation was totally different from what the Zionist information media have put out during the past four decades. And, as a study of the Iraqi Jewish community indicates, the conditions and standards, as well as the progress of the local community was similar to that of the other segments of society, and if it were not for the propaganda agitation of the Zionists during the first half of the twentieth century, the Jewish community of Iraq would have evolved in a similar pattern as the other social groups in the country.

Background

To study social communities in Iraq prior to the rise of the modern state, it is necessary to understand both the inner dynamics of those groupings, and also their relationship to Islam, to the Ottoman ruling authorities, and to inter-group dynamics existent at the time.

The basic legal premise underlying the relationship of an Islamic government to its non-Muslim communities (dhimmis) is that Muslim laws are concerned with the affairs of Muslims, while relationships among the dhimmis are governed separately within each community according to its own canons and institutions. The religious head of a group is responsible to the Muslim caliph, and the individual dhimmi's status is derived from his membership in a protected community. This system came into existence during the Muslim empires, survived them, and continued throughout the Ottoman period.

As part of the contractual relationship between the Muslim caliph and the dhimmis, the latter were granted freedom of worship, travel, residence and education. Their obligation was to pay a special tax for the protection they received and not to assist the enemies of the state. Certain social restrictions were imposed, but they were often left unimplemented and were freely violated. An example of this from the

'Abbasid Empire was the violation of the rule that no new non-Muslim houses of worship were to be built. Rabbi Benjamin ben Tudela, who visited Baghdad in 1168, stated that there were twenty-eight synagogues at that time. None of these could have been built before the beginning of Muslim rule, as Baghdad was founded by the Caliph al-Mansur in 762. Similar evidence of legal laxity in other cities is abundant.

At the zenith of 'Abbasid rule in Baghdad, philosophers, scholars and scientists of all faiths contributed to a flourishing civilization. Jewish merchants, especially the Radhaniya group, played a key role in the international trade of the Empire. When Arab rule declined and tribal-military invasions destroyed the bases of agriculture, commerce and public administration, all communities, without exception, suffered.

Ottoman rule (1534-1914) was punctuated by foreign invasions and local armed conflicts. Chronic instability resulted in stagnation: no public social programs were introduced until the nineteenth century, and Istanbul followed a policy of sheer neglect toward the Iraqi provinces. For example, the reforms, Tanzimat, of the mid-nineteenth century were applied in Iraq several decades after being introduced in Istanbul. However, the Ottoman Empire recognized the protected status of the dhimmis. As early as 1326, the Jewish community (millet), was granted *firmans* permitting Jews to build synagogues and schools and granting them freedom of travel, occupation and residence. At a time when Jews suffered social and religious persecution in Europe, many in the Ottoman Empire were diplomats, wealthy merchants and craftsmen.[1] Nevertheless, despite the legal and institutional reforms of the late nineteenth century, social and economic processes remained backward in the Empire as a whole, and particularly in Iraq. A few Iraqis in the major cities and towns lived prosperous lives, but the majority of the population, regardless of creed, continued to suffer as a result of centuries of economic decadence, exploitation and poor administration. Most Ottoman administrators were ignorant of the language and conditions of the territory. Modern education was limited to the sons of notables, while others received only traditional religious education. The Ottoman governors controlled the local population through a combination of military force and by coopting the notables and the religious elites into their entourage. Natural disasters contributed to the general backwardness of the area; some sixty percent of the inhabitants of Baghdad were killed in the Spring of 1831, when both a flood and a plague attacked the city during the same week.

Social Conditions

The history of the Jews of Iraq is ancient, dating from 586 B.C., if not earlier. From thence onward and throughout the Islamic Empire, Jews played a significant intellectual, religious and commercial role. Well-known accomplishments during this period and before the advent of the Ottomans in the fourteenth century include the academies at Sura, Nehadra and Pumbaditha, the Babylonic Talmud, the offices of the Exilarch and the Geonim, the works of the Responsa, and religious missions to Egypt, North Africa, South Asia and the Far East.

Records concerning the conditions of Iraqi society between the fourteenth and nineteenth centuries are sparse. However, accounts by travellers as early as the seventeenth century describe Baghdad as a town of 20,000 to 30,000 houses, 200 to 300 of them inhabited by Jews. More reliable figures are supplied by travellers in the late nineteenth century, who estimated the total Jewish community of Baghdad at 50,000. This figure corresponds to the census carried out by the British occupation authorities in 1920 which estimated the total population of Iraq at 2,849,282, including 87,484 Jews. Of the latter, 50,000 lived in Baghdad, 15,000 in the North and 7,000 in Basra.[2]

The Jews of Iraq formed an integral part of society. Their cultural and social practices were those of the population at large:

> It was a completely Arabized community . . . (The Jews) spoke Arabic among themselves, introduced Arabic into their religious services, and wrote Arabic in Hebrew characters for their correspondence. Their social life was that of Arabs, their cuisine . . . superstitions, even . . . harem.[3]

In comparison to Jews living in other societies in the East, they fared well economically. Rabbi Israel Benjamin, who travelled the area extensively during the middle of the nineteenth century, found the Baghdadi Jewish community well established: "In no other place in the east have I found my Israelith brethren in such perfectly happy circumstances, and so worthy of their condition."[4] As with other social groups the majority of moderate-income Jews lived in their own sector of Baghdad while their richer counterparts lived in elaborate houses by the Tigris alongside Muslim and Christian notables and Turkish officials. Thus, the socioeconomic conditions of Iraqi Jews differed from one city quarter to another as well as from one area of the country to another, and were closely correlated to their choice of profession; generally they were more frequently engaged in trade, less frequently in agriculture.

Trade was concentrated in central and southern Iraq, particularly in Baghdad and Basra, where a large portion of the Jewish community participated in commerce. Quite a few families engaged in international trade and opened commercial houses in Persia, India and England. The majority were small retail merchants in major cities, and also throughout the rural areas, except for certain districts of the Middle Euphrates.

In the North, there were a few Jewish tradesmen among the Kurdish tribes and serving as advisers to aghas and princes. Most however, were in agriculture. There were also some landlords, whose peasants were themselves Jewish, but the majority lived in the isolated mountains at the same socioeconomic level as other peasants in Iraq. They were heavily armed, paid an annual sum to stronger tribes for protection, and rendered services, such as digging canals and building houses, to their landlords.

Jewish landlords existed elsewhere in Iraq, especially in Basra, Hilla and Diyala, where they owned date groves, grain farms and fruit gardens. In smaller towns, such as Anna and Hit, some Jews were both merchants and landowners.

Members of the Jewish community were also engaged in the primitive industries that existed at the time: textile, silk and leather manufacturing. Except for the silk exports from Kurdistan, their products were consumed locally.

Political Leadership

Throughout this period, when the central administration was weak or nonexistent, communal groups in Baghdad were under the direct political and religious influence of certain families, who retained their power through ancestry, respect for their scholarship and wealth. Because of their small numbers and special privileges, such as exemption from taxes and military service, these families competed with one another and intrigued among themselves. Often a family was connected with a particular governor and as his fortunes fluctuated, so did theirs. Their relationship to the communities they represented was despotic and much corruption and injustice occurred. Becoming part of a governor's entourage, they fulfilled his wishes and shared in the wealth he distributed. The contributions of these families to religious and scientific scholarship were insignificant. The schools they operated graduated religious functionaries, reactionaries in their outlook toward both the spiritual and secular worlds.

The hakham bashi was the leading religious representative of the

Jewish community. The hakham bashi of Istanbul was the representative of all Jews in the Empire in the Council of State. He was responsible for apportioning and collecting taxes from the community and for confirming the appointment of lower hakhamim. In Baghdad, the hakham bashi was selected by representatives of the local community and confirmed by the governor as well as by the hakham bashi of Istanbul. However, in time, he became isolated from the community and served as the governor's lackey rather than as the community's representative. This led to a major conflict within the Jewish community of Baghdad in 1879. The hakham bashi at the time, Sassoon bin Elijah Smooha, had held his office for thirty-five years and enjoyed the support of the local governors and the hakham bashi of Istanbul. One of the community's grievances against him was embezzlement of the military tax. A majority of the Jewish community, including the leading lower hakhamim, addressed a petition to the governor requesting his removal. The governor felt forced to comply, despite his friendship with Smooha, but the hakham bashi of Istanbul reversed the decision. However, Smooha's return to office was brief. His behaviour caused the community to cable Istanbul and, finally, the Sultan himself intervened and forced Smooha's dismissal. By that time the conflict had left a major division within the Baghdadi Jewish community.[5]

In addition to the hakham bashi, the power structure within the Jewish community included a Beth-Din, which adjudicated disputes within the community, while the hakham bashi determined punishments. The Beth-Din was usually made up of members of wealthy mercantile Jewish families. A single family would often, in effect, inherit all these positions for centuries.

A nasi ("noble") was the secular representative of the community and was often the wealthiest of the merchants. He was also the treasurer or financial adviser of the governor. Community financial matters, mainly tax collection, were administered by a millet cha'ush. He was elected by the community, as was a body of ten notables who supervised the educational and social programs of the community. During the seventeenth, eighteenth, and early nineteenth centuries, the nasi of Baghdad, rather than the hakham bashi, held effective political power over the community. The Sassoon family inherited this post generation after generation. They had close ties with Istanbul. When Daud Pasha, the last of the Mamluk governors, attained power in Baghdad in 1817, he had to rely on the Sassoons in order to receive a *firman* from the Sultan. However, this particular intervention created enemies for the Sassoons within the governor's entourage, which ultimately led to the migration of a branch of the family to India and later to England. In the decades that followed the Tanzimat, the office of nasi continued to be held by the wealthiest merchant in town, but political power reverted to the hakham bashi.[6]

Religion

The Jews of Iraq were all rabbinical and adhered completely to the Talmud. With a decline of scholarship within their community and the country in general during the Ottoman period, religious practice became heavily concerned with ritual, especially in the rural areas.

Certain contacts with foreign Jews were maintained and influenced the religious practices and beliefs of Iraqi Jews. Kabbalism and mysticism were particularly widespread in the Jewish communities of Eastern Europe, Turkey and Safed, Palestine. It was with these groups that Iraqi Jewish contacts were especially strong, and their religious publications were familiar in Baghdad. Furthermore, Hakham Yusif Hayim, one of the chief spiritual leaders in Baghdad from 1859 to 1909, encouraged the spread of these practices. As a learned and wealthy man, a great speaker, and the author of thirty-two books of homilies, commentaries, kabbalistic prayers, poems, liturgy and responsa, the hakham had a large following.[7]

Changes in the Nineteenth Century

The introduction of the Tanzimat in the nineteenth century transformed the official status of the dhimmis. The Hatti-Humayun of 1856, and to a lesser extent the Hatti-Sherif of 1839, granted equal citizenship and rights to all the people of the Empire, including assurances of security for life and property, admission to civil and military systems, equal taxation, freedom of worship, special and mixed courts and equality on the witness stand. The communal system was retained only in that religious authorities continued to control civil matters such as marriage and inheritance.

The Constitution of 1876 granted representation to property holders in local, regional and imperial administrative councils and legislatures. These new institutions had great symbolic importance, even if those elected were handpicked by the authorities and their functions limited in scope. Jewish representatives included Minahayim Danyal, one of three Baghdadi representatives to the first parliament of 1877; Sassoon Hisqail, who held that seat in the parliament of 1909; Yusif Kurqui, a member of the Administrative Council of Baghdad in 1873; and Yusif Shantub, a member of the council in 1888. All were wealthy merchants, except for Sassoon Hisqail, who was an official at the Ministry of Commerce. He was later to become the first finance minister of Iraq and held that post for a number of years.

In the last decades of the nineteenth century, Jewish education began to benefit from foreign assistance, not only from the wealthy Iraqi-Jewish communities in India, but also through direct establishment of modern primary and secondary schools by the Alliance Israelite Universelle de Paris and the Anglo-Jewish Association of London. These schools preceded both the military and civilian public systems which began in 1870, and graduated some sixty percent of all the secondary students in Iraq before the turn of the century. The first boys' school was established by the Alliance and the Anglo-Jewish Association in 1865. A girls' school, the first in Iraq, was established in 1897. Among non-Jewish Iraqis, only the sons of notables and a few military cadets were able to receive modern education during the same period. An educational census was taken in Baghdad in 1913. The results are revealed in Table 1.[8]

Table 1: Schools in Baghdad in 1913

		No. of Students	
Number	Type	Male	Female
38	Official primary	1525	300
13	Official secondary (both military and civilian)	2705	–
6	Ja'fariya private	860	–
12	Christian private	995	918
39	Jewish private	4791	1095

Source: Abdal-Razzaq Al-Hillali, *History of Education in Iraq During the Ottoman Regime, 1638-1917* (Baghdad, 1959).

Despite the influence of Western Europe on the Iraqi-Jewish educational system, the intellectual work of the community continued to be limited to religious subjects. Books and newspapers available during the nineteenth century were mainly from Poland and Russia. The first Jewish printing house, established in 1855, published mainly books on religious topics, particularly kabbalism and the zohar. Exceptions included an Arabic translation of Rabbi Benjamin bin Tudela's twelfth-century travels and some works by Maimonides. Two journals appeared: *ha-Dober* (1868-1870) in Hebrew and *Jeshurun* (1910) in Arabic and Hebrew. They dealt with affairs of the local community.

Throughout this period, very few instances of tension between the

Jewish community and other groups have been recorded. The few incidents that did occur were minor. For example, in 1860 a conflict arose when the authorities, for an undetermined reason, stopped the pilgrimage of Jews to the tomb of Esekiel, located a short distance from Baghdad. Upon the intervention of the Anglo-Jewish Association with the Sultan, the matter was settled. In 1889, a shrine outside Baghdad called Nabi Yusha, one of the burial grounds of the Baghdad rabbis, was sold to a Muslim in the course of a dispute between the former hakham bashi, Sassoon Smooha, and the millet cha'ush. Later that year one of the rabbis died and a conflict arose as to the ownership of the grounds. The hakham bashi and a few other persons were imprisoned. Contacts were again established with the Anglo-Jewish Association and the Jewish Board of Deputies in London, who in turn contacted the British ambassador in Istanbul. As a result, the grounds were returned to the community, despite the original sale; the hakham bashi and his followers were released and the governor of Baghdad was dismissed by the Sultan.[9]

The social conditions of Iraqi Jewry continued to prosper throughout the first half of the twentieth century. Education flourished among its young. The number of students multiplied; they attended public institutions as well as private Jewish schools. In the latter, their number increased from 5,886 male and female students in 1913 to 11,435 in 1935.[10] The number of synagogues in Baghdad increased from 29 in 1915 to 41 in 1936.[11] The community prospered economically as well, especially with the advent of the new state and the increase in commercial activity. According to a report published by Joseph Schechtman of the Jewish Agency, commercial activity in Iraq before World War II was estimated as follows: Imports, 95 percent in Jewish hands; contracts, 90 percent Jewish-controlled; exports, 10 percent in Jewish hands.[12]

The basic disturbing element took place with the Zionization of Palestine and the infiltration of the Jewish Agency in the ranks of the Iraqi-Jewish community during the forties. Their agents organized Zionist cells, laid the grounds for the immigration at the latter part of the decade — after meeting stiff opposition from the community itself at the beginning of the decade — and planned sabotage operations and internal disturbances. Tension was deliberately created among the members of the community and between them and the rest of the population, as well as the authorities, in order to create an appropriate domestic and international atmosphere for an immigration campaign. This was clearly demonstrated in the following concluding paragraph of a Jewish Agency report, submitted by one of their agents upon his return from Iraq:

> ... there could be no substantial immigration from Iraq in the fore-seeable future (early forties) and that our main efforts should be directed to the expansion and training of the defence cadres we had set up there and their appropriate training. These cadres would at the same time continue educational work and prepare for immigration into Palestine at all costs and by any means.[13]

Conclusions

The Iraqi-Jewish community, when studied within the developmental process of Iraqi society during the nineteenth century and the overall social conditions that prevailed then, fared well in comparison to the rest of the population. Despite the despotic and corrupt practices prevailing in the country at large, there was freedom of religion, residence, work and travel. Moreover, during the tumultuous political changes that took place within Iraq during the same period, there was little, if any, tension between the Jewish community and other social groups. This situation, was, of course, completely the opposite in Europe at the time.

The people of Iraq took advantage of the period of reforms in the Ottoman Empire and began educating their young at a much larger and wider scale than before. This expansion in the educational system, along with the gradual expansion of trade and rapid economic development, created new social and economic opportunities for the population at large. The Jews of Iraq figured prominently in these two developments.

The disturbing element in modern Iraqi-Jewish history, and what led to their abrupt and sudden immigration after centuries of social harmony and cohesion, and at a critical period of social integration, was the agitation and propaganda directed at them, as well as at the rest of Arab Jewry, by the Jewish Agency and the Zionist organizations. This, coupled with the occupation of Palestine in 1948 and the continuous threats to the security of the Arab people, are major factors in an analysis of the current history of the Middle East.

Notes

1. For a discussion of the rights, duties and roles of the non-Muslim com-

munities during the Islamic and Ottoman periods, *see*: H.A.R. Gibb and Harold Bowen, *Islamic Society and the West* vol. 1, pt. 2, pp. 207-61; and, Majid Khadduri, "International Law", in *Law in the Middle East,* eds. Majid Khadduri and Herbert J. Leibesny (Washington, D.C., 1955), vol. I, pp. 349-73.

2. Yusif Rizq-Allah Ghanimah, *A History of the Jews of Iraq* (Arabic) (Baghdad, 1924), p. 184.

3. Cecil Roth, *The Sassoon Dynasty* (London, 1941), pp. 20-21.

4. Israel Jospeh Benjamin II, *Eight Years in Asia and Africa from 1846 to 1855* (Hanover, 1859), p. 110.

5. David Soloman Sassoon, *A History of the Jews in Baghdad* (Letchworth, 1949), pp. 157-61.

6. *Ibid.,* pp. 149-52 and Ghanimah, *Jews of Iraq,* pp. 168-69.

7. Ghanimah, *Jews of Iraq,* p. 170 and Sassoon, *Jews in Baghdad*, pp. 124-25.

8. Abdal-Razzaq Al-Hillali, *History of Education in Iraq During the Ottoman Regime, 1638-1917* (Arabic) (Baghdad, 1959), pp. 249-52.

9. M. Franco, "Baghdad," in *The Jewish Ecyclopedia* (N.Y., 1912), vol. 2, p. 438. Also, Ghanimah, *Jews of Iraq*, p. 179 and Sassoon, *Jews in Baghdad*, p. 161.

10. *The Iraq Directory, 1936* (Baghdad, 1936), pp. 462-63.

11. *Ibid.,* p. 465.

12. Joseph Schechtman, *On Wings of Eagles. The Plight, Exodus, and Homecoming of Oriental Jewry* (New York, 1961), p. 104.

13. Munya M. Mardor, *Haganah* (New York, 1964), p. 100.

12 ECONOMIC DIMENSIONS OF ARAB RESISTANCE TO ZIONISM: A POLITICAL INTERPRETATION

Joe Stork

The economic weakness of the Arab world and its subordination to the world capitalist economic system was an essential and inseparable precondition for imperialist division and control of the Arab territories after World War I, which in turn provided the political and economic basis for Zionist colonization of Palestine. The capacity of the Palestinian Arab people to resist this Zionist/British imposition in the 1930s and 40s was considerably bounded by the consequences of more than a century of Western capitalist penetration of the region. The relative ease with which the British, and later the Americans, took over the area's oil resources (over the same decades that the Zionist foundations were laid) was directly related to the way the region had been softened up by centuries of Ottoman and later European oppression and exploitation. Prior to the beginnings of the industrial revolution in England and Europe and after the ciritical commercial and trading function of the Middle East had sharply declined under the impact of European naval exploits, surpluses from peasant agricultural production were expropriated and consumed by the local ruling classes or transmitted to the Ottoman capital. There was no sustained process of expanding productive investments. Local manufacturing was limited to artisan and handicraft scale and was not industrial.

Contact between the developing capitalist economies of the West and the traditional economies of the Middle East occurred through trade as well as military expeditions and assaults. The pattern of exchanging Western manufacturers, chiefly textiles and hardware, for Middle Eastern raw materials used in the new industries was laid this early, and smoothed the way for the period of imperialist expansion in the latter half of the nineteenth century. This was partly due to the failure of the Ottoman authorities to impose any kind of protective tariffs or otherwise stimulate local production. Typical of the relationship was the Anglo-Turkish Commercial Convention of 1838 which "confirmed now and forever . . . all rights, privileges, and immunities which have been conferred on the subjects or ships of Great Britain by the existing Capitulations and Treaties."[1] Hershlag describes the effect of the capitulations, which were not abolished until the 1920s and 30s, as follows:

> The low tariff barrier enabled foreign wares, sometimes inferior to local products, to flood Ottoman markets and to deal a serious blow to the productive capacity and competetive ability of local producers, while the markets that were opened to Turkey's raw materials . . . represented only partial compensation for the ruin of prospects for the development of a diversified local economy.[2]

This unequal trading relationship was not the accidental outcome of intangible forces, but represented the fulfillment of a commercial strategy fully shared by the rival European bourgeois regimes. One British commentator, writing in 1838, observed:

> We may calculate, at no remote period, if, indeed, political troubles are arrested, on supplying the necessities as well as the luxuries of the whole of the eastern population, whose attention will thus be directed to agriculture, and the furnishing of raw produce; when we can take from them their produce in return for our wares, or find them the means of exchanging it. These changed circumstances are beginning to produce their effects. Persia, which lately drew raw silk from Turkey for its manufactures, now has commenced to import silk from England; and the current of precious metals, which a few years ago carried L5,000,000 towards the east, is now drawn backwards by the spinning mules and power looms of England.[3]

This division of the world did not go without challenge at the time. The most serious and sustained effort in the Middle East in the nineteenth century was made in Egypt under the reign of Mohammed Ali. He endeavoured to transform Egypt from a subsistence peasant economy to a "modern" industrialized one under state control, independent of the Ottoman Empire, and largely closed off from the expanding European economies. Virtually all this effort was linked to Muhammad Ali's intent to develop and equip an Egyptian military that could defend and extend his rule in the face of opposition from the Ottoman regime and the European powers. The threat was militarily crushed by 1841.

Although the threat of Mohammed Ali did not arise elsewhere in the Middle East, his efforts were not solitary. In Iraq, Dawud Pasha, governor from 1817 to 1831, introduced a modern munitions factory, textile plant, water-oil-pump, and printing press, in a similar attempt to govern independently of the Sublime Porte and of the British

Residency in Baghdad. But the attempt "proved to be abortive owing to the rising forces of foreign economic expansion and penetration in Iraq."[4]

In the decade after 1827, in the Ottoman Empire itself, Sultan Mahmoud II sponsored the establishment of a tannery and boot works, a spinning mill, wool-spinning and weaving facilities, a saw mill, a copper-sheet rolling plant and the conversion of a cannon foundry and musket works to steam power. Almost without exception:

> These early attempts to introduce European industrial methods were devoted exclusively to the manufacture of goods intended for governmental and military use. They concentrated on the final stages of manufacture and ignored or only partly solved associated problems such as internal sources of raw materials, transportation and other economic infrastructure.[5]

Recognition of the need for a more ambitious program of "defensive industrialization" by Ottoman authorities reached a peak in the years of the Tanzimat reform period that lasted from the early 1840s to the eve of the Crimean War. The ultimate failure of these efforts resulted not only from the competetive hostility of the European powers, but from the "hothouse" character of the efforts. Nearly all the machinery was imported from Europe, and "most if not all foremen, master craftsmen, and skilled workers of necessity came from abroad to assemble, operate and repair factories and equipment."[6] Both investment and consumption were confined solely to the state sector, and this proved fatal when the regime's poor financial condition led to cutbacks on both fronts. "With the Crimean War came the first European loans and Ottoman indebtedness, and the Porte was forced to abandon the greater part of its industrialization program."[7] The resemblance between early efforts at industrialization in the Middle East and many of the industrial projects being promoted there today in the wake of what *Business Week* calls the "tidal wave of oil money" is more than coincidental and should give pause to those who think that industrialization is some mere agglomeration of capital and technique, some machine that can be transplanted from abroad with all its component parts.

The development of industrialization under capitalism is dependent not only on the local setting, but on the global context. These early attempts in the Middle East were made at the same time the industrial revolution was on the rise in Europe, creating the need for raw materials,

212 Economic Dimensions of Arab Resistance to Zionism

cheap labor and wider markets that motivated imperialist expansion. This stage was characterized by the export of capital to the Middle East precisely to consolidate the raw material export orientation of those economies and the penetration of those markets. This was the age of great infrastructural projects — railways, ports, the Suez Canal. "The canal, whose ownership was held in common between European banking interests and the Egyptian ruler, was dug almost by hand by tens of thousands of Egyptian peasant laborers performing unpaid corvee labor. About 20,000 reportedly perished in this endeavor."[8] Merchant and investment bankers financed the purchase of European industrial and commercial goods by Middle Eastern rulers, and then refinanced their debts at usurious rates. All the states soon went bankrupt (1976 is the centennial for Egypt's plunge under Khedive Ismail) and European diplomatic residents and bank agents came to virtually rule those countries which they hadn't taken direct control of, like Egypt. By the turn of the century nearly one-third of all state revenue, plus a 3 percent customs surtax and 8 percent *ad valorem* tax went to service the Ottoman public debt. The peasant economies were substantially redirected from subsistence farming to cash crops (notably cotton in Egypt) to raise the foreign exchange necessary to service the public debt. It was this phenomenon which Issawi characterized for Egypt as "a process, consummated only after the British occupation, integrating Egypt as an agricultural unit in the international politico-economic system."[9]

Thus the forced accumulation of capital necessary for industrialization took place in the Middle East under foreign direction rather than that of local capitalists or local state authorities. It was then used to finance the development of European industry. This had consequences not only for the local economies in general but for the peasant sectors in particular, as governments attempted to raise revenues to pay off these debts by intensifying exploitation of the lower classes. M.S. Hasan describes the application of these developments to Iraq:

> Thus the expansion of European demand for Iraq's produce of wool, dates and grain was satisfied by the utilization of Iraq's surplus productive capacity of land and labor. The economic process whereby the surplus productive capacity was used for the satisfaction of rising European demand took the form of a decline in subsistence agriculture and pasture, and an expansion of commercial production for exports.[10]

The shift also included the changeover from tribal to private land-ownership and the local expropriation of surplus value by the sheikhs and urban merchants:

> The tribal system was transformed into the system of private [*tapu*] landownership. They became landlords, entitled to a substantial share in the crops which they sold to merchants; the latter marketed the surplus agricultural produce ... in the towns and abroad. The share of landlords in agricultural produce increased in proportion to the expansion in production, the transformation of tribal into *tapu* landownership, and the decline of subsistence relative to commercial agriculture — but above all in proportion to the growth of exports and the development of law and order which made practicable the effective appropriation of the *tapu* crop share.

> The expenditure of the greater part of the proceeds of surplus agricultural produce on consumption meant that there was very little investment in maintaining, let alone improving, the fertility of the soil, flood control, and the quality of seed. The declining productivity of the land and the growth of rural population more rapidly than production ... resulted in a fall of the output per head of the pastoral and agricultural population. Thus the annual output of grain fell from 1,000 kilos per head of the rural population in the 1880s to 560 kilos during the 1930s and further to 505 kilos during the 1950s. The increasing effective share of the landowners in a relatively declining agricultural production meant a fall in the standard of life of the Iraqi peasantry.[11]

A similar transformation in land tenure took place in Palestine, where peasants frequently registered their lands in the names of local town merchants to avoid taxation and conscription. Reudy states,

> The growing value of cash crops in the late 19th century encouraged the urban bourgeoisie of Beirut, Damascus and Jerusalem to take advantage of the windfall ... thousands of peasants from the 1870s onwards found themselves in fact deprived of the most minimal rights of tenure as they became increasingly under the control of the owner, who might be landlord, tax collector, and moneylender combined.[12]

As Polk points out regarding the application of the Ottoman Land Code of 1858: "Long before the Balfour Declaration, which is often seen as the fount of all contention over Palestine, the inarticulate but ancient peasantry had slipped a rung on the ladder which was to lead them down into the refugee camps in 1948."[13]

The Mandate Period and the 1948 Defeat

The competition among the European powers that led to World War I had decisive impact on the Middle East. The mandate system, a modified form of direct colonial rule, was concocted to provide a facade for the division and subjugation of the Arab world according to the competitive economic and strategic needs of Britain and France. It was in this period that the importance of crude oil for modern warfare in particular and industrial strength in general became apparent. Thus, the British insistence on control of Iraq's northern provinces. After the nationalist struggle was suppressed in Syria and Feisal, the British-sponsored spokesman for Arab nationalist demands, was run out of Damascus by the French army, Britain had need of a pliable king to help pacify the struggle that had erupted in Iraq in May 1920 with the announcement of the British Mandate. The insurrection posed the first serious challenge to British policy in the area, and it was met and crushed as such. Among other tactical innovations, the British used airplanes to bomb and terrorize peasant villages in the countryside. Certainly among the reasons for the failure of resistance was the decades-long deterioration of the living standards of the masses of peasants and the absence of indigenous economic, political and social institutions and relationships that could sustain a protracted struggle.

A similar situation obtained in Palestine, except that it was augmented by the Zionist settler-colonial enterprise which led to the development of a strong capitalist sector within Palestine that, with the help of the Mandate power, quite dominated the non-capitalist traditional Arab sector. Probably the most important single reason for the issuance of the infamous Balfour Declaration on November 2, 1917, was related more to the imminence of the Bolshevik Revolution and the vain hope of mobilizing Russian Jewish influence to keep Russia in the war against Germany. But the value of a friendly colony in such a strategic position was already well appreciated by British policymakers. While not itself a promising candidate as an oil producer, Palestine was an important link in the chain of colonial control of the region.

One of the most important consequences of the heritage of imperialism in the Middle East was the formation and consolidation of a class of local bourgeoisie, their wealth for the most part based in their land holdings, and to a lesser extent in trade (in which sector ethnic compradores were relatively important.) Certainly in Palestine it was this local bourgeoisie, including most of the traditional notables, which made up the political establishment. But now their dominance had a class character as well. They led the political struggle against the Zionists and their sponsors, but their own self-interest dictated a response that would not challenge their own privileges and prerogatives. In Palestine and elsewhere their nationalist ambitions were muted by their stake in the status quo. This class performed a mediating role without which the Mandate could not have functioned.

To grasp the full import of the economic dimension of the struggle during the Mandate period, the transformation of Palestine must be articulated in class terms, along the lines which Talal Asad has advanced. For Asad, the "Jewish sector" must be identified functionally as the capitalist sector, for whose relative and absolute growth the Mandate apparatus was essential: "The Mandate Administration maintained a fiscal structure which facilitated the extraction of surplus from the non-capitalist sector, and its partial transfer to the expanding capitalist sector."[14] Both the rural property tax and the various forms of indirect taxation, concentrated on necessities, were extremely regressive. Peasant indebtedness was increased, facilitating the limited land acquisition of the Mandate period; capital-intensive Jewish agricultural enterprises paid proportionately less tax, and sometimes none at all. Similarly in the industrial sector, tax policies favoring large-scale enterprises (mainly Jewish) "hastened the demise of Arab craft manufacture" and "as in the agricultural sector, the fiscal structure served to support the differential wage rates between Jewish (immigrant) and Arab (native) labor obtaining in the industrial sector."[15]

As for Mandate administration expenditures, these were devoted primarily to improvement of transport, communications and other infrastructural features, "which imparted relatively greater value to capitalist production"[16] and to 'defense' — "the maintenance of a repressive state apparatus, continuously and primarily directed against the Arab producing masses."[17] In the 1930s "security matters" consumed as much as 35 percent of the budget. Moreover the Administration "was intent on amassing a surplus to repay Palestine's portion of the Ottoman public debt, and it strove to make Palestine self supporting and hence less of a burden on the ill-tempered British taxpayer."[18]

The increase of European Jewish immigration in the 1930s meant the growth, with fluctuations to be sure, of the capitalist sector. Owing to the "conquest of labor" policies of the Zionists, it directly and adversely affected the Arab population by causing high unemployment and significant inflation. This increased tensions among the Arab classes as well as providing the direct impetus to strike economically and militarily at the Zionists. For the peasants and poor workers of Palestine, the political conflict with the Zionists was felt most acutely and most frequently on an immediate economic level. It was not an abstract or mystical "love of the land" that motivated the Palestinians to struggle against great odds, but their utter dependence on the land which was only reinforced by the pauperization and sub-proletarianization of the Zionist project. Protests against immigration and land acquisition policies, and against utility concessions to Zionist corporations, were prominent on the agendas of the Palestine Arab congresses in the 1920s.

It is not coincidental that when the Palestinian masses struck, it was via an economic weapon: the general strike of 1936. As Waines correctly points out, both this and other more spontaneous random outbreaks of violence, which make apparent the revolutionary potential of the Palestinian masses, were due to the fact that "the position of the Arab peasant and worker had become intolerable."

> Thus the uprising of 1929 (and more especially the rebellion of 1936-39) was related to the overall ineffectiveness of the mandate administration to cope with the fundamental economic grievances of the peasantry. Implicitly [*sic*], the Jewish national home was called into question, for extensive planning and expenditure on the Arab sector of the economy would seriously retard the rate of the Zionists' progress in their sector.[19]

Waines is one of the few writers who, while not adopting a Marxist framework of analysis, can grasp the fact that in the Arab population

> the perspectives of the upper class and the peasantry were quite different ... The former sought a resolution to the question of political power, while the latter struggled to alleviate their economic plight. Representative institutions would secure the interests of the upper class which would then enjoy the privilege of rule in an independent Palestine; hence the basis of political action of the Arab leadership was direct negotiation with the British for a democratic constitution. The basis of political action for the peasantry was

through violence so long as political negotiations and the demands for economic stability proved fruitless. A strong movement among the peasantry was perhaps [*sic*] the more radical approach, for the transfer of political power from the mandatory to the upper classes did not necessitate the betterment of the peasants' living conditions . . . . the failure of the nationalist program was largely due to the inability and unwillingness of the Arab leadership to co-opt the peasants' full support in bringing about the destruction of the mandate. The upper classes could not think in terms of *being obligated to* the lower classes in the context of a total national struggle; they could only feel *some* obligation *for* the lower classes insofar as this did not conflict with their own vital interests . . . In times of crisis . . . . the Arab leadership seemed to shrink in horror at the prospect of violence from below.[20]

The general strike and rebellion of 1936-39 was the most important blow struck against the Zionists and the Mandate, and its ultimate failure is related to the social and economic structure of the Arab community, and to the high degree of organization and economic coherence of the Zionist community, which by this time equalled one-third of the total population. The Zionists were "on the threshold of a new stage of rapid development and expansion"[21] and took advantage of the Arab strike to consolidate and expand their economic domain. This certainly contributed to the final decision of the Arab Higher Committee to seek an end to the rebellion and rely on political negotiations with the British, pressed now by the shadows of war in Europe. It is also an indication of their relative weakness within the Palestinian community that they had to request the ruling circles of Iraq, Egypt, Saudi Arabia and Yemen to intercede with the Palestinian masses to bring an end to the uprising. Those ruling circles led by Iraqi Foreign Minister Nuri as-Said, were only too happy to oblige, given their similar class interests and their own subservient position vis-à-vis the British.

This episode marks the beginning of the internationalization of the Palestine question. The defeat of 1936-39 was a precursor to the defeat of 1948. The inability of the Arab states to intervene successfully in 1948 can be attributed to the bankruptcy of the local bourgeoisie which had taken over the reigns of state power under the supervision of the former colonial authorities. It is in this period, however, that the use of economic warfare by the Arab states against Israel and its supporters was initiated.[22]

Economic Aspects, 1948-67

The struggle for Palestine after World War II, corresponding to the 'internationalization' of the conflict within the Arab world, brings with it the first application of economic sanctions against the new state of Israel: a general economic boycott of Israel organized under the aegis of the newly-formed Arab League, and specifically an oil boycott and closure of the Suez Canal to Israeli shipping. The general boycott was extended to apply against Western firms trading with Israel, as well as prohibiting any Arab trade with the Zionist state. The main importance of the general boycott was that it prevented Israel's emergence as, in the words of Chaim Weizmann, "the new Switzerland, supplying consumer goods to the untapped markets of the Middle East."[23] British, Dutch, South African and American capital entered Israel, according to *Fortune*, "not . . . out of compassion but in the expectation of profits."[24] But only if the boycott were lifted or rendered ineffective would it be possible for Israel to establish a classically imperialist relationship with its Arab neighbors, which Abba Eban envisioned as being "akin to the relationship between the United States and the Latin American continent."[25]

The early fifties were tough years for the Iraeli economy, a fact to which the Arab boycott surely contributed. The reasons why it was not a more decisive factor are Israeli expropriation and exploitation of virtually the entirety of Palestinian Arab property within its borders, including the property of thse who did not leave as refugees, and the large-scale financial aid from the United States, West Germany and international Jewish organizations. David Horowitz, a leading Israeli economist and former head of the Bank of Israel, admitted that the import of capital in Israel's first twenty years "financed not only investment, but also to a considerable extent, consumption." By mid-1973 Israel had received over $8 billion from foreign sources, an average of $233 per year per capita. By comparison the total per capita income of an Egyptian in 1969 was less than half that amount — $102.[26] The Zionist theft of the property and productive resources of the Palestinians is well documented by Don Peretz from official records:

Abandoned property was one of the greatest contributions toward making Israel a viable state. The extent of its area and the fact that most of the regions along the border consisted of absentee property made it strategically significant. Of the 370 new Jewish settlements established between 1948 and the beginning of 1953, 350 were on absentee property. In 1954 more than one-third of Israel's Jewish population lived on absentee property and nearly a third of the new immigrants (250,000 people) settled in urban areas abandoned by Arabs. They left whole cities like Jaffa, Acre, Lydda, Ramleh, Baysan, Majdal; 338 towns and villages and large parts of 94 other cities and towns, containing nearly a quarter of all the buildings in Israel. Ten thousand shops, businesses and stores were left in Jewish hands. At the end of the Mandate, citrus holdings in the area of Israel totaled about 240,000 dunums of which half were Arab-owned. Most of the Arab groves were taken over by the Israel Custodian of Absentee Property. But only 340,000 dunums were cultivated by the end of 1953. By 1956, 73,000 dunums were either cultivated or fit for cultivation. In 1951-52, former Arab groves produced one-and-a-quarter million boxes of fruit, of which 400,000 were exported. Arab fruit sent abroad provided nearly 10 percent of the country's foreign exchange earnings from exports in 1951. In 1949 the olive produce from abandoned Arab groves was Israel's third largest export, ranking after citrus and diamonds. The relative economic importance of Arab property was largest from 1948 until 1953, during the period of greatest immigration and need. After that, as the immigrants became more productive, national dependence upon abandoned Arab property declined relatively.[27]

The conflict in 1948 also directly linked, for the first time, the fortunes of Zionism and Western oil interests. The former Iraqi Prime Minister Saleh Jabr, revealed that Saudi Arabia had blocked an Arab League plan to cut off all oil production as a result of the U.N. partition decision. In December 1947, Crown Prince (later King) Saud told the American arbassador in Jidda that if other Arab states (chiefly Iraq) insisted on breaking relations with the United States over Palestine, Saudi Arabia would break with them. Nevertheless, the Americans were aware in the first half of 1948 that the King might be forced by popular Arab sentiment to take some action in this regard. There is no question that oil politics was an important factor in shaping U.S. policy in 1948. Top officials in the defense and state departments opposed U.S. support of the Zionists precisely because they saw it would jeopardize the U.S. hold on Middle East oil reserves, and the Joint Chiefs of Staff had already warned (in 1946) against any policy that would require the dispatch of U.S. troops: "The political shock attending the reappearance of US armed forces in the Middle East would unnecessarily risk such serious disturbances throughout the area as to dwarf any local Palestine difficulties."[28]

The United States followed the path of least resistance, both in terms of domestic political pressures and international complications. As it turned out, the only repercussions on the oil front came in Palestine itself, where, after the Zionist takeover of Haifa, Iraq shut off crude deliveries (via pipeline) to the Iraq Petroleum Company refinery there, foregoing about half its normal exports and foreign exchange. The Iraqis steadfastly refused to renew the oil flow, despite considerable pressure from the United States through U.N. mediator Bernadotte.

A related development occured in Syria, where negotiations for the Aramco Trans-Arabian Pipeline project right-of-way were being conducted. An agreement was worked out in September 1947 after a two-week conference of U.S. diplomatic personnel in the region, but the war of 1948 broke out before ratification by the Syrian parliament. Syrian reluctance to proceed was sidestepped when Colonel Husni Zaim seized control of the government at the end of March 1949 and dissolved the parliament. The United States quickly recognized the new regime and the agreement with TAPline was finally signed in Damascus in May 1949.

The limited application of economic warfare by the Arab regimes during and after 1948 must be related to the class character of those regimes, the limited economic resources at their disposal, and their even more limited control over those resources. In almost every instance the regimes were composed of and represented the interests of the landed oligarchies and bourgeoises who had come to power under (British) colonial tutelage. It has been said, not without some justification, that they entered the Palestine war in 1948 as much to fight and checkmate each other as to confront the Zionists in battle.[29] Their corruption and subservience to imperialism was famous. It is a significant example of the interaction of the Palestinian national struggle with the general course of the class struggle in the Arab world that the defeat of 1948 precipitated the overthrow of most of these regimes in the following decade (in order of their proximity and responsibility to Palestine): Egypt in 1952; Syria in 1954; Iraq in 1958. Abdullah of Jordan was assassinated in 1951, but British and later American direct intervention managed to preserve his mercenary state under his grandson, Hussein.

The oil producers were an exception; there was no upheaval in Saudi Arabia, and even in Iraq it took the Baghdad Pact, the Eisenhower Doctrine and the crisis in Lebanon to bring down Nuri as-Said and the Hashemite entourage. This can be attributed to the decision by the oil monopolies to buy off the regimes and at the same time give them a greater stake in perpetuating the status quo by offering them a nominal 50/50 share in their vast profits from Middle East production. George McGhee, then a high state department official and later an oil company executive, described the strategy:

> We felt it exceedingly important from the standpoint of the stability of the regimes in the area and the security of the Middle East as a whole and the continued ownership of our oil concessions there and the ability to exploit them, that the Government of Saudi Arabia receive an increased oil income.[30]

If the 1948 defeat signalled the death knell for the landed oligarchy and bougeoisie, 1956 represented the apogee of the radical nationalism of the petit bourgeois regimes of Nasser in Egypt and the Baath in Syria (and later Iraq). The particular origins of that crisis were of an economic dimension: the decison by Egypt to nationalize the Suez Canal and to enter into aid agreements with the Soviet Union in order to assert some autonomy for the Egyptian economy regarding Western control. The nationalization issue was doubly portentious for the oil-men, for it served as an example to the Arab peoples of what might be achieved in the oil-producing states along similar lines. The United States, for its part, used an array of economic levers to pressure Egypt, Israel and Britain and France to arrive at a settlement. Even before the Suez crisis in November, there were widespread strikes by oil and other workers in April in Bahrain, the administrative center of British rule in the Gulf, demanding, among other things, the dismissal of the British political agent, Sir Charles Belgrave. In June 1956 a visit of King Saud to Dhahran sparked a spontaneous protest against Aramco. Shaken by the massive character of the demonstration and its nationalist anti-imperialist slogans, the King ordered a crackdown on any and all trade union or political activity by workers. The militant and popular character of Nasser's appeal throughout the Arab world was seen as a clear threat to Western economic interests which could be easily detonated by the simmering Palestine conflict. This fear was heightened when in 1958 Egypt and Syria joined to form the United Arab Republic (UAR), since, according to oil industry sources, it seemed to enhance Nasser's ability to disrupt oil operations by controlling the IPC and Aramco pipelines through Syria as well as the Suez Canal. This in turn led to the construction of a pipeline in Israel (with French financial assistance) and increased exploration activity in Libya and Algeria. The formation of the UAR enhanced further the prestige of the radical nationalist forces in the Arab world.

The military coup in Iraq on July 14, 1958 was the first against a puppet regime in an oil-producing country and precipitated the U.S. and British military intervention into Lebanon and Jordan, partly to guard against nationalist victories in those countries, and largely to prepare for a possible invasion of Iraq. Repeated declarations by the new regime that oil interests would not be touched and the absence of any indigenous counter-revolutionary activity removed the possibility of military intervention in Iraq. In the 1960s Iraq took the lead in the Arab world in asserting popular sovereignty over its national resources.

The period between 1956 and 1967 marks the rapid development of an "oil consciousness" on the part of the Middle Eastern regimes and those political forces challenging them. While not of immediate relevance to the Palestine conflict, an understanding of the meaning and implications of the oil weapon requires a probe of the political character of the persons and institutions through which the oil weapon was implemented. It is not necessary to detail the mechanisms by which Western corporations maintained control of Middle East oil, nor the waste and exploitation that characterized their administration of this power. The governments had been totally dependent on the companies for the economic information and analyses used in formulating concession terms and revisions. As late as 1951 none of the Iraqi negotiators knew anything about the function of the posted prices on which their country's revenues were to be calculated, nor did they have access to the economic studies that would help them formulate a negotiating position not effectively predetermined by the company.

By the middle of the 50s, a small but growing number of Arabs with Western technical training in petroleum engineering and economics began to fill positions in the companies and in the state oil ministries. The most influential of these was Abdullah Tariki, who returned to Saudi Arabia from the University of Texas in 1954 at age 29 to become the first director general of petroleum affairs. Tariki's dedication to educating the public about oil affairs, to improving concession terms and opening up management positions for Saudis, to using the country's wealth for the benefit of all the people — made him stand out in a regime where venality and corruption was the rule and where power and influence depended on one's lineage in the House of Saud.

Tariki realized early that real changes in company-government relations could only come about through concerted action by the producing countries. He pressed for the convening of an Arab Oil

Congress under the auspices of the Arab League, which was finally held in April 1959. While results were limited and vague, this communication and contact facilitated the convening of the special meeting of oil ministers in Baghdad in September 1960 after the second round of company-dictated price cuts. OPEC emerged from this meeting. The political transformation of the Middle East during the 1950s, a transformation related in no small measure to the impact of the Palestine conflict, was characterized by increasingly radical popular demands regarding the future of the oil industry. These demands threatened companies and regimes alike. There could be no question of whether things would change, but rather what forces would dominate and control those changes and how extensive they would be.

OPEC must be understood in the context of the political forces contending for power and influence in the region. While it achieved some very limited economic gains during the 1960s, it failed to achieve the measure of control that Tariki, perhaps naively, had envisaged for it. Indicative of the problems it would face was the consolidation of the Saudi monarchy under Feisal in 1962 with U.S. assistance, leading to Tariki's dismissal from his post and eventual banishment from Saudi Arabia. Tariki was the most radical of the technocrats; his departure left OPEC in the hands of those who distrusted the vague Arab nationalist ideology then in the ascendancy and who saw the task of OPEC to lie in "removing oil matters from the realm of ordinary politics" perhaps without realizing that this was in itself a highly political stance which best suited the reactionary regimes by depoliticizing the one area in which they were most politically vulnerable.

In the end, though, it was not the political character and cultural dependency of the technocrats which determined the politics of OPEC, but the fact that they were functioning as agents of regimes who for the most part owed their power to the oil companies and Western governments. It could go no further than allowed by its most conservative members, like Saudi Arabia, for whom OPEC served as a means of diffusing Arab nationalist criticism. The alliance between the companies and the reactionary regimes is perhaps most clearly expressed in the struggle for control of Iraqi oil during this period, precipitated by the issuance of Law 80 under the Kassem regime in 1961 and later by Laws 97 and 123 in 1967. The companies helped ferment the political instability that characterized Iraqi politics in the 1960s by reducing output and therefore the main source of national income. Saudi Arabia, through the ubiquitous Yamani, gave the companies every incentive to avoid making concessions to Iraq by warning that any concession to Iraq would have to be implemented in Saudi Arabia as well. He gave this approach a more general formulation in 1966 by proclaiming his opposition to "unilateral action" (as urged by the nationalists) as "inconsistent with the friendly atmosphere which characterizes our relation with the oil companies at present." "I am sure," he added, "that the oil companies operating in Saudi Arabia have no interest whatsoever in shaking our faith in this philosophy by showing us that other means are more rewarding in safeguarding our oil interests."[31]

On the surface the changes in the Middle East from 1948 to the eve of the 1967 June War were enormous, chiefly related in the success of the radical regimes in nationalizing their resources and main industrial and financial sectors. But underneath the surface another reality was lurking. The political momentum of the radical nationalists had been jolted by the Egyptian fiasco in Yemen and a kind of political modus vivendi was erected by the contending regimes, chiefly Egypt and Saudi Arabia, at a series of summits beginning in 1964 (where not coincidentally a new bureaucratic formation called the Palestine Liberation Organization was put forth, chiefly to compensate for the inability of the regimes to confront the Israeli diversion of the Jordan river waters).

One must look at the underlying economic reality. A United Nations survey of the situation in the early sixties revealed that primary commodities made up 96 percent of the exports of Middle Eastern countries. For the non-oil producers these were mainly agricultural products. Forty-five percent of the imports of these countries were primary commodities, mainly food items, the value of which exceeded machinery and transport equipment imports together. Sixty-five percent of these countries' exports went to the capitalist countries; sixty-four percent of their imports came from those same countries. The other "export" not covered in these statistics is the outflow of capital, including foreign profits, which exceeded capital imports (investments and aid) by $1 billion annually.[32] On the eve of the 1967 war, it was clear that the end of formal colonialism had not ended the subordination of the region's economy to the needs of the industrialized West rather than the needs of its own peoples. This is the fundamental economic dimension that underlies the catastrophe of 1967.

Economic Aspects, 1967-1976

If 1948 represented the utter failure of the landed oilgarchies and comprador bourgeoisie to resolve the national question posed by the Zionist endeavor, 1967 represented the failure of a similar scale of the petit bourgeois radical nationalist regimes represented by Nasser in Egypt and the Baath in Syria. There were, to be sure, many contributing causes to this devastating defeat, and it would be a mistake to over-look, for example, the degree of imperialist collusion that lay behind the Israeli *blitzkrieg*. But the single most important cause lay with the failure of the regimes in question to mobilize their societies for the kind of protracted struggle that is critical for the liberation of Palestine. Behind this failure, and symptomatic of it, was the extent to which the class divisions in those societies had been maintained and accentuated, while the surplus exacted from the masses was used to construct a military machine that was completely inadequate to the task of libera-ting Palestine or even defending the country's borders, but was used instead to discourage and repress indigenous mass actions aimed at social and political change. In Egypt in 1966, 1 percent of the rural population appropriated 25 percent of the agricultural income: 50 per-cent of the population appropriated 25 percent of the agricultural income; 50 percent of the population received less than 20 percent of the income. In Syria 50 percent of the peasants were still landless after a decade of land reform, and the regime published that 60 percent of the state budget was devoted to the defense establishment.[33] The regimes had succeeded in transposing class frustrations to focus on the national question, but then utterly failed to resolve that question.

Politically the radical nationalist petit bourgeois regimes preferred an alternative to both reaction and revolution – socialism without class struggle. Their failure in 1967 resulted foremost in a political polariza-tion between the forces of reaction, led by Saudi Arabia, and a new commitment to revolutionary change sparked by the resurgence of the Palestine resistance movement. The struggle between these forces over the next six years effectively determined the extent to which economic factors would play a paramount role in the next war.

To review the extent to which economic aspects came into play in 1967, particularly with regard to oil: in the immediate aftermath of the Israeli attack there were demonstrations and strikes in the Saudi oil fields. Numerous Palestinian workers were deported and there were over 800 arrests. A strike at Aramco on June 25 resulted in damage to American property. Radio Baghdad broadcast an appeal of the Iraqi oil workers' union calling on members to guard installations against spontaneous sabotage. Libyan oil workers kept facilities there shut down for more than a month. There was a suspension of all oil ship-ments from all the producers for about a week beginning June 7, and an embargo on shipments to Britain and the United States followed.

Abu Dhabi, where popular demands to join the brief boycott had been ignored, finally shut down operations on June 11, after an explosion wrecked a British bank. By the end of the month, Arab oil operations were back to 50 percent of normal, the main exceptions being Iraq and Libya. But in a more fundamental sense things would never be "normal" again. Saudi Arabia was complaining that the boycott of the United States and Britain was costing more than it was worth, while in Syria and Iraq the technocrats were pressing more strongly than ever for nationalization. Iraq unilaterally resolved the dispute with IPC over North Rumaila by authorizing the state company, INOC, to undertake production there.

But the radical nationalists, after the June defeat, could not prevail. Iraq and Algeria among the oil producers, supported by Egypt and Syria, pressed in high-level political meetings for strong measures against the industry. A communiqué after a mid-August meeting in Baghdad of all Arab ministers of finance and oil, did not even mention nationalization proposals. The stage was set for the Arab summit conference in Khartoum, where the "spectacular rapprochement" between Nasser and Feisal was the result of Egyptian capitulation to the Saudi line on the question of oil embargoes. The conference stipulated that "nothing should be done to impair the financial capacity of the Arab oil-producing states to back the unified Arab effort; and that the responsibility for deciding on appropriate measures should be left to the producing countries themselves".[34] In return for this and immediate withdrawal of troops from Yemen, Egypt was granted two-thirds of an annual subsidy of $378 million from Saudi Arabia, Kuwait and Libya; the rest was earmarked for Jordan. The partial embargoes of the United States and Britain were lifted under the formula of using oil as a "positive weapon." Saudi Arabia's determination to hold the financial reins tightly was evident in Feisal's refusal to grant any funds to Syria, which had boycotted the conference.

Polarization continued. Iraq moved in a steadily more assertive direction which culminated in the oil agreement with the Soviet Union in 1969. Pressure built up within OPEC for higher revenues. In effect, the bill for reactionary hegemony on the oil question was passed on to the Western companies and governments. This dimension was outlined by the editor of *Middle East Economic Survey*:

In the present political turmoil the major Arab oil producing countries have on the whole opted for a moderate course and, at the expense of considerable effort on their part in highly explosive circumstances, performed an invaluable service for the whole world in maintaining the flow of oil to international markets. In the process of accomplishing this, they have incurred very heavy financial burdens which, if not made up in some way or another, could result in heavy damage to their developing economies. It is therefore not surprising that the Arab oil producers should now be looking to the consuming countries and the oil companies for a broad measure of understanding when it comes to their current drive for an increase in their revenue from oil.[35]

Under the leadership of Saudi Arabia, the conservative oil states moved to isolate themselves politically from the radical upsurge in the rest of the Arab world following the 1967 war by creating the Organization of Arab Petroleum Exporting Countries (OAPEC). Such an organization had long been demanded by the radical technocrats like Tariki, one which countries like Syria and Egypt would have a stake in as transit states as well as minor producers. OAPEC, though, was restricted to states for which oil production was the main source of income: Saudi Arabia, Libya and Kuwait. Iraq rejected the initial invitation to join. The *Middle East Economic Survey* observed:

> The purpose of this restrictive condition is clearly to ensure that all countries admitted into the organization would be equally anxious to maintain a purely economic approach to the development of the oil sector to the exclusion, as far as possible, of dangerous political crosscurrents.[36]

It proved impossible to keep questions of oil policy isolated from the Palestinian struggle. The main body of the resistance, Fatah, received financial support from Saudi Arabia and other oil states, but radical Palestinians carried their hostility to Arab reaction beyond rhetoric in June 1969 when the Popular Front for the Liberation of Palestine (PFLP) sabotaged a portion of the TAPline running through the occupied Golan Heights. Similar attacks followed. Despite these ominous portents, though, Western control of oil in the Gulf seemed relatively secure. When the "dangerous political crosscurrents" started to blow, they came not from the Gulf, where everyone's attention was riveted, but from the hot North African sands of Libya, where rapid and intense exploitation of oil reserves gave the industry a strategic vulnerability it had not experienced in any other country at any other time, a direct consequence of the 1967 war. On September 1, 1969, young army officers under the leadership of Muammar Qaddafi toppled the monarchy in a bloodless coup: the code words were "Palestine is ours." Despite the cautious moves of the revolutionary regime in its first year, the *Middle East Economic Survey* anticipated that the coup

> could well signify a momentous realignment of the balance of forces in the Arab world . . . and this is likely to have long-term implications on a number of fronts — not the least for the remaining oil-producing monarchies, for the oil industry, and for the Arab struggle against Israel together with the related strategic interests of the big powers.[37]

This study will not review the process that culminated in crude oil price hikes in Teheran and Tripoli in early 1971. The OPEC demands were genuine, albeit prompted by the unilateral initiative of Libya and Algeria. Once the need for an increase had become unmistakably clear, the companies could mold and channel those demands into specific forms that did not threaten the structure of the industry and in fact enhanced its stability and profitability. In this way they were aided by the pliable politics of the dominant OPEC countries, Iran and Saudi Arabia, and were able to short circuit more serious challenges from Libya, Algeria and Iraq. This scenario was even more blatantly repeated in the push for nationalization and the Saudi countermove dubbed "participation": "We want the present setup to continue as long as possible and at all costs to avoid any disastrous clash of interests which would shake the foundations of the whole oil business. That is why we are calling for participation."[38]

During the actual participation negotiations in 1972 Yamani bluntly told a *Financial Times* conference in London that participation represented an alternative to nationalization for "appeasing patriotic sentiments" in the Arab World.[39]

The next opportunity for Saudi Arabia to "appease patriotic sentiments" was the outbreak of the October war. Before discussing the application of the oil weapon in that context, a review of some of the events of 1973 that led up to that war is appropriate. Almost every month of that year was punctuated by incidents that stressed the fragility of the status quo: the Libyan airliner shot down by the Israelis over Sinai in February; the Black September attack on the Saudi embassy in Khartoum in March; the Israeli commando raid into Beirut in April which killed three resistance leaders and numerous civilians. The late spring brought direct reports from Saudi Arabia that Feisal feared he could no longer stand virtually alone in the Arab world as a U.S. ally. A U.S. offer of Phantom jets was turned down as being no substitute for a change in U.S. support of Israel. These energy warnings were sharpened on May 15, the anniversary of the 1948 defeat, by the symbolic shut-off of oil production for one hour in Kuwait, Algeria and Iraq, and for twenty-four hours in Libya. In the spring of 1973 Malcom Kerr ended his review of Nixon administration policies by noting that:

> the Palestine crisis has crystallized the accumulating unhappiness of a whole generation, and continues today to channel it in a rising stream against certain targets that under other circumstances would not be so vulnerable: the United States, their own governments and the established but shaky fabric of institutions and classes in their own society.

Kerr concluded with the following observation:

> Americans may well come to wish that their government had taken decisive steps to stem the drift and give the forces of moderation in Arab society a chance to recover their grip on affairs while there was still time.[40]

By this time pressure had already built up for an Arab oil policy that could be used to pressure the United States. The OPEC success in the price negotiations, particularly Libya's careful use of production curbs, raised the obvious question of why such tactics could not be used to secure a political objective. At the end of 1972 the Economic Council of the Arab League issued a study entitled *Economic Interests in the Service of Arab Causes* which took the view that while Arab interests in the long run would best be served by developing independent and autonomous industrially based economies, in the short run a more restrictive oil production policy would both conserve wasting resources for future use and bring a significant degree of pressure on industrial consuming countries to alter their support for Israel and hostility toward the Palestinian cause. The report did not call for an embargo but a slower expansion rate that would allow maximum flexibility for proportionate degress of escalation. In July 1973 the Palestine Liberation Organization endorsed the tactic of freezing oil production at existing levels.

The Saudi decision to cooperate with the oil embargo after the war had started is closely related to the Egyptian shift to the right under

Sadat, and it was on Feisal's urging that the Russian arms advisers were sent packing in 1972. When this failed to produce any perceptible change in U.S. policy, the Saudis were under some obligation to support Sadat when he finally chose the course of limited war. For the months leading up to the war, the Saudi campaign to use oil as a weapon was restricted to the arena of communiqués and press interviews. Production for the first seven months of 1973 was up to 37 percent over the previous year, with July production up a whopping 62 percent and production scheduled to hit 10 million barrels per day by early 1974. The campaign was aimed at securing a public and superficial indication of change in U.S. policy that would validate Saudi-U.S. ties and preclude the need to actually wield the "weapon." In August, Prince Abdullah, Feisal's brother and head of internal security forces, urged that "all Arab countries, whether oil producers of not, should act to prevent the debate on the use of oil from being transferred to the street."[41] A meeting of Arab oil ministers on September 4 produced no recommendations for the upcoming meeting of heads of state and apparently split between the Saudi-led camp and the nationalists pushing for seizing control of U.S. operations. As it was, Sadat had to put public pressure on Feisal after the war was well under way. Only Iraq had moved to action by nationalizing the U.S. interests in the Basra Petroleum Company. This set a militant tone for future deliberations, but it was more than a week, following Nixon's request to the U.S. Congress for more than $2.2 billion in military aid to Israel, before the OAPEC embargo of selected countries and general production cutback was initiated.

The oil weapon was an integral feature of the October war. The same popular pressures that forced the Sadat regime to undertake a limited military campaign also forced Feisal to implement an embargo of oil to the allies of Israel. The oil weapon was specifically instrumental in cutting into Israel's diplomatic and political support among the Western countries. But just as the war itself was limited in its cope and purpose, the oil weapon's effectiveness was important but limited. None of the contradictions in the Middle East which led to the war have been more than partially defused or deflected. Even the question of the occupied Egyptian and Syrian territories has not been resolved, not to speak of the much more intractable question of Palestinian demands.

The unstated goals of the war included the consolidation of political power and legitimacy by rightist forces in the frontline countries and in the Arab world as a whole. In this sense the oil weapon can best be understood as a class weapon, an instrument for providing the Sadat regime with a political victory over Israel and a means of expanding the political and economic role of Saudi Arabia, Iran and other reactionary forces throughout the Arab world. It thus furthered the political trend set in motion by the defeat of the radical nationalist Arab regimes in 1967. It also furthered U.S. goals of promoting the reactionary regimes against more radical elements. For the United States, under Kissinger's direction, the war provoked the crisis which Kissinger used to justify a shift from almost complete reliance on Zionism to a more equal reliance on Arab reaction as well.

The war proved to be the political tremor that unleashed pressures that had been building for more than a generation for the producing states to take unilateral control of pricing and production policies. The result was the sharp increase in crude prices and significant cutbacks in production for conservation and political reasons. This in turn, though, has not proved to be an unmitigated blessing, as the capitalist countries and corporations have expanded their markets into the Middle East and are lining up secure supplies of raw materials and profits as well. The bulk of the oil revenues are being spent in ways that strengthen rather than weaken the prevailing international system. Even the development of primary industries like steel and petrochemicals comes at a time when the multinational corporations are looking for locations where labor is controlled by regimes whose most modern sector is the police and armed forces, and where pollution can be imposed.

Will the Middle East oil producers be content with moving one rung up the ladder but being no closer to the top? Saudi Arabia under its present regime no doubt will. What about the radical nationalist regimes like Algeria and Iraq? They have made the most serious efforts to develop well-integrated economies relatively less open to the vicissitudes of the international system. But the Algerian program, at least, has been subjected to sharp criticism from Algerian dissidents who argue that its industrialization is being accomplished on the basis of an exchange with international capital, that it is highly dependent on the importation of Western equipment and technology, and that to date it has tended to reinforce the hydrocarbon export orientation of the economy, albeit at a higher stage. The existence of this debate is a reflection of the fact that the highly integrated and pervasive nature of the international capitalist economy calls into question the possibility of development outside that system except along the path of socialist revolution.

The debate further shows the distinct need for a class perspective in discussing the merits of economic nationalism as a development strategy, since that nationalism in and of itself seldom represents sharp disengagement from the international system. Patterns of uneven development and distorted income distribution are reproduced and accentuated within and among the countries and regions. In an age where the most dynamic force is the multinational corporation, economic nationalism may not reflect more than the growth of a techno-bureaucratic class committed to a version of state capitalism and leading to a modification but not a radical change of the country's economic role. It may reflect a shift in the basis of capital accumulation from primary production and industries to technology-intensive producer and consumer goods in which international capital is mainly interested in a reliable and adequate supply of raw materials, even at a higher price and not necessarily maintaining direct control. It is surely no mere slip of the tongue that led Kissinger to discuss Third World demands at UNCTAD in terms of "trade unionism," and from a class perspective economic nationalism may serve as an alternative rather than a stepping stone to socialism.

But this is simply to suggest the shape of the present stage, for the resulting relationship is bound to be anything but stable. The interaction between the class and national struggles of the Arab people will surely produce violent ruptures in the future of which the current struggle in Lebanon is one manifestation. In a study of the significant economic aspects of the struggle from a political point of view, an understanding of the changing class formations of Arab societies and the shifting class character of their leadership is essential. Understanding that leadership is a necessary precondition to changing it. One thing that is clear from this survey, but which has been conveniently shelved by the Arab regimes today, is that the struggle against Zionism can only be won by struggling against imperialism, not by striking deals with future Kissingers.

Notes

1. The text of the convention can be found in Charles Issawi, ed., *Economic History of the Middle East* (Chicago, 1966), p. 39.

2. Z.Y. Hershlag, *Introduction to the Modern Economic History of the Middle East* (Leiden, 1964), pp. 44-5.

3. Urquhart, "Turkey," in Issawi, *Economic History*, p. 42.

4. M.S. Hasan, "the Role of Foreign Trade in the Economic Development of Iraq, 1864-1964," in *Studies in the Economic History of the Middle East*, (ed., M.A. Cook (London, 1970), p. 346.

5. Edward C. Clark, "The Ottoman Industrial Revolution," *International*

Journal of Middle East Studies 5 (1974): 66-7.

6. *Ibid.*, p. 69.

7. *Ibid.*, p. 73.

8. Samih Farsoun, "Changes in Labor Force Structure in Selected Arab Countries," paper presented at the Joint AAUG – Kuwait National Council for Culture, Arts and Letters Conference on Issues in Human Resource Development in the Arab World, December, 1975.

9. Charles Issawi, *Egypt in Revolution* (London, 1963), p. 19.

10. Hasan, "Role of Foreign Trade", p. 349.

11. *Ibid.*, pp. 350-52.

12. John Reudy, "Dynamics of Land Alienation," in *The Transformation of Palestine*, ed. Ibrahim Abu-Lughod (Evanston, 1971), p. 124.

13. William Polk, et al., *Backdrop to Tragedy* (Boston, 1957), p. 236, quoted in Reudy, "Dynamics," p. 124.

14. Talal Asad, "Anthropological Texts and Ideological Problems," in *Review of Middle East Studies I*, eds. Asad and Owen (London, 1975), p. 15.

15. *Ibid.*, p. 15.

16. *Ibid.*, pp. 15-16.

17. *Ibid.*, p. 18.

18. David Waines, "The Nationalist Resistance," in Abu Lughod, *Transformation*, p. 224.

19. *Ibid.*, p. 227. Emphasis in original.

20. *Ibid.*, pp. 227-8.

21. *Ibid.*, p. 230.

22. For an analysis of the motives of the Arab states in this period, *see* Fawwaz Trabulsi, "The Palestine Problem," *New Left Review* 57 (September/October 1969): 65-71.

23. Sheila Ryan, "Israeli Economic Policy in the Occupied Areas," *MERIP Reports* 24 (January 1974): 5.

24. *Ibid.*,

25. Abba Eban, *Voice of Israel* (New York, 1957) p. 111.

26. Ryan, "Israeli Economic," p. 6.

27. Don Peretz, *Israel and the Palestine Arabs* (Washington, 1958), p. 143.

28. *Foreign Relations of the United States*, 1946, VII (Washington, 1969), p. 632.

29. Trabulsi, "Palestine Problem," pp. 68-9, 73.

30. Testimony to the Subcommittee on Multinational Corporations, Senate Foreign Relations Committee, January 28, 1974; released February 24, 1974.

31. *Middle East Economic Survey*, November 18, 1966.

32. United Nations Economic and Social Office in Beirut, *Studies on Selected Development Problems in Various Countries in the Middle East* (New York, 1967), pp. 14-15.

33. Trabulsi, "Palestine Problem," pp. 80, 84.

34. *Middle East Economic Survey*, September 1, 1967.

35. *MEES*, September 22, 1967.

36. *MEES*, January 12, 1968.

37. *MEES*, September 5, 1969.

38. Zuhayr Mikdashi, ed., *Continuity and Change in the World Oil Industry* (Beirut, 1970), p. 220.

39. Joe Stork, *Middle East Oil and the Energy Crisis* (New York, 1975), p. 299.

40. Malcom Kerr, "Nixon's Policy Prospects," *Journal of Palestine Studies*, Spring 1973, pp. 28-9.

41. *MEES*, August 17, 1973.

13 THE EFFICACY OF ZIONIST IDEOLOGY AND ITS IMPLICATIONS FOR THE ARAB-ISRAELI CONFLICT

Michael C. Hudson

There is no doubt that Zionism today remains an exclusivist, particularist ideology, a throwback to the folk nationalisms of the mid-nineteenth century. Nor is there any doubt that the behavioral manifestations of Zionism in the Israeli state have given rise to systematic discrimination against Arabs, both Muslim and Christian, and also against Jews from Arab societies. This pattern of discrimination has been so widely observed by Western journalists, Arab lawyers like Sabri Jiryis, and even by Israelis such as Israel Shahak and Felicia Langer as to require no further elaboration.[1] As the recent events in the Galilee and Hebron indicate, the policy of discrimination has not diminished over the years, despite the relaxation of military restrictions in some areas. Rather, it continues up to this very day and in such an aggressive form as to require the physical displacement of Arab individuals and communities.[2]

It is important, therefore, to dwell upon the exclusivist character of Zionism if a proper understanding of this phenomenon is to be reached. But such a focus should not obscure another characteristic of Zionism that is even more important for an understanding of its remarkable political efficacy. This is what may be called the multiple appeals of Zionism to people, Jews and non-Jews, living outside Israel. If Zionism is understood simply as the racist nationalism of a small state called Israel the main sources of its power are ignored. One of these is the Jewish communities of the Western societies. The other is among important non-Jewish elites of these societies. The fact that a nationalism so exclusivist in its practices, so parochial in its concerns, and so defective in its moral vision could generate interest, let alone support, from outsiders, Jewish or non-Jewish, is seemingly paradoxical. It demands additional explanation.

Today it may seem self-evident that the natural constituency of Zionism should be all the world's Jews. In fact, however, the political congruence of Zionism and Judaism is of relatively recent origin and still far from consolidated. Not until World War II did the Zionist movement become the dominant political tendency in Judaism, and perhaps not until the 1967 war did it succeed in mobilizing Jews on a truly mass scale. It has taken concerted effort by Zionist thinkers and organizers to win world Judaism to their program. How was this accomplished? The answer lies in the multiple faces which Zionism could present to Jews of different orientations. Chameleon-like, it could take on a variety of ideological colorations and thus broaden its appeal in the diverse Jewish communities of the West.

Similarly, Zionism could and still does present a variety of faces to non-Jews. To be able to do so seems incompatible, if not directly contradictory, with exclusivism and particularism; yet these mutliple appeals have had an undeniable reality — and success. Although Zionism is centrally concerned with what it has unilaterally defined as the political aspirations of the world's Jews, it is also — and paradoxically — a movement which has been able to enlist supporters and sympathizers from important non-Jewish elites throughout the Western world. To them Zionism is not racist chauvinism but a moral force, a religious doctrine, a means of assuaging guilt and even latent anti-Semitism, and a strategic and economic interest. An instructive comparison in this respect may be made with Arab nationalism. Although Arab nationalism, in its various forms, has many friends in the Third World, it generates mainly indifference or outright hostility from the Western industrial societies.

Zionism's success among Western gentiles, of course, is due in part to the influential Jewish communties that are found throughout the West, especially in the United States. The distribution of Jewish communities clearly is important in explaining the success of Zionism as an organization. But, contrary to some impressions, the Jewish communities in the West do not control the larger non-Jewish societies. They remain minorities, and still — unfortunately — in several countries, despised minorities to bigots in the majority populations. They are well-to-do minorities in most cases but in no way do they possess the economic or financial influence to control the majority societies. The answer lies in the content of Zionist ideology and the specific appeals which Zionism makes to specific elites.

Whatever the political situation at any given moment may be — such as at the present time when it appears that Israel is once again in a superior position because of inter-Arab weaknesses — the long-term fact is that Israel's future depends increasingly on the support it must have from non-Jewish sources in the West. Anybody interested in the future of Palestine, therefore, must have the best possible understanding of the ideological linkages between Zionism and the world outside.

Appeals to World Jewry

The early history of Zionism affords some interesting insights into the diversity of the Jewish peoples in the nineteenth century and the diversity of ideological appeals embodied in such seminal thinkers of Zionism as Leon Pinsker, Ahad Ha-Am, A.D. Gordon and Theodor Herzl. What emerged in the first Zionist Congress at Basle in 1897 and definitely by the seventh Zionist Conference of 1905 was a program that responded to several strongly felt, if contradictory, concerns in the European Jewish communities.

One of these concerns was fear. Plagued by persecution in the Christian societies of Europe ever since their expulsion from Palestine by the Romans, many Jews dreaded the thought of extinction as an ethnic-religious community. Even during periods of Gentile toleration, such as the post-Napoleonic Enlightenment, there were some who feared the obliteration of their culture precisely because of such tolerance. In the enlightened societies of France, Britain and Germany in the early nineteenth century, the solution to the "Jewish problem" was assimilation. Jews were given the opportunity to merge into the majority's society and culture — and many, especially in the middle and upper classes, took it. Yet some Jewish intellectuals feared that the unique Jewish heritage might thus ultimately disappear. The more predominant and intensely felt fear, of course, was the fear of physical persecution through the progroms. As historians like Arthur Hertzberg have pointed out, the progroms of Russia in 1881 following the assassination of Tsar Alexander II unleashed terror in the ghettoes of Eastern Europe.[3] Then, in the 1890s, the blight of anti-Semitism broke out in the presumably enlightened Western Europe when the Dreyfuss affair rocked French society. In her autobiography Golda Meir paints a vivid description of the fear felt by her family and neighbors in the ghetto of Pinsk.[4] And so, the emerging common element in the European Jewish perspective of the late nineteenth century was a palpable fear — the fear of not belonging. It was an attitude that was given perhaps its most dramatic expression by the early Zionist thinker, Leon Pinsker:

> The essence of the problem, as we see it, lies in the fact that, in the midst of the nations among whom the Jews reside, they form a distinct element which cannot be readily digested by any nation. . . . Among the living nations of the earth the Jews occupy the position of a nation long since dead. . . . This ghostlike apparition of a people without unity or organization, without land or other bond of union,

no longer alive, and yet moving about among the living — this eerie form scarcely paralleled in history, unlike anything that preceded or followed it, could not fail to make a strange and peculiar impression upon the imagination of the nations. . . . He must be blind indeed who will assert that the Jews are not *the chosen people*, the people chosen for universal hatred.[5]

The persecutions perpetrated by Adolph Hitler in the 1930s and 1940s against the Jews and other minorities, far overshadowed anything ever done by the Tsar or even contemplated by pessimistic Zionists. The Nazi holocaust is still too firmly branded on the consciousness of Jews today living in Europe, Russia and the United States to allow them to rest fully at ease in their societies. Many do not believe that "it can't happen here." That, they feel, is what their naïve German Jewish forbears thought, and they paid for their complacency in the ovens of Auschwitz. One's impression is that much of the appeal of Zionism today for even the most comfortable and secure Jewish communties in the United States lies in the idea of Israel as a haven, a place they can retreat to, in case an epidemic of anti-Semitism should break out in the West. The almost hysterical joy which erupted in American Jewish communities in 1967 and again most recently at Entebbe, seems to reflect a deeply rooted insecurity; and any spectacular manifestation of Israeli power has for them an almost cathartic effect.

Insofar as latent fear is an important bulwark of Zionist support among Western Jews, it has very little to do directly with the Arabs. For most Jews the Arabs are basically a primitive people and unable to carry out a holocaust on their own; the real dangers lie among the Christian peoples of the West. Obviously, however, when Jews see both the United States and the Soviet Union providing military assistance to Arab regimes, even when both superpowers are known to support Israel's continued existence, it gives rise to a great deal of alarm. The defeat suffered by the Zionist lobby in Washington over arms to Saudi Arabia and and anti-Arab boycott legislation gave rise to considerable anxiety among American Jews, an anxiety only partly assuaged by the grant of $1 billion in arms to Israel a few days later.

But Zionism does more than relieve fear and anxiety among Western Jews. It also has come to shape for them a specific sense of nationalism which in turn reflects a deep-seated desire for assimilation as a nation in the world of nations. This is the second principal appeal of Zionism for Jews. The historical Jewish dilemma of desiring both acceptance and separateness at the same time is circumvented through the existence of a Jewish state — a state like all states, with sovereignty, territory, coercive power, and national identity; and yet at the same time a state within which the uniqueness of Jewish culture can be preserved and developed. The primary exponent of assimilation-through-nationalism was Theodor Herzl. It was Herzl's audacious idea, expounded in *The Jewish State*, that the Jews could turn European anti-Semitism to their own advantage by arguing that a separate Jewish state would draw Jews out of the Western societies. Furthermore, inasmuch as the Jews of Herzl's class and orientation considered themselves (anti-Semitism notwithstanding) a part of the Western cultural and political tradition, he could even argue that a Jewish state could actually be helpful to the cause of European imperialism.[6] Accordingly, the Jewish people, through the agency of the Jewish state, would become assimilated into the world of nations.

Originally, the specific location of such a state was relatively unimportant, and Zionists were divided between East Africa and Palestine. But once the Palestine adherents had won the day the next step was to begin to fashion linkages with that particular piece of territory. Since the Western European Zionists were essentially secular, the religious ties of the Jews of Palestine played only a subordinate role in their thinking. Among the Jews of eastern Europe the religious importance of Palestine was much stronger; the idea of a Jewish nation-state was subordinate to the goals of establishing essentially non-nationalist settlements with a pious communal or secular socialist utopian character. What the Zionist immigrants who began pouring into Palestine early in this century eventually succeeded in accomplishing was the merging of these original diverse tendencies into a coherent ideology of Jewish territorial and sovereign nationhood. By the mid-1930s the revisionists and the militant Zionists led by Ben-Gurion were in the ascendent, and the goal of a Jewish sovereign state rather than the ambiguous "national home" was virtually undisguised. So, after the Nazi holocaust and the formal establishment of Israel, Zionism developed into a highly nationalist ideology rooted in the land of Palestine. The idea that all the Jews of the world somehow held title to that land because Jewish tribes had migrated into it 4000 years ago and at times had established political control was widely propagated. The fact that the Jews had been largely driven out of Palestine by the Romans in the second century A.D., never to return in numbers until the twentieth century, and the extreme tenuousness of any racial or sociocultural similarity between the modern Western Jews and the Jewish inhabitants of Biblical Palestine, did not prevent this idea from gradually winning wide and fervent acceptance among Jews throughout the world.

In Israel itself, the national passion for archaeology was only the most obvious symptom of the need to establish (or to obliterate nagging latent uncertainties) about the people's link with the land. Many Jews, of course, were disturbed (and continue to be disturbed) about the implications which the loyalty claims of a distinct Jewish nation-state, Israel, hold for their loyalty to the nation-states in which they are citizens and in which they reside. On balance, however, since the 1967 war Zionism appears to have succeeded in winning over many of the world's Jews through its celebration of a *machismo* kind of national identity, one which to people who have been a persecuted minority has an understandable appeal. One receives the impression that for many Jews outside Israel, the Jewish state, with its skill, cunning, and bravado in the martial arts, becomes an instrument for surrogate assimilation into the world of the mighty.

The third way in which Zionism today appeals to Jews outside Israel is through its ideological pluralism. However monolithic and exclusivist it may be in terms of its basic nationalism, it has come to offer a loose compatibility for a variety of ideological currents present among the Jewish communities in the West. This ideological pluralism also exerts an appeal to non-Jews. Philosophic difficulties notwithstanding, it is possible to be a Zionist and also a capitalist or socialist, a pious believer or a secularist, a friend of Western neo-imperialism or a friend of the Third World. Early Zionism or proto-Zionism had its religious humanists like Ahad Ha-Am and its socialists like A. D. Gordon. It had its brazen imperialists like Herzl and its liberals like Magnes. There was philanthropic Zionism, cultural Zionism, messianic Zionism, practical Zionism and revisionist Zionism. One can only speculate as to whether these different and contradictory Zionisms would not have withered away through endless factional struggles if the Zionist leadership had not succeeded, through the Balfour Declaration, in obtaining its toe-hold in Palestine. Once that toehold was achieved, all the Zionist tendencies had a concrete territorial reality to focus upon and support; and the success of the leaders of the *Yishuv* in building national institutions which could accommodate this pluralism and yet contain its natural self-destructiveness, gave Zionism both a structure and a catholicity which in the future would stand it in good stead in mobilizing the Jews outside.

To be sure, there were and still are serious divisions within Zionism both inside and outside Israel. Some small splinter groups, either highly orthodox in their religion or of an uncompromising progressive-inter-nationalist character, reject the all-embracing nationalist shell of modern Zionism. Anti-Zionist Jewish organizations still exist in the United States and Europe. Nevertheless, it appears that just as almost all Israelis accept the basic territorial and national postulates of Zionism, so too do most Jews in the world uncritically accept these assumptions. In the United States, certainly, it is rare to find a Jew opposed to the national legitimacy of Israel; and while one can find a good many Jews (notably on college campuses) that are opposed to specific Israeli policies (some indeed, believe that Israeli policies toward the Arabs are racist) these too are a small minority. Part of the secret of this success is that Zionism is relatively tolerant of ideologies that do not directly challenge its own nationalist core values.

Appeals to Non-Jews in the West

One does not have to be Jewish to be Zionist. Zionism has proven remarkably functional in appealing to a wide variety of constituencies. At first glance it seems incongruous if not illogical that an ideology so exclusively centered on Judaism should excite any important support from non-Jews. A Jew usually explains his or her adherence to Zionist doctrine on the basis of his primordial membership in the Jewish people – an ethnic identification reinforced by religious law – or else by his intellectual and spiritual adherence to the precepts of the Jewish religion. Usually it is some combination of the two. Yet this creed, which owes its appeal to its members to some extent precisely because it excludes the less-enlightened, even misguided or hostile outsiders, still exerts a distinct magnetism for these very outsiders. Much of the success of Israel is due to Christian Zionists like Lord Balfour and President Truman. Respected spokesmen for the Christian churches – Catholic and Protestant – argue the case for Zionism with as much fervor as the rabbis. In the United States, at least, the pro-Zionist orientation of important editors, columnists, journalists and television commentators is conspicuous; yet these people are often as not non-Jewish.

To explain the popularity of Zionism among non-Jews by asserting that the news media are all owned by Jews is not only factually wrong but tends to obscure an important aspect of the strength of Zionism as an ideology. In no way can it be shown that the news media or the educational system are controlled by Jews, and even if they were it would still not be a satisfactory explanation for the general acceptance of Zionism. Nor is it particularly enlightening to explain this phenomenon, in the United States at least, by asserting that Americans gullibly accept whatever they read; such assertions, in the first place, are insults to the intelligence of Americans and, in the second place, are contradicted by the deeply engrained individualism and skepticism in the American character. Explanations such as these simply will not do.

The fact remains, however, that Zionism is widely accepted by non-Jews who, by definition, cannot be said to accept it on the grounds of some primordial identification with the "tribe." There has to be, therefore, a factor of intellectual rationality involved. People consciously choose to support Zionism because they believe that it is congruent with other deeply felt values. Its appeal to non-Jews rests upon its supposed congruence with the Judaeo-Christian tradition, its parallels in Christian fundamentalist theology, its function as restitution for the sins inflicted on the Jews by the West, its pioneering ethos, its egalitarian character, and Israel's alleged position as the weaker party in its conflict with the Arabs. In addition Zionism and Israel exert a purely pragmatic appeal to the political elites of the West, especially the United States; politicians find that support for Zionism pays off in terms of financing and votes in electoral campaigns; and foreign-policy-makers perceive Israel as a strategic asset to the United States, as long as Israel appears militarily preponderant and the Arabs appear militarily weak and politically divided.

Arab-Islamic civilization and the Western Judaeo-Christian tradition have much in common in terms of religious values, rationalism, and humanistic and scientific accomplishments; thus it is difficult to understand the gap which most Westerners perceive between their culture and that of what was quaintly known as "the Orient" or "the mysterious East." In reality, the conventional Western perception of the Arab world is colored by deep-rooted prejudice. Only relatively recently has Islam been regarded in an objective light, and the residue of older biases lingers on, even in reputable American universities. Memories of the Crusades (or the Crusader myth) do not die easily.[7] But, today, the problem of the "gap" is mainly a problem of ignorance rather than of outright prejudice. In the United States, most school children go through the secondary level without any serious exposure to non-Western culture, and what little material they receive about the Arab world is, more often than not, fraught with a degree of bias, often unwitting.[8] Even at the university level, while there are now at least twenty programs that deal with the Middle East (and the Arab world, to some extent), very few university students are involved with them. But the average American is familiar with Israel or "the Holy Land" from learning about it in Sunday schools and reading about it (usually portrayed in a positive light) in their daily newspapers. Israel is portrayed as an outpost of civilization in a region otherwise noted only for backwardness and barbarism.

While a fairly large proportion of Westerners has some general notion of the Holy Land but little else in the Middle East, there is a smaller section of fundamentalist Protestant Christians (mostly Baptists) whose ideas about Israel are much more fully crystallized. These "Bible Belt" Christians sincerely believe that the return of the Jews to Palestine is ordained by Scriptures and is an event to be celebrated. Efforts by non-believers or infidels to thwart the return of the Jews are viewed, accordingly, as sins of the highest order. Perhaps such fundamentalism is more a political factor in the United States than elsewhere; but even the Catholic and Protestant establishments have been supportive of a Jewish return to Palestine, especially in light of the desire for ecumenical cooperation.

Then there is the guilt factor. Zionism owes much of its non-Jewish support in the West, it is argued, because Europeans and Americans feel a deep collective sense of guilt for the destruction of the Jews by the Nazi German regime. The issue has been discussed so fully that there is no need to comment further here except to underline the fact that the horrors of the holocaust have been (and continue to be) presented in grim detail to the entire educated strata in the West. They are, in short, very well-known, an important fact in estimating the significance of the guilt factor. It might be added, however, that "guilt" is perhaps not quite the correct term for what many Americans and Europeans feel. Today, one would surmise, there is less a sense of collective guilt about what happened as there is (in America at least) an attitude that the Jews have been badly treated by historical circumstances and that, consequently, it would be decent and humane to lend them a helping hand. Zionism has provided a ready vehicle for implementing these sentiments in a concrete manner. To many Westerners the idea of establishing, and now maintaining, a Jewish commonwealth is an eminently sensible method for recompensing the Jews for the bad treatment they received at the hands of others. Conversely, not to support the Jewish state when it is threatened by Arab enemies, who, are perceived as alien to Western cultural tradition, is viewed not only as a mean thing to do but also as an abrogation of the obligation implicitly assumed by helping create the Zionist entity in the first place.

Another element in the appeal of Zionism to non-Jews is its seeming compatibility with a variety of other deeply held ideological principles. Just as Zionism could, in a broad sense, embrace a variety of disparate ideological tendencies within Judaism, so too it appears to express values, many of which are mutually contradictory, among non-Jews which have nothing directly to do with the Jewish people. Possibly the most important of these values is democracy. U.S. politicians never tire of justifying their support on the grounds that Israel is "an outpost of democracy." If what is meant is liberal democracy, characterized by meaningful structures of popular representation and freedom of political expression and activity, then the appellation is substantially correct when applied to Israel's Jewish population. The fact that Israel has never treated its Arab population as fully equal to its Jewish nationals is not widely known and where it is known it is justified (as it is in Israel) on grounds of state security. The relevant point here is that to Western elites, the Zionist state appears to embody, or at least strive for, the same political ideals so highly valued by Western societies. This common democratic basis makes it easier for Western elites to *identify* with Israel; it brings Israel psychologically closer to them. In contrast, of course, the Arab political systems — regardless of conservative or progressive ideology — appear alien, to say the least.

The Zionist ideology also holds attractions for socialists and capitalists alike in the West. To progressives, Israel still tries to present itself as a socialist state, even though its private sector is large and flourishing. The ruling Labour party and coalition of Israel is officially socialist, and Israeli leaders regularly attend the meetings of European socialist parties. The distribution of national income in Israel is one of the most equal in the world — a statistical demonstration of one of socialism's central tenets.[9] Once again, the inequalities suffered by the Arab community and the Arab Jewish communities are masked; and the exploitation of Arab labor in the occupied territories, to the detriment of their development, is concealed by the aggregate picture. People looking at Israel from afar perceive only the positive aspects and tend to be ignorant of, or unready to believe, the negative ones.

At the same time, Zionism exerts attractions to a conservative, capitalist audience. Foreign investors are hardly frightened by the fact that Israel's government is socialist; on the contrary, they find that Israelis have the most sympathetic understanding of capitalism and are ready to facilitate and guarantee investments from abroad. Even in the United States, perhaps the last country in the world where socialism is regarded as an intrinsically evil ideology, there is no discernible unhappiness with Israeli socialism; certainly Israeli banks and Israeli products are thriving in the United States, and America's volume of trade and investment in Israel is substantial indeed. It is understandable, though a bit ironical, that Western capitalist enterprise has developed a much greater interest in the Arab world, with its larger market and its petroleum, than it has, or can ever have, in Israel. In terms of political and cultural values, Zionism and Israel have "the inside track" with the West, but in terms of economic interests and opportunities they hold no such advantage; and the desperate attempts by Israel's supporters in the United States to counter the Arab boycott are a dramatic testament to the strong attraction between American capitalism and the Arab economies.

Any list of Zionism's attractions to the outside world would be incomplete without an allusion to the alleged peaceful character of the Zionist state in international relations. Implicit in the European context of Zionism's origins is the idea that the Jewish homeland would be essentially a refuge for persecuted Jews the world over. The idea that this Jewish state could ever be aggressive, or that it might behave in the amoral, if not immoral, way in which other nation-states behave, must have been hard to entertain seriously. Certainly, at the time of Israel's creation, its Western backers tended to regard it as an innocent, almost defenseless creature, which would be lucky to survive in a world of powerful, predatory adversaries. The fact that there was an expansionist strain in Zionism, and that the Zionist movement was being taken over by militants even on the eve of Israel's establishment, might have given people warning of what was to come; but most people believed, and many continue to believe, that Israel only wishes to live in peace and does not covet the territory of its neighbors. References to Zionist claims to southern Lebanon, Syria, and Transjordan, and the assertion by right-wing and religious zealots in Israel to the territory from the Nile to the Euphrates are dismissed by most Europeans and Americans as mere rhetoric. Even the four wars which Israel has waged (including the 1973 war which Israel did not initiate, but which the Arabs launched to try and recover Israeli-occupied territory), as well as its brutal assaults on southern Lebanon, are widely interpreted in the West as evidence that Israel is a victim rather than an instigator of aggression. To be sure, it has not gone unnoticed that Israel has become a modern Sparta and that its armed forces are extraordinarily capable. American military specialists concede privately that they expect that Israel will initiate the next Arab-Israeli war, and American diplomats concede privately that Israel has been far more obstructionist than the Arab states in the effort to reach a diplomatic settlement. Yet among the public at large and the leading politicians, Israel somehow maintains its image as a peaceable society and thus worthy of Western support.

It is especially ironic, therefore, that the final item in the catalogue of Zionism attractions in the West is admiration for the Jewish state's martial capabilities. If, in the United States at least, one feels a certain virtue in supporting the underdog, one feels an added, unexpected gratification, bordering on glee, when the underdog wins a round. It was natural and understandable that the Israelis should have indulged themselves in ecstatic euphoria after the 1967 victory and, more recently, after the successful Entebbe operation; but it is both curious and significant that the same emotions swept through American public opinion. It was almost as if "we" had done it ourselves. Three-quarters of a century after Herzl tried to persuade British policymakers that the Zionist state could be useful to them in a strategic sense, the Israelis have made considerable progress in convincing American policymakers that they constitute a strategic asset to the West, mainly by virtue of their power in the region.

The Political Consequences

The fact that Zionism today exerts multiple appeals to a variety of constituencies in the world has important implications for the course of the Arab-Israeli conflict. In the first place, it distorts rational Israeli foreign policymaking because it persuades the policymakers that they have both the obligation and the ability to involve all the Jews of the world and their sympathizers in the pursuit of Israeli national interests. In the process, such perspectives also lead to an exaggeration of what actually constitute valid Israeli national interests. Second, because Zionism is so influential in the formation of American Middle East policy, U.S. policy is often premised on the assumption of a complete congruence of interests between Israel and the United States. The operative question in American policy thus becomes, "What can we do to support Israel?" rather than "What policy best serves American interests?" Third, the many faces of Zionism tend to confuse Arab policymakers and opinion leaders. This confusion takes various forms and has a number of implications, but possibly the most important is the climate of uncertainty which it generates. It is difficult to come to terms with a force which embodies so many contradictory elements and whose ultimate objectives are by no means clear. While Israel's immediate interests are thus served by keeping the Arabs off balance, the long-term consequence is an ominous and pervasive sense of distrust and insecurity which can easily lead to policy miscalculations.

In his definitive study of the Israeli foreign policy process, Michael Brecher rightly draws attention to the importance of political culture in affecting the decision-making process and then asserts that in Israel the "primordial and pre-eminent aspect of the political culture [is] its Jewishness." He writes that members of the High Policy Elite "perceive Jewry as a world people of which Israelis are an integral part." Emphasizing Israel's link with Jewish antiquity and the experience of the Holocaust, these policymakers

> perceive the State of Israel as the logical, and necessary, and rightful successor to the collective interests and rights of the few who survived. Israel as the voice, the representative, and the defender of Jews in distress anywhere – this is a role which flows naturally from the "Jewish prism." Through this lens too, there is created an expectation that world Jewry will reciprocate with massive and continuous support for that segment of the People resettled in the Homeland.[10]

Jewish policymakers, in short, do not see themselves simply as the leaders of a small nation of three million people; their goals and their perceptions of their policy options are of much broader scope. What has emerged over the years is a curious amalgam of messianic perspectives and highly pragmatic, *realpolitik* practices. Noting that the militant insiders, typified by Ben-Gurion, Dayan, Peres, Allon, and Begin, gained predominance over the moderate outsiders like Weizmann, Sharett and Eban, Brecher observes that militancy and coercion became the norm in Israel's dealings with the Arabs while at the same time there was a cynical exploitation of its links with American Zionism to carry on the struggle.[11]

The American connection today is even more vital for the success of Israeli policy objectives than it has been in the past. The strength of that connection also seems to have increased. While there were some signs just after the 1973 war, during that rare and brief period when Arab strength, determination and unity had been credibly demonstrated, that the U.S. government might place some constraints on its policy of total support for Israel, subsequent developments indicate very little significant change. The bases for the pro-Israel bias in U.S. foreign policy are complex.[12] It suffices to indicate that in a poll conducted in September 1976, designed to compare the differences between Republican and Democratic party workers, the investigators found clear disagreements in every foreign policy area except the Middle East. "In only one area, Middle East policy, did they tend to come together. Great majorities of both groups agreed with a statement that 'the United States has a moral obligation to prevent the destruction of

Israel,' and disagreed with a statement that 'to protect our supply of oil, the United States should be more pro-Arab in the Middle East conflict.'[13] Addressing a Washington conference on Arab and American cultures, Senator James Abourezk, the first U.S. Senator of Arab origin, remarked that he did not see "a nickel's worth of difference" between presidential candidates Gerald Ford and Jimmy Carter on the Middle East question. And in the second Ford-Carter debate, on foreign policy, the two candidates tried to outdo each other in courting the Jewish vote with the extravagance of their promised support for Israel. Shortly thereafter President Ford gave $1 billion in arms aid to Israel. Nothing had changed on the internal scene since the Truman-Dewey campaign of 1948.

One can only surmise how Arab policymakers now analyze the Zionist phenomenon. Some of the past perceptions and reactions have been simplistic, for example, the view that equated Zionism and international communism, or that conceived of a Jewish conspiracy to take over the world. Hopefully, such erroneous views are no longer seriously entertained. The fact remains, however, that Zionism still poses dilemmas for rational Arab policymakers. The multifaceted appeals of Zionism to important constituencies outside Israel, and Israel's cynical manipulation of the Western Jewish communities cannot but be disquieting. Israel's persistent unwillingness to define its borders may be nothing more than a sensible bargaining maneuver, but it can also be interpreted as evidence of latent expansionist tendencies. The unwillingness or inability of Israeli governments to renounce historic claims or to oppose effectively the militant Jewish settlers in the occupied territories cannot but be disturbing. As long as the same militance which has characterized past Zionist policy toward the Arabs continues, Arab policymakers must face its implications in terms of military, and nuclear, possibilities. The fact that Zionism historically has been unable to perceive the Arabs as human beings carries grave doubts about the possibility of military restraint in the future. If Israeli leaders feel that they can count on American backing in almost any adventure (whether or not this feeling is correct), then Arab leaders are not unreasonable to expect adventurous behavior on their part. Furthermore, the position of moderate Arab opinionmakers and policymakers can only be weakened by militant inflexible Israeli stands. In short, the hardline *realpolitik* of Zionist policymakers tends to strengthen the case for militancy on the Arab side, in strictly rational terms. Given the multidimensional nature of Zionism and its successes in building up a variety of constituencies, the Arabs find themselves driven to responses which appear emotional and irrational, even though they can be supported by logic and prudence.

What does seem beyond dispute, however, is that Arab policies to counter Zionism and Israeli expansion, have thus far been almost completely unsuccessful. They have not only failed to prevent the establishment of the Jewish state on Arab land, they have also failed to contain it. These failures have been accompanied by catastrophic human, material and territorial losses. There have been some successes in terms of losses inflicted on Israel and the isolation of Israel from the greater part of world opinion. But Israel's lifeline to the United States remains as solid as ever, while the Americans for the most part remain either ignorant, indifferent or hostile to Arab aspirations. Only when objective knowledge about the Arab world has been widely diffused over a long period of time is the situation likely to change.

From an Arab point of view, therefore, it would seem that there is a great need for further study of the Zionist phenomenon. Such a study must go beyond the discovery that Zionists are racist in their attitude towards Arabs. What requires study are the implications of such attitudes in the formation of Israeli policy and, just as important, the functions of Zionism as an ideology instrumentally capable of mobilizing a diverse group of powerful constituencies outside Israel itself and even outside the Jewish communities of the world. Above all, it is important to remember that Zionism has been an effective instrument for political mobilization; its leaders, as Erskine Childers states, were superb long-range planners.[14] No matter how obvious the parochial atavism of Zionism may be, it serves a political movement unexelled in the rationality — and ruthlessness — of its methods.

Notes

1. *See* Sabri Jiryis, *The Arabs in Israel* (New York, 1976); Felicia Langer, *With My Own Eyes* (London, 1975); Uri Davis and Norton Mezvinsky, eds., *Documents from Israel 1967-1973* (London, 1975). A casual sampling of articles in *The Washington Post, The New York Times* and *The Christian Science Monitor* since October 1975 which are critical of Israel's discrimination against its Arab inhabitants includes William J. Drummond, "Zionism Gives Israel's Arabs an Uphill Life," *Washington Post*, 12 November 1975; Eric Silver, "Israel Applies Pressure in Nazareth Election," *Washington Post*, 9 December 1975; William J. Drummond, "Christians Pressure Israel for Old Lands," *Washington Post*, 6 May 1976; John K. Cooley, "Political Dissenter in Israel Fearful of Another War," *Christian Science Monitor*, 14 July 1976; William E. Farrell, "Fence Touches a Nerve with West Bank Arabs," *The New York Times*, 11 August 1976; Jason Morris, "Israel Draws Line in West Bank," *Christian Science Monitor*, 26 August

1976; John Chadwick, "Settlement Efforts of Israel Rightists Anger Arab
Hebron," *Washington Post*, 27 August 1976; and William J. Drummond, "Israeli
Settlements Called Obstacle to Peace Accord," *Washington Post*, 26 September
1976.

2. *See*, for example, on the current dispute over the "Koenig Report,"
William E. Farrell, "Israeli Arabs Call a Strike in Galilee," *New York Times*,
23 September 1976; and William E. Farrell, "Israeli's Proposal on Arabs
Disputed," *The New York Times*, 9 September 1976.

3. For an enlightening and sympathetic analysis of Zionist thought, *see*
Arthur Hertzberg's introduction in Hertzberg, ed., *The Zionist Idea* (New York,
1959), pp. 15-100.

4. Golda Meir, *My Life* (New York, 1975), pp. 17-27.

5. Pinsker, excerpts from "auto-Emancipation," reprinted in Hertzberg,
Zionist Idea, pp. 182-85.

6. Theodor Herzl, *The Jewish State* (1896).

7. Some examples of this prejudice, *see* Phillip K. Hitti, *Islam and The
West: A Historical Cultural Survey* (Princeton, N.J. 1962), Chap. 4, "Islam in
Western Literature."

8. Committee on the Image of the Middle East, *The Image of the Middle East
in Secondary School Textbooks* (New York, 1975). "In far too many texts the
Committee found not only errors but also bias. This often occurs in regard to
Islam and the Arab world when authors display latent prejudices abetted by care-
less research, poor writing, and inadequate editing," p. 25. The committee was
chaired by Professor Farhat J. Ziadeh of the University of Washington, Seattle.

9. For income inequality estimates, *see* Charles L. Taylor and Michael
C. Hudson, *World Handbook of Political and Social Indicators*, 2nd ed. (New
Haven, 1972), pp. 263-66.

10. Michael Brecher, *The Foreign Policy System of Israel* (New Haven, 1972),
pp. 229-31.

11. *Ibid.*, pp. 246-47.

12. Michael C. Hudson, "Domestic Politics and American Policy in the Arab-
Israeli Conflict," *Politique Etrangère* (Paris) 39, no. 6 (December 1974): 641-58.

13. Barry Sussman, "Elites in America: a Washington Post-Harvard Survey,"
The Washington Post, 27 September 1976, p. A2.

14. Erskine Childers, "The Worldless Wish: From Citizens to Refugees," in
The Transformation of Palestine, ed. Ibrahim Abu-Lughod (Evanson, Ill. 1971),
pp. 165-202, esp. pp. 166-78.

14 SECTARIANISM AND ZIONISM: TWO ELEMENTARY FORMS OF CONSCIOUSNESS

Halim Barakat

Sectarianism in Lebanon and Zionism in Israel are two ideologies based on primordial sentiments and committed to rigid orders that foster the dominance of one religious community over others. Both have negative consequences for Arab society. Their basic task is to maintain a specific religious community in power, to preserve the existing hierarchical arrangements, and to spread their models into the neighboring countries. In fact, Arabs are faced with two alternative designs for themselves. One is more in continuity with the prevailing trends and aims at further dismantling of Arab society by the establishment of small states as national homes for the different ethnic and religious communities in the area. The alternative design represents a departure from the status quo and aims at the establishment of a unified, secular and democratic Arab country.

The first design is partly intended to secure Western domination and the legitimization of the existence of Israel. It is most significant to point out that the prevailing conditions in Arab countries provide the needed climate for dismantling of the Arab society, the legitimization of Israel, the fostering of sectarianism in Lebanon, and the diffusion of these models in the whole area. These prevailing conditions are not merely political. Much more basic is the dominance in Lebanon and other Arab countries of traditional ties and vertical loyalties represented in grouping on the basis of religion, kinship, ethnic, regional and similar identification.[1]

The alternative design, namely, the establishment of a unified secular-democratic Arab country requires liberation from traditional ties and value orientations and the development of a higher order of national and social class consciousness. The current civil war in Lebanon which witnessed drastic shifts in alliances (particularly the support of several Arab countries to the isolationists) demonstrates beyond doubt that there is an urgent need for redefining Arab nationalism toward incorporating class analysis in a much more genuine and accurate manner.

Two arguments will permeate the discussion of the similarities between sectarianism and Zionism: First, sectarianism, Zionism, and other

250

similar communal systems based on traditional loyalties represent some sort of an elementary form of consciousness that undermines the development of a higher order of national and social class identification; second, a set of hypotheses will be posed that stands in diametrical opposition to the claims that Zionist and other communal models serve the cause of modernization in the Arab society. On the contrary, all sorts of evidences demonstrate that they serve as deterrent forces in the whole area. Both of these ideologies (1) were created to secure national homes for one religious community against the welfare of others; (2) serve as bases for imperialism; (3) practice discrimination and promote inequalities; and (4) suffer from inability to correct injustices and transform themselves.

National Homes for Religious Communities

Lebanon and Israel were created with the help of Western powers as national homes for Maronites and Jews respectively. The republic of Lebanon in its present form was carved out of Syria by the French Mandate on August 20, 1920 and externally imposed on a significant segment of the Christian Arab and Syrian nationalists and the great majority of the Muslim communities. Formal protests and petitions were made by Christian and Muslim nationalists. Some of these petitions were signed by family representatives in several districts, cities and towns including Beirut, Tripoli, Sidon, Tyre and Baalbeck. In their attempt to create and maintain Lebanon as an independent and sovereign state, the Maronites have presented themselves as a persecuted and constantly threatened community that needs a national home of its own, and insisted on talking in the name of other Christians. Even after independence, they continued to reinforce the image in the minds of their own people, particularly the young. Hence the image of Lebanon as a victim, as a modern country in a backward region, as a Christian state that needs to preserve its identity or "melt in a Muslim sea," and as a democratic society in an area controlled by authoritarian military or traditional dictatorships. They have continued to promote this image to justify converting the country into a base for Western imperialism for the control of other Arab countries.

With time Maronites and some other Christians tended to believe that they are entitled to hold the larger share of power. This is rationalized by pointing out that "it is they who have more frequently tended to feel responsible for national leadership" and that the "Muslim Lebanese masses ... are unprepared to appreciate the virtues of a liberal way of life."[2]

Because of the insistence on reinforcing this image and asserting the religious identity of Lebanon, the Muslim community never reconciled itself to the new state and relationships between the different religious communities have continued to waver between outright conflict and hypocritical accommodation. Unfortunately, the religious cleavages disguised the socioeconomic cleavages — a situation which has contributed to political organization and polarization between communities rather than classes.

Unlike the Zionists, the Lebanese sectarian isolationists are natives of the area and tried to establish a relatively open pluralistic system with the help of the traditional Muslim leaders. The Zionists, being colonial settlers, created Israel by uprooting the Palestinian natives and dispersing them from their native land. In 1948, more than 726,000 Palestinians (estimate of the U.N. Economic Survey Mission for the Middle East) left their homes, lands, livelihoods, villages, towns and country under conditions of war and sought safety in Jordan, Lebanon, Syria and Gaza where they have continued to live stateless and under the mercy of authoritarian governments. The part of Palestine which was assigned to the Zionists by the U.N. partition plan in 1948 to form a Jewish state had a total of 495,000 Arabs as compared with 489,000 Jews. Were the Arabs allowed to stay, the dream of a Jewish state would not have been realized. There were 340,000 European Jews waiting in Cyprus for immigration to Israel as soon as the new state was created. Don Peretz tells us that

> the property abandoned by the Palestinian Arabs was a valuable resource helping to make room for hundreds of thousands of Jews who replaced the Arab refugees. The abandoned Arab fields, orchards, vineyards, homes, shops, factories, and businesses provided shelter, economic sustenance, and employment for a significant percentage of the nearly 700,000 new immigrants who came to Israel between May, 1948, and the end of 1951. Israel would have found it far more difficult to more than double its population during this period without access to abandoned Arab property.[3]

Yet, Zionists have promoted the image of Israel as a victim constantly threatened to be thrown into the sea, as the only civilized democracy in the Middle East, as a Western model for modernization and as a pioneering society that converted the desert into bloom. This image continues to be reinforced and the security of Israel has become the most significant criterion for morality within Israel as well as in the

United States. In the name of Israeli security, boundaries are changed and the most sophisticated arms are supplied to drive the Palestinians into submission.

Again, reality is disguised as evidenced in the current civil war in Lebanon. The Palestinians are presented to the world as ungrateful terrorists and they, rather then the Israeli colonizers, become the target of the military genius of the present Syrian regime in complicity with several Arab states, Israel, and the United States. These are facts that no academic objectivity can deny or disguise.

Bases for Western Imperialism

Both Lebanon and Israel have served as bases for Western imperialism in the area helping to maintain Western domination over Arab resources as well as checking the advancement of Arab unity. Israel participated in a military invasion of Egypt in 1956 to prevent nationalization of the Suez Canal and to depose Nasser. It has also continually threatened to invade Jordan and Lebanon in the event of any real threats to the existing traditional regimes and particularly in case of a nationalist take-over. Threats were even made to Saudi Arabia, Kuwait and Libya in case of oil boycotts agains the West.

Similarly, Lebanon was used directly in 1958 against the Egyptian-Syrian unity and Iraqi revolution by inviting American military intervention. The 1958 civil war should be seen against the background of an on-going struggle between forces for Arab unity and forces for enforcement of the Western design for a fragmented area. The emergence of the United Arab Republic alarmed the West, Israel, and the isolationist elements within Lebanon. Thus, a pro-western government controlled by Camille Shamoun and Charles Malik was formed prior to the civil war in an attempt to play a more direct role in undermining Arab unity. Lebanon became the center for active plots against the emerging Arab Republic. These moves were considered by the Lebanese Muslim community and the Christian Arab nationalists as a break from the spirit of the National Pact whose tenets states that Lebanon (1) is an Arab state and follows a policy of cooperation with the rest of the Arab world, and (2) would refrain from seeking Western protection. In fact, the isolationists continued to collaborate against the Arab cause and to look up to the West for protection and as a model. The Christian Lebanese isolationists, particularly the Maronites, exposed themselves most willingly, freely and uncritically to Western influence. As pointed out by Kamal S. Salibi, they saw "Western nations as protectors rather than conquerors or masters . . . Hence, when they westernize, they do so without apology. Although their understanding of Western ideas is frequently shallow, they nevertheless adopt them with enthusiasm."[4]

This tendency to Westernize and allow Lebanon to serve as a base against Arab unity had long been seen by the isolationists as the best way to preserve the Christian domination in Lebanon. To that end, as shown by William Haddad, "some Lebanese Maronites viewed with favor the establishment in Palestine of a Jewish state which would be a seemingly natural ally against the Muslim sea surrounding these two states."[5] To support this claim, William Haddad quotes the Maronite Archbishop Mubarak who said in an interview in Beirut in 1946, "Development of the Lebanon is tied up with that of Palestine. We Christian Lebanese know that. We realize that Zionism is bringing civilization to Palestine and to the entire Middle East."[6]

Great commotions were caused by such a point of view, one that many Maronite politicians had to denounce. Yet, it actually stemmed from deep-rooted sentiments that escape the censorship of diplomatic inhibitions whenever Christian domination is threatened. For example, in the recent civil war, having failed to get direct American or French military intervention, they accepted Syrian intervention and sought Israeli support. The Lebanese rightists continue to view with alarm and suspicion any reformist inclination in the country let alone the development of a progressive nationalist movement.

Similarly, the Zionist claim that Israel would serve at least as "a catalyst of the modernization process in Arab society" was proved wrong as shown by the Israeli sociologist Yochanan Peres. His data based on focused interviews with 472 Israeli Arabs carried out in the Fall of 1967 by Arab students at the Hebrew University proved "quite surprising. They [results] completely contradict Israeli propaganda which tends to stress the relative progress of Israeli Arabs as compared with the population of Arab countries, and are furthermore not in accordance with statistical data, which are published intermittently by Israeli sources."[7]

Practice of Discrimination

Sectarianism and Zionism have grown to be increasingly rightist particularly in terms of discriminating against other communities, contributing to the widening and deepening of the gap between the privileged and deprived, and collaborating with imperialism and racist regimes in Africa and Asia.

Contrary to the liberal heritage of the Jews in Europe, the Zionist movement has grown to be increasingly rightist, militaristic, racial, nonsecular, and repressive. The Zionist dream of a Jewish state in Palestine could be realized only at the expense of Palestinian Arabs and the Zionists have continued to feel that there is no place in Palestine for Arabs and Jews together. To be an Arab in Israel is to be totally alienated in your own country. As pointed out by Uri Davis in his introduction to Fauzi el-Asmar's *To Be An Arab in Israel*, an Arab faces "a political reality which excludes apriori, by the elementary terms of its motivating raison d'etre, equal participation of non-Jews, first and foremost, the native population of the land: The Palestine-Arabs. To the extent that the state is Jewish it must deny equality of economic, political and national rights to its native non-Jewish population."[8]

Lebanese sectarianism has been bound by its very nature to develop in the same direction. Again, discrimination against non-Christian communities occurred in spite of the professed principles and goals as expressed by Michel Shiha (one of the major architects of the Lebanese sectarian system): "Lebanon is a country of associated confessional minorities. All minority groups should find their places and obtain their rights in it. This is the raison d'etre of this country and this is its originality."[9]

The fact of the matter, however, is that the raison d'etre of the country was to establish a national home for the Christians. This, coupled with the fact of scarcity of powers and rewards, contributed to the emergence of greater disparities between the Lebanese religious communities and to further polarization rather than assimilation. The influence of religion on parliamentary elections has been increasing rather than decreasing and a process of polarization between the Christian and Muslim communities has been taking root — a situation which will render the political system less capable of resolving accumulating problems from within the system.[10]

Similarly, in spite of the great wealth that poured into Lebanon (rendering it the finance center of the area), prosperity has continued to be confined to some areas and groups. Mount Lebanon and some neighborhoods in Beirut have been growing prosperous at a much more rapid pace than the South, the North, and the Beqa' Valley. Two poverty belts inhabited predominantly by Muslims emerged and evidence the disproportion of wealth and rewards. One belt includes the poor districts of the South, the Beqa' and the North which surround the prosperous Mount Lebanon. The other belt surrounds Beirut whose suburbs were rapidly converted into overcrowded slums. The disparities are many, including educational opportunities and availability of roads, hospitals and other basic facilities. To illustrate the immense disparities in educational opportunities — about 40 percent of the children between the ages of 6 and 10 do not attend schools in South Lebanon compared to about 4 percent in Mount Lebanon. While the population of the deprived areas constitute 38.5 percent of the total population, official statistics show that 63.95 percent of their students attend ill-equipped public schools. In contrast, the great majority (78.18 percent) of those who attend expensive private schools come from Mount Lebanon and Beirut. The percentages of those who attend public schools were found to be 83 percent in Nabatieh (a Shi'ite town in the South) and 84 percent in Akkar in the North in comparison to only 21 percent in Northern Matn and 18 percent in Kisrwan (Maronite districts in Mount Lebanon).[11] Wide discrepancies in educational opportunities have also existed on the bases of rural-urban residency, social class, sex and religious affiliation. The illiteracy rate (1970) for Lebanese males aged 25 years and over in rural areas is almost twice as much as that for the same population in Beirut (40.1 percent vs. 22.1 percent). Likewise, 7.1 percent of this male age group in rural areas have earned intermediate and secondary education in comparison to 23.4 percent in Beirut. Finally, only 1.5 percent of this male age group in rural areas have earned university education in comparison to 12.4 percent in Beirut. Similar discrepancies between rural and urban areas exist in the case of the female population; 59.9 percent of the female population aged 25 years and over are illiterate or have less than primary education in Beirut in comparison to 91.1 percent of the corresponding population in rural areas.[12]

These disparities extend to other areas and can be easily documented. The point to be established, however, is connected with the tendency of the sectarian and Zionist systems to favor some religious communities and discriminate against others. While the dominating groups grow more conservative, nonsecular and discriminating, their victims become increasingly revolutionary, secular and socialist in orientation. The Palestinian cause has merged with the cause of the deprived Lebanese in the current civil war and both have changed through involvement in the struggle for liberation from confessionalism and Zionism. The change has been moving gradually away from traditional loyalties and elementary forms of consciousness and in the direction of secularism, socialism and democracy. By liberating themselves from primordial ties and adopting a secular-socialist-revolutionary ideology, the Palestinians and other Arab leftists could cooperate with socialist Jews and work together in opposition to the emerging confessional-Zionist alliance.

Rigidity of Confessionalism and Zionism: Their Inability to Transform Themselves

Both confessionalism and Zionism are born rigid and unable to transform themselves in response to emerging conflicts and challenges. Communal conflicts in particular gain momentum with time provoking violence and generating unexpected difficulties. Discrimination and oppression are built in the very nature of the systems and the existing communities never get assimilated into one unified nation. On the contrary, as Milton Esman points out, "where communal and class cleavages coincide, the probability of severe conflict increases."[13] To be sure, several mechanisms of conflict management are used to bring conflicts under control, but "the conflict management perspective has an inevitable bias toward conservatism and system maintenance, toward the orderly and peaceful continuity of a conflict-ridden or violence-prone political system."[14] Such a built-in inclination toward conservatism is rooted not in communal differences as such but in the determination of the dominant strata to preserve their privileges and powers. This explains why Lebanon and Israel have not been able to effectively use conflict-regulating practices such as those suggested by Eric Nordlinger, namely, stable coalition, the proportionality principle, depoliticization, mutual veto, compromise, and concessions by the stronger to the weaker party.[15] Simply, confessionalism and Zionism are committed to preserve the dominance of Maronites and Jews over others who are expected to adjust to a condition that renders them inferior, powerless and deprived. They subscribe to a democracy in form not out of concern for justice and freedom but because dominant communities benefit from laissez-faire competition.

The rigidity does now even allow for liberal change. Injustices cannot be corrected. Amos Elon wonders about the reason for the outcry in Israel over the Arab villages of Ikrit and Berem whose inhabitants were expelled about twenty-five years ago and prevented from returning to their homes by the military in spite of the Supreme Court's reaffirmation of their rights to repossess their houses and lands. He concludes that one reason for the outcry may be "an undercurrent of guilt feeling toward the Palestinian Arabs, caught as they are under the wheels of history. Indeed, a certain sense of guilt toward individual Arabs runs like a red thread through a great number of novels, plays and poems of the post-1948 period."[16] Elon further states that Mrs. Meir (then premier of Israel) defended her position of refusing to allow the people of Berem and Ikrit to go back to their homes. She stuck to three main reasons. First, there is a security consideration. Second, there is a grave danger of setting a precedent. She feared that

> all sorts of claims may be put forward by hundreds of thousands of Arab refugees of the 1948 war. What begins as Ikrit and Berem, Mrs. Meir was said to fear, might end in Tel Aviv-Jaffa . . . Therefore, although the original expulsion might have been a mistake, it is now too late, too dangerous to redress the wrong done. Third, there is the concern over a crisis of Zionist ideology for the restoration of the two towns might intensify the doubts in the righteousness of the Zionist cause.[17]

The point here is the inability of the system to redress injustices. By attempting to do so it erradicates its very foundation. As mentioned by Noam Chomsky, the Supreme Court of Israel decreed that "there is no Israeli nation apart from the Jewish people and the Jewish people consists not only of the people residing in Israel but also of the Jews in the Diaspora." Israel, thus,

> is a Jewish State governing a society that is in part non-Jewish. This fact . . . has always been the Achilles heel of political Zionism. If a state is Jewish in certain respects, then in these respects it is not democratic . . . (and) a non-Jewish citizen suffers various forms of discrimination. He is not permitted to lease or work on state lands. He is not able to reside in all-Jewish cities, such as Karmiel, built on lands confiscated from Israeli Arabs. To mention a recent case, a Druze, formerly an officer with 20 years service in the Israeli Border Police, was denied the right even to open a business near Karmiel by decision of the Israel Land Authority. [18]

Consequently, Israel is not only unable to be democratic and redress its injustices, it is an embodiment of the concept of Jewish nationhood and racism and stands in diametrical opposition to the 'democratic secular state' proposed by the Palestinian revolutionary movement.

The Lebanese political system was conceived and arranged according to a sectarian formula which rendered it highly rigid and static. Representation in the Parliament and distribution of major and minor posts on a sectarian basis did not take into account the fact that religious ratios do change. It has been constantly feared that any basic reforms would certainly upset the delicate balance. Hence, the tendency of the Lebanese ruling class to resist change.

The inability of the system to transform itself and the tendency of resisting change are reflected in several interrelated phenomena:

1. Christian elites have refused to take a census of the Lebanese population since 1932 even though planning, scientific research, developmental projects, the social security plan, etc., have been hampered by this refusal. The government has also failed to adopt a policy on immigration, naturalization and citizenship rights. While some groups were rightly granted citizenship (such as Armenians), others were wrongly deprived of it (such as Kurds).

2. The traditional leaders of Lebanon have continued to control the country and perpetuate themselves. Political positions have been inherited like family names, and some children could not wait the death of the father. Hence, the phenomenon of voting both father and son into Parliament (as in the case of Pierre Jumayil and his son Amin). Some liberal professionals and newly prosperous businessmen were able to reach the Parliament and Cabinet but only under the wings of the traditional leaders and by buying their nominations on their slates. Once in power the liberal technocrats and businessmen could maintain their positions only by adhering to the policies of these traditional leaders. Those liberal technocrats who were appointed to the Cabinet in the early 1970s (reference is made here to Ghassan Tueini, Elias Saba, Emile Bitar, Henry Eddeh) took their jobs seriously and tried to introduce such reforms as the imposition of higher taxes on luxury items, lowering the soaring prices of medical drugs, enforcing laws governing taxation, improving public schools and revising educational curricula. All these attempts were vehemently resisted and all of these ministers had to resign; in one instance a minister (Henry Eddeh) was expelled from office upon refusal to resign.

Simply, the political system has proved non-responsive to public opinion. A research survey conducted by Iliya Harik and myself in Beirut (1972) showed that the majority of the Muslim (86 percent) and Christian (61 percent) respondents favored ending Maronite monopoly over the office of the president — rather that it should be accessible to all Lebanese regardless of their religious affiliation. In fact, increasing powers had been centered in the office of the presidency undermining the office of the premier reserved for Sunni Muslims. The results of a research study conducted on a representative sample of Lebanese students at the American University of Beirut in 1969 showed that 84 percent were dissatisfied with the political conditions at that time; 73 percent expressed basic disagreement with the political trends and activities of the Lebanese government; 71 percent believed that the political system was not really democratic; and 94 percent agreed that there was a great deal of corruption and favoritism in the political administration. Yet, the dissatisfied Lebanese isolationists felt they had to defend the system and oppose change out of fear of upsetting the delicate balance. Hence the decline in the capacity of the Lebanese establishment for institutional adjustment and the potential dilemma observed by Michael Hudson: "To adjust to the new social justice and the newly politicized elements may lead to a derangement of the traditional balance of power . . . ; not to adjust may invite the total destruction of the political system."[19]

3. There had been a great disparity between popular support to progressive groups and their representation in parliament and the cabinet. The immensity of this disparity has been clearly demonstrated in the current civil war. This in turn has contributed to further aggrevation of the polarization process gradually taking place between the Christian and Muslim communities. The more the gap widened and deepened, the more the confessionalists tended to publicly deny the existence of disunity and not tolerate criticism.

Conclusion

In spite of the national and social struggle, Arab society continues to be threatened with further deterioration. What undermines the struggle and contributes to the gap between dream and reality is the failure to develop a scientific secular-revolutionary vision. The prevailing traditional loyalties provide the necessary climate for the survival and the sustenance of sectarianism and Zionism. Unless the Arabs liberate themselves from the traditional loyalties, the dream will be that distant from realization. Human will makes a difference as long as reality allows for a choice. A choice will have to be made, for there can be no comfort in the successive tragedies that have haunted Arab life. The choice is in revolutionary confrontation.

Notes

1. For more details on this thesis, *see* Halim Barakat, *Lebanon in Strife: Student Preludes to the Civil War* (Austin, Texas, 1977).

2. Kamal S. Salibi, "The Personality of Lebanon in Relation to the Modern World," in *Politics in Lebanon*, ed. L. Binder (New York, 1966) pp. 268-269.

3. Don Peretz, "The Palestine Arab Refugee Problem", in *Political Dynamics in the Middle East*, eds. P.Y. Hammond and S.S. Alexander (N.Y., 1972), p. 281.

4. Salibi, "Personality", p. 266.

5. William W. Haddad, "Lebanon, Officially and Unofficially, and Palestine," unpublished manuscript presented at the annual convention of the Association of Arab-American University Graduates in New York, October 1-3, 1976, p. 10.

6. Quoted from *Palestine Post*, 21 March 1946.

7. Yochanan Peres, "Modernization and Nationalism in The Identity of the Israeli Arab," *Middle East Journal*, Autumn, 1970, pp. 479-492, p. 488.

8. Uri Davis, "To Be an Arab in Israel", in *Documents From Israel 1967-1973: Readings For a Critique of Zionism,* eds. Uri Davis and Norton Mezvinsky (London, 1975).

9. Michel Shiha, *Politique Interieure* (Beirut, 1964), p. 44; cited in William W. Haddad, "Lebanon, Officially," p. 1.

10. Halim Barakat, "The Religious Factor and Parliamentary Elections in Lebanon: A Tendency Toward Sectarian Polarization", *Mawaqif*, no. 19/20, 1972, pp. 6-16.

11. These official statistics are reported in *Educational Statistics for the Year 1974-75,* Center for Educational Research and Development, Ministry of Education, Lebanon.

12. *See* Liban, Ministere du Plan – Direction Centrale de la Statistique, *L'Enquete Par Sondage sur la Population Active au Liban,* November 1970, Fascicule No. 4 Scolarisation et Education, March 1972; and Joseph Antoun and Khali Abou-Rujaily, *The Outputs of the Lebanese Educational System* (Beirut, 1975) (in Arabic).

13. Milton J. Esman, "The Management of Communal Conflict," *Public Policy* vol. 21, no. 1 (Winter 1973): 49-78, p. 50.

14. *Ibid.*, p. 52.

15. For details on these six conflict-regulating practices, *see* Eric A. Nordlinger, *Conflict Regulation in Divided Societies,* Occasional Papers in International Affairs, No. 29 (Cambridge, Mass., 1972).

16. Amos Elon, "Two Arab Towns that Plumb Israel's Conscience," *The New York Times Magazine*, 22 October 1972, p. 69; *see* also Amos Elon, *The Israelis: Founders & Sons* (London, 1971).

17. Elon, "Two Arab Towns."

18. Noam Chomsky, "Israeli Jews and Palestinian Arabs," *The Holy Cross Quarterly* 5, no. 2 (Summer 1972): 16-17.

19. Michael C. Hudson, *The Precarious Republic: Political Modernization in Lebanon* (N.Y. 1968), p. 12.

Part Four

ZIONISM AND THE
INTERNATIONAL COMMUNITY

15 ISRAEL AND SOUTH AFRICA: A COMPARATIVE STUDY IN RACISM AND SETTLER COLONIALISM

Richard P. Stevens

In parallel developments, remarkable not so much for their occurrence but as for the reluctance of Western opinion to acknowledge their reality and interrelationship, Israel and South Africa today present the world with the predictable responses of two surviving settler states as they struggle to ward off the demands of the original inhabitants seeking the full exercise of their natural and political rights. In addition, a further challenge is presented to both states at the international level where the demand has grown for their exclusion from the United Nations and other world bodies. Faced with such pressures it is small wonder that the relationship between these two settler entities, long played down for a variety of motives, has recently assumed an open character.

There is a pattern of behavior which is identical in its general lines exhibited by those European settlers who have formed political entities in non-European lands. This pattern of behavior is quite recognizable in South Africa and Israel. It also is observable in Rhodesia but this state merely reproduces most of the historical phenomenon which gave rise to South Africa. The same pattern was present in Algeria and in part in Kenya. In the latter two cases, however, the metropolitan power still retained ultimate authority and thus saw fit to bring about majority rule. Such an approach to the study of settler colonialism is not only valid, but it is useful in comprehending the past and rewarding in attempting to predict the course of future events.

As settler colonialism is different from traditional colonialism because the settlers are permanently there, and permanently in contact with the indigenous inhabitants, the "natives," the discriminatory treatment imposed upon the latter is more intense, systematic and brutal than that which the natives were subjected to by overseas imperial authorities. A declared espousal of discrimination on the basis of race, color or creed without apology also distinguishes settler colonialism. Because the settlers are well-entrenched in the lands they have occupied, indeed, many being cut off after several generations from any alternative home, new approaches are required which were not essential to the dismantling of the old colonialism. Although not overseas agents who came to the colonies on duty, for a variety of historical and cultural reasons they continue to derive support from their Western sources. Because of their success in establishing strong fortified positions these states are able to stubbornly hold on to power. This does not mean, however, that they are without challenge, internally and externally. Although the future is uncertain, if there is any lesson in history it is that a people will not be displaced in their own land without a fight. And today, with the objective international environment changing so dramatically, it is difficult to believe that the settler colonial phenomenon can continue to receive the unqualified Western support it has traditionally expected.

Fundamental to an understanding of the policies of both Israel and South Africa is the fact that the character of each is ultimately determined by the processes employed by an external element in acquiring, occupying and maintaining control of the land whether through purchase, force, legal enactment or judicial interpretation. For it is this dependence upon the acquisition and holding of land, presumably in perpetuity, and the policies adopted to dispossess the original inhabitants, which gives settler colonialism its distinctive character. Once set in motion the process carries within it a logic and a rationale almost predictable in its ideological and practical elaboration including a wide range of tactical stratagems designed to deal with internationl *realpolitik*. But whatever the tactics adopted by Israel and South Africa, their inability to contain internal dissent, to ward off international criticism, to sustain external support, or to prevent that fatal erosion of conviction and dedication among the dominant augurs ill for the continued survival of these states, at least in their present form.

Zionism and Afrikaner Ideology: Response to Internal 'Threats'

Of primary importance in understanding the character of Afrikanerdom and Zionism is the fact that both developed more in response to threats from within the community than, as customary among nineteenth-century nationalistic movements, from fear of external elements. Briefly, the intermingling of disparate elements in South Africa, while resulting in instability and conflict, also witnessed an intermingling of various groups which promised to lead to mutual assimilation and combination. The final product of such a response would necessarily have been a blend of the contributions of each according to their respective strengths, whether Dutch, Hottentot, Bushmen or Bantu. But it was not the challenge of the indigenous elements to Dutch arrival at the Cape in 1652 which precipitated the evolution of Dutch or Afrikaner nationalism into unmitigated racism as nationalism. Rather, it was in the challenge presented by the more advanced English, who themselves first arrived as occupiers in 1795, that the core of Afrikaner ideology developed. For while the Dutch (Boer) offshot could maintain itself while mingling with the less-advanced indigenous culture and technology, the British presence revealed all too clearly the latter's cultural and technological superiority. Hence, the determination of the most extreme element, always the prime mover of Afrikaner nationalism, to use language, religion, and their own way of life as proof of separate divine mission. Group consciousness, introversion, ethnocentrism and loyalty to the group as a supreme end in itself was thus enshrined at all levels of society and government. Over the next century and a half, culminating in political victory in 1948, Afrikaner nationalism reached its full flower with racism, in the form of apartheid, enunciated as state policy.

To view Zionism as embodied in the Israeli state in historical perspective the circumstances giving rise to that nationalistic Jewish phenomenon must also be observed. Accordingly, it can be postulated that the vital thrust behind the Zionist movement came neither from those Jews living in eastern Islamic societies where centuries of interaction and accommodation had testified to the strength and capacity for survival of the Jewish tradition, nor from those of Jewish faith in the Western Hemisphere where religious belief, as distinct from "nationality" or "race" was well on the way to formal disassociation. Not only did the American Reform rabbis declare in 1869 that "the messianic aim of Israel is not the restoration of the old Jewish state," but in 1885 they said that they considered themselves "no longer a nation, but a religious community and, therefore, expect no return to Palestine."

Where then did Zionism derive its impulse? Primarily from eastern and central Europe where, against the background of the less-developed Tsarist and Austro-Hungarian empires, a new freedom, whether the product of liberal democratic philosophy or Marxian socialism, threatened the integrity of Jewish life as traditionally practiced. For if the ghetto or restrictive class employments were to be overthrown along with serfdom and other relics of political stagnation, so also would those internal and external constraints which had long molded Jewish life in eastern and central Europe presumably be weakened. In short, a new ghetto, psychological, cultural and political, was to be erected in the form of Zionism, only then, it was assumed, could the processes of assimilation be countered. If no actual physical threat existed it was nevertheless stated as dogma that the non-Jew, the goyim, was by nature anti-Semitic and must be regarded as such. In short, only separation could save the group.

Asserting that the God of Abraham and Moses had given the Jews the right as the Chosen people to a land of their own in Palestine, the Zionists would also marshall cultural, historical and political arguments in support of their claim. Some Zionists cared less about Palestine as the end product, but all were concerned about assimilation. While the chief argument employed, the religious, was properly Judaic and acceptable in its spiritual sense to Christians and Muslims (two other faiths which shared the Biblical legacy) as well as to "spiritual" Zionists, once linked with land occupation through political stratagems, Zionism increasingly unfolded as a racist phenomenon. Step by step through the Balfour Declaration, the Mandate, and finally the creation and expansion of the state of Israel, a land allegedly promised to Jews and no others, was to be occupied at whatever cost. The sacralization of the state and its people was thus enshrined as religious duty. The foremost enemy would be those Jews who would refuse to accept the identification of Jewish faith with possession of the land. And for those non-Jews who, like the Caanites of old, were, according to fossilized Jewish tradition, outside the Covenant, not only could their claim to the land not be recognized but their eviction, indeed, their extermination, was strongly recommended by the most militant leaders. Racism as nationalism was again effected, and the fear of that Jewish intellectual giant, Albert Einstein, was rapidly borne out:

> I am afraid of the inner damage Judaism will sustain, especially from the development of a narrow nationalism within a Jewish state. We are no longer the Jews of the Maccabee period! A return to a nation in the political sense of the word would be equivalent to turning away from the spiritualism of our community, which we owe to the genius of our prophets.[1]

It is of more than passing interest that the same Biblical tradition which served Zionist exclusivism also provided the ideological basis for Afrikaner nationalism. In the view of the Afrikaner he, like the Children of Israel, was in search of a promised land. His victories were the Lord's victories. Kaffirs, "pagans," were predestined, as the offspring of Ham, to serve the "new Israelities" as "hewers of wood and drawers of water." From Calvinism the Afrikaner took his belief in predestination and infallibility of the Bible as he read it. As if to reinforce his title to the land this offspring of Dutch and Huguenot settlers thus appropriated to himself the title of "African" or "Afrikaner". The land was his by right just as much as it was for those Jews who would emigrate to Palestine. With such a motor force and under the leadership of the most extreme elements, one succeeding the other, it became the avowed end of both Jew and Afrikaner to make of the indigenous people strangers in their own land. If Mrs. Meir found no Palestinian people in Palestine when the Jews arrived, the Afrikaner found no Africans, only kaffirs or at best a language group of Bantu. In both cases the land of the indigenous population was to be secured and the inhabitants coerced to leave the land of their fathers. In short, the condition of settler survival was the nonexistence — physical or psychological — of the original inhabitants of the land.

But if the racist-based Union of South Africa founded in 1910 under joint Anglo-Afrikaner direction could ignore the local populace even while enjoying the blessing first of Britain, then the Commonwealth and the League of Nations and even be numbered among the founding members of the United Nations, by the late 1950s history had caught up with this charade of democracy. Thus, despite strong objections from Britain, France and the United States that apartheid was a matter of domestic jurisdiction and outside the competence of the United Nations, in 1957 the General Assembly, considerably more representative of world opinion than in 1945, called upon South Africa to revise its racial policies. In 1961 even the United States and Britain reluctantly concurred that apartheid, because of its exceptional character, was a fit topic for U.N. debate. Three years later, in 1964, every member of the United Nations except South Africa and Portugal saw fit to vote in condemnation of apartheid although the United States, the Western allies and Israel declined to join any coercive action.

Just as expanded U.N. membership and the realities of a changing world economic and political order led to South Africa's isolation, so also over the next decade those same factors led to a reappraisal of Israel and Zionism on the part of many states, especially after Israel's expansion in 1967. Accordingly, by resolution on November 10, 1975 the U.N. General Assembly determined "that Zionism is a form of racism and racial discrimination." Although denounced by the United States and some of its dwindling number of allies as "obscene, racist and immoral", this U.N. action was a measure of Israel's growing isolation. American and allied prevention of South Africa's ousting the same year from the United Nations further underscored the dependence of both settler states upon American support.

As mentioned earlier, the linkage of a nationalist ideology to the possession of land the occupation of which necessarily requires the displacement and permanent subjection of the indigenous inhabitants, properly speaking, gives such a movement its settler-colonialist and racist character. The fact that in the case of Palestine, as the spiritual Zionist Ahad Ha'am had pointed out in 1891, the land desired was not empty caused as little problem for the Zionists as did the presence of Africans in the land coveted by the Boer Voertrekkers. From the Zionist point of view the first object was to secure "the creation in Palestine of a homeland for the Jewish people guaranteed by public law." In historical context this meant autonomy for a Jewish Palestine under the sovereignty of the sultan and with the guarantee of the great powers. The underlying desire for an independent Jewish state, though not expressed, was clearly in the background and it could be expected that unlimited Jewish immigration would eventually lead to that realization. Thanks in part to the perception of Weizmann and the dominant politicians of the day, Zionist goals were successfully linked to British imperial interests. Thus, the Balfour Declaration, which referred to the Arab majority in Palestine simply as the "non-Jewish communties," not only signalled that the Zionist project was well on the way to accomplishment but demonstrated that an imperial power could still assume the right to dispossess the indigenous populace.

Smuts and the Appeal of Zionism

In a remarkable convergence of imperial design and Western liberal philosophy — a philosophy which placed the burden of costs on alien if not "inferior" peoples, the sanctioning of eventual Jewish control over Palestine through the Balfour Declaration was effected essentially by the same handful of politicians — indeed, by some of the outstanding representatives of the British ruling class — who eight years earlier had legitimized white minority rule in South Africa. For the South Africa Act of Union of 1909 and the Balfour Declaration both owed their existence in large part to Lord Milner, Lord Selbourne, Lord Balfour, Joseph Chamberlain and General Smuts. As for South Africa, the important thing for both Liberals and Conservatives in Britain was to hold the Empire together, and this could be done by placating the Boers, represented by such imperial converts as Botha and Smuts, and entrusting to them the real exercise of power. Consequently, knowing full well that by passing the South Africa Act the British Parliament would be relinquishing its right to intervene on behalf of South Africa's Black population, both parties proceeded to ratify the Act and left the indigenous majority to the mercy of its white rulers. In the final analysis it was the argument advanced by Balfour which carried the day: "You cannot," he declared, "give the natives in South Africa equal rights with the whites without threatening the whole fabric of white civilization." More accurately he might have stated that without the adoption of such a discriminatory act, the defeated but "moderate" Afrikaner leadership would not willingly play its part in serving the British Empire.

Intimately involved in the discussions leading both to the Act of Union and the Balfour Declaration was Jan Christian Smuts, noted Boer general, politician and eventual prime minister of South Africa. Considering the greater acknowledgement of South African and Israeli ties in recent months it is important to note that the organic embodiment of this relationship was established decades ago in the persons of Smuts and Chaim Weizmann, the Anglo-Zionist leader and first president of the state of Israel. The close identification of Smuts with imperial decision-making not only provided dramatic testimony to the importance Britain attached to South Africa but also indicated that the British factor continued to play a vital role in Union politics. "The special relationship . . . formed during the Botha-Smuts period," was then a two-sided arrangement involving gold and diamonds, trade and defense, emigration and investment; in short, it spoke to the very special way in which both parties interpreted dominion status and imperial security.[2] Together with Balfour, Churchill and Milner, Smuts would contribute to the development of a new imperial approach to the Middle East question. As the bearer of Cecil Rhodes' vision of the future of Africa, Smuts would throw himself wholeheartedly into those questions affecting the continent's security, and for Smuts as for Rhodes, the continent clearly began at Suez.

Although there is no evidence that Smuts actively concerned himself with Zionism before 1916 (although he reportedly joined a South African branch chapter in 1906), it is important to understand his attitude toward Jews in general and South African Jewry in particular. At the same time the special characteristics of South African Jewry must be taken into consideration for these, as will be shown later, continue to mold the very special relationship which exists today between Israel and South Africa. On one level Smuts' attitude toward Jewry was a necessary corollary to his belief in the dominant historical role of Western civilization and the role of Jewry in that context, all of which was underpinned by his Calvinist and Afrikaner-modified religious beliefs. On another level were the facts of South African political life and Smuts' association with a political party which essentially represented the interests of mining, banking and industry, sectors in which Jews were well represented (although not dominant). Smuts touched on some of these factors when he spoke on the future of southern and central Africa in London in 1917. In this speech, remarkable for its candor, the only non-British member of the Imperial War Cabinet confessed that there were many intelligent South Africans who doubted that they could ever succeed in making a white man's land of southern Africa. "Nevertheless," said Smuts, "we have started by creating a new white base in South Africa, and today we are in a position to move forward towards the North and the civilization of the African continent."[3] But this venture could succeed, he said, only by establishing "as an accepted axiom in our dealings with the natives that it is dishonourable to mix white and black blood." While strongly affirming the necessity for implementing the Christian moral code in dealing with Africa, he said it must be understood that "natives have the simplest minds, understand only the simplest ideas or ideals, and are almost animal-like in the simplicity of their minds and ways." Therefore, "political ideas which apply to our white civilization largely do not apply to the administration of native affairs." Thus spoke the defender of white interests on the African continent, the man heralded in the Western world as one of its greatest liberal thinkers, a founding father of the League of Nations and the mandate system and of the United Nations Organization.

In short, if the defense of civilization, which Smuts so insistently equated with "white civilization," required white unity, particularly in its South African base, it also meant the permanent subjection of the black race. As Smuts' admirer and biographer, Sarah G. Millin, herself a South African Jew, observed, Smuts computed the worth of white civilization as sufficient reason to deny black liberty. While Smuts occasionally spoke of "self-government for the native," this was to be in areas granted by whites and on white sufferance – the prototype of modern day Bantustans. Only in the context of racial separation could he speak of liberty – white man's liberty was distinct from black man's liberty. No sooner had Smuts and his colleague, General Botha, set about forming their Het Volk party after their military defeat in the Boer War than they declared that it was "open to all white men whether Boer, Jew or Briton."[4] Since it was only through white unity, according to Smuts, that white civilization could be preserved, anti-Semitism was rejected.

Against this background it is understandable that Smuts enthusiastically supported the resolution of the South African Jewish Congress unanimously adopted in 1916 which requested that "the claim of the

Jewish people to Palestine" be recognized at the peace conference following the war. The next year, when approached by Weizmann in London for his support, Smuts related that he had already promised to champion the Zionist cause. Smuts' endorsement of Zionism, while reflecting his own cultural and racial bias, at the same time demonstrated his understanding of the fact that Jewish institutions in South Africa reflected the Zionist priorities and interests of that community. Indeed, the main organs of Jewish life were the South African Zionist Federation, founded in 1895, and the South African Jewish Board of Deputies, founded in 1912. Fully 99 percent of South African Jews were Zionist-affiliated and these formed the majority of the Board of Deputies. Zionism was without question the primary cultural expression and group concern of South African Jewry and in the context of a Western parliamentary political system and unrestrained capitalism, its success in South Africa would foreshadow its victories elsewhere in the Western world.

With the small but influential South African Jewish community committed to the Zionist philosophy, Smuts readily saw the political wisdom of embracing the Zionist vision. The fact that Zionism would fit in nicely with the imperial scheme of things was all the more reason to accept it wholeheartedly. And in what better way could Britain provide continental security, in the most economical manner, than to deliver Palestine, at the very crossroads of Africa and Asia, to the Jews. British politicians listened to the arguments advanced first by Herzl and then by Weizmann linking the Zionist program to British imperial interests. In the thinking of such imperialists as Sir Mark Sykes, Balfour, and Lord Milner, Palestine would be an important strategic point in the British empire, and it would be worthwhile to develop it after the war. But as one of Smuts' biographers observed, "the only people with the money, energy, and the inclination to do that would be the Jews; both for the present crisis and future needs, Zionism ought to be backed to the full. To Smuts also the idea appealed in every way. Rhodes had dreamed of an all-British Africa. Smuts dreamed the same dream. Palestine developed and made strong would be an auxiliary to that dream."[5]

Land Acquisition and Distribution

If General Smuts and the ruling elements in South Africa could speak openly and competitively of their intentions to preserve control of the land and dominate the indigenous population, in the years before Jewish statehood had been openly acknowledged as the Zionist goal it was necessary for the Zionist leadership to take a different road. Fearing that international opinion might be alienated at a time when the mandates under discussion were supposedly to be operated in the name of the inhabitants and intent upon securing financial support for immigration projects from non-Zionist, philanthropic Jews, the Zionist leadership argued that the land of Palestine would never be acquired by force. In this vein, Albert Hyamson, an English Zionist later appointed to the Palestine mandate administration, advanced the argument that "there will be a new incentive, and a strong one, for a Moslem Arab emigration from Palestine." "Close at hand," he said, "there is to be a Moslem Arab State ... which should of itself be a magnet to Moslem Arabs settled in other lands.... It should be unnecessary to say that no Arab will be dispossessed or forced by any means to leave his home."[6] In a more honest and logical vein, however, Israel Zangwill, president of the Jewish Territorial Organization, spoke pointedly of the only alternative if a Jewish State were to be established:

> The whole planet is in the grip of Allied Might and it needs but Allied Right to reshape all racial boundaries and international relations.... But a Hebrew Palestine, if it is to exist at all must be a reality, not a sham.... The power in every country ... always remains in the land-owning classes. Yet over 30,000 Arab landlords and some 600,000 fellahin are to continue in possession of the bulk of the Holy Soil ... And hence we must suppose that this new system of creative politics ... will be carried out in Palestine as elsewhere. Thus the Arabs would gradually be settled in the new and vast Arabian Kingdom.... Only thus can Palestine become a "Jewish National Home." ... Only with a Jewish majority ... can Israel enter upon the task of building up that model State.[7]

Central to the Zionist effort at land acquisition and population displacement was the establishment in 1901 of the Jewish National Fund (JNF). Created "exclusively for the purchase of land in Palestine and Syria," this body would, by 1948, next to the government, be the largest landowner in Palestine holding title to 54 percent of the Jewish-owned land on which 85 percent of all Jewish settlements were located. Directed first from Vienna the JNF laid down as policy that it "could either itself develop the land or lease it, but only to Jews," The result, as John Hope Simpson noted in 1930 was that the "land has been extraterritorialized. It ceases to be land from which the Arab can gain any advantage either now or at any time in the future."[8] Nevertheless, despite the fact that there were no legal impediments to Jewish land purchase from 1920 to 1930, and only ineffective ones after that, the JNF had succeeded by 1948 only in securing title to 3.55 percent of the total land area. Few Arabs would sell their land and those who did were for the most part absentee landowners. Under these circumstances it was obvious that without the panic created by the Dir Yassin massacre of April 1948 and like atrocities, as well as actual military expansion, the land could not have been secured for Jewish settlement.

Forceful occupation also provided the basis for white land ownership in South Africa although a handful of shameful purchases paid for in trinkets are on record. But it was essentially through a series of battles, the so-called "Kaffir Wars" beginning in 1779 and lasting over a century, that the bulk of African land was brought under white control. From the mid-nineteenth century on, however, the British authorities at the Cape thought of another alternative to driving the Africans back, while at the same time keeping them under control. After all, the whites' hunger for land was not now so demanding, as labor for mines and industry, under British influence, assumed greater importance. The new alternative was to keep Africans in occupancy of a part of the newly-conquered territories, while the government sent some of its agents to take charge of certain administrative tasks. This alternative provided the foundations for native reserves, or, as they have been known under the Afrikaner regime, Bantustans. The Native Land Act of 1913, vigorously protested by black leaders, gave immediate proof of the newly created Union's intentions. In this act, 7 percent of the territory of the Union was set aside for Africans and they were prohibited from acquiring land outside those reserves. In 1936 the Native Trust and Land Act increased the amount of land available to 13 percent for three-quarters of the country's inhabitants, and this land, by all estimates, was decidedly the most barren and least productive.

Coming to power in May 1948 the Afrikaner Nationalists soon announced their intention of implementing territorial apartheid or "separate development." Not only was this to mean more stringent enforcement of the thousands of discriminatory laws already on the books, but in the late 1950s it was announced that territorial separation, based on the reserves, was to be carried to its conclusion. These plans were accelerated following the Sharpeville massacre of early 1960 as Dr. Verwoerd, the prime minister, worked against time to create the image of a total, credible separation of the races with ultimate justice and autonomy for each. The government declared that all Bantu reserves, numbering over 250, would be consolidated, enlarged and developed as "homelands" for eight "national units" (a ninth was added in 1970). But whatever the terminology employed, a terminology which interestingly enough, utilized such Zionist words as "homeland" and "commonwealth," it was the transformation of images rather than of reality which was intended. Under the able direction of Verwoerd, a former professor of applied psychology, a massive transformation of the laws and social system was launched to make the new image believable. Two concessions, and two only, were made in the face of the most powerful, united, and sustained political and diplomatic pressure on a single nation in history: the long-term nature of separate development was to be telescoped, especially for the Transkei, the largest of the rural reserves, where self-government was to be initiated in 1963. Secondly, in contradiction to years of denunciation of "one-man-one-vote" for Africans, the "full franchise" was to underlie the constitution advanced by the government. Until this point, what Verwoerd called "the sound foundations of the Bantu's own essentially democratic system of self-government" had been rule by chiefs, a rule the whites found very easy to manipulate through the chiefs' position as paid government servants, through the exploitation of tribal rivalries, and through the resurrection of obscure genealogies which revived extinct chieftainships, or created mere government puppets as chiefs. That these concessions were made as a result of pressure was admitted by Verwoerd to Parliament but he affirmed that he was "thereby buying the white man his freedom and the right to retain domination in what is his country."

Within the Transkei the government chose to work through an able and ambitious minor chief, Kaiser Matanzima. Matanzima fell for the government's bait of tribal advancement and of local political power, in return for collaboration in the apartheid policy. A qualified lawyer, he had scarcely ever left the Transkei and the traditionalist in him appealed to the other chiefs. But his reputation as a collaborator and his personal harshness with dissenters denied him popular support. Although the elective principle in the new constitutional arrangement was introduced as promised, the government's power was to be maintained in the new legislature by 64 appointed chiefs who comfortably outnumbered the 45 elected members. Consequently, despite the fact that the great mass of Transkeians defied the government, the existing emergency regulations, the police and the chiefs to vote for their own and not the white nominees, it provided an accurate commentary on the reality of self-government in the Transkei that the people nevertheless got the white man's nominee, Chief Kaiser Matanzima and his followers, by the working of that very constitution which they had been obliged to implement with their votes.

Over the past thirteen years the opposition within the Transkei parliament or Bunga has been largely dissipated through fear and bribery. Today the chief minister's power comes, as before, from the powers that the Emergency Regulations of 1960 gave the chiefs. They can banish critics and opponents, refuse permission for gatherings of more than ten persons, burn the homes of suspected political opponents and have all the power they need to force acceptance of their views on their subjects. They also have near absolute power over banned and exiled persons from towns who have been sent back to the Transkei after serving sentences for political offenses. It is with this structure of self-government that the Transkei's "independence" as a South African "commonwealth" was set for October 26, 1976. As selected Transkeians are sent abroad on good-will missions and are posted to various South African diplomatic missions, the government seeks to receive foreign sanction for its charade. Needless to say, diplomatic recognition on the part of some African government would constitute a major South African victory.

But whatever the formal trappings of "independence," the fact remains that the Transkei offers little hope to its people politically or economically. Over 300,000 Transkeians continue to work as migrants while of the remaining 1.2 million perhaps a third are adult males of working age who spend a period of their working life tilling their fields and raising families in the Transkei. Many of them have been "endorsed out" of the areas where they once worked under the Influx Control regulations aimed at stemming the tide of Africans moving into the new industrial complexes except on government terms. A very large portion of the old and the young are in their care. Thus the Transkei, like all the "Bantu homelands," is both a labor reservoir and a refuse dump for the unwanted "surplus Bantu" — the diseased, the aged, the politically suspect — of the cities. Populated thus it is hardly surprising that its people are so poor and its development so feeble as to be almost nonexistent. The only changes the Verwoerd and present-day Vorster theories have brought to this rural slum are the increase of traditionalism, a further demoralizing of the younger generation by the imposition of inferior Bantu education, and the hindrance of the natural movement into the towns of South Africa of workers and families. These conditions are further aggravated by the establishment of so-called "border industries." Designed to give white entrepreneurs on the borders of the Bantustans the benefits of cheap black labor while keeping them out of South African cities, they are also intended to prevent the industrialization of the Bantustans themselves. Border industries, by their very nature, cannot benefit the "homelands" since the profits flow back into the province where they are actually situated. The only benefit to the "homeland" worker is that he must work away from home, across a border, and must carry a pay packet far lower than he could earn in distant Cape Town, Durban or Johannesburg. For how else is the government to attract industry to the remote borders of the "homelands" but by the attraction of the lowest wages, to make up for the lack of facilities for the privileged white staff, factory maintenance and necessary infrastructure? According to the Bantu Homelands Citizenship Act of 1970 every African was made a "citizen" of one of the nine Bantustans; outside of these "national units" the African was to be a foreigner. As such, discriminatory legislation in wages, services, etc. could presumably be rationalized more easily both at home and abroad. The right of Africans to home ownership in their own urban areas was withdrawn in 1967 and only restored on a limited leasehold basis in 1975-76 as concessions in the face of growing internal violence. In short, as Chief Albert Luthuli once stated, the aim of separate development or apartheid has been to justify total political domination by white or black in an economic system more aptly called "paid slavery."

Racism and the Ideology of Survival

At the core of all legislation in South Africa and Israel is the question of race. In South Africa the law differentiates three main racial groups — white, colored and Bantu. A person is classified as white if both parents have been classified as white. Citizenship, however, is not irrevocable. Instead, it can be withdrawn if it is proved that the citizen's ancestors were not of the correct genealogy in the case of an immigrant; a citizen, he can be reclassified as colored. According to Israeli law any Jew in the world has the right to instant citizenship in Israel provided that he is born of a Jewish mother. All Jewish marriages in Israel, however, must be conducted by an Orthodox rabbi since civil marriage is not recognized. By interpretation of the rabbinate certain persons who assumed themselves to be Jewish, such as certain Black American groups and Ethiopians, have been denied Israeli citizenship. Others, as a result of conversion from Judaism to another faith or lack of proper credentials on the part of parents, have lost their right to citizenship.

For the dominant group, in each case meticulously defined in law according to the method described, there is an ideology of survival as well as of nationalism. And in the name of survival the rights of non-whites and non-Jews, as the case may be, are sacrificed to the interests of the dominant group. The similarity between the two has been acknowledged by none less than the editor of the *Zionist Record* of South Africa, H. Katzew, who stated: "You cannot in one breath claim the right of Jews to political power and sovereignty in one corner of the earth (Israel), as South Africa's fervent Zionists do, and in the next breath approve attitudes which seek to take away the same hard-won right from the children of the Boers."

In South Africa, in addition to the legislation directly geared to Bantustan existence, some of the more appalling enactments provide that a non-white may be removed from any area at any time whether or not he has been born and lived there all his life; no judicial recourse is available. Further, he may not leave his municipal area without a special permit; he may not be employed in professions exclusively reserved to whites; he may not strike; he may not organize or attend a meeting of more than ten people without a permit; he cannot share in the welfare benefits which exist only for whites, and he must receive a type of education especially designed to assure his proper place in society. In short, white survival requires that legislation and restrictions be directed toward two ends: forcing Africans off the land into a labor market which will fuel South Africa's growth while at the same time preventing any resistance on the part of the subject population.

Israel's survival policy, on the other hand, has been more exclusively oriented toward acquiring land and simply replacing the previous inhabitants. The Law on the Acquisition of Absentee Property (1950) was applied to the refugees before and after the 1948 war. Under this law the land and property of a person declared an "absentee" is transferred to the Custodian of Absentee Property. The law defines an absentee as any person who is a citizen of Israel, but who left his place of residence between November 29, 1947 and the day on which the State of Emergency was abrogated, if that person went (a) to a place which before September 1, 1948 was outside the land of Israel or '(b) to a place inside the land of Israel but occupied at that time by hostile forces. By this law those Palestinians who left their villages or had been driven out of them by the Israelis, even if they remained under Israeli control, were prevented from returning to their villages. Thus the government was able to confiscate their lands. Even though this law was dated 1950 its effect was back-dated to 1947.[9]

Among the Emergency Laws promulgated by the minister of defense in 1949 was the "Emergency Articles for the Exploitation of Uncultivated Lands" which empowered the minister of agriculture to take possession of uncultivated land.[10] Applying this legislation the minister of defense would declare a certain area a "Closed Area," admission to which could only be secured from the military governor. For "reasons of State security" owners of such areas were not granted permission to occupy their lands which were then declared "uncultivated." Thereafter, the minister of agriculture could ensure the cultivation of the land by engaging laborers or allowing another party to cultivate it. According to the 1951 report of the U.N. Palestine Conciliation Commission, four-fifths of Israel's area and two-thirds of her cultivable land belonged to Palestinian refugees prevented from returning home. One-third of Israel's Jewish population was thus living on absentee Arab property.

In the aftermath of the 1967 war, similar policies were pursued on the Golan Heights, in Jerusalem, in Gaza and on the West Bank of the Jordan. Thus, in Israel as in South Africa, the alienation of the indigenous peoples from the land has occurred as part of the pattern of establishing and maintaining a settler state. Unlike South Africa, however, Israel does not assign to the "native" a primary role as laborer although this role, through force of circumstance, is steadily growing. Israel, like South Africa, will increasingly need the cheap labor whose physical presence it equally fears. Ironically, it was the official proscription of the use of Arab labor on Jewish land — intended to build up a Jewish agricultural class rooted in the soil and determined to resist native displacement — that the Zionists frequently cited as proof of their noncolonial character. But this policy calculated to prevent that fatal weakening which led to other colonial abandonments, to the dismay of many Zionists, has, since the 1967 expansion, added more than one million Arabs to state control and these have been increasingly subjected to treatment on the South African model. Thus, from their areas of residence there are weekly or monthly migrations of Arab workers into Jewish towns and farms most of whom are paid below the Jewish wage. As with South Africa which, despite its racial policies, attracts migrants from neighboring black countries as well as the reserves because of economic circumstances Israel in turn cites such movement as proof of its positive and beneficial policies.

While the dominant group both in Israel and South Africa disagree on the best means of maintaining control there is agreement in both countries on hostility toward the subordinate groups. Israeli sociologist Peres reported that 91 percent of his 1968 sample of Israeli Jews agreed that "It would be better if there were fewer Arabs"; 76 percent agreed that "the Arabs will never reach the level of progress of Jews"; and 86 percent said that they would not rent a room to an Arab. [11]

In other areas the similarity between South Africa and Israel is more than accidental as well. Thus, while South Africa has its Bantu education, Israel, as even the *New York Times* noted, presents a wide gap between Jew and Arab in post-primary education. Almost 60 percent of the Jews but only 20 percent of the Arabs between the ages of 14 and 17, it stated, were regular students.[12] Sabri Jiryis has outlined in his admirable book, *The Arabs in Israel*, that the educational standards in the Arab schools are extremely low, not only in comparison with Jewish schools in Israel but also with present standards all over the Middle East and with those prevailing in Palestine under the Mandate. While Israeli officials justify the lack of equality for Arabs on the basis of their low education yet it is precisely in the field of education, notes *Newsweek*, that the most pervasive inequities exist.[13] Curriculum manipulation plays down those elements in Arab or Islamic history which would undercut Israeli assumptions; the Israeli version of history is required. The unequal position given to the Arabic language, despite the fact that it is described as an official language of the country, has further undermined the educational process among Arabs and has diminished the prospects of Arab advancement.

Although the documentation of inequality in Israel and South Africa is beyond the scope of this study, it should be mentioned that the tools of repression are broadly similar. While the pass system provides an efficient instrument for pressure on Africans in South Africa and results in the daily arrest of approximately 2,000 people, it has been supplemented by a wide variety of laws permitting preventive detention, banning (a form of flexible house arrest) and imprisonment for extended sentences under charges of "sabotage" or "communism," the definitions of which can include almost any kind of activity designed to upset the existing social order. In Israel the foundation of control largely rested upon emergency laws enacted in Palestine in 1936, 1939 and 1945. These laws, vigorously opposed at the time by many who are today high government officials in the Israeli state, have governed the lives of hundreds of thousands of Palestinians since 1948. These and other Defense Laws have been used not only to restrict movement in "closed areas," but they have provided for house arrest and indefinite detention. Other measures taken in the wake of the 1967 war include deportations of Palestinians without trial and "collective punishment" of villages. This latter tactic, so reminiscent of German occupation policy during World War II, has resulted in the total destruction of villages such as Beit Nuba and Yalu. Individual houses may be destroyed simply because someone suspected of guerrilla activity has lived there. In addition, some villages, like Emmaus, have been totally depopulated and destroyed for strategic military or political reasons. This duplicates exactly those decrees in South Africa which permit the burning of homes in the reserve areas suspected of anti-government activity.

Conclusion

Despite the general denial by Zionists and their supporters of any similarity between Israeli and South African policies, a host of witnesses, Israeli and Arab, have given ample evidence to the contrary. Moreover, the logic of Israeli survival, which has led so naturally to expansion and further occupation, must of necessity bring forth the same constraints which ushered in South Africa's Bantustan philosophy, at least in its economic if not territorial-political aspects. For indeed there are only two choices a settler state can follow unless total dependence is to be placed on military-police repression, integration or separation. But if integration would destroy the racial basis of the state, separation, while perhaps allaying international and domestic criticism in the short run, can only stimulate group feelings of deprivation arising from economic inequality. In the latter instance the risk is also run, as many South Africans today argue, of a Trojan horse being planted in their midst. For given the right combination of circumstances there is the strong possibility that even the most compliant subordinate authorities will act or be used for purposes of state subversion.

Realizing the dangers posed by any subordinate Arab regional government Israel declined to establish such an arrangement even though for some years there were at hand a number of traditional leaders who might well have cooperated. By 1976, however, as the April municipal elections on the West Bank and the violent protests of Arab youth thereafter indicated, it was the PLO which had clearly caught up the loyalties of Palestinians. Under these circumstances even more reliance was place on immigration and external support as the *deus ex machina* to stave off the inevitable. But immigration, as Rhodesia and South Africa know only too well, and external support are fickle guarantees of continued settler domination. In short, whatever path is followed, since the settler character of the state remains, the same end result can be expected.

In the final analysis Israel and South Africa find themselves dependent, directly or indirectly, upon external support. Not only do they naturally converge together, economically and politically, as Vorster's

visit and subsequent agreements have indicated, but the United States'
dominant role in supporting both, daily becomes more evident. For
whether it is the internal political, the economic or the strategic, under
one or other of these impulses America finds itself involved. In the case
of South Africa it is the fear of a radical change in the economic-
political structure, a change which could have grave consequences for
the traditional movement of capital and possible jeopardy for Western
strategic interests, which has dictated the U.S. position. Having long
advocated a "let-alone" policy toward South Africa, the consequences
of the unexpected Portuguese collapse in Africa and its ramifications
for white control of Rhodesia and South Africa, have stimulated a
direct U.S. initiative. In essence, however, the Kissinger mediation
vis-à-vis Vorster on the one hand and neighboring black African leaders
on the other parallels exactly the Kissinger mediation between Egypt
and Israel. In both cases the real issue and the real actors have been
ignored. But because both Israel and South Africa are so organically
linked to U.S. and, to a lesser degree, certain other Western interests, it
can be expected that U.S. policy will also be reinforced at the societal,
non-official level. In short, labor unions, a variety of professional
organizations, civic groups and newspapers will act to bolster both
policies. Those elements which perceive interlocking interests will
generate strong support for the status quo. This has recently been
demonstrated by the visit to South Africa of twelve Jewish newspaper editors from the United States, who, upon return, were reportedly "impressed with the logic and sincerity of the 'Separate Development program'" of the regime.

Whatever the temporary successes of settler policy, whether through
internal manipulation or external support, those central to the conflict
have refused, physically and psychologically, to deny their own existence. In a simultaneous show of rejection of any approach which denies
their own right as a people to exist, Arab youth on the West Bank and
black youth in South Africa have shown the world their determination
to resist. Marches, boycotts, demonstrations, work stoppages, all
involving loss of life at the hands of the dominant element, have also
served to weaken the propaganda picture of a happy, compliant albeit
subject people. As the challenge from within mounts there are also
those in both camps who have begun a serious questioning of their own
right as a dominant people. To what extent this erosion of self-assured-
ness, so vital to the settler psychology, will develop, is uncertain, but it
also carries its consequences for external support. Nor can it be forgot-
ten that those millions of Americans of African origin, of other racial

minorities, and ordinary citizens who believe in America's mission to save its own soul, once aware of the true nature of their country's involvements, may yet act to force a restructuring of official policy.

In retrospect, the poignant warning of Anstruther MacKay, British military governor of part of Palestine during World War I, writing in 1920, remains to be disproved:

> It will be seen that, to fulfill their aspirations, the Zionists must obtain the armed assistance of one of the European powers, presumably Great Britain, or of the United States of America. To keep the peace in such a scattered and mountainous country the garrison would have to be a large one. Is the League of Nations, or any of the Western powers willing to undertake such a task: But without such armed protection, the scheme of a Jewish state, or settlement, is bound to end in failure and disaster.[14]

That this would be the natural expectation for a settler entity founded in alien land was further prophesied by Lord Sydenham of Comb, a Liberal governor of Bombay, in 1921, when he asked:

> Can the "Arabs" be bribed or cajoled into parting with their hereditary lands, and can the great schemes projected be carried out on an economic basis? Money will accomplish much; but I do not believe that the Palestinians will tamely submit to the loss of their birthright, or be turned into labourers by the operations of Zionist capital.[15]

In occupied Palestine as in South Africa the answer has been given by the inhabitants; it now remains to be seen how long it will take for those now dominant and their supporters to come to grips with that reality.

Notes

1. Albert Einstein, *Out of My Later Years* (New York, 1950), p. 263.
2. Dorothy F. Wilson, *Smuts of South Africa* (London, 1946), p. 80.
3. Jan C. Smuts, *War-Time Speeches* (London, 1917), p. 85.
4. Sarah G. Millin, *General Smuts* (London, 1936) vol. 2 p. 108.
5. H.C. Armstrong, *Grey Steel: J.C. Smuts: A Study in Arrogance* (London, 1937), pp. 300-01.
6. Albert Hyamson, "Problems of the New Palestine," *The Quarterly Review*, no. 459 (April 1919): 324.
7. Israel Zangwill, "Before the Peace Conference," *Asia*, February 1919,

pp. 105-6.

8. John Hope Simpson, *Palestine: Report on Immigration, Land Settlement and Development*, Cmd. 3686 (London, 1930), p. 53.

9. *Laws of Israel*, 1950 vol. 37, p. 86.

10. *Official Gazette* 27 (15 October 1948):5.

11. *American Journal of Sociology*, May 1971.

12. *New York Times*, 29 January 1971.

13. *Newsweek*, 8 February 1971.

14. Anstruther MacKay, "Zionist Aspirations in Palestine," *Atlantic*, July 1920.

15. Lord Sydenham of Comb (George Sydenham Clarke), "Palestine and the Mandate," *The Nineteenth Century and After*, April 1921.

ISRAEL AND SOUTH AFRICA: THE RACISTS
ALLIED

Peter Hellyer

Two member states of the United Nations have been condemned as racialist, in conception, formation and practice: Israel and South Africa. Both have been the subject of United Nations resolutions, as well as those of other international bodies, and both, in consequence, are considered as, and, to a considerable extent, treated as pariahs within the world community. In April 1976, the governments of the two virtually acknowledged their common position, with the visit by Prime Minister Balthazar Johannes Vorster of South Africa to Israel, setting the seal on what has become over the past few years a well-founded, rapidly expanding, yet relatively secret alliance. The two racialist states, for the first time, came publicly and nakedly together.

On the surface, the grounds for the Pretoria-Tel Aviv axis seem, in the eyes of the Western world at least, to be offset by the different histories of the Zionist movement in Palestine and the Afrikaaner nationalists who, since the general election of 1948, have dominated South African politics. Thirty or forty years ago, the two ideologies were on opposing sides in the division of the world community over the ideologies of fascism and Nazism. Nazism in Germany, under Adolf Hitler, took as one of the bases for its ideology, and its program, the need to cleanse the German people of the taint of alien blood, in particular that of the German Jewish community. During the Third Reich, from 1933 to 1945, literally millions of European Jews, not only in Germany, but also in the countries occupied by the Nazis, were eliminated, not as a result of the hazards of war, but as a result of a conscious policy of extermination, Hitler's "final solution" to the "Jewish problem."

For the world's Jews, the Nazi extermination policy was of crucial importance in determining their present belief that the cancer of anti-Semitism is always latent, within Europe at least, and reinforcing their support for the Zionist program. The Zionists of the past, like the government of the state of Israel today, based their appeal to the Jews of the world upon the fear that another "holocaust" might occur.

The Afrikaner nationalists, on the other hand, were closely linked with Nazism during the 1930s and 1940s, and, indeed, the present prime minister, Vorster, was interned by the South African government during World War II for acts deemed to be of assistance to the Nazi cause. In 1940, one of the Afrikaaner leaders, former Prime Minister Hertzog, openly welcomed the possibility of a Nazi victory: "In considering the future relations between blacks and whites in South Africa, the nationalists (i.e. the Afrikaaners) would welcome a new division of Africa if Germany would reign over a territory in central Africa, stretching from the Atlantic Ocean to the Indian Ocean. They would regard that German territory as a welcome barrier against other concepts of racial policy."[1]

Two other Afrikaner leaders, Strijdom and Verwoerd, both later to serve as prime minister, studied in Germany before the war, and had links with Nazi party officials.[2] The Afrikaner secret society, the Broederbond, had discussions with a Nazi party envoy in 1934.[3] A variety of paramilitary groups, notably the Greyshirts led by Oswal Pirow, the Ossewa Brandwag which carried out sabotage during the war, and the South African Gentile National Socialist Movement, also emerged among the Afrikaner community in the pre-World War II period. All had anti-Semitic overtones, sometimes organizing demonstrations against Jews fleeing from Nazi Germany to refuge in South Africa, and, in every case, their leaders later became key figures in the Afrikaner National Party.[4]

Perhaps the most concise explanation of the links between Afrikaaner nationalism and Nazism was that of Vorster himself, when, in 1942, in an outline of his political philosophy, he stated: "We stand for Christian Nationalism, which is an ally of National Socialism. . . . In Italy it is called Fascism, in Germany Nationalism, and in South Africa Christian Nationalism."[5] The identification of the ideology of the Afrikaners' mainstream leaders with Nazism was clear and thorough — covering not only anti-Semitism, but also the attitude toward the African population.

Since the victory of the National Party in the South African general election of 1948, the country's prime ministers, from Malan to Vorster, have been people with a past history of adhering not only to the most anti-African, but also the most anti-Semitic tenets of Afrikaner nationalism. Yet the government of Israel has carefully maintained good relations with each of them. And with the playing down of anti-Semitism within South Africa itself, there has emerged a clear alliance not only in an economic sense, but a political one as well. Today, both regimes consider each other as major partners in all fields. The protestations of opposition to apartheid uttered by Israeli spokesmen in the United Nations and elsewhere during the 1960s have withered away, and are now no more than a rarely observed ritual. For all practical purposes, South Africa and Israel are now tightly linked and if the Zionists have chosen to forget the past anti-Semitism of Mr. Vorster and his colleagues, so have the South African leaders abandoned that anti-Semitism, in public at least, in pursuit of the higher goal of the preservation of white supremacy.

Economic Links

In the economic field, ties have expanded rapidly. Before 1956, there was only a limited trade, with both sides still dependent on other markets, and with their political positions protected by the survival of the great European empires. Between 1956 and 1967, the Egyptian presence in Sinai rendered the Red Sea trade route usable but potentially insecure, and, in any case, the period coincided with the heyday of the attempts by the Israelis to win friends in newly independent sub-Saharan Africa. The latter made South African links a temporary embarrassment. Since the 1967 June War, however, links in the economic field have grown dramatically.

Between 1961 and 1966, Israeli exports to South Africa averaged between US $2.0-2.7 million per year. By 1968, the figure had risen to US $5.7 million, and by 1969 to US $8.2 million. In 1973, it was US $12.0 million and 1974 saw a leap to US $28 million. Preliminary figures indicate that the total was further increased by a substantial amount in 1975.

The growth in trade the other way was even more dramatic. In 1966, Israel imported goods worth US $3.4 million from South Africa; in 1968, US $5.2 million; in 1969, US $5.8 million. By 1972, the figure was US $11.6 million; 1973 saw a jump to US $32 million and in 1974, Israeli imports from South Africa totalled US $38 million. Once again, preliminary figures for 1975 showed another enormous jump. The rapid expansion has been boosted both by the South African government's decision to open major lines of credit for exports to Israel, and also by the inauguration of a variety of joint ventures, in both countries, producing goods designed either for local consumption, or for export to Africa and Western Europe. Today, South Africa is Israel's biggest trading partner outside the countries of Western Europe and the United States.

These figures are made more significant by the fact that they do not include Israel's diamond imports, largely of South African origin, but purchased through the Central Selling Organisation in London. For more than twenty years, beginning in 1949, the export of polished diamonds, produced by Israeli diamond-polishers from imported stones, provided from one-third to one-half of Israel's total industrial exports, and although today Israel's arms exports are now cutting into the figure, diamonds remain a key factor in Israel's external trade pattern. If the diamond trade is also taken into consideration, South Africa becomes even more important to Israel in the economic field.[6]

Political and Military Links

In the sphere of political relations, the visit by Vorster was but a culmination of years of conversations and visits. The new Afrikaner government in South Africa was the fifth state to extend *de jure* recognition to the state of Israel, within a month of Israel's creation — *de facto* recognition had been one of the last acts of the outgoing government of the United Party, led by General Smuts. Since that time, there have been regular visits, at top level, in both directions. In 1950, Moshe Sharett, then the Israeli prime minister, visited South Africa, ostensibly to confer with the South African Jewish community. In 1953, South African prime minister Malan visited Israel — the first "Western" prime minister to do so while still in office.[7]

Moshe Dayan and Yigal Allon visited South Africa in the 1950s[8] as did a variety of lesser figures. Shimon Peres, then secretary general of the ruling Israeli Labour Party, visited South Africa in 1968,[9] as did Knesset member and former Attorney General Gideon Hausner, who had been intimately involved in the trial of former Nazi leader Adolf Eichmann.[10] David Ben-Gurion and former Israeli intelligence chief Chaim Herzog visited in 1969, the former meeting with Prime Minister Vorster,[11] while a couple of years later, Menahem Begin of the Herut Party — a minister in the Israeli cabinet from 1967 to 1970 — also met with Vorster.[12]

Until this time, there seemed to be an unwritten convention, in operation from the early 1960s onwards, that no Israeli minister should visit South Africa while in office, and also that all leading Israelis visiting South Africa should do so ostensibly under the aegis of the local Zionist or Jewish community organizations. In 1973, that convention began to disappear, with the visit of Israel's deputy minister of communications, Gad Yaacobi, who, in the midst of various communal activities, met with his South African counterparts.[13] In May of the same year, Yitzhak Rabin also visited South Africa, on a fund-raising visit.[14] By 1974 the situation had changed completely, following the destruction of Israel's African policy before and during the October war. Moshe Dayan, for example, returned to South Africa in August as a guest of the South Africa Foundation, a group of businessmen aiming, with government backing, to improve South Africa's overseas image. Dr. Shlomo Peer, a former colleague of Dayan in the Rafi Party in Israel, is on the committe of the Foundation.[15] The pretence that Israelis only visited South Africa to talk to fellow Jews was dropped.

The traffic was also in the other direction, although there was a period in the 1960s when little official visiting was done, even though leading members of the South African Zionist groups continued, of course, to visit Israel. The resumption of trips, at a high level, came around 1971. In that year, a senior South African parliamentary delegation visited Israel, at the invitation of the Knesset.[16] The next year, the South African minister of water affairs and forestry, Stephanus Botha, went to Israel and held talks with his Israeli counterpart.[17] In September 1973, the South African minister of information and the interior, Connie Mulder, met with Foreign Minister Abba Eban and Interior Minister Yosef Burg.[18] He has returned to Israel on at least one other occasion since, to pave the way for the Vorster visit. A number of other people, of lesser political importance, or spanning the fields of politics and economics, have also made visits, such as General Meir Amit, Dayan's second-in-command when the latter was chief of staff of the Israeli army, and now head of Koor Industries; and Eschel Rhoodie, the South African secretary of information.

The pattern of economic and military ties, which can be outlined only in brief, have been parallelled, especially since 1967, by other developments in the field of the exchange of military expertise and equipment. In October 1967, the chief of staff of the Israeli air force, General Mordechai Hod, lectured to the South African Air Force Staff College on the tactics of the June war,[19] while in the same month, a delegation from Israel Aircraft Industries (IAI), visited the factory of Atlas Aircraft Industries in South Africa to discuss the possibility of sales for their Arava multi-purpose transport craft.[20] By 1969, IAI had secured a South African agent for their Commodore jet,[21] and, at the beginning of 1970, the Jewish Telegraphic Agency referred to reports on the initiation of a plan for South Africa to export heavy tanks to Israel — though the plan was later denied.[22] In the same year, Tadiran, partly owned by, and supplying much of its equipment to the Israeli ministry of defence, set up an agreement with a South African firm for the production of its sophisticated electronic equipment under license.[23] In 1971, IAI offered to sell planes to the South African air force to replace three which had crashed, though the offer was turned down. In September 1971, a trade in explosives was revealed as a result of a fire on board a ship in Durban harbor.[24]

In 1973, the Head of South Africa's bureau of state security (BOSS), General Hendrik Van den Bergh, made a secret trip to Israel for talks both with his intelligence counterparts and with Prime Minister Golda Meir.[25] During the October war, South African Mirages were sent to assist Israel on the Sinai front[26] while, as in 1967, large numbers of South African volunteers arrived to help Israel.

Since then, the relationship has expanded rapidly. Israeli officers have trained South African troops in counter-insurgency techniques,[27] and were involved in South African planning for the Angola operation in late 1975 and early 1976.[28] There have also been reports from the South West African Peoples Organization (SWAPO), that Israeli troops have been helping the South African army in Namibia.[29] Israel sold the sophisticated Gabriel sea-to-sea missile to South Africa in 1974,[30] while following the Vorster visit, there were well-authenticated reports that South Africa was to purchase Reshef missile boats — possibly to be built under license in South Africa — and IAI's Kfir fighter.[31]

There is also a clear possibility that the two regimes may now be collaborating in the field of nuclear energy, in its military usage. Research cooperation for non-military use is already a matter of public knowledge. The possibility that military cooperation now exists makes the alliance of even greater potential danger, not only for the states in the immediate neighborhood, but for the continent of Africa and the Arab world as a whole.

There have been other forms of collaboration as well. Israel has consistently breached attempts by the United Nations to enforce a sporting and cultural boycott of South Africa, examples being the visit of an Israel sports group in December 1973,[32] and the tour by the Israeli Philharmonic Orchestra in August 1974.[33] These breaches took place even during the period in the early 1960s when the Israeli government generally supported anti-apartheid resolutions at the United Nations. By 1973, however, that token opposition to South Africa disappeared; in the voting on resolutions at the twenty-eighth General Assembly, Israel abstained on two resolutions, voted against one, and was absent from all of the other votes.[34] When the 1974 General Assembly voted to refuse to accept the credentials of the South African delegation — a resolution passed by 125 votes to 1 (South Africa) — Israel was one of the nine abstentions.[35]

The simple facts of collaboration in the economic, political and military fields are clear. Since the establishment of the state of Israel in the land of Palestine in May 1948, and the gaining of power by the

South African National Party (the Afrikaners) in the same month, there have been close relations between the two. Following the 1967 June War, and particularly since the 1973 October War, those relations have developed at great speed, becoming of considerable importance to both sides. On a purely practical level, therefore, the alliance exists, and flourishes.

What an examination of the bare facts does not achieve, however significant they may be, is any real explanation of the reasons for the closeness between the two regimes in a broader, more ideological sense. There are, after all, other states which have close ties with South Africa — such as the United Kingdom and France, which, at the same time, do not hesitate at least to make a *pro forma* condemnation of apartheid. For them there is a distinction, however finely, or even hypocritically drawn, between approval of the ideological basis of the apartheid regime and trading with it. Accepting and promoting the trade on the one hand, they condemn, to a greater or lesser extent, the racialism of South Africa on the other.

The basis, therefore, for the South Africa-Israel alliance is not merely one of trade; it has deeper, and, in the long run, potentially more durable roots. These include, for both, their conception as to their origin and destiny and their attitudes toward their native populations. The role of the South African Jewish community is also of some significance.

South African Jews and Zionism

The Jewish community in South Africa, largely of Eastern European origin, represents only a small percentage of South Africa's white population — around 110,000 of a total of over four million. Their importance in white politics, however, is far more than mere figures would suggest. They are extremely active in the spheres of business, mining and banking, the cornerstones on which the wealth of the white community has been built. In addition, a large proportion of the Jewish population is urban, concentrated in Johannesburg and other towns along the gold-bearing Reef. In some parts of Johannesburg, they represent as much as ten percent of the white electorate, and their influence, because of financial power, is even greater. Thus, though small in numbers, the community's political and economic weight is considerable.

The Jewish community of South Africa has been controlled by Zionists for decades, long before the foundation of the state of Israel. Indeed, the Zionist Federation in South Africa was formed as early as

1895, and gained control of the representative organs of the community in the early years of the century, long before the resistance of British Jewry's officials to the Zionist program had been defeated. Under Zionist control, the community first formed a close relationship with the leading white South African political figure of the first half of this century, General Smuts. Formerly a leader of the resistance to the British during the Boer War, Smuts became Britain's strongest defender in the southern half of the continent. His commitment to empire, on the British model, was sufficiently accepted in London for him to be made a member of the Imperial War Cabinet during World War I. In that capacity — as has been amply documented by Richard Stevens in his *Weizmann and Smuts*[36] — he played a key role in the formulation and granting of the Balfour Declaration in 1917.

Smuts' connection with Zionism, however, predates his links with Chaim Weizmann. In the first years of the century, he became a member of the Jewish Territorial Organization (JTO), which, though opposed to Herzl's plans for a Jewish state in Palestine, supported the idea of a Zionist-Jewish colony anywhere in the world that Britain thought fit.[37] His view of Zionism was that it was a movement that could be put to use to strengthen British imperialism, and when, later on, he supported the Balfour Declaration and worked from 1917 to 1948 to secure the creation of a Jewish state in Palestine, he did so in the belief that it was in the best interests of the British empire.

Smuts' support had concrete results. In the period before the establishment of the state of Israel, Smuts was occupying the post of prime minister of South Africa for the last time; he permitted money, supplies and men to be passed to the underground Haganah in Palestine, even though he disapproved of the conflict raging between the Jewish settlers and the British mandatory authority. Benjamin Kagan, in *The Secret Battle for Israel*, commented: "Haganah's representative there (i.e. in South Africa) recruited 'volunteers' freely and without any obstacle from the Government. The Haganah in 1947-48 had no more than a handful of pilots in its own forces, and South African pilots constituted the second largest group after the Americans."[38]

When Smuts died in 1950, the South African Jewish community eulogized him, while the acting prime minister of Israel, Joseph Sprinzak, declared: "General Smuts is written on the map of Israel, and in the heart of our nation."[39] While his commitment to the Zionist ideal was important up until 1948 and recognized by Zionists in both South Africa and Palestine, by the time of his last election defeat, in 1948, the South African Jewish community was turning away from him. Indeed, the election victory of the South African National Party in that year was to a large extent due to the defection of sectors of the previously solidly pro-United Party Jewish community. That shift helped to lay the groundwork for the collaboration between the National Party and both the South African Jewish community and Israel that was to come.

First, the South African Zionists, feeling closely involved in the Haganah struggle in Palestine against both the Palestinians and Britain, were less inclined to support the apostle of British imperialism that Smuts had become. Secondly, the National Party, besides having a long history of opposition to Britain, had begun to lay aside its anti-Semitic past. This was partly because the end of World War II and the defeat of Nazism had rendered that particular viewpoint publicly intolerable — something that even Ossewa Brandwag members like Vorster, newly united with the mainstream of Afrikaner politics in the National Party, accepted. Moreover, there was a recognition among the Afrikaners that white supremacy in South Africa could only be preserved through white unity. In South Africa, in contrast to the situation in Palestine, all the Jews were of European origin and counted as "white." Furthermore, some Afrikaner politicians, sensing a chance of winning power, feared that an exodus of South African Jews, frightened away by anti-Semitism, "would shake the country to its foundation" because of the consequent flight of capital.[40]

The South African Jewish community, therefore, led by its Zionist chiefs within the South African Jewish Board of Deputies, came to make an accommodation with the Afrikaners and with apartheid. It was not until 1951 that the Transvaal region of the National Party lifted its ban on Jewish membership and some isolated outbursts of anti-Semitism continued into the 1960s and even more recently, but the issue, at an official level, was buried.

From the time of the establishment of the state of Israel, the South African Jewish community has pushed hard for greater economic and other links with Israel. As previously indicated, dozens of leading Israelis visited South Africa long before the burgeoning alliance caught public attention a few years ago. The Israelis ostensibly came to meet with communal bodies, but also took the opportunity on many occasions to meet with South African businessmen and politicians. And after the 1967 war, it was a member of the Johannesburg community, Stanley Kaplan, who set in motion the process that led to the establishment of the Israeli-South African Trade Association (ISATA).[41]

More than nine thousand South African Jews emigrated to Israel through 1973, including Abba Eban and Michael Comay. For many

years, the community held the record for the highest per capita donation of cash for Israeli appeals. The links were rendered stronger by the
apparent ease with which some South African Jews emigrated to
Israel for a few years, and then returned, adding their weight to the
pressure for closer ties. The relationship was deep and strong, but at the
same time almost natural. Upon its foundation was to be built the
direct link between the ideologists of apartheid and the leaders of the
Zionist movement in Israel itself.

The apartheid chiefs — Malan, Strijdom, Verwoerd and Vorster —
never had real grounds for suspecting the commitment of the South
African Jewish community to apartheid itself even at times when for
reasons of world politics Israel felt itself obliged to adopt a transient
position of public hostility. On the assassination of Verwoerd in 1966,
for example, the senior rabbi of the Progressive Jewish Congregation,
Arthur Super, delivered an eulogy in which he referred to Verwoerd as

one of the greatest, if not the greatest Prime Minister South Africa
has ever produced. Here was a man who, like Moses of old, has led
his people to the promised land after sixty years of wandering. He
had the courage and the strength to establish the Republic of South
Africa (by breaking the link with the British Crown and leaving
the Commonwealth) and so dissolve in one act the old heritage of
hatred, communal jealousies, blurred loyalties, old grudges and
grievances which were preventing South Africa becoming one nation.

Rabbi Abraham described him on the same occasion as "a man of
sincerity and deep integrity . . . a moral conscience underlay his policies; he was the first to give apartheid a moral ground."[42]

The same thread has run through statements of leaders of the
South African Jewish community ever since 1948. In 1953, for
example, Rabbi Weiler told the Eighth International Conference in
London of the World Union for Progressive Judaism that the Jews as a
community had decided to take no stand on the native question,
because they were involved with the problem of assisting Jewry in other
lands.[43] In 1960, Chaim Hoppenstein, a member of the Board of
Deputies for more than thirty years, wrote to the *Jewish Chronicle* in
London: "A Majority of us are supporting the Union Government's
policy in connection with apartheid."[44] And in 1972, the chairman of
the Board of Deputies, D. K. Mann, was reported in the South African
press as saying that the community "has no reason to be ashamed of its
attitude to social ills in South Africa."[45] The position was neatly

summed up in a 1973 article by Geoffrey Wigoder in the *Jerusalem Post*: "Unlike the position in the United States, the Jewish representative organisation in South Africa has never endeavoured to fight for other under-privileged groups."[46]

Indeed, it has done precisely the opposite. There has been a tiny minority of the community which has stood out against apartheid, and has allied itself with African organizations fighting for freedom. Over a period of thirty years, that minority has been subjected to pressure from the Board of Deputies to cease its activity.

Thus the South African Jewish community, by and large, has shown that it can be Zionist and support the racialist ideology of apartheid without difficulty. For them, racialism, whether it involves dispossessing the people of Palestine, or oppressing the people of South Africa, has become part of their lives.

Among the rest of the white community, too, there has been a clear willingness to accept and identify with the Zionist state in Palestine. For the Afrikaners, the majority of the white population, there has been a feeling akin to religious mysticism. They too consider themselves to have been chosen by God, and although they and their leading Churchmen in the Dutch Reformed Church claim to be Christian, there is little in their beliefs and teachings of the love and charity of the New Testament. Instead, they have drawn their religion from the harsh fundamentalist texts of the Old Testament, from such verses as the division of mankind into "the hewers of wood and the drawers of water." Basing their own racialist views on a distorted version of the Bible, the theologians of the Dutch Reformed Church, who have a religious stranglehold over the bulk of the Afrikaner community, have, at the same time, developed an innate sympathy for the racialism implicit in the claim that the Jews, *per se*, are God's Chosen People. Such an attitude has led to a real feeling of identification with Israel — exemplified by the large donation given during the June war to Israel's emergency financial appeal by the Broederbond, the secret society at the heart of Afrikanerdom.

Mysticism aside, there have been other, more political grounds for common feeling. On both sides, there has been a steadily growing recognition that the two settler states are in a similar geopolitical situation: embattled minorities, of foreign origin, implanted on the land of people now struggling for their birthright. In August 1967, for example, the journal of the South African Foundation, *Perspective*, commented:

The recent war in the Middle East aroused fevered interest and passionate concern in many parts of the world, but in few so deep a feeling of personal involvement as in South Africa. Sympathy with Israel was not confined to the Jewish community, however. White South Africans generally identified themselves personally with the plight of the Israelis . . . all were aware of the analogy between the situation of Israel, surrounded by hostile neighbours, and the situation of South Africa. . . . In the circumstances, it seemed only natural that white South Africans generally should view the Israelis as comrades in peril, and seek to assist and succor them accordingly.

Again, on May 29, 1968, *Die Burger*, organ of the National Party in the Cape, editorialized:

Israel and South Africa have a common lot. Both are engaged in a struggle for existence, and both are in constant clash with the decisive majorities in the U.N. Both are reliable foci of strength within the region, which would, without them, fall into anti-Western anarchy. It is in South Africa's interest that Israel is successful in containing her enemies, who are amongst our own most vicious enemies, and Israel would have all the world against it if the navigation route around the Cape of Good Hope should be out of operation because South Africa's control is undermined. The anti-Western powers have driven Israel and South Africa into a community of interests which had better be utilised than denied.

During the October war, South African Defence Minister P. W. Botha commented: "There is a deep feeling on the part of thousands of South Africans for Israel, in her battle against the forces supported by communistic militarism, which also poses a threat to us."[47]

That feeling of common problems in the politico-military sphere has led to collaboration, as for example in the Israeli provision of counter-insurgency training to South Africa, or in the exchange of information between the intelligence services of the two regimes.

In many ways, it is not surprising that such an attitude has emerged. Both states are of the same type, as George Jabbour has pointed out in his *Settler Colonialism in Southern Africa and the Middle East*,[48] even though there have been differences in their histories and differences remain today. Israel, for example, does not have a "native" problem of the same scale as South Africa, because the majority of the Palestinians were expelled. The definition of racial purity for each varies: for one

298 Israel and South Africa: The Racists Allied

it is enough to be 'white', for the other enough to be a "Jew," though in neither case has the classification been quite as easy as the ideologists pretended. There have been times when their interests have diverged, and consequently their relations have been temporarily ruffled, during the period of Israel's diplomatic honeymoon with independent Africa, for example. On balance, however, the common features have shown through.

Zionism began and developed under the wing of, though occasionally in conflict with, British imperialism, and owed its successful establishment of a state largely to that relationship. Afrikaner nationalism followed a similar path, despite the hostility that characterized relations with London. The protection of Britain fallen away, both regimes sought more friends, and, to some extent, succeeded. As international condemnation of both has mounted, however, they have come closer together, and their common interests have come to the fore, a process aided by, but not exclusively because of, the activities of the South African Jewish community. With the old empires gone, the surviving specimens of settler colonialism (with the shaky addition of the Smith regime in Rhodesia) have come together, partly by choice, and partly by force of circumstance, in the same final defence position.

The nature of their relationship goes far deeper than trade figures, or even military collaboration against liberation movements. It has been able to develop in the way it has precisely because of the underlying similarity between the two regimes. Both apartheid and Zionism are racialist ideologies, and although both claim to derive their justification from the Old Testament, it is their present-day attitudes, formed within the framework of their settler-colonialist institutions that determine not only their nature and identity, but also the intimate relationship between them.

It is that relationship — between two racialisms whose very raison d'etre is the dispossession of others — that makes the Israeli-South African alliance so deep, so dangerous, and potentially so durable.

Notes

1. *Sudafrika-Bericht*, 26 September 1940.
2. A. Kum'a N'dumbe, *Relations between Nazi Germany and South Africa*, U.N. Centre Against Apartheid, document 12/76, p. 6.
3. Brian Bunting, *The Rise of the South African Reich* (London, 1964) pp. 44-5.
4. Kum'a N'dumbe, *Relations*, pp. 7-8.
5. Quoted in *Israel and Southern Africa* (Madison Area Committee on Southern

Africa, n.d. p. 13.

6. The quoted figures are from Peter Hellyer, *Israel and South Africa – the Development of Relations 1967-74*, (United Nations, 1974); and Peter Hellyer, "Israel's Diamond Industry," *IDOC Bulletin*, no. 6 (April 1973).

7. Bunting, *South African Reich*, p. 65.

8. Henry Katzew, *Rand Daily Mail* (hereafter *RDM*), 27 February 1969.

9. *Sechaba*, journal of the African National Congress of South Africa, April 1970.

10. *RDM*, 9 September 1968.

11. *RDM*, 10 May 1969.

12. *Jewish Chronicle* (London) (hereafter *JC*), 5 November 1971.

13. *JC*, 2 February 1973.

14. *RDM*, 10 and 14 May 1973.

15. *JC*, 2 August 1974.

16. *RDM*, 11 October 1971.

17. *Kuwait Times*, 13 June 1972.

18. *The Star* (Johannesburg), 22 September 1973.

19. *RDM*, 10 October 1967.

20. *Sunday Times* (Johannesburg), 10 October 1967.

21. *RDM*, 27 November 1969.

22. Jewish Telegraphic Agency, 20 January 1970.

23. *South African News and Press Review*, published by South Africa Foundation, (London), December 1970.

24. *RDM*, 11 September 1971.

25. *Yediot Aharanot* (Tel Aviv), 16 August 1973.

26. *Daily Telegraph* (London), 31 October 1973.

27. *Guardian* (London), 8 July 1975.

28. *RDM*, 4 March 1976.

29. "Focus on Africa," BBC African Service, 8 July 1976.

30. *Daily Telegraph*, 8 September 1974.

31. E.g. *see The Middle East*, June 1976; and *Les Flottes de Combat* (Paris, 1976).

32. *JC*, 7 December 1973.

33. *Jerusalem Post* (Weekly Edition), 13 August 1974.

34. *See* UN Document: A/AC 115/L.383, 29 April 1974.

35. UN Information Centre (London), Weekly Summary, WS/74/39, October 1974.

36. Published by the Institute for Palestine Studies (Beirut, 1975).

37. Reported in Joseph Leftwich, *Israel Zangwill* (London, 1957), p. 227.

38. *See* George Tomeh, *Israel and South Africa* (1st edition, 1970).

39. *South African Jewish Chronicle*, 22 September 1950.

40. According to Edwin Munger, "Jews and the National Party," American Universities Field Staff Reports, 1956, p. 2.

41. *RDM*, 1 August 1967.

42. *RDM*, 12 September 1966.

43. Quoted in Document no. 14, *Jews-South Africa*, issued by Fritz Flesch, (Michigan, 1973).

44. *JC*, 2 September 1960.

45. *RDM*, 11 October 1972.

46. *Jerusalem Post* (weekly edition), 25 May 1973.

47. *RDM*, 15 October 1973.

48. Published by PLO Research Centre (Beirut) and the University of Khartoum, April 1970.

INDEX